Policing Notting Hill

FIFTY YEARS OF TURBULENCE

Tony Moore

Policing Notting Hill
Fifty Years of Turbulence
Tony Moore

ISBN 978-1-904380-61-0 (Paperback)
ISBN 978-1-908162-41-0 (Adobe E-book)
ISBN 978-1-908162-43-4 (Kindle /Epub E-book)

Cataloguing-In-Publication Data A catalogue record for this book can be obtained from the British Library.

e-book *Policing Notting Hill* is available as an ebook and also to subscribers of Myilibrary, Dawsonera, ebrary and Ebscohost.

Printed by CPI Antony Rowe, Chippenham, UK.

Main UK distributor Gardners Books, 1 Whittle Drive, Eastbourne, East Sussex, BN23 6QH. Tel: (+44) 01323 521777; sales@gardners.com; www.gardners.com

North American distribution Ingram Book Company, One Ingram Blvd, La Vergne, TN 37086, USA. Tel: (+1) 615 793 5000; inquiry@ingramcontent.com

Published 2013 by
Waterside Press Ltd.
Sherfield Gables
Sherfield on Loddon
Hook, Hampshire
United Kingdom RG27 0JG

Telephone +44(0)1256 882250
E-mail enquiries@watersidepress.co.uk
Online catalogue WatersidePress.co.uk

Policing Notting Hill

FIFTY YEARS OF TURBULENCE

Tony Moore

With a Foreword by Lord Blair of Boughton

❧ **WATERSIDE** PRESS

CONTENTS

ACKNOWLEDGEMENTS

This book has been over 20 years in the writing but I could not have put together the story of these 50 turbulent years without the assistance of a number of the police officers who either served on Notting Hill Division or were connected to its policing activities in some way during this period. Under the former category come Jim Busby, David Cooke, David Gilbertson, Rod Havard, Tim Hollis, Stan May, Matt Nicholls, Denis O'Connor, Charles Rideout, Colin Searle, Alan Shave, and Anthony Wills, who were all either gracious enough to allow me to interview them or exchanged correspondence with me, often despite busy schedules.

I am particularly indebted to Graham Sharp who served as an inspector for four years during what was probably the most difficult period and then returned, firstly as the Deputy Divisional Commander before becoming the Divisional Commander for the final stage of the journey.

Amongst those who did not serve at Notting Hill but had knowledge of some of the events described in the book were John Purnell, Larry Roach and Ken Diccocks. During the late-1980s, a number of the senior officers deployed at the 1976 Notting Hill Carnival were kind enough either to allow me to interview them or took the time to exchange correspondence with me whilst I was completing a thesis on public order policing at the University of Southampton. These included Brian Dovey, Wilfred Gibson, Robert Hunt, John Perrett, and Ron Patterson. I am extremely grateful to them all.

Over a period stretching from the late-1980s until well into the 1990s, I regularly visited the library at what was then the Police Staff College at Bramshill where Sue King and her staff were most helpful in response to my requests for obscure pieces of information relating to the policing of Notting Hill. Two other libraries gave me assistance insofar as researching newspapers: the British Museum Newspaper Library at Colindale and the public library in Kensington.

I am grateful to Bryan Gibson and his team at Waterside Press, firstly for agreeing to publish the book and, secondly, for the helpful advice given during its preparation. Also to Kate Whittingham for drawing the various maps that are included at appropriate places in the book.

My final and most important thanks go to my wife, Hamide, who showed great patience and understanding whilst I was writing the book and who kept me supplied with numerous cups of tea and coffee. For all this, I am eternally grateful.

Where comment or discussion is not original I have taken care to acknowledge other sources. Where I express my own comments or observations I should emphasise that they do not necessarily represent the views of the Metropolitan Police, either then or now, or of the police service in general.

Tony Moore
May 2013

ABOUT THE AUTHOR

Tony Moore was Divisional Commander at Notting Hill for two years at the start of the 1980s: at what the film-maker Roger Graef described as 'the most widely publicised 'nick' in Britain' (*Evening Standard*).

After a year in the Metropolitan Police Cadet Force, he spent four years in the British Army, seeing service in Germany and Aden.

He then spent the next 28 years in the Metropolitan Police, serving successively at Commercial Street, Holborn, Bethnal Green, City Road, New Scotland Yard, Islington, Caledonian Road, Leyton, Kensington, and finally, on reaching the rank of Chief Superintendent, two years as Divisional Commander at Notting Hill.

Twice on the staff of the Police Staff College at Bramshill and an experienced public order commander, he was involved in a number of high profile policing events, including the Iranian Embassy Siege, Notting Hill Carnival, the wedding of Prince Charles to Lady Diana Spencer, football hooliganism at a major ground, and various clashes between right and left-wing demonstrators.

On leaving the police, he lectured at Cranfield University, based within the Defence Academy of the United Kingdom at Shrivenham, specialising in crisis and disaster management and counter-terrorism.

He holds an M.Phil from the University of Southampton and is Deputy President and a Fellow of the Institute of Civil Protection and Emergency Management. Apart from some 40 articles on aspects of policing, his publications include *Tolley's Principles and Practice of Disaster Management* (as co-editor) (three editions 2002–2006); *Jane's Facility Managers Handbook* (as co-editor) (2nd edn. 2006), *Disaster and Emergency Management Systems* (British Standards Institution, 2008).

FOREWORD

Tony Moore is well fitted to write the history of Notting hill and its relationship with the Metropolitan Police Service.

I served there for a year as a detective sergeant in 1979 and it was a real eye-opener for a young man whose previous police service had been spent in the less controversial areas of the West End, Wembley and Chelsea.

In 1979, the police in Notting Hill were struggling to build a new relationship with a very distrustful and at times very angry African-Caribbean population: at the same time, it was an area of great wealth and extreme deprivation.

Individual incidents, let alone the Carnival, which I policed throughout my career, were capable of exploding into violence, which would have an impact throughout London.

I learned a great deal there, which was why I chose it to be the location of a photocall and interview on my first day as Commissioner.

Lord Blair of Boughton

INTRODUCTION

Notting Hill has never been officially defined as an administrative area but, generally, it is understood to be that part of the Royal Borough of Kensington and Chelsea, sometimes referred to as North Kensington, which falls north of Holland Park Avenue and Notting Hill Gate and south of Harrow Road. It broadly corresponds to the old London postcodes of W10 and W11 and the western end of W2. Despite its lack of definition as an administrative area, it is an extremely well-known and popular part of London. Today, it is probably best known for its annual Carnival, for the Portobello Road Market, for the film *Notting Hill* starring Hugh Grant and Julia Roberts, and as the place where David Cameron, British Prime Minister, had his home before entering Downing Street in 2010. But, during the second half of the twentieth century, a small part of Notting Hill was known by many of those that frequented it as the 'Front Line' and by the police as a 'Symbolic Location'.

Notting Hill first hit the national headlines in 1958 when four nights of rioting between white and black inhabitants, supported by many people on both sides from outside the area, severely tested the ability of the police to preserve the peace. The following year a young black carpenter, Kelso Cochrane, was murdered by white racists in circumstances that bore similarities to the murder of Stephen Lawrence over 30 years later. Two of Stephen Lawrence's killers were eventually brought to justice, but the murderers of Kelso Cochrane have never been identified.

In 1963, a notorious landlord, Peter Rachman, who had died the previous year, was exposed, primarily because of his connections to two women, Christine Keeler and Mandy Rice-Davies. Both played prominent parts in one of the biggest scandals to hit post-war British politics, the downfall of the Secretary of State for War, John Profumo, after it was found that he had an affair with Keeler at the same time as she was having a sexual relationship with the Assistant Naval Attaché at the Russian Embassy, at the height of the Cold War. On the face of it, this would appear to have nothing to do with Notting Hill and it would not if Keeler had not also been involved with two 'hustlers', Aloysius 'Lucky' Gordon and Johnny Edgecombe, who frequented the illegal clubs and coffee bars in that area.

Rachman had built a property empire in and around Notting Hill over a number of years and, in order to maximise his rental income, sitting tenants, mostly white, who, at that time had protection against rental increases, were driven out by dubious means to enable him to house newly-arrived immigrants, mainly from the West Indies, at greatly enhanced rents. Illegal drinking clubs and prostitutes operated in some of the properties, although Rachman was never prosecuted in respect of either. However, his exploitation of tenants led to the word 'Rachmanism' entering the Oxford English Dictionary, as a synonym for any greedy, unscrupulous landlord.

Notting Hill was frequently in the news between 1959 and 1965 when the bodies of eight naked women were found in West London; all were prostitutes. Although none of the bodies were actually found in the Notting Hill police area, a number of the dead women frequented its pubs, illegal drinking clubs and coffee bars and much of the subsequent investigation was concentrated in that area. The officer finally leading the enquiries, Detective Chief Superintendent John du Rose, compared the killer, nicknamed Jack the Stripper, to both Jack the Ripper and the Boston Strangler but he (it has always been assumed that the culprit was a man) was never brought to justice. Theories abound as to who the killer was; one even suggested he was a former police officer who had been dismissed from the Metropolitan Police and was seeking revenge for the way he had been treated.

In 1965 and for the first time, Notting Hill became the home of what was to become the annual Notting Hill Carnival. For the first few years it was hardly noticed but, by the mid-1970s, it was attracting larger crowds each year. As the crowds grew, criminals were attracted to the event and police attempts to deal with them were, arguably, a main cause of the rioting that occurred in 1976, when over 400 police officers were injured. Indeed, it was this single event that led the police to acquire protective shields for use in public order situations. By 1980, the Carnival was the largest regular police operation mounted by the Metropolitan Police each year, in which up to 11,000 officers were deployed over a single weekend. Whilst that number was reduced in succeeding years, there were, nevertheless, outbreaks of serious disorder in 1987 and 1989. But disorder was not confined to the Carnival for the 1980s saw scenes of ferocious violence within predominantly ethnic minority areas of Britain. First to erupt was St Paul's in Bristol in 1980, followed by Brixton in London, in April 1981, and Moss Side in Manchester, Handsworth in Birmingham and Toxteth in Liverpool in the summer of 1981. In the same year there was minor disorder in a number of other areas, including Notting Hill. Violence erupted again in Notting Hill in 1982, shortly after the anniversary of the first Brixton riot.

Meanwhile, the southern half of All Saints Road, a fairly narrow street running from Tavistock Road at its northern end to Westbourne Park Road at its southern end, increasingly become known to those who frequented it as the 'Front Line', and, as already mentioned, to the police as a 'Symbolic Location', as its international reputation for the purchase of illegal drugs grew. And where there were drugs, other crimes were never far away. Insofar as the African-Caribbean community was concerned it was a place where criminals sought refuge and where the ready availability of illegal drugs and other unlawful activities such as unlicensed drinking and gambling clubs, brought those that frequented the area into regular conflict with the police.

The term Symbolic Location arose primarily because the large scale opposition by many of those who frequented these places to any attempt by the police to curtail these activities meant that the law could only be enforced by mounting special operations, involving careful planning and using a substantial number of officers. Such was the case with All Saints Road for something like 25 years; indeed, despite denials by senior officers, All Saints Road effectively became a 'no go' area, insofar as normal policing was concerned, for a period in the late-1970s and most of the 1980s in which the law could only be upheld by mounting such operations.

All Saints Road first came to national prominence in 1971. Frank Crichlow, who for ten years had run the Rio Coffee Bar in Westbourne Park Road, opened the Mangrove in All Saints Road in early-1969, hoping that it would become an upmarket African-Caribbean restaurant. Although it started out like that, attracting such people as Nina Simone, Vanessa Redgrave, Sammy Davis Jnr, C L R James and Lord Gifford, breaches of its licence on a fairly regular basis brought Crichlow and his staffs into conflict with both the licensing authority and the police. Consequently, in August 1970, there was a protest against police harassment which turned violent, resulting in a number of arrests. Nearly three months later, seven men, including Crichlow, and two women were charged with riotous assembly and affray. When the case eventually came to court, amidst accusations that there was a police 'heavy mob' operating in the area at the time, all nine were acquitted of riotous assembly, although some were convicted of affray and other lesser offences; however, the sentences were suspended for two years. The case had received widespread publicity in the national media putting All Saints Road, Frank Crichlow and the Mangrove firmly on the map.

Subsequently, two major raids on the Mangrove, in 1977 and 1988, in which Frank Crichlow was arrested, with others, and charged with drug offences on each occasion, did little to improve the reputation of the Metropolitan Police; instead, arguably his acquittal on both occasions did much to raise his personal profile as the underdog being persecuted by the police. Indeed, following his acquittal on the second occasion he accepted a substantial financial settlement at the High Court after he had brought proceedings against the Commissioner of the Metropolitan Police for false imprisonment, battery and malicious prosecution.

Periodically, the police mounted successful operations in All Saints Road itself without involving the Mangrove. One of the earliest, Operation Michael, was in February 1980; another was Operation Trident in 1987. But, whilst they had some short term success, they did little to curb the availability of drugs on a permanent basis. For many years the police saw it as a law and order problem which only they alone could deal with and a group of police officers set up to patrol All Saints Road became known as the Black Watch. Some attempt was made to enlist the cooperation of other agencies and the public from 1982 onwards, but it was arguably not until towards the end of the 1980s that a multi-agency approach was seriously developed.

The police continued to conduct operations against the drug trade but, at the same time, with Government funding, the Royal Borough of Kensington and Chelsea and others, including the police, formed the North Kensington Task Force and, acting together, renovated many of the crumbling Victorian buildings and improved physical security. Followed by another government funded initiative, City Challenge, under which, amongst other things, closed circuit television (CCTV) was installed in some crime-ridden areas, this was eventually successful to the extent that the illegal drug trade and other associated illegal activities were driven from All Saints Road and, as the 1990s were drawing to a close, Notting Hill had lost its tag both as a Front Line and as a Symbolic Location, although shades of the Front Line still return on two days of the year for the annual Carnival, now nearing its 50th year.

Notting Hill is nowadays a smart, gentrified part of London, no different from many other urban areas, other than that, perhaps, it has a relatively high proportion of well-known residents. But, as the book shows, that was not always the case. For a period of its history it was an area that became increasingly difficult to police and was rarely out of the news. This then is the story of that turbulent period.

CHAPTER 1

IN THE BEGINNING...

Introduction

Some of the 8,000 African-Caribbean people, who had either served in the Armed Forces or worked in the munitions factories, remained in Britain at the end of the Second World War.[1] But it was the arrival of the *Empire Windrush* in June 1948, with 492 passengers on board, which was the start of what was eventually to become a wave of immigration from that part of the world. For many years, Notting Dale had contained a fairly large white criminal population, to some extent isolated from the respectable districts around it.[2] It was an area of dilapidated houses, and one of four areas in London which were amongst the most notorious 'for crime, violence and prostitution.'[3] Policing was inadequate. Being at the end of a highway which effectively was in a straight line from Soho, which was regarded, certainly during the early years, as the 'vice capital of Europe, renowned for its gambling, drinking and prostitution,' the location of Notting Hill 'was crucial' to the events that were to plague the area for much of the next 50 years or so.[4]

Although many of the immigrants managed to get work, it was a struggle to save sufficient money to bring their families from the Caribbean or for them to find somewhere better to live. The housing conditions were appalling and this was 'compounded by the hostility they encountered in the streets and often at work.'[5] Others, 'relatively untroubled by the character of the district'

---

1. In a letter to the author, dated 15 April 1993, from Stan May, who served as a constable at Notting Hill from the end of World War II until 1957.
2. Wickenden, James (1958). *Colour in Britain*. Institute of Race Relations. Oxford: Oxford University Press, p.36.
3. Phillips, Mike and Trevor Phillips (1998). *Windrush: The Irresistible Rise of Multi-Racial Britain*. London: HarperCollins, p.105. According to this source, the other areas were Jago (in the East End), Hoxton and Hackney.
4. *Ibid*, p.108.
5. *Ibid*, p.109.

found the 'aura of vice and violence' exciting, constructing 'a network of clubs and gambling joints which rivalled Soho' because the area allowed them to live 'wild and free', virtually 'uninhibited by laws and respectability.'[6] For them, it was a place where the norm was to go 'out at four in the afternoon' and come 'home at five the next morning.'[7]

Against this background five crucial problems arose which were to plague the area for much of the next 50 years. The first was housing, the second employment, the third prostitution, the fourth a lack of entertainment and the fifth, particularly insofar as the police were concerned, the disputes that arose from the first four.

Housing

A report by Clarence Senior and Douglas Manley, published in 1955, placed housing first amongst the difficulties faced by the migrants from the West Indies.[8] The Colville area of Notting Hill still consisted of four and five-storey terraced buildings constructed during the reign of Queen Victoria; many had been turned into one room bedsits to accommodate the floating population of largely, single white people, attracted to London by the prospects of jobs over the previous 50 years. Therefore, the people from the West Indies did not initiate the process of sub-division and decay that existed in Notting Hill; they were merely the latest group who had to look for lodgings in the streets which had the physical and social characteristics of 'zones of transition'.[9] By the 1950s these once elegant, terraced houses were crumbling under 'the pressure of extreme overcrowding and neglect,' with plaster 'falling away from outside walls, exposing large patches of bare brick'. The balconies, too, 'were failing apart; and the windows were unpainted and rotten.'[10]

---

6.   *Ibid,* p.110.

7.   Olden, Mark (2011). *Murder in Notting Hill.* Winchester: Zero Books, p.20.

8.   Senior, Clarence and Douglas Manley (1955). *The West Indians in Britain.* Quoted by Wickenden, *op. cit.* 2, p.9.

9.   Glass, Ruth assisted by Harold Pollins (1960). *Newcomers: The West Indians in London.* London: Centre for Urban Studies and George Allen & Unwin, p.49.

10. Pilkington, Edward (1988). *Beyond the Mother Country: West Indians and the Notting Hill White Riots.* London: I. B. Tauris, p.60.

Notting Dale, a relatively small triangle bordered by Latimer Road, Walmer Road and Lancaster Road, with Bramley Road running through the middle, was arguably worse. At the beginning of the 1950s, it was a

'massive slum, full of multi-occupied houses, crawling with rats and rubbish. The people who lived there were poor. Their wages were low or they were unemployed…In some parts of the district there were pockets of Poles, Irish and blacks, competing for jobs and living with the natives. Mostly born and bred in the Notting Dale area, these natives, like the immigrants, were at the bottom of the ladder…'[11]

Racial prejudice was rife. Advertisements in windows and on notice boards regularly said, 'Room for rent — No coloureds.'[12] In a survey of London landlords in 1956, 90 per cent admitted they would not take black lodgers[13] and a survey by a local newspaper in 1958 found that 'one in eight of "To Let" advertisements had "No Coloured" tags'. But this did not mean that the remaining seven would let to black people.[14] Frequently, when a black person called to ask to rent the room, they were told that it had just been let. Whilst some were openly hostile to taking black people, others were quick to place the blame elsewhere, suggesting it was other white tenants, or white neighbours who would not like it.[15]

Merchant seaman, Michael de Freitas from Trinidad, who settled originally in Cardiff, found a place to live in Southam Street which was at the northern extremity of Notting Hill, when he decided to settle in London, with his girlfriend, Desiree, and her daughter, in 1957. De Freitas described the experience, as they approached the property:

'It was impossible to believe you were in twentieth-century England: terraced houses with shabby, crumbling stonework and the last traces of discoloured paint peeling from their doors, windows broken, garbage and dirt strewn all over the road, derelict cars…every second house deserted, with doors nailed up and rusty,

11. Phillips Mike and Trevor Phillips, *op. cit.* 3, p.107.
12. *Ibid,* p.136.
13. Pilkington, *op. cit.* 10, p.42.
14. *Ibid,* p.41.
15. *Ibid,* p.43.

corrugated iron across the window spaces, a legion of filthy white children swarming everywhere and people lying drunk across the pavement ...'

Once they reached the house,

'the African owner led us up the decrepit stairway to a room practically filled with
ugly furniture. The single gas ring for cooking was outside on the dismal landing,
there was no bath in the house—and he wanted £2.15 shillings a week. We were
desperate and we moved straight in.'[16]

The Rent Act 1957, a highly contentious piece of legislation, had only
recently been introduced. The government argued that by abolishing rent
controls it would 'halt the decay of private property' because landlords would
be encouraged to maintain, improve and invest in the rental market. Instead
'it became a charter for the exploitation of poor tenants in areas like North
Kensington.'[17]

By 1958, it was estimated that 114,000 people from the Caribbean had
arrived in Britain since the end of the Second World War. From an early stage,
some gravitated to Paddington but the available accommodation quickly
filled up 'before the peak influx of 1955–56.' Located immediately to the west
of Paddington, Notting Hill became 'a logical overspill area.'[18] Three thousand
had quickly settled in that part centred on the Colville area and it was literally
'bursting at the seams.'[19] Certain unscrupulous landlords, the infamous
Peter Rachman[20] amongst them, immediately recognised the financial
benefits of letting rooms to black people who were having difficulty finding
accommodation elsewhere, 'because they could be charged extravagant rents,
with often four people per room, paying per head.' Police Constable Stan
May, who was at Notting Hill at the time, subsequently recalled that 'they
were exploited right, left and centre by both white and coloured property

---

16. Malik, Michael Abdul (1968). *From Michael de Freitas to Michael X*. London: Andre Deutsch,
    p.56.
17. Phillips and Phillips, *op. cit.* 3, p.190.
18. Wickenden, *op. cit.* 2, p.36. (Olden in his book *Murder in Notting Hill, op. cit.* 7, p.18, puts the
    number at 125,000).
19. Glass, *op. cit.* 9, p.50.
20. See *Chapter 4*.

speculators, forced by circumstances to pay outrageous rent for crumbling properties in areas that were already depressed, in particular St Stephen's Gardens, Powis Terrace and the Colvilles.'[21] In some cases as many as ten West Indians would be sleeping in one room, sometimes in shifts, whilst in others, whole families lived. In an effort to reduce extravagant rents, some newcomers hid friends in their rooms without the landlord's knowledge. If they could get 'five people into a room which the landlord thought was only occupied by one, each would pay one fifth of the rent.'[22] At the time of the 1958 riots, described in *Chapter 2*, it was estimated that 'the total coloured population of the North Kensington' was 'about 7,000.'[23]

Despite the problems, the newcomers quickly became established, in many cases living side-by-side with white families. Indeed, there were only a very few streets 'where the majority of people, or almost a majority,' were 'coloured'. Usually, more white people than coloured people were 'seen at the windows, on the doorsteps and in the streets' even in the districts in which the African-Caribbeans were concentrated and lived near to one another.[24] Therefore the image which some people tried to paint by referring to Notting Hill as a 'ghetto'[25] was 'far from reality'. It was certainly not a ghetto in the American sense of the word.[26]

Employment

The report by Senior and Manley placed employment second amongst the difficulties faced by migrants from the West Indies.[27] Although many were able to get work, albeit mainly in unskilled jobs, others found it impossible. Nevertheless, in 1956, the Conservative Government made a conscious decision to recruit people from the Caribbean to ease the post-war labour shortage, particularly on London Transport—the buses and the underground

---

21. May, *op. cit.* 1.
22. Ramdin, Ron (1987). *The Making of the Black Working Class in Britain*. Aldershot: Wildwood House, p.192; see also Pilkington, *op. cit.* 10, p.56.
23. Wickenden, *op. cit.* 2, p.36.
24. Glass, *op. cit.* 9, pp.41–42.
25. Malik, *op. cit.* 16, p.55–56.
26. Glass, *op. cit.* 9, pp.41/42; see also Ramdin, *op. cit.* 19, p.190. *Collins English Dictionary* defines a ghetto as 'an area that is inhabited by people of a particular race, religion, nationality or class'.
27. Senior and Manley, *op. cit.* 8. Quoted by Wickenden, op. cit. 2, p.9.

system—and in nursing. By 1958, there were something like 8,000 African-Caribbeans working for London Transport. However, the Suez Crisis and subsequent shortage of oil led to a recession and the return of high levels of unemployment in some areas. Even though black people were invariably the first to be laid off, white working-class people felt that their presence was the cause of unemployment amongst the white population too.[28]

Wickenden suggested that West Indian immigrants fell into two categories. Firstly, there were those who had, on the whole, made good in Britain which was the majority. On the other hand, a minority, for a variety of reasons failed to make good—Wickenden referred to them as misfits. Such people believed their failures were due 'to prejudice' and once unemployed, easily became 'a tool for the sale of marijuana or hemp', or they found 'it easier to live off women'. As a result they quickly became unemployable.[29] Michael de Freitas described how on the second day following his arrival in Notting Hill, he registered at the local Labour Exchange as a painter, which was one of the skills he had learned on board ship.

> 'It took me three minutes flat to find out I wasn't going to get [a job]. They told me straight out that there were jobs, but none for coloured people. It was the room scene all over again. No coloured for this, no coloured for that.'[30]

De Freitas went on to become a ponce, i.e. one who knowingly lives off the earnings of a prostitute, a shebeen owner, strong-arm man for Peter Rachman and, later to gain notoriety as Michael X. Invariably, black people were in a no-win situation with white people, the latter either claiming that black people had taken their jobs or, when they could not find work or chose not to work, referring to them as layabouts.

Prostitution

Well before the mass immigration from the West Indies commenced, Notting Hill already provided 'reinforcements for the army of prostitutes who lined

---

28. Vague, Tom (1988). *Vague 30: London Psychologeography—Rachman, Riots and Rillington Place*. London: Ladbroke Grove, p.17.

29. Wickenden, *op. cit.* 2, p.22.

30. Malik, op. cit. 16, p.57.

the Hyde Park railings every few yards all the way down Bayswater Road and along Park Lane.'[31] The Italian Messina brothers, who controlled much of the prostitution in the West End, had even installed two girls in a flat in Lancaster Road, but generally the local girls were 'run' locally by Maltese or Cypriot men,[32] together with a few from Ireland.[33] By the mid-1950s, it was claimed that 'there were prostitutes occupying virtually every street corner from Marble Arch to Shepherds Bush' and by 1957, approximately 15 prostitutes were arrested each night just on Notting Hill's sub-division alone.[34] By the 1960s it had become a 'well-established offshoot of the Soho vice empire'. Whilst many of the inhabitants deeply resented this, 'others plunged enthusiastically' into the opportunities it provided to make easy money.[35]

During the early years of migration the vast majority of men coming from the Caribbean came alone. It was, therefore, 'perfectly natural for them to seek female companionship'[36] but, only the prostitutes, most of them white, showed them 'any generosity of spirit' or gave them 'a friendly smile or a helping hand.'[37] This, in turn, 'started to sow the seeds of racial disharmony jealousy.'[38] Whilst white men had lived on the immoral earnings of prostitutes for years it was not until it became 'a major occupation amongst black men living in Notting Hill' that it became a real issue.[39] Green summarised the situation, suggesting that

'a disconcerting proportion of young black men lived off white prostitutes, partly because women have never enjoyed a very high status in West Indian eyes, but

---

31. Phillips Mike and Trevor Phillips, *op. cit.* 3, p.25.
32. Scott, Sir Harold (1954). *Scotland Yard.* London: Andre Deutsch, p.66.
33. May, *op. cit.* 1.
34. *Ibid.* To reinforce May's recollection, Phillips and Phillips, *op. cit.* 3, p.109, described how on one evening in November 1958, between 10 p.m. and 10.30 p.m., 73 prostitutes were seen operating between Notting Hill and Shepherds Bush. Twelve were arrested but only four appeared at court; the remaining eight 'disappeared into the warren of streets' in Notting Hill.
35. Phillips, Mike and Trevor Phillips (1991). *Notting Hill in the Sixties.* London: Lawrence & Wishart, p.50.
36. May, *op. cit.* 1.
37. Phillips Mike and Trevor Phillips, *op. cit.* 3, p.114.
38. May, *op. cit.* 1.
39. Phillips Mike and Trevor Phillips, *op. cit.* 35, pp.52–54.

mainly because, whereas living off immoral earnings proved extremely easy, finding an honest, well-paid job proved extremely difficult.'[40]

In the two years leading up to the 1958 riot, 24 men (20 from Jamaica; one from British Guiana and three from West Africa) were arrested and charged with living on the earnings of prostitution in the Notting Hill area.[41] However, it is likely that this number represented only about one quarter of those who were actually living off such earnings.[42]

Later, a number of black girls, principally from Jamaica, earned their living by working as prostitutes, soliciting in the nearby Bayswater Road. One young man who took advantage of the situation was De Freitas. He described how, when he first settled in Notting Hill with his girl-friend, Desiree, the area would take on 'a sexual quality' at night with many of the young women plying 'their bodies for hire'[43] and he, too, took advantage of the situation.[44] But, as one café owner said at the time of the 1958 riots, 'a lot of black men live off prostitutes and a lot of teddy boys would like to.'[45]

A source of annoyance to the police arose when the black ponces[46] started buying expensive cars, driving the girls to and from the place where they solicited and buying and wearing expensive clothes. Not all white women who were seen in the company of black men were prostitutes, but any white woman, prostitute or not, who associated with black men, was immediately ostracised by the white community who saw such an association as 'working-class degeneracy on the part of the women' in meeting 'with the legendary and indiscriminating lust of black men.'[47]

---

40. Green, Shirley (1979). *Rachman*. London: Michael Joseph/Hamlyn, p.90.
41. Metropolitan Police (1958). 'Report on The Notting Hill Race Riots 1958'. Typescript, pp.83–84. Copy in the author's possession.
42. Wickenden, *op. cit.* 2, pp.37–38.
43. Malik, *op. cit.* 16, p.57.
44. *Ibid*, pp.58–65.
45. Phillips Mike and Trevor Phillips, *op. cit.* 35, p.51.
46. Ponce is another word, similar to pimp, used to describe someone who lives on the earnings of a prostitute.
47. Phillips Mike and Trevor Phillips, *op. cit.* 35, pp.51.

Lack of Entertainment

Illegal clubs, frequented by white people, many of them criminals, already existed in the early-1950s, particularly in Notting Dale. Some were set up legally in that they were licensed for members and only but became illegal when the rules relating to membership or the hours during which they were allowed to sell alcohol were not adhered to. Indeed, some, known as 'afters', would not open until the pubs had shut, and drinking would continue until the early hours of the morning. In others, known as 'spielers', illegal gambling also took place. Police Constable Bob Davis, who was stationed at Notting Dale at the time, described how 'there were fights and God knows what going on till four or five in the morning, until we eventually got to grips with them.' The crime associated with them was violent, including some very serious assaults with 'people with their legs shot off with shotguns and axes in their heads and this kind of thing.' And it happened 'night after night after night.'[48]

Any black person attempting to gain admittance to these 'white' clubs would run the risk of hostility, at the very least, and most probably serious injury. In addition, pubs and dance halls were 'equally inhospitable' to the newly arrived immigrants. Many dance halls operated outright colour bars whilst others would only allow entry if the man was accompanied by a white partner. In those pubs which did allow black men to congregate it was only in the public bar, not in the saloon bar.[49] One such pub in All Saints Road, The Apollo, accepted black men from an early stage, and was to figure regularly as one of the dominant features of the Front Line for the next 25 years until its closure in 1983.[50]

In any event, pubs in Notting Hill were not particularly hospitable places to visit. Talking of his early visits to Notting Hill in 1952, Police Constable Joe Nixon described how 'ill-clad and dirty children' squatted 'on the steps of public houses while their mothers guzzled beer inside and their fathers quarrelled or exchanged bawdy anecdotes'. Even then, groups of white youths

---

48. Pilkington in conversation with PC Bob Davis on 21 December 1983. Quoted in Pilkington, *op. cit.* 10, p.96; Olden *op. cit.* 7,
49. Vague, *op. cit.* 12, p.18.
50. Pilkington, *op. cit.* 10, p.61; Olden, *op. cit.* 7, p.19 describes how 'black' people from all over London came to drink there.

would gibe at 'coloured men' when they passed, and 'drunkenness, cars turned over, violence, and obscenity stalked the shadows'.[51]

Those from the Caribbean who wanted to set up their own entertainment were confronted with two major problems — the strict liquor licensing laws and the equally strict gambling laws. Therefore the black people started to open their own, usually unlicensed, clubs in ground floor and basement flats in residential areas. As one black resident of the time pointed out, no magistrate would grant a liquor licence for such a place and, therefore, if anyone wanted to provide a place of entertainment for black people they 'had to break the law.'[52] Not unnaturally, perhaps, this was deeply resented by many white residents.

By the mid-1950s 'a complete sub-culture had sprung up in Notting Hill which centred on various kinds of clubs that West Indians were illegally running from their houses.' Green described two types, 'the cellar clubs where people could smoke or gamble during the day' and the 'after-clubs,' which derived their name from being a place to visit 'where people could smoke and drink and dance' as well as purchase alcohol after the licensed premises had closed.[53] These were more commonly known as shebeens. Sometimes, the shebeens doubled as gambling clubs, although frequently they were separate. De Freitas described how often during the day he and his friends would go to 'cellar clubs — quiet basements with a table, where people would gamble with dice or cards.'[54] Claiming there were 'no social amenities, no community hall, no public place where a band could play to people and amuse them' in Notting Hill, he described how blues dances were 'a regular happening'. Because West Indians were 'basically a drinking people' who wanted a place where they could 'sit and drink as well as dance,' there had to be a bar and this made 'the whole thing illegal.' Describing how such things were organized, he said:

---

51. Richardson, Anthony (1965). *Nick of Notting Hill*. London: George G. Harrap, pp.54–55.
52. Phillips Mike and Trevor Phillips, *op. cit.* 35, p.55.
53. Green, *op. cit.* 53, p.93.
54. Malik, *op. cit.* 16, p.57.

'We simply cleared the floor, put a table across the kitchen door to serve as a counter and stocked up with a load of canned beer. We charged 2s. 6d. to come in and 2s. 6d. for each beer.'[55]

Johnny Edgecombe, later to become famous as a result of his involvement with Christine Keeler and the Profumo case,[56] claimed he opened the very first shebeen in London in Colville Terrace although there is some doubt about this. It was, he said, a flat on the first floor which would hold between 20 and 30 people:

'There was a front room where you could listen to the latest sounds, sitting in low chairs. In this room was a bar, where we served any type of drink you wanted. Next door in the bedroom was the casino. The only furniture in the bedroom was a table with chairs, where people sat and played poker. .... In the front room would be some nice jazz going down, with people drinking and smoking dope. I would roll joints myself, and sell them for five shillings a spliff. While the men were gambling, the chicks sat around getting stoned and drunk. The gambling room was mainly occupied by pimps where they would gamble their night's wages away. There were also some professional gamblers who, more often than not, would win the pimps' money from them. The game played was mostly five-card stud poker, with quite heavy stakes of up to £100 — a lot of money in those days.'

Claiming that his landlord was Rachman and he was earning £400 per week from the card games in 'house' money, the shebeen had no fixed hours but would stay open until the last people left. One of the people who allegedly frequented his shebeen was Lucky Gordon, who was also to hit the headlines during the Profumo scandal.[57]

Precisely how many of these clubs there were at any one time is difficult to calculate. Countering Edgecombe's earlier claim to be the first, Vague suggested that the first was in fact Duke Vin's in Talbot Road.[58] Another was a basement gymnasium at 32a Powis Square which became a shebeen

---

55. *Ibid*, pp.71–72.
56. See *Chapter 4*.
57. Edgecombe, John (2002). *Black Scandal*. London: Westworld International, pp.56–57.
58. Vague, *op. cit.* 28, p.19.

at night, run by Roy Stewart, who also worked as a part-time film extra and stuntman.[59] The *Kensington News* referred to them as 'mushroom clubs', suggesting they had 'all the appearance of private parties' but drinking went 'on until the early hours of the morning.' But, more importantly, the continual comings and goings throughout the night and the fights,[60] which often broke out when 'drunken guests' came 'out into the street to settle their differences', caused friction between black and white people living in the areas around these clubs. Initially, there was some attempt at respectability by some West Indians to the extent that, at the end of 1958, there were five clubs that, on the face of it, were operating legally. One, the Calypso Dance and Social Club in Westbourne Park Road, had opened in 1957; the remainder—Club New Orleans in St Stephen's Gardens, Club Blues in Talbot Road, Club Montparnasse in Chepstow Road, and the Phoenix Club in Colville Road, had all opened in 1958. Most were open until four or five o'clock in the morning but were legally only entitled to sell alcohol until 11 p.m. (weekdays) and 10 p.m. (Sundays).[61] Because the licensing laws were not adhered to, these clubs were not in existence for very long before they were raided by the police and the licence was revoked. The end result of all this was that a sizeable minority of West Indians spent their time gambling, smoking cannabis and drifting into petty crime.[62]

Disputes

Whilst successive governments made some efforts to inform those in the Caribbean intending to migrate to Britain, what it would be like, no steps were taken 'to educate and inform the host community on the implications of the mass migration of black people to Britain.'[63] No-one predicted 'the consequences of more or less uncontrolled immigration and there was no leadership from government, churches or local authorities to whom the police

---

59. Olden, *op. cit.* 7, p.19.
60. These fights frequently involved 'black American servicemen, West Indians, Irish and English [Notting] Dale locals, and police.' *Kensington News*, 15 August 1958.
61. Metropolitan Police, *op. cit.* 41, pp.88–89
62. Green, *op. cit.* 40, p.93.
63. Whitfield, James (2004). *Unhappy Dialogue: The Metropolitan Police and Black Londoners in Post-war Britain.* Cullompton, Devon: Willan, p.20.

would normally look for guidelines.'[64] The greatest failing was at central government level. There being 'no strategic plan or directions from the centre', the police, along with local government, and other statutory and voluntary agencies 'were left to sort out the situation as best they could.'[65] It was not surprising, therefore, that, as time passed, there was a noticeable increase in the number of occasions when police were called to disputes between black and white people either living in the same property or in adjacent houses. These took a number of forms. Firstly, the dispute often related to the accommodation itself. Glass described how 'tensions and frictions' would develop as the West Indians were 'wedged in and forced to compete for scarce space and amenities' with white tenants, many of whom had for a long time 'been badly housed themselves'. And, invariably, it was 'the newcomer' who was 'made the scapegoat for physical and social claustrophobia' especially if they were coloured and their 'mode of living' had 'not yet adapted to dense quarters in a cold climate.'[66]

Stan May, described how the police were 'frequently called to rent disputes which often became emotional and highly charged'. But there was rarely any satisfaction for the immigrants, partly, it seems, because in the Caribbean, the 'West Indies police could arbitrate on the spot in such disputes' and they expected the English policeman to do the same. Instead, British police officers would refer them to 'their civil remedies' which meant either going to a rent tribunal or to a magistrates' court. The result was a loss of confidence in the British police and accusations that they were always on the side of the property owners or the indigenous population. May claimed that the Police Service could not 'be entirely exonerated' from this state of affairs. Whilst 'individual officers did their best to be impartial and do their job properly, the foretaste of things to come was clearly visible' both to the constables and the sergeants, who dealt with many of those early disputes, but no-one of more senior rank appeared either interested or saw the danger signs.[67]

In addition, there were also a number of cases where white tenants suffered at the hands of their new African-Caribbean landlords. Having purchased

---

64. *Ibid*, p.21.
65. May, *op. cit.* 1.
66. Glass, *op. cit.* 9, p.56.
67. May, *op. cit.* 1.

the house and let some of the rooms to their fellow countrymen they would then turn their attention to any white tenants who had been in residence at the time of purchase. Quickly the new landlords made life unbearable for those people, forcing them eventually to seek alternative accommodation.[68] This tactic was highlighted when, in late-August 1958, a white woman, living with her two children in accommodation, which had recently been purchased by two Jamaicans, was asked to vacate her room but she refused. From then onwards she was the victim of insults from her landlords who often came into her room uninvited, both when she was present and when she was out. Indeed, her life became so unbearable that she attempted to gas herself and her two children. She was subsequently charged with administering gas with intent to murder but at the trial no evidence was offered and she was given an absolute discharge for exposing the children in a manner likely to cause unnecessary suffering and injury to health. The children were taken into care by the Greater London Council.[69]

Two weeks earlier, the position was summed up by a tenant talking to the *Kensington News* when she said:

> 'Coloured landlords have — as white landlords have been doing since the passing of the Rent Act — been trying to get their tenants out so they can get higher rents for their rooms. In some cases they have been stopping at nothing to do so. There have been reports of trumped-up charges to get us out. Last week I was served with four summonses alleging assault on the landlord and his wife. I've never laid a finger on either of them.'[70]

Another tenant complained that the landlord had taken over his room whilst he was still paying for it; another that he had been 'thrown out onto the street with all his belongings, on the grounds that he was 'trespassing'.[71]

A second cause of disputes was noise arising from the different lifestyles. West Indians were 'an extrovert and music-loving people' who 'liked their music loud enough to make a home shake to its foundations,' and one of the

---

68. Metropolitan Police, *op. cit.* 41, p.4.
69. *Kensington News*, 15 August 1958.
70. *Kensington News*, 1 August 1958.
71. Green, *op. cit.* 40, p.90.

first priorities was to make 'a down-payment on a record player.'[72] For many, 'home was a place to invite one's friends for a party, or general get-together, as well as to reminisce about life 'back home', frequently to musical and alcoholic accompaniment.' However, in London, they 'predominantly lived in multi-occupancy accommodation, often with grudging white neighbours who had little empathy with West Indian cultures.' This meant the police were, not surprisingly perhaps, 'frequent and unwelcome visitors' to these Caribbean 'get-togethers.'[73] But some of these so-called parties were not parties at all in the generally accepted sense of the word; rather they were shebeens, where, although the people attending were likely to know one another and even be friends, the food and drinks were on sale for the purpose of making the owner a tidy profit. Similarly, in those places where gaming occurred, the owner would take a percentage from each pot.

According to one black resident, a lot of things 'annoyed' the police. Loud music, the illegal sale of alcohol, large gatherings of black people all brought the police into contact with them. Consequently, the clubs were raided regularly. However, whilst the seizure of the alcohol found on the premises was, to some extent acceptable to the black inhabitants of the club, the fact that the police would also 'kick in' the sound systems, including the speakers, caused great resentment. One frequenter of the clubs during that period suggested that anything which happened subsequently between black people and the police arose from their earlier 'stupidness' in 'breaking their sound systems, costing them money, and indirectly disrupting their social pattern.'[74] This pattern of behaviour by the police unfortunately continued with one West Indian writer, Cecil Gutzmore suggesting that, 'throughout the 60s, and early-70s, blacks were systemically brutalised in shebeens and house parties.'[75]

72. Phillips Mike and Trevor Phillips, *op. cit.* 35, p.55.
73. Whitfield, *op. cit.* 63, p.29.
74. Phillips Mike and Trevor Phillips, *op. cit.* 3, p.112.
75. Gutzmore, Cecil (1993). 'Carnival, the State and the Black Masses in the United Kingdom'. In *Inside Babylon: The Caribbean Diaspora in Britain* (eds: Winston James and Clive Harris). London: Verso, p.214.

Conclusions

When the *Empire Windrush* arrived in 1948, post-war reconstruction was in its early stages and the arriving West Indians found 'racialism, particularly in employment, and housing' in abundance. At first, they 'found it difficult to cope with British prejudices', and, as a result, they took refuge within their own communities, organizing 'their own churches, clubs and welfare organizations' and congregating in 'barber shops, cafés or street corners, if the weather was fine.'[76] This was an early cause of friction, because there was a lack of understanding amongst the police of black street culture. Former Metropolitan Police Commissioner, Sir Peter Imbert explained:

> 'It's often been said that the young Caribbean youth had a street culture whereas the indigenous youth didn't have a street culture in quite the same way. I think we in the police didn't understand that. When we saw black youth hanging around street corners we couldn't understand why. We automatically thought — quite wrongly of course — on every occasion that they were up to no good. But that was because of a lack of understanding of their culture and their way of life.'[77]

Former police officer turned academic, James Whitfield, pointed out that 'neither Whitehall nor the Met had initially envisaged a role for the police in areas of immigrant settlement other than the time-honoured ones of law enforcement and regulation.'[78] Like the general public, the police at Notting Hill, and, indeed, police officers throughout the United Kingdom generally, 'were ignorant of, and lacked empathy with, Caribbean cultures and lifestyles.' This was a failure that, from 1945 onwards, 'successive governments' did 'little to correct.'[79] So whilst none of these factors actually led to the Notting Hill riots in 1958, there was a background of increasing resentment between white and black people living in the area, and between those living in the area, both black and white, and the police.

---

76. Ramdin, *op. cit.* 22, p.493.
77. From an interview, Whitfield had with Sir Peter Imbert. Quoted from Whitfield, *op. cit.* 63, p.147.
78. *Ibid*, p.54.
79. *Ibid*, p.55.

CHAPTER 2

RACE RIOTS OF 1958

Prelude to the Riot

During the early hours of Sunday, August 24, 1958, nine young men, all in their teens, crammed into one car and set out 'on a pleasure tour of West London'[1] after a drinking session in a local public house. In the car were a number of weapons, including an air pistol, a starting handle, iron railings shaped as spears, chair legs and wooden staves, each between three and four feet in length. All the young men were white.

Between 3 a.m. and 5.30 a.m. on that August morning, they attacked black people in Notting Hill and the surrounding area on five separate occasions. The first three attacks occurred in quick succession. In Lancaster Road one man was stabbed and another beaten about the head; both were taken to hospital. Five minutes later, in Ladbroke Grove, a man was left with a head wound requiring six stitches. Following the third assault, in Oxford Gardens, a man was taken to hospital with cuts and bruises to his head. They then moved away from the immediate Notting Hill area. As a result, there was a lull before the fourth attack occurred at shortly after 5 a.m. in Shepherds Bush Green. This time the victim required 12 stitches to a head wound. The final attack took place soon afterwards in North Pole Road when another man was attacked. In each attack iron bars and other weapons were used.[2]

Although the police had been alerted to the gang after the first attack it was not until shortly after the fifth incident that the car containing the nine young men was seen. The police gave chase but the occupants abandoned the car in Loftus Road, Shepherds Bush, and escaped, leaving their weapons

---

1. Pilkington, Edward (1988). *Beyond the Mother Country: West Indians and the Notting Hill White Riots*. London: I. B. Taurus, p.109.

2. Metropolitan Police (1958). 'Report on The Notting Hill Race Riots 1958'. Unpublished, pp.9–10. See also Olden, Mark (2011). *Murder at Notting Hill*. Winchester: Zero Books, pp.21–22 for a more detailed account which is slightly at variance with that contained in the Metropolitan Police Report.

behind. Extensive enquiries followed and some 12 hours later all nine men were in custody. They were all charged with wounding two men and causing actual bodily harm to two others; four of the nine were also charged with wounding a fifth man.[3]

All remained quiet for the five days following the attacks but, on Friday, 29 August, the nine youths made their first appearance at West London Magistrates' Court where the magistrate, E R Guest, pointed out, in response to an application for bail, that some men had been injured in the attacks and commented, 'I can only say that if ever there was a case in which it would be contrary to the public interest to grant bail, it is this case.' He went on to say:

> 'It is a matter of considerable public importance that something should be done seriously to stop street disorders in Fulham, Hammersmith and North Kensington. They are not only a disgrace to the neighbourhood, but extremely dangerous for ordinary citizens. They are only committed by a minority of nuisances who could be very quickly stamped out by any court with true powers.'[4]

What happened in Notting Hill over the next five days should have surprised no-one given that a similar area in Nottingham, St Anne's, had erupted a week earlier in a series of clashes between white and black men.[5] Indeed, the local newspaper warned on that same Friday:

> 'Kensington has a colour problem whether you care to admit it or not. It must exist where people of greatly differing outlook, emotions and appearance are living side by side.'

Pointing out that 'petty problems become magnified out of all proportion', it went on to suggest that 'Nottingham must be a warning to

---

3. *Ibid*, p.10. For a more detailed account of the arrest and investigation relating to the nine youths, see Olden, *op. cit.* 2, pp.22–25.
4. *Kensington Post*, 29 August, 1958.
5. See Pilkington, *op. cit.* 1, pp.107–113 for a brief description of the riots in Nottingham; see also Phillips, Mike and Trevor Phillips (1998). *Windrush: The Irresistible Rise of Multi-Racial Britain.* London: HarperCollins, pp.166–170.

North Kensington, to Paddington, to Brixton, wherever coloured people in large numbers are living and working side-by-side with long-established Londoners.'[6]

National newspapers like *The Guardian,* too, were warning that Notting Hill was showing all the signs of being the next area where racial conflict might break out.[7] Despite this, the Metropolitan Police took no immediate action to increase its presence on the streets and neither did it arrange for any officers to be on reserve.

Friday 29/Saturday 30 August

The first incident occurred that same Friday evening outside Latimer Road Underground Station. An argument between Majbritt Morrison, a pregnant Swedish woman, and her Jamaican husband, Raymond,[8] drew a crowd of white people. Thinking it was their duty to protect the white woman, men in the crowd started shouting at her husband. But Majbritt then tried to protect Raymond, which was anathema to the white crowd. Fortunately, a group of her husband's friends arrived and, although there was a small skirmish, no-one was hurt. Later that evening, white youths broke the windows of two houses, occupied by black people, 'but these were treated as ordinary cases of criminal damage' rather than a foretaste of what was to come.[9]

Saturday 30/Sunday 31 August

The following day the weather was warm. Throughout the afternoon, word spread around Notting Dale 'that it was time to teach the "niggers" and their "white trash" a lesson.'[10] By early evening the five public houses in Bramley Road were full and groups of white people were gathered on the streets, talking. Only now, did the police take some precautions. In addition to the normal night-duty patrol strength at Notting Hill—an inspector, a sergeant and eleven constables—two wireless cars, each crewed by three

---

6. *Kensington News and West London Times,* 29 August 1958.
7. *The Guardian,* 27 August 1958.
8. The couple had met in 1955 when Majbritt was visiting London with a group of Swedish students. Raymond was already living on the immoral earnings of prostitution and, according to Olden, once the baby was born, Majbritt became a prostitute. Olden, *op. cit.* 2, p.26.
9. Metropolitan Police, *op. cit.* 2, p.12.
10. Pilkington, *op. cit.* 1, p.113.

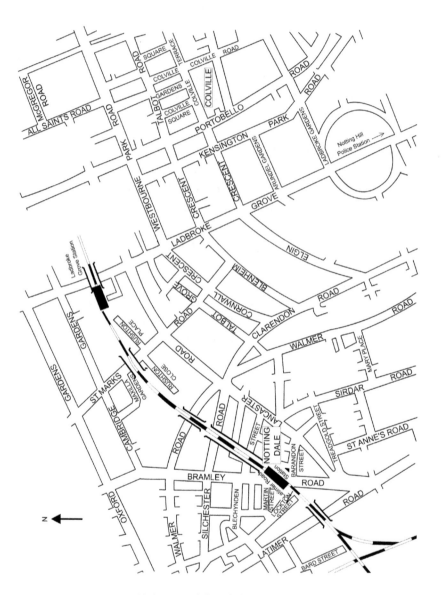

Main area of the 1958 Race Riot.

Map drawn and © Kate Whittingham.

constables, and three dog handlers patrolled the area. Another ten constables were on stand-by at the police station.[11] As things turned out, this was woefully inadequate.

The relative calm in the early evening sunshine was the lull before the storm. Once darkness descended, a large crowd of white people surrounded eight black men outside Latimer Road Underground Station, and attacked them with empty milk bottles and sticks. Serious injury was only prevented by the timely arrival of one of the three dog handlers, Police Constable Sayce. With the help of his dog, he managed to separate the two groups and lock the black men in the underground station for their own protection. Attracted by the noise, Constables Rhodes and Main appeared on the scene and helped Constable Sayce disperse the crowd.[12]

It was the first of a number of incidents. A petrol bomb was thrown through the window of No.63 Bramley Road, by white youths, starting a small fire. With one exception, the house, divided into separate rooms, was occupied solely by black people. The exception was the ground floor flat, occupied by Majbritt Morrison and her husband but both were out at the time. The incident attracted a large number of people but the fire brigade were quickly on the scene to prevent serious damage. However, whilst they were engaged in fighting the fire, Morrison, suddenly appeared from the direction of Blechynden Street, and walked towards No.63 Bramley Road. She was recognised by the crowd who jeered and jostled her, calling her, amongst other things, 'Nigger lover!'[13] She was escorted to her home by Sergeant Shearn who advised her to go in the house and remain there for her own safety which, initially, she did.

Unfortunately, she emerged a few minutes later. Sergeant Shearn told her to go back inside the house; in addition to his concern for her personal safety, he was also worried that her presence was likely to make it far more difficult for the police officers present to keep the peace. She refused; Sergeant Shearn offered to have her escorted away from Bramley Road but again she refused. He therefore arrested her for obstructing a police officer in the execution of his duty and she was taken to Notting Hill Police Station. As soon as the

---

11. Metropolitan Police, *op. cit.* 2, p.13.

12. *Ibid*, p.14.

13. Pilkington, *op. cit.* 1, p.113.

fire brigade had extinguished the fire, they left the scene and the police were able to disperse the crowd without further incident.[14]

The senior officer on duty, Acting Superintendent Simmonds, had, meanwhile, increased the number of officers at his disposal to 35 by arranging for another ten constables to be sent from adjoining police stations.[15] The crowd, having been dispersed from Bramley Road, next sought confrontation with 70 black people holding a party in the basement of a house in nearby Blechynden Street. Bottles were thrown at the windows and an attempt by the black occupants to leave the house to confront the white crowd was only prevented by the timely arrival of Inspector Coventry and five constables. More officers arrived shortly afterwards, enabling the inspector to disperse the crowd and arrange for the party-goers to be escorted to their respective homes.[16] Pilkington subsequently suggested that Inspector Coventry's action in escorting the West Indians away from the party in Blechynden Street 'averted a potentially disastrous confrontation' but 'it did little to avert further rioting, for in the eyes of the white rioters these tactics seemed to confirm their belief that through violence they could drive black people out of Notting Dale.'[17]

There were four further incidents that night. In the first, two black men who had been escorted to their home were seen shortly afterwards on the street armed with empty milk bottles. They were told to return to their home, refused and were arrested for obstructing the officer in the execution of his duty; windows were broken in two houses occupied by black people, whilst in the fourth, a white man walking alone at about 2 a.m. was attacked by a group of black men. The toll that night was relatively light. Two police constables and one white man were slightly injured. Two white men and two black men were arrested and four houses had been damaged.[18]

---

14. Metropolitan Police, *op. cit.* 2, pp.14–15.
15. *Ibid*, pp.15–16. The charge was subsequently dismissed at the magistrates' court pursuant to the Magistrates' Courts Act 1952. *Ibid*, p.64.
16. *Ibid*, p.16.
17. Pilkington, *op. cit.* 1, p.11.
18. Metropolitan Police, *op. cit.* 2, p.17.

Sunday 31 August/Monday 1 September

In anticipation of disorder on the Sunday night, arrangements were made for the late shift—normally an inspector, a sergeant and eleven constables—to be doubled from 7 p.m. Anticipating that any violence was most likely to occur after the pubs closed, the night shift was strengthened at 10 p.m. by drafting in two serials, i.e. two inspectors, four sergeants and forty constables but, as the evening wore on, it became clear that even this was insufficient.[19]

This was the worst night of violence. The first incident of note occurred at about 8 p.m. when a black man was confronted by two white youths carrying iron bars as he left Latimer Road Underground Station. The black man immediately took to his heels but was chased by the two youths who, in turn, were followed by a crowd of white children. The black man managed to gain the shelter of a house and the two youths disappeared. But, on the whole that evening, black people stayed inside their houses.[20]

Robbed of the target of their venom, white youths turned against the police, accusing them of being 'all for the niggers' and 'nigger lovers.'[21] People gathered in Bramley Road. Many were between 15 and 18-years-of-age and were dressed in the 'Teddy-boy' style of the day. Some were armed with makeshift weapons and were clearly out to attack black people, voicing such sentiments as 'We'll kill the black bastards.'[22]

In an attempt to forestall outbreaks of disorder later in the evening, the police, operating in groups of five, tried to clear the crowd from the street but, in doing so, found themselves the principal target for the crowd's hostility. Milk bottles, stones and iron railings were thrown at them. Hopelessly outnumbered, some were injured.[23]

In one particularly nasty incident, Police Constable Golding was struck on the leg by a white man wielding an iron-bar as he attempted to disperse a crowd in Bramley Road. The man, William Woodrow, was arrested but Golding was quickly surrounded by a crowd intent on freeing the prisoner. With the assistance of other officers who were nearby, Woodrow was eventually

---

19. *Ibid*, pp.17–18.
20. *Ibid*, p.19.
21. Pilkington, *op. cit.* 1, p.114.
22. *Ibid*.
23. Metropolitan Police, *op. cit.* 2, p.18.

placed in a police car and driven away to Notting Hill Police Station. However, the remaining police officers then came under attack.

Hemmed in by the crowd they were forced back against some shop windows and were then subjected to a hail of missiles.[24] Whilst this incident was ongoing, a black man, who had become entangled with the crowd, attacked two white men, father and son, seriously injuring the former when he slashed him across the neck and head with a pair of scissors. The man was arrested and subsequently charged with causing grievous bodily harm; other arrests made at this time included three white men, one of them the son of the injured man.[25]

At about 9 p.m., the Divisional Commander, Chief Superintendent Fieldsend, arrived in Bramley Road. Realising that 'the crowd was now thoroughly roused and Bramley Road was a scene of complete confusion' he returned to Notting Hill Police Station where he immediately arranged for the two serials due to arrive at 10 p.m. to be increased to five, giving him over 100 officers. By the time these officers began to arrive in Bramley Road the crowd had increased to between 600 and 700.[26] In the meantime, Police Constable Saunders received multiple cuts to his face when a bottle smashed into the windscreen of the car he was driving.[27]

Many of the youths cleverly switched the centre of activity by moving quickly from one place to another in their efforts to keep ahead of the police. In Blenchynden Street and Loxton Street, wooden and iron railings were torn from their fixings for use as weapons[28] and police vehicles bringing reinforcements into the area were attacked by missile-throwing youths.

At 10.30 p.m., Acting Commander Manuel, the deputy chief officer in charge of No 2 Area,[29] of which Notting Hill and F Division was a part, arrived to assume

---

24. *R v Woodrow, Cooper and Harrington*, Court of Criminal Appeal, 9 February 1959.
25. Metropolitan Police, *op. cit.* 2, p.19.
26. *Ibid*, pp.19–20.
27. *Ibid*, p.52.
28. Metropolitan Police, *op. cit.* 2, pp.20–21.
29. At the time, the Metropolitan Police District (MPD) was divided into four areas, numbered 1, 2, 3 and 4, with a commander in charge of each. Within each area there were a number of divisions, each under the command of a chief superintendent, and within each division, a number of sub-divisions under the command of a superintendent. At the time, the sub-division of Notting Hill was part of F Division within No.2 Area of the MPD.

overall command. As more police were drafted into the area around Bramley Road, small groups of white youths marauded further afield and black people were attacked in Lancaster Road, Clarendon Road, Cambridge Gardens and Westbourne Grove.[30]

As the evening wore on, more policemen were injured in Latimer Road, Lancaster Road and Silchester Road as they attempted to disperse crowds. In one incident, at about 11.30 p.m., two police officers, Constables Bending and Duphie fell to the ground and were kicked in the face by a white youth who was subsequently arrested and charged with assaulting the officers. At about the same time, Police Constable Taylor was struck by an iron railing which had been thrown through the window of the police van he was driving.[31] In another incident, at about midnight, the window of a shop in Bramley Road, being guarded by policemen, was broken when a jeering crowd threw bottles at it.[32] There were four more attacks by white people on black people and a fifth incident occurred in Portobello Road when a white person was struck over the head by a black person causing a wound which required four stitches.[33]

By 1 a.m., order had been restored and the crowds had dispersed; 19 people (15 white and four black) had been arrested. In addition to 12 police officers, at least ten members of the public (five white; five black) were known to have been injured. Seven police vehicles and four buildings were damaged.[34]

Thirteen of those arrested in Bramley Road that night (ten white men and three black men) later stood trial at the Central Criminal Court for what was then a little used common law offence of 'making an affray'. Five, including Woodrow, were found guilty and given prison sentences varying between 18 months and two years. The other eight, including the three black men, were acquitted.[35]

---

30. Metropolitan Police, *op. cit.* 2, p.20.
31. *Ibid*, p.53.
32. *The Times*, 1 September 1958.
33. Metropolitan Police, *op. cit.* 2, pp.23–24.
34. *Ibid*, pp.20–21.
35. *The Manchester Guardian*, 20 September 1958.

Monday 1/Tuesday 2 September — The Police Gain the Upper Hand

The following morning, the police reviewed their strategy and tactics. It was clear that they faced an escalation in violence and a more co-ordinated response was necessary if disorder was to be prevented. A re-appraisal of the problem revealed that:

(a) The number of people involved in the disorders was about 700, although they were rarely all in one place at the same time. They were predominantly white; however, many did not take an active part, confining themselves to giving moral support and encouragement to those involved in the violence and disorder.

(b) Although initially it was a clear case of white on black, a general feeling of hostility between the two factions was increasingly apparent. Attempts by the police to keep the two groups apart were becoming more difficult because sections of the white population, finding themselves prevented from attacking their primary target, turned their hostility on the police.

It was decided, therefore, that the police's principle tactic would be one of disruption, i.e. moving people on as soon as they began to gather on the streets and breaking large groups down into smaller groups. In doing so, it was hoped to forestall a repetition of the previous night's violence.[36]

Early in the day, Labour Member of Parliament for North Kensington George Rogers toured the district in a loudspeaker van, appealing to the residents 'for common sense, decency, and tolerance in this matter of race relations.' He continued, 'I ask you to remain calm, to stay indoors in your homes tonight and to obey the police.' His appeal largely went unheeded.[37]

Attracted by the many press reporters and newsreel cameramen roaming the streets, approximately 300 people, predominantly women and children, with a smattering of young men among them, had assembled in Bramley Road by 3 p.m. Notting Dale and the Colville area of Notting Hill was 'gripped by an unhealthy mood' and white people 'looked preoccupied and

---

36. Metropolitan Police, *op. cit.* 2, p.
37. *The Times*, 1 September 1958.

tense.' Despite the presence of this large crowd there was only one minor incident during the afternoon. A young West-African student, Seymour Manning, who was visiting London to see a friend and was unaware of the disturbances on the previous days, emerged from Latimer Road Underground Station at about 3.30 p.m. and sought directions to Walmer Road from a passer-by. He was immediately spotted by a large number of white youths who moved towards him shouting abuse. Pursued by the youths, the man ran along Bramley Road eventually seeking refuge in a greengrocer's shop at No. 95, where the shopkeeper's wife, a female friend and a teenage boy kept the crowd at bay until two constables arrived on foot, followed by two in a car. It eventually took mounted police and 20 constables on foot half-an-hour to disperse the crowd before they could escort him away from the area.[38]

At 8 p.m. that evening, the police implemented a number of measures designed to prevent a repeat of what had already taken place:

(a) Twenty constables, in pairs, under the command of an inspector and a sergeant, commenced patrols in the Bramley Road area on foot.[39]

(b) A 'mobile strike force', consisting of two inspectors, four sergeants and 40 constables, was on stand-by at Notting Hill Police Station, ready to respond rapidly to any incident. The transport available for their use consisted of two tenders,[40] two vans and three cars.[41]

(c) Four officers, in plain clothes, patrolled near the area on cycles to gather information and report back to the Operational Headquarters which had been set up at Notting Hill Police Station.[42]

(d) Two wireless cars patrolled the area with the intention of radioing back information of likely flashpoints.[43]

---

38. *Ibid.*
39. Metropolitan Police, *op. cit.* 2, p.34.
40. Tenders were green coaches, some with bars across the side windows, designed to hold about 30 police officers, and normally driven by civilian employees of the Metropolitan Police.
41. Metropolitan Police, *op. cit.* 2, p.34.
42. *Ibid.*
43. *Ibid.*

(e) Elsewhere, an inspector, a sergeant and 40 constables were on standby at Shepherds Bush Police Station in case the violence spread westwards and a further 30 constables in total were on standby at Chelsea, Putney and Ealing Police Stations respectively, to travel to Notting Hill if required.[44]

Between 8 p.m. and 9 p.m., a meeting by the National Union Movement in Baradon Street, addressed by Oswald Mosley's deputy, Jeffrey Hamm,[45] was, according to the police, attended at one point by about 200 people.[46] The police report claimed that a strong presence of police officers ensured there was no disorder but Pilkington suggested that, at the end of Hamm's speech, there was a great cry 'Kill the Niggers' from the crowd which then rushed off in all directions, avoiding police attempts to cut them off. Within half-an-hour, now 1,000 strong, it had broken scores of windows.[47] The truth is likely to be somewhere between the two versions. As the whole story of Notting Hill unravels it will be seen that, invariably, police reports tend to play down an incident, whereas the version put out by 'the other side' is prone to exaggeration.

As the evening wore on, the police acted quickly to prevent crowds from gathering but they were unable to stop small gangs of white youths moving rapidly around the area. But the character of the riots was changing. Firstly, due to reports appearing in the media, people, both black and white, were being drawn to the area from other parts of London and some of the surrounding towns, arriving by bus, car and van, and by train at Latimer Road and Ladbroke Grove Underground Stations; 'some came to ogle and gape, others to participate in the actual fighting.'[48] Secondly, a black response was now gaining momentum, with an increasing number of them coming onto the streets, some armed with wooden clubs, iron bars, knives, missiles and even petrol and bottles to make improvised Molotov cocktails. The West Indian community had held a meeting that afternoon in the Calypso Club

---

44. *Ibid.*
45. For the role of the Union Movement and other Fascist organizations during and immediately following the riots, see *Chapter 3*.
46. Metropolitan Police, *op. cit.* 2, p.23. Pilkington suggested as many as 700 were present, *op. cit.* 1, p.118.
47. Pilkington, *op. cit.* 1, p.118.
48. *Ibid*, p.119.

in Westbourne Park Road to decide on a course of action and, as night fell, 300 of them assembled in Nos. 6 and 9 Blenheim Crescent. And thirdly, the geographical area of the violence had widened. Consequently a series of incidents occurred over a fairly wide area—in Notting Hill and Notting Dale and beyond, in Shepherds Bush and the Harrow Road—throughout the evening and into the night, both white against black and black against white.[49]

Under the former category, white youths attacked black people or their property, as had been the pattern on the two previous evenings. Shortly before 8.30 p.m., a gang of between ten and 15 white youths threw bottles and pieces of wood at the windows of a black man's house in Latimer Road. Forty-five minutes later, windows were broken at two houses, one in Bard Road and one in St Marks Road, both buildings occupied by black families. Later that evening, a black man was chased into his house at Shepherds Bush Green by a gang of white youths. Meanwhile, another black man was confronted by white youths in Maxilla Gardens. In this latter case, although his coat was torn, he suffered no injury. Between 10 p.m. and 10.40 p.m., there were three further cases in which white youths assaulted black men, twice in Uxbridge Road and once in Norland Road.[50]

Other cases involved attacks by black on white. Around 8.45 p.m., a white man was struck on the forehead by a black man holding a broken bottle; the resultant wound required four stitches. Shortly after 9.30 p.m., the windows of a greengrocer's shop in Cornwall Crescent, owned by a white man, were broken. At about 10.10 p.m., a white man was stabbed in the back by a black man in Blenheim Crescent; fortunately the wound was not serious. Later, around 11.30 p.m., four white youths were attacked by a gang of black men in Westbourne Park Road. Still later, a group of some 15 black youths threw bottles at a house occupied by a white man in St Stephen's Gardens, breaking glass in the front door and a ground floor window.[51]

In all, between 600 and 700 people were involved, but police tactics ensured there were never more than 200 gathered in any one place. The 'mobile strike force' was constantly in action—a sergeant and ten constables

---

49. *Ibid*, pp.121/122.
50. Metropolitan Police, *op. cit.* 2, pp.23–25.
51. *Ibid*.

being sent to minor incidents, a full serial of an inspector, two sergeants and 20 constables, going to the more serious ones. By 9 p.m., the reserves from Chelsea, Putney and Ealing had been called to Notting Hill. The transport they travelled in was retained to supplement the vehicle fleet already at Notting Hill. As the crowds and the number of incidents increased, a further two inspectors, six sergeants and 26 constables were mustered from surrounding divisions and sent to Notting Hill, arriving between 10 p.m. and 11 p.m.[52]

The most serious incident occurred in Blenheim Crescent where, as already mentioned, something like 300 West Indians were crammed into Nos.6 and 9. Knowing that No.9 was a West Indian café, a large crowd of white people began to gather outside. Suddenly,

> '... up shot the third floor windows and out flew the Molotov cocktails. Pandemonium ensued as the white crowds scattered, dodging pieces of flying glass, with the West Indians in hot pursuit brandishing knives and choppers. .... Only a hard core of white people stayed to confront the West Indians, running between the two houses and hurling missiles back.'[53]

The police arrived on the scene within minutes. Eight black men and three white men were arrested and charged with affray. As Pilkington pointed out, this was an alarming development for the police because they were now caught between 'a mass of violent white youths intent on killing "nigs", and black people determined to defend themselves by any means necessary.'[54] Later, in another incident in Bard Road, over 50 white youths attacked a house, hurling a paraffin lamp through a ground-floor window which landed on a bed, causing a fire to break out. But again, the white youths were sent packing by a West Indian response.

The police tactics, consisting of a strong force patrolling potential trouble-spots, backed up by the 'mobile strike force', began to prove their effectiveness in preventing serious outbreaks of disorder. A total of 38 people (20 white; 18 black) were arrested, nine buildings were slightly damaged and eleven

---

52. *Ibid*, pp.25–26.
53. Pilkington, *op. cit.* 1, p.122.
54. *Ibid*, p.123.

members of the public (seven white; four black) were known to have been injured. No police officer was injured.[55]

Tuesday 2/Wednesday 3 September

On Tuesday, 2nd September, Notting Hill was described as looking 'like a scene from a film set in the American South' with people standing 'about in the heat outside their doors', leaning 'on balconies', or sitting 'sweating behind the blistered window-sills of Rachman's properties.'[56] Police officers 'walked about trying to look casual, and Black Marias were positioned at intersections.'[57]

A re-appraisal of the carefully laid plans made for the previous night revealed one main flaw. Only two wireless cars were in radio communication with the Operational Headquarters. Information from the plainclothes cyclists either had to be passed by telephone, using the police network that then existed in London or public call boxes, or it had to be taken personally. As Notting Hill Police Station was about a mile from the main area of disorder, the latter method took too long for the information to be used effectively. As a result, two police vans, fitted with radios, were sent, one to be parked outside Notting Hill Police Station whilst the other patrolled the area. This speeded up the flow of information.[58]

That evening, the officer in charge of No.2 Area, Commander Evans, assumed overall command, leaving Chief Superintendent Fieldsend as the ground commander. In addition, there was a superintendent, an acting chief inspector, seven inspectors, 12 sergeants and 130 constables available for deployment. Transport consisted of three tenders, four vans, three radio telegraphy (R/T) vans and five traffic patrol cars. Finally, Commissioner Sir Joseph Simpson spent four hours in the area.[59]

Throughout the evening, the police were engaged continuously in preventing outbreaks of disorder. By 8 p.m., crowds had begun to re-assemble in the areas around Bramley Road, Westbourne Park Road, Shepherds Bush

---

55. Metropolitan Police, *op. cit.* 2, pp.26–27.
56. Pilkington, *op. cit.* 1, p.123. Peter Rachman was unknown outside Notting Hill at the time but would become widely known later: see *Chapter 4*.
57. *The Guardian*, 3 September 1958.
58. Metropolitan Police, *op. cit.* 2, p.36.
59. *Ibid*, p.27.

Green and Paddington, but there were only minor incidents. In Lancaster Road, a large crowd of youths chanted 'Down with niggers'.[60] Once again, the tactic of having a strong force of police patrolling potentially troublesome areas, supported by the 'mobile strike force', began to take effect.[61] Despite this, gangs of youths, both black and white, toured the area in cars clearly looking for trouble. In the Colville area, several hundred white youths were roaming about shouting 'we want a nigger'.[62] But the police struck quickly, rounding up gangs of white youths, a number of whom were charged with possessing offensive weapons.[63]

Unlike previous days when there had been numerous incidents involving black and white people, there were only three of note during the course of the evening, two of which occurred outside the immediate Notting Hill area. At 11 p.m., the windows of a house in Cathnor Road, Shepherds Bush, which was occupied by black people, were broken. Shortly afterwards, a gang of white youths attacked a black man in Shepherds Bush Green; the resultant wound required six stitches. And finally, at about 11.30 p.m., police were called to Talbot Grove where it was alleged that a number of black men had emerged from the 'Blues Club' and broken the window of a tobacconist's shop, which was owned by a white man.[64]

By 12.30 a.m. all the crowds had dispersed. The police made 37 arrests (26 white; 11 black) that day. Only two properties had been damaged and only two people were known to have been injured. For the second night running, no police officer was injured.[65]

Rain Signals the End

On 3 September, the crowds had thinned considerably. Even so, shortly before mid-day, three white men threw bottles at a car being driven by a black man in Talbot Road. But, during the afternoon it started to rain. This got steadily heavier until, by evening, there were some torrential outbursts, followed by further rain throughout the night and into the next morning.

---

60. *The Times*, 3 September 1958.
61. Metropolitan Police, *op. cit.* 2, p.27.
62. Pilkington, *op. cit.* 1, p.123.
63. Metropolitan Police, *op. cit.* 2, p.29.
64. *Ibid*, p.28.
65. *Ibid*, pp.28–29.

This had the effect of keeping people in their houses and there was only one incident during the night when, in Norland Road, two black men had an altercation with two white men.[66]

However, it is interesting to note that the police report, in suggesting that 'conditions in this racial conflict had now returned to something like the conditions prevalent before the serious disorders commenced on 30th August', listed a further eleven incidents between 3 and 8 September. Eight involved attacks by white people on black people or their property; three involved attacks or threatened attacks by black people on white.[67] By the end of September, there had been a further nine attacks on black people or their property. None of the incidents were serious and consisted, in the main, of missiles being thrown through windows.[68]

Rain and increasingly effective police tactics had joined forces to bring the Notting Hill Race Riots to an end.

Conclusion

In five days, Notting Hill had become a focus of international attention. For the first three days, the 'West Indians were dazed and shocked and they stayed indoors in the hope that the violence would pass.' But, by the Monday they had had enough and 'it began to dawn on them that some more drastic form of defence was required.'[69]

According to Pilkington, there was 'no evidence on which one could base an accurate estimate' but it did appear 'the rioters were acting with the blessing of the majority of Notting Dale's white community.' In any event that was the perception of West Indians. Many white people were passive throughout the long weekend but, if any white person went to the help of a black person — and a few did — they were 'treated severely by their own people.'[70]

---

66. *Ibid, p.30.*
67. *Ibid*, pp.30–32.
68. *Ibid*, pp.32–33.
69. Pilkington, *op. cit.* 1, p.121.
70. *Ibid*, p.123.

Gutzmore suggested that the attacks on black people took place 'with the tacit and sometimes active approval of the Metropolitan Police.'[71] Bowes made a similar allegation, suggesting that 'the inadequacy of police protection ... could have been deliberate' for political reasons but 'it could have been because the Metropolitan Police were incapable of providing anything better.'[72] In his autobiography, Michael de Freitas, who was arrested during the riots, described the police as being 'very hostile to the blacks.'[73] All three were wrong. As Miles pointed out, the role of the police 'was often to protect the West Indians and their property from attack' and there was 'no evidence that the riotous behaviour involved conflict between the police and West Indians.'[74] Indeed, on a number of occasions, the police prevented attacks on black people by white gangs and, in doing so, some officers suffered quite serious injuries.

Phillips, on the other hand, suggested that 'part of the reason for the scale and intensity of the riots had been inept policing, and the failure to recognise that anything out of the ordinary was happening as the Saturday skirmishes escalated.'[75] Similarly, Pilkington suggested that it wasn't until the 'fourth night of rioting that the police, who had until then been virtually overpowered by the uncontrollable crowds, finally gained the upper hand.'[76] Both are correct. That the police grossly under-estimated the scale of the disorders, certainly during the first two days, and were not therefore in a position to respond effectively, was abundantly clear. Also, whilst the police in the United Kingdom were generally, but not always, well-prepared to handle planned demonstrations where disorder might arise, they received virtually no training in countering spontaneous disorder of this type, as was

---

71. Gutzmore, Cecil (1993). 'Carnival, the State and the Black Masses in the United Kingdom'. In *Inside Babylon: The Caribbean Diaspora in Britain* (edited by Winston James and Clive Harris). London: Verso, p.212.

72. Bowes, Stuart (1966). *The Police and Civil Liberties*. London: Lawrence & Wisehard, p.64.

73. Malik, Michael Abdul (1968). *From Michael de Freitas to Michael X*. London: Andre Deutsch, p.77. De Freitas's fuller part in the riots is described in *Chapter 4*.

74. Miles, Robert (1984). 'The Riots of 1958: Notes on the Ideological Construction of "Race Relations" as a Political Issue in Britain'. In *Immigrants and Minorities*, November 1984, p.255.

75. Phillips, Mike and Trevor Phillips (1998). *Windrush: The Irresistible Rise of Multi-Racial Britain*. London: HarperCollins, p.159.

76. Pilkington, *op. cit.* 2, p.123.

evident over 20 years later in Bristol in 1980, and in Brixton and other parts of the country in 1981.

The failure of the Metropolitan Police, particularly those officers who had a specific responsibility for the policing of Notting Hill, to equate what had happened the previous week in the St Anne's district of Nottingham with what could happen in Notting Hill was paramount. This was recognised, in hindsight, by Chief Superintendent Fieldsend, who, in his subsequent report, made a number of recommendations as to the action to be taken on future occasions:

> '[A] strong force of police must be in the disturbance area prior to the anticipated time of the start of any disturbance. They should be in double patrols and so posted that they are always within sight of another double patrol. [Radio telegraphy] vans ... should patrol to give immediate information of disorders and pass requests for assistance ....'[77]

The report continued by suggesting that 'the ideal method of using the reserves of police was found to be in a division of small units' each comprising one sergeant and six constables (including the driver) in a police van, with three such units under the command of an inspector.[78] Interestingly, many years later, that became the standard format of a Police Support Unit.

Finally, the report noted that 'hostile crowds had a healthy respect for the police dogs and it was possible to keep roads clear by the mere presence of the dogs.' However, it pointed out that their use was limited in the event of 'a wave of bottle throwing' because of 'the danger of broken glass.'[79] But, as will be seen later, Lord Scarman expressed a contrary view about the use of police dogs to control crowds in his report on the Brixton disorders of 1981.[80]

---

77. Metropolitan Police, *op. cit.* 2, p.42.
78. *Ibid.*
79. *Ibid*, pp.42–43.
80. Scarman, The Rt Hon The Lord, OBE (1981). *The Brixton Disorders 10–12 April 1981*. Cmnd. 8427. London: Her Majesty's Stationery Office, p.69, para. 4.84 and p.97, para. 5.73.

Postscript

When the nine young men who had carried out the attacks on 24 August appeared at the Old Bailey on 15 September, they pleaded guilty to all charges. On each of the wounding charges they were sentenced to four years' imprisonment; on each of the assault charges they were sentenced to nine months' imprisonment. The sentences were to run concurrently. In sentencing them, Mr Justice Salmon said that the nine men had formed themselves into a gang and

> 'set out on a cruel and vicious manhunt. You armed yourselves with iron bars and other weapons. Your quarry was any man, providing there were not more than two of them together, whose skin happened to be a different colour from your own. Your object was to instil stark terror and inflict as much pain and grievous injury as you could.'

He went on to say, 'it was you men who started the whole of this violence in Notting Hill', before concluding, 'everyone, irrespective of the colour of their skin is entitled to walk through the streets in peace, with their heads erect and free from fear.'[81]

Including these nine, a total of 108 people were arrested during the Notting Hill riot of which just over two-thirds were white. Amongst the weapons seized were axes, belts studded with nails or bolts, bicycle chains, bottles, carving knives, iron bars, sheath knives and scissors.[82]

---

81. Metropolitan Police, *op. cit.* 2, p.11.
82. *Ibid*, p.45.

CHAPTER 3

AFTERMATH OF THE RIOTS

The Immediate Response

By the standards of the American riots of the 1960s, what occurred in Notting Hill and Nottingham was pretty mild, but it nevertheless 'came as a savage shock to a Britain which preserved a myth about its own standards of tolerance.'[1] Many years later, it was revealed how senior officers tried to dismiss the riots as the work of 'ruffians, both coloured and white, who seized on this opportunity to indulge in hooliganism.' But statements from some of the police officers on the street at the time told a different story.[2] Most reports at the time condemned the white hooligans of Notting Hill and urged racial tolerance, but, at the same time were quick to point out that the disorders had occurred at a time of increasing unemployment, appalling living conditions, and concerns about prostitution and the growth of shebeens, often in residential streets.[3] A leading article in the local newspaper also pointed out that the events took place 'within a community' which was 'not sympathetic to the law.' It continued:

> 'The proper conception of the friendly kindly policeman waiting to help at the other end of a 999 call is not held by certain sections of the population who are too often on the wrong side of the law themselves and hesitate to approach it even in innocence. When they are in trouble they seek their own solutions in the law of mob rule...'[4]

1. Walker, Martin (1977). *The National Front*. London: Fontana/Collins, p.32.
2. Travis, Alan (2002). 'After 44 years secret papers reveal truth about five nights of violence in Notting Hill'. *The Guardian*, 24 August 2002. The quote comes from a report by Detective Sergeant Walters of Special Branch.
3. Glass, Ruth (1960) (assisted by Harold Pollins*). Newcomers: The West Indians in London*. London: Centre for Urban Studies and George Allen & Unwin, pp.147–150.
4. *Kensington News*, 12 September 1958.

Two particular observations did emerge which were to prove extremely relevant, the first in the short-term, the second would emerge time-and-time-again over the next 20 years or so. The first came from Dan Jacobson, who suggested the response of the majority 'of articulate and liberal minded people' to the riots 'was one of studied and deliberate indifference.'[5] The second came in a relatively short report produced by James Wickenden of the Institute of Race Relations and this reinforces what has already been described in *Chapter 1*. Wickenden claimed that 'the majority of the West Indians were ... well-behaved and decent citizens, often with a charm that was refreshing'. But, at the same time, 'there was a small minority of "wide boys", recognisable by their bright and flashy clothes and off-hand manners'. Wickenden went on to suggest that it was the latter group who were known to carry knives, who had begun to organize the prostitution of young white girls, who became involved in increasingly noisy parties and who consistently barged to the front of the queue at the Employment Exchange in front of the white unemployed.[6]

The Politicians

The response by politicians, both in the United Kingdom and elsewhere, was predictable. George Rogers, went to the Home Office where he left the Conservative Under-Secretary of State, Timothy Renton, in no doubt that 'the Government were at fault in not introducing legislation to deal with the racial problem a long time ago.' Pointing out that 'there were between 5,000 and 7,000 coloured people living in an area two-miles square' in Notting Hill, he claimed they were 'living in over-crowded accommodation badly needed by white people.'[7] Rogers made three suggestions as to how things might be improved. Firstly, there should be a restriction on the entry of immigrants into overcrowded areas such as North Kensington. Secondly, legislation should be introduced which would enable people convicted of crimes of vice and violence to be deported. Thirdly, the authorities should be given greater powers to close 'undesirable clubs'. Outside the meeting,

---

5. Jacobson, Dan. 'After Notting Hill'. *Encounter*, December 3–10, 1958, p.9.
6. Wickenden, James (1958*). Colour in Britain.* Institute of Race Relations. Oxford: Oxford University Press, p.25.
7. *The Times*, 4 September 1958.

he also suggested that the Metropolitan Police should form 'a coloured section' of the Criminal Investigation Department to detect 'crime among the coloured community.'[8] Finally, in a statement to the local newspaper the next day, he said:

> 'The main cause of the trouble of the unrest in North Kensington is housing. People are living in crowded houses, living cheek by jowl in vastly overcrowded conditions. To add to the difficulties some of the West Indians make no attempt to adapt themselves to the way of life here. Whilst I thoroughly deplore the riots and violence, naturally there is resentment that West Indians can buy houses here.'[9]

Meanwhile, in a statement made from the Prime Minister's Office, it was made clear that 'the immediate aspect' involved 'the maintenance of law and order.' The statement went on:

> 'The Government and the authorities concerned wish to make it clear that the utmost strictness will be observed in the impartial enforcement of the law and in preventing the illegal carrying of offensive weapons. As regards the wider aspects of policy, Her Majesty's Government have for some little time been examining the results of this country's time-honoured practice to allow free entry of immigrants from Commonwealth and colonial countries. Whilst the study of major policy and its implications and effects on employment will continue, Her Majesty's Government do not think it right to take long-term decisions, except after careful consideration of the problem as a whole.'[10]

The government statement was criticised for not condemning 'in forthright terms the outbreaks of violence and colour prejudice.'[11]

After meeting Rogers and Tom McGregor, the Labour Party Agent for North Kensington, Labour Party leader Hugh Gaitskill agreed that 'the deplorable outbreaks of street violence ... must be suppressed with the utmost firmness.' He went on:

---

8. *Kensington News*, 5 September 1958, p.1.
9. *Ibid.*
10. *The Times*, 4 September 1958, p.10.
11. *Ibid.*

'Whatever local difficulties there may be, nothing can justify the rioting and hooligans of the past days. Such behaviour can only damage the reputation of our country in the world, weaken the unity of the Commonwealth and increase racial tension without in any way solving the underlying social and economic problems.'[12]

Two days later, McGregor issued a statement through the local newspaper:

'It has come to my notice that there are lots of rumours that the Labour Party generally are responsible for the coloured people being in North Kensington. This is completely untrue. For three years the offices of this party have been advocating for some form of control, if not in the country, then at least in the numbers allowed into the already crowded areas like North Kensington. Not only in the interest of the people of North Kensington, but of the coloured people themselves.'[13]

At the same time, some of the Ministers from the parent countries of black people added to the debate. Principal amongst them was Norman Manley, the Chief Minister for Jamaica, who arrived in London on 5 September 'to make representations to the Government about the racial disorders in Nottingham and London.'[14] Two days later, Manley shared a platform with Rogers at a meeting at Friends House in Euston Road attended by 2,000 black people. Manley's speech was punctuated by applause and he received a standing ovation at the end of it. In contrast, Roger's speech was interrupted by boos, hisses and insults.[15] On 13 September, Manley and his wife, together with Rogers and McGregor, toured Notting Hill, listening to complaints. A white woman living in Colville Road, who was one of many who had signed a petition which was presented to him, told Manley 'of the trouble caused by a nearby coloured club, where the juke box blares all afternoon and evening, and even up to three or four o'clock in the morning.' Another group of white people complained of all-night parties, brothels and 'the eviction of white tenants from houses that had been bought up by coloured people.'[16]

---

12. *The Times*, 4 September 1958, p.4.
13. *Kensington News*, 5 September 1958, p.6.
14. *The Times*, 5 September 1958, p.7.
15. *Kensington News*, 12 September 1958, p.1.
16. *Kensington News*, 19 September 1958, p.1.

The Fascists

The Union Movement, led by Sir Oswald Mosley,[17] had been active in Notting Hill for a number of years prior to the riots. As long ago as 1949, a Union meeting at Kensington Town Hall, attended by some 700 people, had been disrupted by tear gas bombs whilst, outside, one hundred police officers kept Mosley supporters, who could not gain entry into the hall, and their opponents apart.[18] The Union Movement had four regular meeting places, two on Notting Hill sub-division in Pembridge Gardens just south of Notting Hill Gate and at Walmer Road near the junction with Lancaster Road, and two on adjoining divisions in Queensway and Shepherds Bush Green. The main antagonists at their meetings prior to the riots came from the Jewish 43 Group who would lay in wait and try to break up the meetings resulting, occasionally, in some people being arrested.[19]

But the riots had provided the Union Movement with a new and potentially explosive focus. Mosley, who was in Ireland at the time of the riots, saw them as an opportunity to revitalise his political career, although he did not return until the beginning of October. But in the meantime, led by Hamm, who lived in Notting Hill, a campaign was mounted to have the sentences reviewed following Mr Justice Salmon's decision to jail the nine youths. A letter was distributed to every house in Notting Hill and the Union Movement held weekly public surgeries.[20] On Mosley's return, it was arranged for him to address a series of meetings in Birmingham, Derby, Leicester, Liverpool, Leeds, North London in Hornsey, and West London in Kensington Town Hall. The meeting in Kensington, due to take place on 7 October, was cancelled by the local authority; so too were those at all the venues except Birmingham. This meeting which was held on 12 October, ended in disorder, suggesting that the authorities had, on each of the other

---

17. Sir Oswald Mosley, became a Conservative Member of Parliament after he returned from fighting in the First World War. Disillusioned with the slowness with which traditional political parties reacted to change, in subsequent elections he stood as an Independent Conservative, as an Independent, as a Labour candidate and then as a member of the New Party which he had set up. However, the life of the New Party was short lived; it collapsed in 1931 and the following year he launched the British Union of Fascists.
18. Walker, *op. cit.* 1, p.26.
19. In a letter to the author, dated 15 April 1993, from Stan May, who served as a constable at Notting Hill from the end of World War II until 1957.
20. Olden, Mark (2011). *Murder in Notting Hill.* Winchester: Zero Books, pp.32–33.

occasions, been right to cancel. In the run-up to the 1959 parliamentary elections, in which he stood as a candidate, Mosley poured all the Union Movement's resources into Notting Hill. On some weekends, he had 'up to 200 canvassers, all preaching [his] message of sending the coloured immigrant back.' Mosley himself did stress that it was to be done humanely, 'the process being sweetened by gifts of money, and justified by the argument that immigrants who had learned about industrial life and methods in Britain could make an enormous contribution to the development of their homelands.' But the leaflets published and handed out by the movement preached a different message. One example read 'People of Kensington — Act Now: Your country is worth fighting for — fight for the Union Movement.' Such messages were hardly helpful when fed 'into a community where gangs of whites roamed the streets looking for black people to beat and kick into unconsciousness.'[21] Mosley eventually lost his deposit for the first time in his electoral career, polling less than 3,000 votes. However, the police had been 'very much encouraged' by the fact that there was no serious disorder throughout his election campaign.[22]

Other groups saw the riots as an opportunity to preach their own brand of fascism. The League of Empire Loyalists had been founded in 1954 by a former member of Mosley's pre-war British Union of Fascists, A K Chesterton. The League was anti-Semitic, anti-Communist and anti-American, but Chesterton also believed in 'British racial superiority' and 'of the need for the white man to continue to rule Africa.'[23] Another organization which quickly became involved in the area was the National Labour Party under the chairmanship of Andrew Fountain;[24] the secretary was John Bean, who had been a campaigns director with the League of Empire Loyalists until three months before the riots when, together with a dozen other members

---

21. Walker, *op. cit.* 1, p.32.
22. Kelland, Gilbert (1989). *Crime in London.* London: Grafton Books, p.99.
23. Walker, *op. cit.* 1, pp.28/29.
24. A Norfolk landowner, Fountaine had fought for Franco in the Spanish Civil War. During the Second World War, he enlisted in the Royal Navy as an Ordinary Seaman but rose to Lieutenant Commander. He was adopted as Conservative candidate for Chorley, in Lancashire, in 1949, but his candidacy was withdrawn after he launched a verbal onslaught on the Conservative Party at its annual conference 'for permitting Jewish people to achieve positions of public importance'. Despite his views, when he stood as an Independent Conservative in the 1951 election, he only lost by 341 votes. *Ibid,* p.28.

including John Tyndall, he had left, claiming the league's policy was 'too limited and negative.'[25]

At the time of the riots, an anti-Semitic publishing company, the Britons' Publishing Society, which had been set up in 1919 by Arnold Leese,[26] was still operating from an address in Princedale Road, Notting Hill. Leese, who had formed the Imperial Fascist League in 1929, was imprisoned during the Second World War under section 18B,[27] because of his devotion to Hitler, but was released on the grounds of ill-health in 1944. In 1946 he recruited Colin Jordan, a Cambridge graduate, and, after the death of Leese in 1956, Jordan worked closely with his widow, Mary. This gave Jordan the necessary resources to build up the National Socialist Movement and it subsequently became the headquarters and base of operations for his White Defence League.[28] Very soon after the riots, a six page publication, edited by Colin Jordan, called *Black and White News*, consisting of articles about black people that had appeared in national newspapers, plus editorial and other features that condemned immigration, began to find its way onto the streets.[29]

In reply to a question during an interview on the BBC's Panorama in early 1959, Jordan said, 'If it is true, as you suggest, that a large number of influential people of Notting Hill are trying to mix the two races, are trying to bring about a coffee coloured population in Britain, then I regard it as no disgrace for the White Defence League to come on the scene and stand up for white interests.'[30] Jordan also published and circulated a series of leaflets in the area, one of which claimed that 'The National Assistance Board pays the children's allowances to the blacks for the coffee coloured monstrosities they father, regardless of whether they are legitimate or illegitimate,' before suggesting that 'material rewards' were 'given to enable semi-savages to mate with the women of one of the leading civilised nations of the world.'[31]

---

25. *The Times*, 10 September 1958, p.5.
26. Leese was a former veterinary surgeon, after returning from France, where he served in the British Army during the First World War.
27. 18B of the Defence (General) Regulations 1939 allowed the Home Secretary to order the detention of people whom he believed were hostile to the country during the Second World War.
28. Walker, *op. cit.* 1, pp.27 and 33.
29. *Kensington News*, 19 September 1958, p.1.
30. 'Panorama', BBC 1, 13 April 1959.
31. Walker, *op. cit.* 1, pp.33/34.

The West Indian Community

The West Indian Standing Conference (WISC) was set up in the aftermath of the riots as a co-ordinating body for the various organizations representing the interests of West Indians living in London. Initially, this organization was largely ignored by the Metropolitan Police, which preferred to discuss African-Caribbean affairs with the government-funded National Committee for Commonwealth Immigrants (NCCI), chaired by the Archbishop of Canterbury.[32] In May 1959, Herbert Hill, the Labour Secretary of the National Association for the Advancement of Coloured People, claimed that he 'was particularly disturbed by the many allegations against the police' in Notting Hill, pointing out that 'coloured people' in the area were 'upset and anxious about abuses of police power.' The allegations included claims that black people were being beaten up in police stations, harassed by police officers on the streets and having their clubs and homes raided by police officers who did not have search warrants. In addition, it was alleged that not only did the police not give them any protection from racist attacks, but, instead, they sided with white racists. Hill warned that coloured people felt 'completely deserted, and that, if effective and reasonable forms of protest and redress' were 'not provided, irrational forms of protest and explosions of anger [were] inevitable.'[33]

The Commissioner, Sir Joseph Simpson, did meet senior staff at the West Indies Federation (WIF)[34] offices in London in July 1959, not long after the murder of Kelso Cochrane, but he was apparently more concerned with pre-empting allegations that the police were uncooperative in their dealings with such organizations rather than enhancing 'the cause of racial and cultural harmony.' Simpson subsequently suggested, in his report of the visit, that the staff at the WIF had 'acknowledged the sort of weaknesses and defects' which the police experienced 'in coloured people' and claimed that they had

---

32. Whitfield, James. *Unhappy Dialogue: The Metropolitan Police and Black Londoners in Post-war Britain.* Cullompton, Devon: Willan Publishing, p.27.

33. *New Statesman*, 9 May 1959, pp.635/636. Quoted in Cashmore, Ellis and Eugene McLaughlin (eds.). *Out of Order: Policing Black People.* London: Routledge, 1991, p.24.

34. The West Indies Federation was a short-lived arrangement whereby ten territories in the Caribbean, including Barbados, Jamaica and Trinidad, formed themselves into a federation in 1958. The demise occurred in early-1962 after Jamaica voted in a referendum to withdraw from it.

'deplored the circulation of rumours and the making of allegations' which were 'unsupported by reasonable evidence.'[35]

In the event his visit had little effect. Fifteen months later, in October 1960, Chief Superintendent Best, who had been appointed by Simpson as the chief point of contact between the Metropolitan Police and the West Indian community, received a letter from the Secretary for Migrant Services at the WIF, expressing concern about the situation in Notting Hill:

'From reports received from leaders of the West Indian Organizations in the area of North Kensington (Notting Hill) over the past three months, I have gathered the impression that there is some latent tension between West Indians and white residents in the area, together with a growing atmosphere of unhappy relations with the police.'[36]

By the early-1960s, the police, in general, were regarded by the West Indian community as 'racially prejudiced and unhelpful [but] in certain areas, like Notting Hill, things were much more highly charged.'[37]

The Rio Coffee Bar

In 1959, Frank Crichlow opened the Rio Coffee Bar at 153 Westbourne Park Road. Born in Trinidad in 1931, he had arrived in Britain at the age of 21 and initially worked for British Rail. Three years later, he became a band leader with the Starlight Four, before opening the Rio. Crichlow subsequently recalled that 'West Indians in London felt a little like Englishmen in Africa; they wanted to club together — especially after the race riots.' His purpose in opening the Rio was an attempt to integrate the immigrants from the various West Indian islands. Never closing, people came throughout the 24 hours and this, inevitably, set Crichlow on a collision course with the judicial system, including the police at Notting Hill, which was to last for at least the next 30 years. But that is hardly surprising given Crichlow's own description of the place, likening it as he did unto 'a school, a university'. He explained, 'It got a lot of hustlers' and 'attracted people who were rebellious

35. Whitfield, *op. cit.* 31, pp.65/66.

36. NA NEPO 2/9854. Quoted by Whitfield, James, *op. cit.* 31, p.66.

37. In a letter, dated 3 April 2001, quoted by Whitfield, James, *op. cit.* 31, p.81.

and a bit smart, those with street intelligence, those for whom the factory was not their speed.'[38]

Leading West Indian radical, Darcus Howe, claimed that it originally catered for the 'unemployed section of the West Indian Community' and had a gambling club in the basement that 'operated outside of the discipline of the Gaming Act.'[39] Although there is no direct evidence for this, or, indeed, confirmation from other sources, Howe alleged that these illegal gaming clubs were a source of police corruption with 'some of the proprietors [being] forced into paying sums of money to the police so that they could operate freely.' They also provided a source of money from which bribes were paid to the police so that they would not oppose the bail of those who had been arrested and not mention previous convictions at the conclusion of a court case in which the defendant had been found guilty.[40]

Crichlow opposed such practices and, together with Colin MacInnes and Michael de Freitas, set up an organization called Defence, the aim of which was to provide legal 'assistance to those victimised by the police.' Claimed to 'give blacks better representation and protection in courts and prisons through the arrangement of legal aid, sureties to stand bail and prison visits', it was the setting up of Defence which marked out Crichlow 'as a trouble maker with anti-police sentiments.'[41]

For Crichlow, it was a nerve-wracking experience as well as an exhilarating time because, so he claimed, he carried a heavy responsibility, which drove him nearly to breaking point. 'It was,' he said, 'like running a hostel for "bad boys".' Subsequently, as will be seen in *Chapter 4*, 'the Rio became a fashionable place for whites to go in the hippy era, acquiring a certain glamour … from its connection with the Profumo affair through Christine Keeler's association with a West Indian hustler called 'Lucky' Gordon.'[42]

---

38. Gould, Tony. *Insider Outsider: The Life and Times of Colin MacInnes.* London: Allison & Busby, p.194. From conversations that Gould had with Frank Crichlow on 6/9 December 1978 and 7 April 1979.
39. Howe, Darcus (1988). *From Bobby to Babylon: Blacks and the British Police.* London: Race Today Publications, p.40.
40. *Ibid.*
41. *Ibid.*
42. Gould, *op. cit.* 38, p.194.

The Murder of Kelso Cochrane

Saturday, 16 May 1959, started as an ordinary day for a 33-year-old carpenter from Antigua, Kelso Cochrane who rented a flat at 11 Bevington Road, just off the Portobello Road. In the afternoon he went shopping in Portobello Road market with his girlfriend, Olivia Ellington, a trainee nurse from Jamaica, returning to the flat they shared for the evening. However, a few days earlier, Cochrane had broken his thumb in an incident at work and, although he had received treatment at Paddington General Hospital, as this particular evening wore on it became more and more painful. He therefore returned to the hospital late in the evening where his arm was put in a sling and he was given some painkillers.

Returning from the hospital in the early hours of the Sunday morning, in a scene reminiscent of the death of Stephen Lawrence some 32 years later,[43] he was set upon by five or six young white men in Southam Street,[44] near the junction with Goldborne Road, which was close to his flat.[45] Two black men, Horatio Lewis and Ken Steele, approached the scene, and the men ran away, leaving Cochrane slumped on the ground. They helped him to his feet and Cochrane apparently said to them, 'They asked me for money but I told them I didn't have any.' At the same time, a taxi was dropping off four people in Southam Street and Lewis and Steele took him to St Charles Hospital in the taxi but he died shortly after being admitted.[46] The cause of death was a single stab wound to the chest made by a stiletto-type knife.[47]

The response to the death of Kelso Cochrane was, in hindsight, predictable for that time. Less than 48 hours into the investigation, the officer in

---

43. Black teenager, Stephen Lawrence, was stabbed by five white youths in a South London street on 22 April 1992. For more details see MacPherson, Sir William (1999). *The Stephen Lawrence Inquiry.* Cm 4262-I. Norwich: The Stationery Office.
44. Southam Street was where Michael de Freitas first set up house with his girl-friend, Desiree: see *Chapter 1.*
45. In Phillips, Mike and Trevor Phillips (1998). *Windrush: The Irresistible Rise of Multi-Racial Britain.* London: HarperCollins, p.184 it is suggested there were six; Glass, *op. cit.* 2, p.165, suggests there may have been six or seven, although five to six seems to be the generally accepted number.
46. Olden, *op. cit.* 19, pp.39–40.
47. *Manchester Guardian*, 6 August 1959.

charge, Detective Superintendent Ian Forbes-Leith,[48] issued a statement to the press which read:

> 'The stabbing has absolutely nothing to do with racial conflict. The motive could have been robbery. We are satisfied that it was the work of a group of about six anti-law white teenagers who had only one motive in view robbery or attempted robbery. The fact that he happened to be coloured doesn't come into the question.'[49]

This claim was received with apathy by both black and white residents in Notting Hill, many of whom believed 'in the wisdom of the announcement but not in its truth.'[50] The African-Caribbean community firmly believed that Cochrane had been killed because he was black. The white community just didn't care or its attitude could be summed up in the statement:

> 'One less of the blacks—that's the way I look at it. We've got too many of them about here.'[51]

Following the murder there was an increased presence of uniformed police officers on the streets, with policemen patrolling in pairs, and on stand-by at Notting Hill Police Station on the basis that 'it would not have taken much to spark off an incident that might lead to further rioting.'[52]

A murder squad of 24 officers was set up at Harrow Road Police Station.[53] Divided into three sections, one group interviewed all likely suspects amongst the white population living in the area; the second group searched for the murder weapon and the third group conducted house-to-house enquiries.[54]

---

48. Forbes-Leith had joined the Metropolitan Police in 1936 under the 'Trenchard Scheme'. During the war he had served in North Africa and taken part in the Normandy landings; afterwards he had returned to the Metropolitan Police where he quickly rose through the ranks to become, at 38, the youngest officer ever to become a detective superintendent.
49. 'Who Killed my Brother, Kelso Cochrane?' BBC2 documentary, 8 April, 2006.
50. *Kensington News*, 22 May 1959, p.1.
51. *The Times*, 19 May 1959.
52. *Ibid.*
53. Much of the Notting Hill area to the north and east of Portobello Road at that time came under X Division with the remainder falling under F Division. Not until 1965 did the whole of Notting Hill come under one police station.
54. Olden, *op. cit.* 19, pp.49—50.

Despite an extensive search, which included 'excavating 30 drains in five streets around the murder spot', the search of sites still derelict, caused by Second World War bombs, the railway lines that ran through that area of Notting Hill, and various stretches of water, including the Grand Union Canal, the murder weapon was never found. However, what did emerge were several coshes, including short lengths of iron piping, milk bottles with jagged tops, a knife, a razor and a bicycle chain, enough, suggested Mark Olden, the only person to write a full account of Cochrane's murder and subsequent investigation, for a future anthropologist to be able to 'draw a vivid portrait of the area's street life.'[55] For some time, enquiries centred on a bottle-party, attended by young white people, which had been held on the Saturday night at 18 Southam Street. A number of people were detained for questioning including, on 20 May, seven men and four women. Two leading suspects were kept in for more than 50 hours.[56]

On the Monday after the murder, African and West Indian organizations sent a joint letter to the Prime Minister, Harold Macmillan, claiming that they had 'lost confidence in the ability of the law-enforcement agencies to protect them.'[57] A few days later, together with a number of English associations, they formed the Inter-Racial Friendship Co-ordinating Council (IFCC).[58] A week after its formation, representatives went to the Home Office to complain about the lack of police officers available to patrol Notting Hill, particularly the 'back streets'.[59]

Black activists demanded new legislation to outlaw racial hatred and for the Metropolitan Police to recruit black officers. Failing that, at a meeting at the Home Office on 2 June 1959, leaders of the West Indian community in Notting Hill recommended that 'suitable people of all races should be recruited as special constables to assist the regular police, as they believed it would be helpful in reducing racial difficulties in the area.' The Commissioner, Sir Joseph Simpson, thought otherwise. Opposing the recruitment of special constables in the Notting Hill area, he said he 'did not feel it desirable

---

55. *Ibid*, p.51.
56. *Ibid*, pp.54-55.
57. *The Times*, 19 May 1959.
58. *The Manchester Guardian*, 22 May 1959.
59. *West Indian Gazette*, June 1959; quoted in Glass, *op. cit.* 2, p.169.

to recruit "coloured" policemen.'[60] It wasn't until 1967 that the first black officer passed out from Hendon Training School.[61]

The funeral service for Kelso Cochrane was held at St Michael's Church in Ladbroke Grove on June 9. Attended by 500 people, with another 700 gathered outside, it was conducted by the Bishop of Kensington, supported by Canon John Collins of St Paul's Cathedral and the local vicar. After the service, the cortege wound its way in a dignified silence through the streets to Kensal Green Cemetery where Kelso Cochrane was buried. Born into obscurity, there were suggestions that between the time of his death and the holding of the funeral service, he had become a martyr. The African-Caribbean community and their supporters turned the occasion into the equivalent of 'a state funeral, a demonstration which would leave an indelible mark on the area and its people' and made them all the more determined to stay put in Notting Hill.[62] It was, suggested Phillips, a great event which brought the 1950s to a close 'and began the West Indian decade of Notting Hill.'[63]

Meanwhile, the police spoke to over 900 people but only nine gave them any information. They were, in fact, faced with a virtual wall of silence as Police Constable Frank Pulley recalled many years later:

> 'There was no doubt there was a conspiracy of silence after the Cochrane murder and regardless of whether it was just a robbery or a racial murder the fact is that nobody was prepared to give up the perpetrators. I am a little surprised that they [the police] didn't get to the bottom of it because usually in those sort of gang fights and that kind of assault, usually somebody from among the confederates would have got afraid and didn't want to get — in those days — hung himself so he would have given up the perpetrators.'[64]

The difficulties of the police were summed up in a leading article in the *Kensington News* in which it posed the question:

---

60. NA HO 325/9. Quoted in Whitfield, *op. cit.* 31, p.116.
61. The first black officer to join the Metropolitan Police was Norwell Roberts in 1967. He retired as a detective sergeant after 30 years. He was awarded the Queens Police Medal (QPM).
62. Phillips, Charlie and Mike (1991). *Notting Hill in the Sixties*. London: Lawrence & Wishart, p.56.
63. *Ibid*, p.57.
64. BBC documentary, *op.cit.* 49.

'How can the police do their job to the fullest of their ability if the people they serve will not work with them? North Kensington must trust the men whose unenviable job it is to keep the peace in their area — if they don't there is no hope for us.'[65]

Olden found the parallels between Cochrane's murder and that of Stephen Lawrence in south-east London in 1992 'striking' and 'overwhelming.' According to him, the police knew the identity of Cochrane's killer but there was insufficient evidence on which to charge him.[66] However, there were a number of disturbing aspects to the investigation into his death which although not identical with defects in the Lawrence investigation,[67] were, nevertheless, a cause for concern. The *Daily Express* had printed the first news of Cochrane's murder within three hours of it occurring which suggested that it had received a tip-off from a police officer. This was confirmed when a cheque for £10 was received from the newspaper by a police constable at Harrow Road Police Station; the only problem was that the police constable knew nothing about it and reported it to his superiors.

As a result two senior detectives from Scotland Yard were appointed to investigate. They quickly narrowed the source down to a detective who was close to the inquiry, finally settling on three; Detective Sergeant Sid Coomber who had visited St Charles Hospital when police received the information that Cochrane had died from a stab wound; Detective Inspector Ferguson Walker and Detective Superintendent Ian Forbes-Leith, who had both been summoned from their beds as soon as it became apparent that Cochrane had been murdered. Pointing out that, rather unusually, Forbes-Leith retired from the Metropolitan Police less than two years later, having completed only 25 years' service, Olden suggests it was the last of the three, before going on

---

65. *Ibid.*
66. Olden, *op. cit.* 19, pp.75 — 80. In January 2012, Gary Dobson and David Norris were both jailed for life for the murder of Stephen Lawrence in 1993. Both had been amongst a group of five youths who were originally arrested in 1993 for the murder but the Crown Prosecution Service dropped the case. In August 2012 they were refused leave to appeal. See *The Guardian*, 3 and 4 January 2012; *The Guardian*, 23 August 2012.
67. See McPherson, *op. cit.* 43 for further details.

to query whether the early release of details surrounding Cochrane's death could have had any effect on the investigation.[68]

But, there were other disturbing aspects to the investigation. Firstly, the placing of the two leading suspects in adjoining cells at Harrow Road Police Station which enabled them to 'get their stories straight' by talking through the adjoining wall.[69] Secondly, despite the publicity given to the search for the knife in public places, Olden claimed that he could find no evidence that the homes of the suspects were searched for the weapon. Thirdly, a witness, who was sitting in a window of an upstairs flat overlooking the scene when the attack occurred, although she could not recognise the youths, had seen one of them attempt to rip a railing from a nearby garden, presumably to use as a weapon, but that railing was never fingerprinted. Fourthly, the rules for retaining evidence in those days were different to those of today, so Cochrane's clothes, which had been 'tested for blood and fibres after the murder' were destroyed in 1968.[70] But the most striking similarity between Cochrane's murder and that of Stephen Lawrence was the speed with which the police announced, almost from the outset, that it was not a racist murder.[71]

Some sections of the media ran a campaign which suggested that Cochrane was drunk and that he was a troublemaker. An article on the front page of *The People* only eight days after the murder cast him in a poor light, which could only have come from a police source. The article claimed that Cochrane 'had been drinking on the night of his death and was known to be truculent after a few drinks', that he liked to carry a knife and it was this one that he had been killed with after he had drawn it and there had been a struggle, and that he was married to a woman living in the USA.[72] In fact, he had been charged with assaulting his wife in the USA and had been deported because his visa had expired after she dropped the charge. The post-mortem

---

68. Olden, *op. cit.* 19, pp.81 - 91.
69. *Ibid*, p.148.
70. *Ibid*, p.149.
71. See the statement above made by Detective Superintendent Forbes-Leith less than 48 hrs after the murder; see also Olden, *op. cit.* 19, p.48.
72. *The People*, 24 May 1959.

carried out by Home Office pathologist, Dr Donald Teare, revealed no alcohol in his system.[73]

In addition to the 'leaks' to the *Daily Express* and *The People*, evidence of an anonymous telephone call to a journalist was revealed in a subsequent BBC documentary:

> 'The man phoned up and said he wanted to tell us about a murder in Goldborne Road, Notting Hill. I asked him for his name and address first and he was reluctant to give it. He said three white youths had stabbed a darkie named Cochrane.'

The programme suggested that the caller might have been Detective Superintendent Forbes-Leith himself but this was never verified.[74]

Despite a review of the case in 2003, Cochrane's murder remains unsolved. Pulley suggested what happened to Cochrane was yet another indication of the increasing racial tensions that existed in Notting Hill at the time. He explained: 'Bad housing, low level crime, gang territory warfare amongst the white population ... there were families which had been involved in crime over many, many decades and when the families weren't fighting each other they would fight with anybody else who raised their head over the parapet.' But he also claimed that:

> 'There's no doubt that although a very large percentage of the West Indian population that came here were law-abiding—even more law-abiding than many of the indigenous people in the area—there was an element of criminality that came with them, hustlers as they called themselves.'[75]

The Fascists' Response to Cochrane's Death

Fascist groups attempted to make capital out of Cochrane's death. The White Defence League, led by Colin Jordan, held a meeting together with the National Labour Party, then effectively led by John Bean, on May 24,[76] at which Jordan suggested that the murder 'was a conspiracy involving

---

73. Olden, *op. cit.* 19, p.41.
74. BBC documentary, *op. cit.* 49.
75. BBC documentary, *op. cit.* 49.
76. Walker, *op. cit.* 1, p.33.

Jews and Communists, whose motive was to smear groups like his and get anti-discrimination laws passed.'[77] Mosley, who held a rally on the precise spot where Cochrane was murdered, issued the following statement:

'On 17th May a negro was reported murdered in the Notting Hill district. The next day some daily papers suggested that this was due to racial tension and that I was responsible on account of my prospective candidature although I had just circulated to every house in the area an appeal to settle the question by "votes not violence". Leading Conservatives were even quoted as having suggested that I should in future be held responsible for my repetition of troubles which had occurred before I even arrived. The same evening the police brought this particular nonsense to an end by saying the motive of the murder appeared to be ordinary robbery. This experience surely marks not only a new low in a smear campaign, but also indicates a new political technique.'[78]

The Police

All the evidence points to the fact that during the late-1950s and early-1960s, the Metropolitan Police 'was seriously concerned about the role of West Indian men in the vice trade' and 'it was also determined to keep a firm control' on the unlicensed black social clubs.[79] The fact that the police were so concerned with African-Caribbean involvement in these types of crime, rather than the indigenous population of Notting Hill as a whole, was supported by the police report of the 1958 riots. It included appendices listing details of: (a) coloured men prosecuted for living on the immoral earnings of prostitution in the Notting Hill area in the year leading up to the riots; (b) coloured prostitutes operating in the Notting Hill area who had been arrested in the previous year; and (c) registered coloured men's clubs in the Notting Hill area, of which there were five.[80]

Quite why the report should only highlight black men living off immoral earnings and black prostitutes, when it was known that many white

---

77. Olden, *op. cit.* 19, p.62.
78. *Kensington News*, 22 May, 1959, p.7.
79. NA HO 325/9, quoted in Whitfield, *op. cit.* 31, p.116.
80. Metropolitan Police (1958). 'Report on The Notting Hill Race Riots 1954–8'. Typescript. Unpublished, p.5 and 6 and Appendices H, I and J.

prostitutes solicited in the area, and had both black and white men living off their earnings, and coloured men's clubs was perhaps indicative of police attitudes at the time, because, 'although there were some West Indian clubs which flouted the law by after-hours drinking and gaming, it was from the bogus clubs run by the indigenous criminals and their stooges that most of the trouble and violence came.'[81] Whitfield suggested that this, what he calls 'racialisation of the police', occurred at 'a time when black and Asian people were regarded as generally law-abiding, and long before relations were blighted by mutual hostility.'[82]

The response to the riots by the hierarchy of the Metropolitan Police was to post two chief inspectors to assist the superintendent at Notting Hill. The idea was for them to alternate for six months periods, with one acting as the deputy to the superintendent whilst the other concentrated on vice work, which included clubs. It was only the second sub-division to be organized in this way; West End Central, which covered Soho, was the first.[83]

One particularly notorious club in Notting Dale, totally unconnected with the newly arrived immigrants, was run by Ernest Bell, who, in May 1960, was arrested along with his three sons, Ernest Bell Junior, Sydney and Peter, together with a friend, George Baker, for the murder of 'Billy' Smith, after a long-running feud between the two families. George Baker and Ernest Bell Junior were eventually convicted of manslaughter and sentenced to five years and seven years imprisonment respectively, whilst the remaining members of the Bell family were acquitted.[84] The Bells and a number of their associates had been interviewed about the Cochrane murder.[85]

In an interview with Assistant Commissioner John Gerrard, who, along with Gilbert Kelland,[86] was a chief inspector at Notting Hill during this period, Whitfield reported him as saying:

'You could raid a club and the doorman's got one [a gun] in the shoulder holster, that sort of thing. Ultimately this was all brought under control, but the people

---

81. Kelland, *op. cit.* 21, p.84.
82. Whitfield, *op. cit.* 33, p.4.
83. Kelland, *op. cit.* 21, p.82.
84. *Ibid*, p.87. See also Olden, pp.105–114.
85. Olden, *op. cit.* 19, pp.52–56.
86. Gilbert Kelland also rose to the rank of assistant commissioner before he retired.

who were running the clubs were people with long criminal records and prostitution was rife as well. Vice was the number one priority of the day at Notting Hill because we realised that if we could control vice we could control the area. But it took two-and-half-years.'[87]

The African-Caribbean Community in Notting Hill

Summing up the situation in Notting Hill at the end of the 1950s, Phillips suggested that 'being an immigrant anywhere else in London meant that out in the open, you ran a gauntlet of hostility until you were safely forted up behind locked doors.' But, in Notting Hill, it was different. Here the immigrants, many of them operating beyond the limits of the law, provided clubs, shebeens, restaurants, cafes and music.[88] In an area no more than 800 yards square, there were a number of shebeens. In addition to the one run by Fullerton's in Talbot Road, already mentioned in *Chapter 1*, there was Bajy's next door, which had a café upstairs with a club downstairs. Michael de Freitas ran a shebeen in Powis Square. In 1961, Fiesta One opened on the corner of Ledbury Road and Westbourne Park Road; next door was the Calypso. At the corner of Colville Road and Elgin Crescent, there was a club in the basement run by a Barbadian. Totobag ran a place at 9 Blenheim Crescent. On the corner of Blenheim Crescent and Kensington Park Road was another, mainly used by 'the real heavy, heavy white guys.' There were also 'two gambling houses, one in St Stephen's Gardens and one in Lancaster Road.'[89]

During the early days, some of the clubs attracted aristocrats and other people from the upper-classes, as well as intellectuals, who thought it was a sign of the times to 'slum' in such places.[90] Others attracted to Notting Hill were black American servicemen of whom there were many stationed in various parts of England and there was friction between them and the local Irish which often resulted in fights. This rather unsavoury situation

---

87. In an interview with Whitfield on 24 July 2000, quoted from Whitfield, *op. cit.* 31, p.145.

88. Phillips, *op. cit.* 61, pp 46/47.

89. *Ibid*, pp.48/49.

90. Phillips, *op. cit.* 45, p.117; Pilkington, Edward (1988). *Beyond the Mother Country: West Indians and the Notting Hill White Riots.* London: I. B. Taurus, pp.65 and 93.

eventually drove the upper-class clientele away from the African-Caribbean places of entertainment.[91]

Despite Cochrane's death and the failure of the police to find the murderers, there was a feeling within the police throughout much of 1959 and 1960 that their increased presence on the streets, with 'firm action against all forms of violence, and sustained pressure against bogus drinking clubs and vice-pedlars, had reduced racial tension and general anxiety in the Notting Hill area.'[92] In a contrary view, Whitfield, who, it should be noted was, himself, a former policeman, claimed that 'the downward spiral in relations between the Met and the Caribbean community, which had begun in the 1950s continued through the following decade.'[93]

---

91. Phillips, *op. cit.* 33, p.72.
92. Kelland, *op. cit.* 21, p.99.
93. Whitfield, *op. cit.* 33, p.125.

CHAPTER 4

THREE HUSTLERS FROM NOTTING HILL

Introduction

Following the riots of 1958, two significant events, which were inextricably linked, occurred in the early-1960s which not only ensured that Notting Hill stayed in the news but emphasised the seediness of the area. It also brought three hustlers from Notting Hill to prominence. The first was Michael de Freitas, who worked for a time for the notorious property speculator, Peter Rachman, before changing his name first to Michael Abdul Malik and then to Michael X. The other two were Aloysius 'Lucky' Gordon and Johnny Edgecombe, both of whom found 'fame' as a result of relationships with a call-girl, Christine Keeler, and her role in bringing about the resignation of a government minister.

Rachman

Peter Rachman[1] was, arguably, one of the most notorious names to come out of Notting Hill during the early-1960s and the stories about him are legion. A Polish immigrant, he had arrived in Britain as a penniless refugee shortly after the end of World War II but he reportedly died a millionaire in 1962. He did not hit the headlines until 1963, about a year after his death, when he was named as the 'protector' of Mandy Rice-Davies during the committal proceedings in the trial of Dr Stephen Ward which is mentioned later in this chapter.

Rachman made his money 'through the cunning manipulation' of his tenants and due to the rent laws that existed at the time. His first property, 'an eight-bedroom house on the north side of Harrow Road' was purchased in the early-1950s for £1,000, which was cheap even in those days, 'because all but one of the rooms were let to controlled tenants paying pre-war rents.'

---

1. His real name was Perac Rachman (1987). See Kelland, Gilbert. *Crime in London*. London: Grafton Books, p.88 *et seq.*

However, he would then 'persuade' the sitting controlled tenants to leave, install some cheap furniture in the place, and let it as furnished accommodation at a greatly inflated rate.[2] Ian Crawford described how an 'empty room was let to eight hand-picked West Indians—"all accomplished musicians"—to whom Rachman said he did not care how many parties they held.' As a result, 'all the statutory tenants left within three months.' As each statutory tenant left, his place was taken by a number of West Indians. Soon 'the house was filled with West Indians, packed into the rooms like sardines and paying excessive rents because it was so particularly difficult for them to find accommodation.'[3] Rachman then sold the house for five times what he had paid for it. Shortly after he first entered the property market, a prostitute named Gloria suggested to Rachman that he could make more money by letting flats to prostitutes at increased prices. As a result his 'business expanded rapidly,'[4] and, within a short space of time, his property empire spread through Bayswater, Paddington and Notting Hill.

By 1957 the area around Powis Square had 'become something of a lawless ghetto.'[5] But Rachman was a shrewd operator, quickly distancing himself from the occupants of his houses. Whilst retaining ownership of his properties, Rachman had turned over control of the houses occupied by black people and prostitutes to black middle-men. Some people 'managed' a number of houses on his behalf; provided they paid him a fixed amount each week anything they received over and above that amount they could keep. In other cases, people were made responsible for collecting the rent from the house in which they lived in exchange for a rent-free flat. In some properties overcrowding was so bad that people slept in shifts. Others had clubs in the basement and prostitutes sitting at many of the windows. In addition, it was suggested, there were 'a disproportionate number of West Indian pimps living off white prostitutes.'[6]

To keep control, Rachman employed a number of strong-arm men whose methods were, to say the least, questionable and sometimes extremely violent.

---

2. Crawford, Iain (1963). *The Profumo Affair*. London: White Lodge Books, p.126.
3. *Ibid.*
4. Williams, John (2008). *Michael X: A Life in Black and White*. London: Century, p.65.
5. Vague, Tom (1988). *Vague 30: London Psychogeography—Rachman, Riots and Rillington Place*. London: Ladbroke Grove, p.37.
6. *Ibid.*

Ivan Weekes, who lived in a Rachman property when he first came to England in 1955 and went on to serve as an alderman on the Kensington and Chelsea Council in the 1970s before becoming one of the first black lay magistrates in England, described 'Rachman and his middlemen [as] terrorisers', claiming that 'he had a whole gang of bully boys with Alsatian dogs' who would be used against any African-Caribbeans who were behind with their rent. However, as Weekes pointed out, although Rachman was unscrupulous, he was one of the few people who would provide housing for black people. Additionally, Weekes suggested that Rachman was 'fairly reasonable' with what he charged in rent. It was 'the middle-men who would bump the charges up by 300 per cent,' thus making 'a killing for themselves,' paying Rachman perhaps a third of that.[7]

Two people who became involved in managing an increasing number of Rachman's properties, particularly in the Colville and Powis areas of Notting Hill, were 'an African who was always known simply as Edwards' and 'a vast and genial West Indian ex-policeman called Vernon Hunte'. Edwards was much the leading figure in this particular partnership and, under his management, illegal clubs and prostitution thrived in Rachman's properties.[8]

Although he had yet to become a prominent figure, there was an increasing awareness of Rachman's activities; so much so that the Rent Tribunals, the Borough Council, the Public Health Authorities and the police all began to take an interest in him. But, Rachman was alive to the dangers, covering his tracks so well that he was never caught. According to Crawford 'ownership and responsibilities for property were so constantly being shuffled, assigned to nominees, and transferred that only a major investigation could have dug out the truth about who owned what.'[9] In May 1959, Hunte and Edwards appeared, as landlords of three properties, before the West London Rent Tribunal where the flats were described by counsel appearing for the tenants as 'scruffy', 'dirty' and 'unfit for human habitation'. Hunte and Edwards claimed to be only the agents of the landlord who was in fact Rachman. As a result of this disclosure, two reporters from the *Kensington News*

---

7. Phillips, Mike and Trevor Phillips (1998). *Windrush: The Irresistible Rise of Multi-Racial Britain*. London: HarperCollins, pp.191–192.

8. Green, Shirley (1979). *Rachman*. London: Michael Joseph/Hamlyn, pp.74/75.

9. Crawford, *op. cit.* 3, p.127.

attempted to trace Rachman but they were unable to find him and gave up after two weeks.[10]

Police investigations into Rachman's activities

The police mounted two investigations against Rachman. The first, by Detective Inspector George Taylor, in early 1959, arose out of allegations made at Rent Tribunal hearings regarding his enforcement methods and, whilst this inquiry had some effect in that it curbed some of the more outrageous activities of his strong-arm men, it did not produce sufficient evidence to prosecute him personally.[11]

Later that year, a small team led by Chief Inspector Kelland, consisting of an inspector, a sergeant and four constables, was set up at Notting Hill Police Station. The aim was to gather evidence with a view to prosecuting Rachman and/or his associates for living on the earnings of prostitution and knowingly allowing premises, of which he was the owner, to be used as brothels.[12] The investigation was organized in three phases. The first was to carry out a survey and keep observation 'on a sample of 50 properties with about 300 separate lettings owned by Rachman companies.' The second phase was to keep observation on his estate office in Westbourne Grove. The third phase was to keep observation on Rachman himself.[13] The investigation revealed that Rachman was either a director or principal shareholder of 33 different companies. In many cases, the company secretary was a man named Brian O'Donnell, who was the brother of Audrey O'Donnell, with whom Rachman shared his Hampstead home and eventually married. But, Rachman 'was a cunning operator, well briefed by his legal and financial advisers.'[14] Consequently, the result of the investigation was disappointing.

Despite the fact that he was the owner of at least one of the premises in which the police subsequently gained a conviction against a prostitute for running a brothel, they were unable to show that Rachman knew what was going on. Kelland described how Rachman reacted when he was told of the

---

10. *Kensington News*, 12 June 1959.
11. Kelland, *op. cit.* 1, p.91.
12. Both offences under the Sexual Offences Act 1956.
13. *Ibid*, p.90.
14. *Ibid*, p.91.

conviction. Together with the two police officers who had been watching the premises, Kelland went to Rachman's Hampstead home and handed him a letter, notifying him of the conviction. Rachman claimed it was not his property but belonged to Hunte. When Kelland told him that he was the rateable occupier according to the records held by Paddington Borough Council, Rachman spoke to Edwards on the telephone. After confirming with Edwards that the property was the responsibility of Hunte, Rachman said:

> 'Well, tell him to get the place cleared by 12 o'clock today or I'll get my solicitor to cancel the lease. I've had a letter about a brothel at the house. I will send Serge to change the locks. I'm fed up with all this.'

When he had put the telephone down, he turned to Kelland and said, 'There, you heard what I said, the place should be right soon.'[15]

There is no doubt that Rachman knew that some of his properties were being used for the purposes of prostitution. Indeed it was claimed on this occasion that, although the prostitutes were thrown out of the property referred to by Kelland, at least one of them duly turned up in 'another Rachman associated property.'[16] Also, during the early days of his property acquisitions he charged 'a higher rent' if it was to be used for prostitution, at the same time insisting that there was only 'one girl per house'. But, although Rachman had distanced himself from his properties he still received a substantial income from them. Even so Rachman continued to encourage 'a limited amount of prostitution in his houses, and connived at unlimited prostitution in his West-Indian run houses.'[17]

The First Hustler — Michael de Freitas

One of Rachman's employees towards the end of his life was the first of the Notting Hill hustlers, Michael de Freitas, who came to London in 1957. Although he signed on at the Labour Exchange in the hope that he would get a decent job, he soon realised this was futile, so he took to visiting 'cafes

---

15.   *Ibid*, pp.92–93.
16.   Vague, *op. cit.* 5, p.35.
17.   Green, *op. cit.* 8, p.122.

like Totobags … blues clubs like Bejays — or the basement of Fullerton's the tailors on Talbot Road.'[18]

De Freitas was not alone in London for long, meeting a young West Indian girl, Desiree, at a party and persuading her to move in with him. Their experience in relation to finding accommodation in Southam Street is described in *Chapter 1* but soon after setting up house with Desiree, De Freitas met up with a prostitute named Sylvia whose ponce had just been sent to prison. From then on Michael led a double life, spending time with Sylvia, and taking money she earned to pay the rent on Southam Street and give Desiree spending money, passing it off to Desiree as 'a business enterprise'.[19] This 'business enterprise' lasted for some months until he and Desiree accidently bumped into Sylvia at a party. De Freitas was forced to choose and he decided to stay with Desiree, leaving Sylvia to look for a new ponce.[20]

By now De Freitas had built up a reputation as a hard man and he briefly tried his hand at armed robbery at which he and his cohorts were singularly unsuccessful. But, before he could become involved in anything else, the riots occurred in August 1958. On the second night of the riots, he was arrested for obstructing a constable in the execution of his duty. Although he was kept in custody overnight at the police station he was granted bail the next morning from the court after he pleaded not guilty.[21] He then attended the meeting at the Calypso Club mentioned in *Chapter 2*, where, after listening to an elderly West Indian suggest that they must form committees, and 'elect officers and make representations to the Police Commissioner and our MPs,' he reportedly leapt to his feet and said:

> 'You don't want committees and representations. What you need is to get a few pieces of iron and a bit of organization so that tonight when they come in here we can defend ourselves.'

18. Williams, *op. cit.* 4, pp.36–38.
19. *Ibid*, pp.48–49.
20. *Ibid*, p.50.
21. Despite his plea of not guilty, he was eventually convicted when his case was heard on 16 September and was fined £3 and ordered to pay two guineas costs, or given the alternative of 14 days in prison. He claimed that he told the magistrate he would 'do the 14 days' but within an hour, much to his annoyance, a friend paid the fine and the costs. Malik, Michael Abdul (1968). *From Michael De Freitas to Michael X*. London: Andre Deutsch, p.76.

De Freitas claimed that 'the effect was electrifying' and 'there was an uproar of supporting cries' because, so he claimed, he had 'told them all just what they wanted to hear.'[22] Williams and, indeed, others, have pointed out that De Freitas 'had a tendency to take individual credit for collective actions, and there was quite likely an element of that here, but there was no doubt that he was at the forefront of what went on that afternoon and evening.'[23] People began 'bringing in all sorts of implements for weapons' and a few black American servicemen demonstrated 'how to make petrol bombs.'[24]

Following the riots, De Freitas was on hand to assist with some of the many 'do-gooders' and others who were attracted to Notting Hill, including a group of MPs. Apparently at their request, they were taken to a shebeen where they bought drinks, mixed with prostitutes and learnt 'how to roll a marijuana cigarette.'[25] At about this time, a local councillor Donald Chesworth started a campaign to get tenants to join together in taking their landlords before tribunals to get their rents reduced. His first target was Rachman and he sought the assistance of De Freitas, who was a Rachman tenant. De Freitas expressed doubt about the plan, but was eventually persuaded and, led by him, over 30 tenants eventually signed up to take their landlords to court but all but four withdrew before the due date.[26]

Following this brief episode, Rachman paid De Freitas a visit during which he promised him a better flat for the same rent and a job, which he accepted. De Freitas was, therefore, effectively back to hustling for a living.[27] Working for Rachman gave him an insight into property speculation. Exactly how is unknown but De Freitas apparently became the 'owner of several former Rachman properties in the Notting Hill area over the next couple of years, including a house in Colville Terrace, at the top of which he set up home with Desiree, her daughter Jennifer by a previous relationship, and their new daughter, Kerine Michelle.'[28]

22. *Ibid*, p.76.
23. Williams, *op. cit.* 4, p.54.
24. De Freitas, *op. cit.* 21, pp.76–77.
25. *Ibid*, pp.81–82.
26. Williams, *op. cit.* 4, pp.63–67.
27. *Ibid*, p.70.
28. *Ibid*, p.70.

De Freitas was joined by his mother, Ioana, who travelled over from Trinidad and who quickly got involved in brothel-keeping.[29] Much as he tried to stay in the background directing his illegal activities, he was arrested shortly after his mother's arrival for keeping a brothel in the basement of his Colville Terrace house. Williams suggested that 'Michael was able to sidestep the charges [by] providing alibis for the time when the police alleged they had seen him receiving money from prostitutes.'[30]

Kelland remembered it slightly differently. He claimed that after his abortive attempt to nail Rachman, De Freitas came under police observation. The basement flat in the house he occupied in Colville Terrace was used by two prostitutes in the evenings; thus, in law, it was a brothel. Other tenants in the same house had rent books showing De Freitas as the landlord and it was alleged he was often around when the prostitutes solicited in the street and took men back to the basement flat. A warrant was obtained and he was arrested. He appeared at Marylebone Magistrates' Court on 20 October 1960 but claimed he was not, in fact, the owner and therefore not the landlord. The magistrate found in favour of De Freitas but this decision was overturned on appeal on the basis that as he had issued the rent books, collected the rents and was regarded by the tenants as their landlord so there was a legal contractual relationship.[31] The case was therefore returned to the magistrates' court and he was eventually found guilty, given a conditional discharge and ordered to pay ten guineas costs.[32]

De Freitas now decided he had a simple choice in terms of hustling—dealing in drugs, living off immoral earnings from prostitution or gambling. He chose the last of these, opening 'a gaming house in a basement in Powis Terrace [which] consisted of little more than a couple of tables covered in green baize, one for cards, the other for dice.'[33] However, 'the strains and stresses of the hustling life' coupled 'with the constant police harassment'—given what he was doing was mostly against the law, it is hardly surprising that the police were interested in his various undertakings—and the fact that

---

29. *Ibid*, p.73.
30. *Ibid*, p.75.
31. Kelland, *op. cit.* 1, p.96.
32. *Ibid*, p.97.
33. Williams, *op. cit.* 4, p.73.

Rachman was, by this time, 'busily selling off all his properties,' De Freitas sold the house in Colville Terrace at a 'decent profit' and moved his family to a flat in Stoke Newington. Because Desiree was, by this time, pregnant again, he quit hustling and returned to sea.[34] Following the birth of his second daughter, he spent some time ashore, again hustling in Notting Hill, but this only lasted for a short while before he again returned to sea. However, after about ten months, he was charged with stealing a can of paint from the ship with which to decorate his flat — he likened it unto using office stationery for private correspondence — and was sentenced to three months imprisonment, during which time his marriage deteriorated. Following his release he left Desiree in Stoke Newington and returned to Notting Hill where he 'turned a room in a house into a shebeen and quickly made some serious money'; sufficient to allow him to put down a deposit on a house in Islington for Desiree and the children. Rachman was now dead but the 'housing rackets' in Notting Hill continued.[35]

De Freitas ended up working for a con man, Robert Jacobs from whom he learned that the real money was to be earned by 'gentrifying the neighbourhood.' Using the money he had acquired by working for Jacobs, he opened another gambling house in a large basement. This time, he decorated it, painting the walls white, laying green carpet on the floor and kitting it out with 'luxury fittings'. He 'hired a doorman to usher guests discreetly in and a couple of attractive French girls to serve free tea, coffee and sandwiches to the gamblers.' The outgoings were 'negligible compared with the clients' spending, but it proved a major draw with the gamblers of Notting Hill.'[36]

De Freitas then met with a Canadian woman, Nancy Bacal, and began a five-year relationship which took him away from Notting Hill to a flat in Primrose Hill and a host of new acquaintances in the world of art and literature.[37] Amongst those he met, in February 1965, was Malcolm X, the leader of the Nation of Islam in the USA, when the latter was on a visit to England and De Freitas invited him to the flat he shared with Bacal in Primrose Hill. Later they both took Malcolm X on a tour of Notting Hill.

---

34. *Ibid*, p.84.
35. *Ibid*, p.86: see also De Freitas, *op. cit.* 21, p.114.
36. Williams, *op. cit.* 4, p.86.
37. *Ibid*, pp.92–97.

It was as a result of this meeting that De Freitas became interested in the Black Power movement that was gathering force in the States, but within three weeks of returning to the USA, Malcolm X had been assassinated in Harlem. Shortly after this, De Freitas took a Muslim name, Michael Abdul Malik, later changing it to Michael X.

In becoming Michael X, De Freitas was able to turn 'to advantage his hustling background — his pimping and his unsavoury record as one of Rachman's bully boys.'[38] He founded the Racial Adjustment Action Society (RAAS) and became a self-appointed Messiah at the Black Power Commune, a house in Holloway Road, North London. In 1967, he was sentenced to 12 months imprisonment under race relations legislation 'for publicly urging the shooting of any white man seen with a black girl.' Two years later, together with four fellow Black Power members, he was committed for trial to the Old Bailey on charges of robbery and demanding money with menaces. He jumped bail and fled to his native Trinidad where some of his followers, including a young English woman, Gale Benson, joined him.[39]

In February 1972, De Freitas decapitated a member of his gang who had refused to carry out a raid on a country police station and Gale Benson was reported missing. De Freitas went to Guyana to give a series of lectures. Whilst he was away the Trinidad police became suspicious, dug up the garden of his house and found two bodies. De Freitas was brought back from Guyana to stand trial and was convicted of the murder of the gang member. He was hanged in Trinidad in 1974.[40]

Christine Keeler and Stephen Ward

At about the same time, in 1959, that Hunte and Edwards were appearing before the West London Rent Tribunal, Christine Keeler arrived in London getting a job at Murray's Cabaret Club in the West End, where the 'showgirls walked bare-breasted onto the stage, and the hostesses, all cleavage and chat, moved among the wealthy and aristocratic middle-aged drinkers and

---

38. *Ibid*, pp.111–112.
39. Kelland, *op. cit.* 1, p.97.
40. Williams, *op. cit.* 4, pp.197–272.

diners'.[41] Shortly after she started working there she met Stephen Ward, an 'osteopath with [a] fashionable clientele'.[42]

Ward liked 'glamorous women around him'[43] and was involved with a variety of people who took part in sexual activities of one kind and another. Some of the women he knew were 'heavily into sadistic sex' and 'group sex sessions'.[44] Although homosexual activity was illegal, even between consenting adults until 1967, he also knew what went on in the gay community. Claiming she never had any real friends other than Ward, Keeler said of him 'he was my companion, my confident [and] would tell me stories about his nocturnal escapades with prostitutes.'[45]

Ward had a fascination for black women and it was this that was to lead to a strong link with Notting Hill. Ward 'would drive around London alone late a night looking at the girls' and even talking to them. Sometimes, claimed Keeler, 'he brought a prostitute back with him.'[46] Later, Ward took Keeler with him, 'driving through the rough areas of Notting Hill late at night' stopping 'for a coffee in a rough café full of black men.' Keeler described Notting Hill as:

> '[A] tough area in 1961. There was always trouble on the streets and the police did
> not seem to patrol although their sirens were as constant and irritating as piped
> music. It wasn't just fights but the threat of riots. Peter Rachman ran the place
> and his clients—the white ones—were usually on the fringes of the underworld
> or prostitution.'[47]

Keeler described how, on one occasion, she was with Ward in his car, when they saw a black prostitute hand some money to a black man who was clearly her ponce, in Westbourne Park Road before the prostitute continued soliciting. She eventually picked up a client and Ward suggested to Keeler

---

41. Keeler, Christine with Douglas Thompson (2001). *The Truth at Last: My Story*. London: Sidgewick & Jackson, p.1.

42. *Ibid*, p.22.

43. *Ibid*, p.36.

44. *Ibid*, p.39.

45. *Ibid*, p.43.

46. *Ibid*, p.82.

47. *Ibid*, p.89.

that she should try her hand at soliciting by walking from the car to a nearby milk-machine. A number of men tried to pick her up but when one got too close, she fled back to the relative safety of Ward's car.[48]

The Second Hustler — Aloysius 'Lucky' Gordon

Ward made friends with prominent people, some of whom he took on his nocturnal trips to Notting Hill where he was keen to visit some of the dives in search of drugs and 'a black girl'. It was on one of these trips, in October 1961, that Keeler met the second of the Notting Hill hustlers, Aloysius 'Lucky' Gordon.[49] Ward, accompanied by a tall, distinguished, upper-class writer on race relations, Lord de Laszlo, and Keeler stumbled upon the Rio Coffee Bar in Westbourne Park Road. In trying to impress his friend, Ward persuaded Keeler to buy some 'weed' or 'grass' whilst the two men waited in the car. Described as 'an extraordinary example of just how squalid a place could be,'[50] Keeler entered and bumped into Gordon, a West Indian jazz singer, living in Leytonstone, who had been thrown out of the British Army and had 'thirteen convictions for crimes, including fraud, theft and shopbreaking'.[51] After buying a small amount of drugs from him, she told Gordon she was also looking to acquire a black girl for Ward and gave him her telephone number at Wimpole Mews.[52]

Forty-eight hours after their initial meeting, Gordon telephoned Keeler, saying he had a black girl for Ward, and asked her to meet him in the Rio. Keeler went with Ward but, on this occasion, she became ill from the effects of a mixture of alcohol and cannabis and Ward, much to Gordon's annoyance took her back to Wimpole Mews. But Gordon was persistent eventually persuading Keeler to meet him on the pretext of showing her some jewellery he had stolen. Keeler claimed that, on getting her back to his flat, he effectively raped her at knife-point and kept her prisoner for nearly 20 hours until she eventually managed to persuade him to let her go by promising to see

---

48. *Ibid*, pp.89–90.
49. Denning suggested this was in October 1961. Coates, Tim (2003). *The Scandal of Christine Keeler and John Profumo: Lord Denning's Report*, 1963. London: Tim Coates Books, p.26.
50. Keeler, *op. cit.* 41, p.92.
51. *Ibid*, pp.97–99.
52. Keeler, *op. cit.* 41, pp.97–99; Crawford, *op. cit.* 3, p.34.

him again.[53] On another occasion, Gordon went to Wimpole Mews to see Keeler whilst Ward and a friend were there, created a scene and was asked to leave.[54] On yet another occasion, Keeler described how Ward took the actor and comedian, Alfred Marks, his wife and herself to the Rio. Although Gordon was present he made no move towards them.[55]

For the next year or so, Keeler was pursued relentlessly by Gordon. On one occasion he kept Keeler and a girlfriend prisoner in a flat for two days at the end of which Keeler managed to escape and telephone the police. Gordon had hit her a number of times and there were noticeable marks and bruises on her body. Gordon was arrested and charged with causing her grievous bodily harm but Gordon's brother persuaded Keeler to drop the charges.[56] On another occasion, she voluntarily spent three days with him in his flat in Leytonstone where he treated her very gently. She left, saying she would see him again but was afraid of his normally violent nature.[57]

The Third Hustler — Johnny Edgecombe

On a visit, in September 1962, to one of her friends, 23-year-old Paula Hamilton-Marshall, who was pregnant by a black USA Air Force officer, Keeler bumped into another West Indian, Johnny Edgecombe, who said he knew Gordon and would have a word with him. Edgecombe became her protector and, for a short time, her lover.[58] The police knew Edgecombe as 'a troublesome petty criminal and dope addict';[59] he had three convictions at this stage, for stealing in 1951, for living on the immoral earnings of a prostitute in 1959 and for the unlawful possession of drugs in 1962.[60]

Immediately, following his enlistment as her protector, Edgecombe spent approximately eight weeks with Keeler in a luxury flat in Sheffield Terrace which was in a fashionable part of Kensington, known as Holland Park, between Kensington High Street and Notting Hill Gate. The only time they

---

53. Keeler, *op. cit.* 41, pp.91–99.
54. *Ibid*, pp.100–101.
55. *Ibid*, p.126.
56. *Ibid*, pp.128–130.
57. *Ibid*, pp.132–133.
58. *Ibid*, pp.139–140.
59. Crawford, *op. cit.* 3, p.2.
60. Coates, *op. cit.* 49, p.80.

ventured out they did so separately, with Keeler going to various secret rendezvous with her 'sugar daddies' and Edgecombe going to Ladbroke Grove to replenish his supply of 'dope'. In the evenings they apparently smoked the dope together during which time Keeler told him how Ward 'had a habit of befriending young girls who worked in night clubs' and then introducing them 'to influential men for sex.' Two of these men were John Profumo, the Minister of State for War, and a Russian Naval Attaché, Captain Eugene Ivanov. Edgecombe claimed that it was never Ward's intention to earn money for supplying the girls but rather 'his fee was government secrets at the highest level.'[61] Edgecombe alleged that, on one occasion, Profumo visited Sheffield Terrace and had sex with Keeler whilst he hid in a cupboard but this has never been verified.[62]

On 27 October, Edgecombe and Gordon were involved in a disturbance at the All Nighters Club in Wardour Street, Soho, during which Edgecombe sliced Gordon's face with a knife;[63] the wound requiring 17 stitches.[64] Edgecombe claimed that when the stitches were removed, Gordon put them in a box and posted them to Keeler at Wimpole Mews 'saying that for each one she would get two in her face.'[65] Edgecombe never admitted to cutting Gordon. He claimed that he was listening to the music in the club when Gordon arrived and immediately came over and punched him. Edgecombe went after him, jumping over a table, but Gordon picked up a chair and threatened him before he was grabbed by the bouncer and dragged out of the club and into the foyer. According to Edgecombe, 'there was a scuffle, during which Lucky got cut.'[66] Edgecombe left the club with Keeler and went to a shebeen in Powis Terrace in Ladbroke Grove[67] where the owner told him that Gordon, accompanied by police officers, had just visited looking for him.

Shortly before this incident, Edgecombe and Keeler moved from Sheffield Terrace to a flat in Lancaster Road. However, they quickly left this flat and went into hiding with a friend of Edgecombe's in Brentford. Keeler,

---

61. Edgecombe, John (2002). *Black Scandal*. London: Westworld International, pp.65/66.
62. *Ibid*, pp.72–73.
63. See Keeler, *op. cit.* 41, pp.143–144.
64. Coates, *op. cit.* 49, p.26. Edgecombe, *op. cit.* 61, p.87 says 14 stitches.
65. Edgecombe, *op. cit.* 61, p.87.
66. *Ibid*, p.86.
67. *Ibid*, pp.86–87.

now tired of living with Edgecombe because she missed the lifestyle she had become accustomed to whilst living with Ward, contacted a retired solicitor, Michael Eddowes, whom she knew. He arranged for her to move back into Central London and she and Edgecombe split up after a fearful row. Later, Edgecombe contacted Keeler and asked her to help in finding a solicitor before the police found him. Keeler refused, saying she would testify against him if the case came to court. But, Edgecombe 'was determined to get her back if he could.'[68]

The Beginning of the End

Things quickly came to a head. On 14 December, Edgecombe arrived in Wimpole Mews in a mini-cab. He rang the front door-bell of Ward's flat, where Keeler was visiting Mandy Rice-Davies. Three of the people who were there, Edgecombe, Keeler and Rice-Davies, have written about the events of that day, and are in broad agreement about what happened although there are some minor discrepancies.[69] When he arrived and asked to see Keeler, but from an upstairs window, Rice-Davies told him she was not there at which he pulled out a gun. Keeler then appeared at the same window and tried to reason with him but Edgecombe fired two shots at the window and three at the front door. These five shots were to catapult the two girls to international prominence. They were also to lead to the resignation of John Profumo from his post as Secretary of State for War, the death of Stephen Ward, and the imprisonment of the two hustlers from Notting Hill.

The mews was soon swarming with police and journalists. Edgecombe escaped in a taxi but was later arrested when he arrived back at the flat he had been staying at, in Brentford. On 17 January 1963, he was committed for trial at the Old Bailey on four charges: shooting with intent to kill Christine Keeler; shooting with intent to cause her grievous bodily harm and two charges of possessing a firearm. That same day, Captain Eugene Ivanov left England to return to Russia.[70] Nine days later, Keeler was interviewed by the police about the evidence she was to give at Edgecombe's trial and,

---

68. Coates, *op. cit.* 49, p.26.
69. See Edgecombe, *op. cit.* 61, pp.92–95; Keeler, *op. cit.* 41, pp.148–149; and Rice-Davies, Mandy with Shirley Flack (1980). *Mandy*. London: Sphere, pp.118–119.
70. Crawford, *op. cit.* 3, p.9.

during the course of the interview, the name of the then Minister of War, John Profumo was mentioned.[71]

Edgecombe appeared at the Central Criminal Court on 14 March. The principal witness, Christine Keeler, failed to attend—she was subsequently brought before the court and ordered to forfeit her recognizance of £40—but both Mandy Rice-Davis and the taxi-driver were able to give evidence that Edgecombe had been in possession of a gun and had fired at the door of the house in Wimpole Mews. The absence of Keeler meant the charges of attempted murder and the attempt to cause her grievous bodily harm were dropped. The following day, Edgecombe was found guilty of the possession of a firearm with intent to endanger life and was sentenced to seven years' imprisonment. Whilst the jury was considering their verdict in this trial, another trial involving Edgecombe commenced. This time it related to wounding Gordon with the knife. Keeler was also a key witness in this trial as she was present when the wounding occurred, but again she failed to appear. On this occasion, Edgecombe was acquitted.[72]

Keeler suddenly resurfaced in Madrid and, in an interview with a television journalist before returning to London, she admitted that she and Profumo had been lovers. On June 6, Keeler visited a friend, Paula Hamilton-Marshall, at her flat in Bryanston Mews. Visiting at the same time were two West Indians, Rudolph 'Truello' Fenton and Clarence Commachio and the two girls decided to go out with them. But, as they left the flat, the four were suddenly confronted by Gordon who had been waiting outside. He attacked Keeler with a 'sudden savagery' before either Fenton or Commachie could react. Paula Hamilton-Marshall, meantime, rushed back into the flat to telephone for the police. Eventually Fenton and Commachie pulled Gordon away from Keeler, who had 'blood pouring down her face', and, hearing that the police had been called, Gordon fled the scene.[73]

Subsequently, Keeler claimed that Fenton and Commachie were terrified of seeing the police. One was on bail awaiting trial; the other, who had six children, was afraid he would be evicted from his flat if it became known that he had been mixed up in any trouble. Therefore, when the police arrived,

71. *Ibid*, pp.11–12.
72. *Ibid*, pp.14–15.
73. Keeler, *op. cit.* 41, p.195.

both men were hiding under the bed in Hamilton-Marshall's room.[74] Gordon was arrested three days later and charged with wounding Miss Keeler, with intent to maim, disfigure, disable or cause grievous bodily harm. When he appeared at the Old Bailey in June, he was found not guilty of wounding Keeler but he was convicted of assaulting her and sentenced to three years' imprisonment. At the trial, Gordon had demanded the attendance as witnesses of the two West Indians, Fenton and Commanchie, but Keeler, Marshall and the only other witness for the prosecution, Olive Booker, Paula's housekeeper, denied that they had been there.[75]

John Profumo

In July 1961, Keeler had met John Profumo whilst she was staying with Stephen Ward at a cottage on Lord Astor's Estate at Cliveden. Profumo, together with his wife, the actress Valerie Hobson, was spending the weekend with Lord Astor. Also amongst Ward's guests that weekend was one of Keeler's 'latest acquisitions, the assistant naval attaché at the Russian Embassy, Captain Eugene Ivanov'.[76] According to Lord Denning, Ward was an admirer of 'the Soviet regime and sympathised with the communists' as a result of which he had become 'very friendly' with Ivanov.[77]

On his return to London, Profumo began to see Keeler regularly, giving her 'presents and "money for her mother" in return for her amorous favours'.[78] Most of the time, they met at Stephen Ward's home at 17 Wimpole Mews whilst he was at work. Another visitor to 17 Wimpole Mews was Captain Ivanov. Within a month, this somewhat dangerous liaison whereby Britain's Secretary of State for War and the assistant Russian Naval Attaché were both known to be visiting Ward's house in Wimpole Street had been brought to the attention of the Cabinet Secretary, Sir Norman Brooke. He warned Profumo that his association with Ward was perhaps unwise in view of the latter's apparent friendship with Ivanov.

---

74. *Ibid*, pp.195–196.
75. Crawford, *op. cit.* 3, pp.32–34.
76. *Ibid*, p.4.
77. Coates, *op. cit.* 49, p.4.
78. Crawford, *op. cit.* 3, p.4.

However, as mentioned earlier, Keeler had mentioned Profumo's name in an interview with the police. This coincided with rumours about Keeler's association with Profumo circulating behind the scenes in newspaper offices which had reached the ear of the Government. As a result, the Attorney-General met with Profumo, who admitted that he had seen Keeler on a number of occasions at parties at Ward's flat, but he strongly denied any sexual relationship with her, and continued to do so for over four months. But rumours persisted.

Also, people 'began openly to ask questions about the sort of company Mr Profumo kept.' Whilst most agreed that a perchant for 'pretty girls' was one thing, 'girls who kept getting involved with West Indians with known criminal records, and in whom the police took an almost exaggerated interest, suggested a more sinister background to the affair.'[79] Rumours were also circulating that Ward was managing a vice-ring. On 4 June, Profumo admitted he had lied about his relationship with Christine Keeler and resigned, not only as Secretary of State for War, but also as a Member of Parliament.[80]

The arrest of Stephen Ward

The following day, Ward was arrested and charged with 'on divers dates between January 1961 and June 1963' living 'wholly or in part on the earnings of prostitution at 17 Wimpole Mews, W1.'[81] Initially, when he appeared at Marylebone Magistrates' Court, he faced eight charges. Two related to living on the immoral earnings of Christine Keeler and Mandy Rice-Davies respectively; three related to the procurement of girls who were under 21 years of age to have unlawful sexual intercourse with third persons; two accused Ward of procuring an unknown person to perform abortions on two women, identified merely as Miss M and Miss W; and finally, he was accused of conspiring with other persons to keep a brothel at 17 Wimpole Mews.[82] Ward denied all the charges. However, he was committed to the Old Bailey to stand trial.[83]

---

79. Crawford, *op. cit.* 3, p.24.
80. Keeler, *op. cit.* 41, p.194.
81. Crawford, *op. cit.* 3, p.35.
82. *Ibid*, p.106.
83. *Ibid*, p.126.

Four things happened between the time Ward was committed for trial and the commencement of his trial on 22 July 1963. Firstly, Lord Denning was asked by Prime Minister Harold Macmillan to inquire into the circumstances leading up to Profumo's resignation and any security aspects relative to it.[84] Secondly, because he had been mentioned, particularly by Mandy Rice-Davies in her evidence at the committal proceedings, the name of Rachman became a household name. Thirdly, doubt was cast on the evidence Keeler had given at the trial of Gordon. Fourthly, the two Notting Hill hustlers, Edgecombe and Gordon, both by then serving prison sentences, were brought to Treasury Chambers in Great George Street, to be interviewed by Lord Denning.

By the end of the proceedings on Tuesday, 30 July 1963, the judge was midway through his summing-up. Before adjourning, he announced, in reference to the following day, 'I have no doubt this will be the last day.'[85] That night Ward took an overdose of Nembutal. He was discovered the next morning by the friend in whose house he was staying and rushed by ambulance to St. Stephen's Hospital. Later that morning, the judge completed his summing-up. After deliberating on the evidence for four-and-a-half hours, the jury returned, finding Ward guilty of living on the immoral earnings of Keeler and Rice-Davies but not guilty of the other charges. The judge said he would pronounce sentence when Ward was well enough to attend court. In fact, sentence was never pronounced, for Ward did not recover from the overdose. He died at St Stephen's Hospital on 3 August after being in a coma for 80 hours.[86]

Tidying Up Loose Ends

On 30 July 1963, Gordon's conviction for assaulting Keeler was quashed by the Court of Appeal on the grounds that there were two witnesses to the events, Fenton and Commachie, that Gordon had wished to call 'which might have led the jury to have reasonable doubt.'[87] Later that year, Keeler was imprisoned for nine months for committing perjury and obstructing

---

84. *Ibid*, p.95.
85. *Ibid*, p.169.
86. *Ibid*, pp.149–172.
87. Coates, *op. cit.* 49, p.123.

the course of justice, at Gordon's trial. Her friend, Paula Hamilton-Marshall received six months imprisonment and Olive Booker was given a one year probation order.[88]

It was clear during his inquiry that Denning formed a low opinion of Ward, describing him as 'utterly immoral'. He went on:

> 'He used to pick up pretty girls at the age of 16 or 17 ... and induce them to come and stay with him at his house in London. He seduced many of these himself. He also procured them to be mistresses for his influential friends. ... He catered also for those of his friends who had perverted tastes. ... He attended parties where there were sexual orgies of a revolting nature.'[89]

In relation to the two hustlers from Notting Hill, Denning described how Ward introduced Keeler 'to the drug of Indian hemp [to which] she became addicted [and she] met coloured men who trafficked in it [and] went to live with them.'[90]

Keeler described Rachman as 'a dark shadow over London in the late-1950s and early-1960s.'[91] There is little doubt that Rachman exploited a situation in which increasing numbers of immigrants arriving from the Caribbean found themselves desperately looking for somewhere to live but he was not the cause of the situation. Many black people felt as De Freitas did, that Rachman was not 'the real villain'; rather it was 'all those who put up notices saying "no coloured".' Although, De Freitas admitted that he charged exorbitant rents, he claimed that 'if it hadn't been for him a lot of black people would have slept in the streets.'[92] People would still have lived in overcrowded accommodation and would still have found it difficult to get jobs, as they had before Rachman came on the scene. Criminality and prostitution would still have thrived without Rachman.[93]

Not surprisingly, perhaps, Keeler was damning in her criticism of Lord Denning's report, calling it 'one of the greatest miscarriages of British justice

88. Keeler, *op. cit.* 41, p.224.
89. Coates, *op. cit.* 49, p.3.
90. *Ibid*, p.6.
91. Keeler, *op. cit.* 41, p.47.
92. De Freitas, *op. cit.* 21, p.93.
93. Green, *op. cit.* 8, pp.90–91.

ever …' and 'the ultimate whitewash'. Her claim that Ward was a Russian spy was ignored as was her descriptions of 'high society decadence.' She also claimed that many of his dates as to when certain events occurred were incorrect and suggested she was ignored 'for the national interest.'[94] Ludovic Kennedy, too, was scathing in his criticism of Denning accusing him of indulging in 'gossipy titbits of the women's magazine variety which had no bearing on his brief', stating 'hearsay as fact', despite claiming, at the outset, that 'no man was to be condemned on suspicion,' and defaming the dead.[95]

Postscript

Some years later, the fall of another Government minister resulted from his liaison with a prostitute who had brief connections with Notting Hill. In May 1973, Lord Lambton, then a junior Minister in the Ministry of Defence, resigned after being exposed in the *News of The World* for consorting with a call-girl, Norma Levy, during which time he took drugs. On 13 June, at Marylebone Magistrates' Court he was fined £300 for the illegal possession of cannabis and amphetamine tablets. The prostitute at the centre of the Lambton case was Norma Levy, who ran away from home in Stockton-on-Tees at the age of 17 years, and found a bedsit in Notting Hill before starting work as an escort at a gentlemen's club, Churchill's, in Bond Street. As a result of her earnings and, in some cases, large tips from the clients she entertained through Churchill's, she was able to move to the more fashionable Maida Vale in North London and was subsequently 'taken on the books' of one of London's leading madams, Jean Horn. As a result, Levy was introduced to a series of high profile customers, one of which was Lord Lambton, entertaining them either at her flat or when she went to visit them.[96]

---

94. Keeler, *op. cit.* 41, pp.208–209.
95. Kennedy, Ludovic (1991). *The Trial of Stephen Ward*. London: Chivers Press, pp.247–250.
96. Jones, David (2007). 'Call girl who nearly toppled a government reveals all'. *Daily Mail*, 26 January 2007.

CHAPTER 5

MURDER MOST FOUL

Heath and Haigh

Notting Hill is no stranger to murder. Three notorious murderers, all of whom were serial killers and all of whom were executed for their crimes, were associated with the area within eight years of the end of World War II. The first was Neville Heath. In June 1946, Heath met part-time actress Margery Gardner and took her back to his room at the Pembridge Court Hotel in Notting Hill Gate where they were involved in sadistic sexual activity. The following morning, Gardner was found dead in bed; she was naked, had 17 slash marks on her body, and her wrists and ankles were bound. There was evidence that a poker, found in the fireplace, had been inserted into her vagina, and both her nipples had been bitten savagely. Heath was eventually arrested after he had murdered a second woman in a similar way. Convicted of murder he was hanged on 16 October 1946.[1]

The second was Acid Bath Murderer, John Haigh, so-called because he dissolved the bodies of his victims in vats of sulphuric acid and, whilst he committed none of the six murders attributed to him in Notting Hill, two of his victims were associated with the area. Haigh had already killed three people when Dr and Mrs Henderson, who lived at 22 Ladbroke Square, advertised their house for sale. Haigh was amongst the first to make enquiries but it is doubtful whether he had serious intentions of buying it. Having befriended them because they obviously 'had money', they sold the house and moved to Fulham. Haig then lured them to a workshop he had rented in Crawley, Sussex, shot them both and disposed of their bodies in vats of

---

1. See Murder UK at http://www.murder.uk.com/serial_neville_heath accessed on 22 November 2011, for further details.

acid. He was to kill a sixth person before he was caught. Convicted of murder, he was hanged on 10 August 1949.[2]

Evans and Christie

But Notting Hill is probably best-known for the serial killer, John Reginald Harold Christie who lived at No.10 Rillington Place, a three-storey end of terrace house, with 'peeling paint and rotting stucco.'[3] Few murder cases, with the exception, perhaps, of those committed by Jack the Ripper in the 1880s have produced as much controversy as the events which took place in that house between 1944 and 1953. Two people, Timothy Evans and Christie stood trial separately for murders that had taken place at the address as a result of which it was suggested that 'no murder case in England has been so difficult to solve, created such uproar, and spawned so many words'.[4] At the conclusion of the second trial, it was described as 'the most notorious trial in modern times.'[5] Although considerable doubt still exists as to the truth of the events that occurred at that address, there is a strong suspicion that a man was hanged for a murder he did not commit.

At about the time the *Empire Windrush* was gliding into London Docks, Evans and his wife, Beryl, moved into the top floor flat of No.10 Rillington Place.[6] The ground floor flat was occupied by Christie and his wife Ethel, who had lived there for about ten years. Unbeknown to anyone at that time, except Christie, the bodies of two women were already buried in the back garden and had been for the previous four to five years.[7]

Evans was fairly well-known in the area, frequenting The Elgin public House and Kensington Park Hotel (or the KPH as it was more commonly known) both of which were in Ladbroke Grove. Following the birth of his daughter, there were constant rows between Evans and his wife. Eventually the bodies of his wife and daughter were found in the outside wash-house

2. See Lefebure, Molly (1958). *Murder with a Difference: The Cases of Haigh and Christie*. London: Heinemann.
3. Kennedy, Ludwig (1971). *Ten Rillington Place*. London: Grafton Books, p.27.
4. Eddowes, John (1995). *The Two Killers of Rillington Place*. London: Warner Books, p.xiii.
5. Kennedy, *op. cit.* 3, p.259.
6. *Ibid*, pp.62/63.
7. *Ibid*, pp.52–55; see also Eddowes, op. cit. 4, pp.8–9.

of No.10 Rillington Place; both had been strangled. Evans was convicted of the murder of his daughter and hanged.[8]

And there the matter might have rested except for the fact that, in March 1953, Christie left his flat after taking three months' rent, in advance, plus another pound for some fittings, from a Mr and Mrs Reilly. Unfortunately, for the Reilly's and for Christie, the landlord, a Mr Brown, visited the flat chasing Christie for rent which had not been paid since January. Mr and Mrs Reilly were forced to leave and the landlord gave his namesake, a Mr Beresford Brown, who was already occupying a room on the top floor, permission to use the ground floor kitchen. Four days later, Brown was trying to fix some brackets to the wall in the kitchen when he realised that the area was hollow. He ripped off some of the wallpaper, exposing some rough wooden boards, through which he could see a woman's naked back. He immediately contacted the police. In the alcove the police found the bodies of three women. Later that night, police found the body of Christie's wife, Ethel, underneath the floorboards and still later they found the two bodies in the garden.[9] Christie's trial opened at the Old Bailey on 22 June. He was accused of the murder of his wife. The trial was short and Christie was found guilty. He was hanged on 15 July 1953.[10]

The discovery of four bodies in Christie's flat, plus a further two in the garden, immediately raised doubts about the guilt of Timothy Evans. As a result there have been two judicial inquiries, the first by the Recorder of Portsmouth, John Scott Henderson QC, in 1953,[11] who found that Evans had murdered both his wife and daughter, and the second by a High Court Judge, Sir Daniel Brabin, in 1965,[12] who found that Evans probably murdered his wife but did not murder his daughter.

In addition to the two inquiries there are at least four leading books on the subject. Most people, including the Court of Appeal,[13] and Scott Hen-

---

8. Eddowes, *op. cit.* 4, pp.58 and 83.
9. Lefebure, *op. cit.* 2, pp.204–217; Kennedy, *op. cit.* 3, pp.242–243.
10. Kennedy, *op. cit.* 3, pp.259–260; Eddowes, *op. cit.* 4, p.94.
11. The Inquiry Report by Mr J Scott Henderson, QC, is contained in the book by Ludwig Kennedy, *op. cit.* 3, pp.271–307.
12. An edition of The Inquiry Report by Daniel Brabin was published by the Stationery Office, London, as part of its 'Uncovered Editions' series in 1999.
13. Brabin, *op. cit.* 12, pp.173–174; Kennedy, *op. cit.* 3, pp.223–224.

derson agreed that, in respect of Beryl and Geraldine, whoever had killed one had killed both. In her book, published in 1958, Molly Lefebure[14] took the view that Christie had killed Beryl but Evans had killed Geraldine. On the other hand, Rupert Furneaux,[15] in his book published in 1961 expressed an opposite view, that Evans killed Beryl and Christie killed Geraldine, which was the finding of the Brabin Inquiry in 1965. However, Ludovic Kennedy,[16] in his book, also published in 1961, expressed the view that both Beryl and Geraldine were killed by Christie and, in a later edition of his book, published in 1971,[17] claimed that there was virtually no evidence to support Brabin's view that Evans had killed his wife. However, in his book, published in 1994, John Eddowes[18] suggested the exact opposite; that Evans murdered both his wife and daughter, thus agreeing with the Scott Henderson inquiry, and attempted to lay the blame for their deaths on Christie. The year after the Brabin inquiry, the Home Secretary recommend to Her Majesty The Queen, that Evans should be given a posthumous free pardon which she did.[19]

As a postscript to this particularly gruesome case, Chief Inspector Kelland described how, in June 1960, the police raided Christie's former flat — the street had been renamed Rushton Close by this time[20] — which was then known, in the evenings at least, as Charlie Brown's Celebrity Club, with alcohol being sold without a licence. The recess in which Christie had hidden the bodies of three of his victims was being used as the bar.[21]

'Jack the Stripper'

But that was by no means the end of Notting Hill's connection with murder. Between 1959 and 1965 the bodies of eight naked women were found in West London. All were prostitutes and all were believed to have been

---

14. Lefebure, *op. cit.* 2, p.250.
15. Furneaux, Rupert (1961). *The Two Stranglers of Rillington Place*. London: Panther Books.
16. Kennedy, Ludovic (1961). *Ten Rillington Place*. London: Victor Gollancz Ltd.
17. Kennedy, *op. cit.* 3.
18. Eddowes, John (1995). *The Two Killers of Rillington Place*. London: Warner Books.
19. Kennedy, *op. cit.* 3, p.7.
20. Vague, Tom (1998). *Vague 30: London Psychogeography — Rachman, Riots and Rillington Place*. London: Ladbroke Grove, p.14.
21. Kelland, Gilbert (1987). *Crime in London*. London: Grafton Books, p.87.

murdered although open verdicts were recorded at the inquests of the second victim, Gwyneth Rees, and the third victim, Hannah Tailford. They became known as the 'nude' murders and were described as the 'most notorious unsolved crimes' since those ascribed to Jack the Ripper nearly 80 years previously. Indeed, Detective Chief Superintendent John du Rose, who was recalled from holiday to take charge of the investigation after the body of the last woman had been found, described the killer, Jack the Stripper as he became known, as having 'as prominent a place in the annals of crime as that of Jack the Ripper and the Boston Strangler'.[22] Whilst none of the bodies were discovered on Notting Hill's ground, the circumstances surrounding the deaths of a number of them, exemplified the seediness that existed in Notting Hill at the time.

Du Rose discounted the first two victims in his autobiography, written in 1971, suggesting that the first victim was Hannah Tailford. Indeed, he makes no mention of the first two. However, in his book, *Found Naked and Dead*, first published three years later in 1974, Fleet Street Crime Reporter, Brian McConnell, links all eight together;[23] so, too, does David Seabrook in *Jack of Jumps* first published in 2006.[24]

Both McConnell and Seabrook suggested the first victim was Elizabeth Figg, also known as Ann Phillips. Born in Cheshire, she had become a prostitute by early-1959, soliciting on the streets in various parts of London, including Holland Park in Notting Hill. Late on the evening of 16 June 1959, she had been picked up near Finsbury Park by a man named Ernest Patrick Forrest. Forrest had wanted to spend the night with her but she claimed that she had an appointment in the early hours of the following morning, at 2 a.m. to be precise, at Holland Park. After having sexual intercourse in his car in Hornsey, Forrest agreed to drive her to Holland Park and then pick her up at 3.30 a.m. so he could spend the rest of the night with her. He dropped her off at 1.10 a.m. and went to a coffee bar in the West End. At about 3.20 a.m., he was seen in his car in Lansdowne Road by two patrolling constables from Notting Hill Police Station, PCs Nash and Dalton. They

22. Du Rose, John (1973). *Murder Was My Business*. St. Albans, Hertfordshire: Mayflower, pp.1–3.
23. McConnell, Brian (1975). *Found Naked and Dead*. London: NEL Books published by the New English Library.
24. Seabrook, David (2007). *Jack of Jumps*. London: Granta Books.

pointed out that they regularly received complaints from people living in the area about motorists soliciting prostitutes and advised him to move on. Forrest was then seen to drive off.[25]

Less than two hours later, Figg's body was found by the crew of a patrolling police car close to the banks of the River Thames near Chiswick Bridge. She was lying on her back with her dress open revealing her breasts. Her head was turned slightly to the right and her eyes were open. She had died as a result of manual strangulation, later estimated by pathologist Dr Donald Teare to be between midnight and 2 a.m.[26] A murder squad, under the command of Detective Superintendent Jim Mitchell, was set up at Chiswick Police Station but no prosecution followed. Forrest came forward voluntarily on hearing of the discovery of Figg's body. He was interviewed at length by Mitchell and his car underwent a detailed forensic examination but it was clear that he had not been involved in Figg's death.[27]

There was then a four year gap before the murderer—if, indeed, it was the same person—struck again. The victim, Gwynneth Rees, who used a number of aliases, had no connections with Notting Hill Division. Her body was found at the Barnes Borough Council Refuse Disposal Plant, some 40 yards from the Thames towpath, on 8 November 1963.[28] According to pathologist Dr Arthur Mant, it is likely that she had been dead for between four and eight weeks and the body, naked except for one nylon stocking rolled down around her ankle, was in an advanced stage of decomposition.[29] She operated as a prostitute in the East End of London and, at the time of her death, had been convicted on 13 separate occasions, 12 for soliciting and once for theft.[30] A murder squad, led by Detective Superintendent Frederick Chadburn, was set up at Richmond Police Station. There was some speculation that Rees's death was not murder at all—rather it was as a result of an illegal abortion that had gone wrong—and indeed at the Coroner's Inquest an open verdict was returned. However, she was murdered, almost certainly by

---

25. *Ibid*, p.4.
26. *Ibid*, p.4; McConnell, *op. cit.* 23, p.36.
27. Seabrook, *op. cit.* 24, p.22.
28. *Ibid*, p.35; McConnell, *op. cit.* 23, p.44.
29. Seabrook, *op. cit.* 24, pp.36–37; McConnell, *op. cit.* 23, pp.45–46.
30. Seabrook, *op. cit.* 24, p.38; McConnell, *op. cit.* 23, says 11 on p.64.

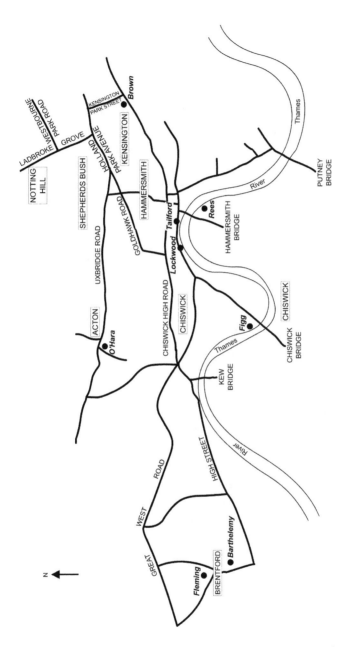

Locations in which the eight bodies from the Nude Murders were found.

Map drawn and © Kate Whittingham.

strangulation, according to a colleague of Dr Mant's, Professor Warwick.[31] But again Du Rose makes no mention of her death, claiming that the so-called nude murders started with the death of Hannah Tailford.

Tailford's body was found on the foreshore below the Corinthian's Clubhouse, located some distance west of Hammersmith Bridge, by two members of the club at 1.15 p.m. on 2 February 1964, less than two months after the body of Rees had been found. She was naked except for a pair of nylon stockings bunched around her lower legs; in her mouth was a piece of her panties.[32] It was estimated that she had been in the water for between two and seven days and the pathologist, again Dr Teare, gave the cause of death as drowning.[33] Tailford came from Northumberland and had a string of convictions, mainly for theft, before she came to London. Her first conviction for soliciting as a prostitute was in Hyde Park in 1954 and she had two further convictions prior to her death. In 1961, she gave birth to a baby girl and met up with a man called Alan Lynch, who had just left the Merchant Navy and was the manager of a billiards hall. He provided a home for Tailford and the baby, firstly in Battersea, then in West Norwood before she moved, alone this time, to Pembridge Villas, Notting Hill. Despite Lynch's job, Tailford continued to work as a prostitute at night, using a string of aliases.[34]

On this occasion, a murder squad was set up at Shepherds Bush Police Station under the command of Detective Chief Inspector Devonald, but, despite interviewing some 700 people during the investigation, little of value was obtained.[35] However, what the investigation did discover was that she did not just solicit on the streets but also attended parties involving 'perverted sexual practices' in houses in Kensington and Mayfair, organized by a foreign diplomat who employed an agent to recruit the women. She had also posed for pornographic photographs involving group sex sessions and was,

---

31. Seabrook, *op. cit.* 24, p.37.
32. Du Rose, *op. cit.* 22, p.103.
33. Seabrook, *op. cit.* 24, pp.93–94.
34. McConnell, *op. cit.* 23, p.84.
35. McConnell, *op. cit.* 23, states that Detective Chief Superintendent Frederick Gerrard was in charge and describes many of the enquiries being undertaken by Detective Inspector Frank Ridge (pp.81–85). Du Rose, *op. cit.* 22, suggests Ridge was in charge but then goes on to say that Devonald questioned 700 people (p.104)

believed, at one time, to be in possession of copies of those photographs.[36] Because of the pathologist's view that the cause of death was drowning, an open verdict was recorded by the inquest.[37]

The fourth victim was Irene Lockwood who, under the name of Sandra Russell, lived successively at 138 Westbourne Grove and 118 Ledbury Road before, on 3 January 1964, moving to 16 Denbigh Road, to share a flat with another prostitute, Maureen Gallagher.[38] Lockwood generally solicited in Westbourne Grove, Bayswater Road and Queensway although on 18 January she had been arrested by PCs Langman and Barringer at 2 a.m., for soliciting in Kensington Church Street. On this occasion she had been taken to Notting Hill Police Station where she was charged. The following morning, she was given a conditional discharge for 12 months at Marylebone Magistrates' Court.[39] On her own admission, she had 14 previous convictions since 1956, including five for soliciting and one for indecency in a public place.[40] Gallagher, on the other hand, tended to confine herself to Westbourne Grove. Although Lockwood occasionally conducted her business in a car, both girls regularly took clients back to the flat in Denbigh Road, taking it in turns to use the bedroom.[41]

It was suggested that Lockwood too, had been involved in some shady deals involving 'purple hearts' and 'blue films'. At one stage, it was thought that both Tailford and Lockwood could have been murdered by people they had been trying to blackmail.[42] Kenneth Archibald was eventually arrested and charged with Lockwood's murder. How this came about is a story in itself.

In early-1964, Archibald a 54-year-old bachelor, was the resident caretaker of the Holland Park Lawn Tennis Club. Joe Cannon, a well-known Notting Hill villain, had recently been released from prison and had already opened an illegal drinker called the Basement Club in Russell Road, Kensington, which provided him with a good income and was on the lookout for other

---

36. Du Rose, *op. cit.* 22, p.104; McConnell, *op. cit.* 23, pp.84–85.
37. McConnell, *op. cit.* 23, p.85; Seabrook, *op. cit.* 24, p.127.
38. Seabrook, *op. cit.* 24, p.130.
39. *Ibid*, p.128.
40. *Ibid*, p.129.
41. *Ibid*, p.131.
42. Du Rose, *op. cit.* 22, pp.105–106.

premises when he was approached by Archibald, whom he knew vaguely. Archibald told him about the lawn tennis club and suggested it would be ideal as a 'late-night drinker'. After visiting the premises, which were luxurious to say the least when compared with the average illegal club in the Notting Hill area, Cannon entered into a partnership with Archibald and it opened from 11 p.m., when the legitimate members of the club had long since left, until 4 a.m. Cannon went on to described how the arrangement worked:

> 'I had recruited a pair of very tasty bodies to help me to keep order, but the customers were allowed to do pretty well what they liked short of breaking up the furniture or otherwise damaging the fixtures and fittings. There was one inflexible rule. At four o'clock in the morning they were all out. Then Archibald and myself with the aid of a gang of helpers, tidied the place up, replaced the stock we had used and departed.'[43]

It quickly became the place 'to go for a late night drink' but its clientele was a 'very mixed bag'; as Cannon explained 'there were brasses and their ponces rubbing shoulders with villains and well-known figures from the world of sport and arts.'[44] However, as Seabrook pointed out, attracting prostitutes was a 'tricky proposition'. Whilst they generally attracted men to the club, they also encouraged them to leave.[45] Amongst the prostitutes who attended the illegal drinker in Holland Park was Irene Lockwood.

The arrangement lasted for just over two months. Then the inevitable happened. In the early hours of 14 March, the Mills brothers beat up a man who had upset them. As a result of the fracas, which took place in the women's toilets, there was blood all over the walls and floor and a large mirror had been smashed, before Cannon and his helpers could intervene.[46] The premises were quickly vacated and Archibald telephoned the police to allege that a break in had occurred. The call was allocated to F2 radio telegraphy (R/T)car, which immediately attended, and following information from Archibald, they arrested two people found nearby, a Patrick Crawford and

---

43. Cannon, Joe (1983). *Tough Guys Don't Cry*. Great Britain: Magnus Books, p.72.
44. *Ibid*, p.163.
45. Seabrook, *op. cit.* 24, p.165.
46. Cannon, *op. cit.* 43, p.73.

Moira Fleming. Both admitted having been in the pavilion but claimed they had been at a party. Archibald initially denied that any such party had taken place but under persistent questioning by the police at Notting Hill Police Station he eventually admitted it. His activities were brought to the attention of the club secretary and he was forced to abandon the all-night parties.[47]

Less than a month after the closure of the Holland Park Lawn Tennis Club as an all-night drinker, on the morning of 8 April 1964, Lockwood's naked body was discovered on the foreshore of the River Thames about 300 yards upstream of where Tailford's body had been found. She was four months pregnant. Only 35 days had elapsed between the discovery of Tailford's body and that of Lockwood. Lockwood was known to have been alive on 7 April, because she had visited a confectionary shop in Westbourne Grove from which she would regularly purchase cheap cigarettes.[48] A murder squad was set up, also at Shepherds Bush Police Station under the command of Detective Superintendent Frank Davies. When the police searched Lockwood's flat in Denbigh Road they found a visiting card with the name 'Kenny' on it together with a telephone number PARK 7157. Enquiries revealed that the telephone number was that of the Holland Park Lawn Tennis Club but when Archibald was shown Lockwood's photograph he denied knowing her.[49]

On 27 April, Archibald appeared in court charged with stealing a hearing aid from a department store. Later, when drinking with friends in the Colville public house, he bragged that he was in serious trouble following which he went to Notting Hill Police Station and confessed to Detective Constable Mooreshead that he had murdered Lockwood before pushing her body into the river. Archibald was taken to Shepherds Bush Police Station where he made a written statement admitting to killing her. He was charged with murder but the evidence relied almost wholly on his admissions and he pleaded not guilty at Acton Magistrates' Court. Nevertheless, the magistrates committed him for trial at the Old Bailey. However, on 23 June 1964, the jury took just 55 minutes to find him not guilty and he was acquitted. Why did he confess to the murder of Irene Lockwood? The confession was

---

47. Seabrook, *op. cit.* 24, p.163.
48. *Ibid*, pp.170–171.
49. *Ibid*, p.166.

apparently made 'in a fit of depression' at a time when Archibald saw the loss of his job and the accommodation that went with it as a major problem.[50]

Sixteen days after the discovery of Lockwood's body, the fifth victim, Helen Barthelemy, was found naked in an alleyway off Swincombe Avenue, Brentford, early on the morning of 24 April 1964, about a mile from where the bodies of Tailford and Lockwood had been found. This was the first body to be found away from the river. The cause of death was asphyxia, probably as a result of her clothing being twisted around her neck but, although four of her teeth were missing, there was no sign that she had been struck by a blow. However, dark rings around her waist suggested her panties had been removed after death.[51]

As far as is known, Barthelemy never lived on Notting Hill's ground—her last known address was in Harlesden—but she did frequent the Jazz Club at 207 Westbourne Park Road and Wraggs Café in All Saints Road, and solicited in the area of Notting Hill and Shepherds Bush. On the night she disappeared (there seems to be some doubt as to whether this was Tuesday/Wednesday 21/22 April or Wednesday/Thursday 22/23 April)[52] she was dancing and talking with African-Caribbean men and women in the Jazz Club until near dawn. She then asked someone to look after her handbag, which suggested she was coming back, went outside and was never seen alive again.[53]

The investigation on this occasion was led by Detective Superintendent Bill Baldock but Detective Superintendent Maurice Osborne was appointed from Scotland Yard's murder squad to collate and coordinate the previous investigations.[54] However, the investigations in an area like Notting Hill were seriously hampered because 'the coloured community' was not only unable but 'unwilling to help' in the investigation into Barthelemy's death.[55] Nevertheless, it was this case that threw up an abundance of clues. According to McConnell, the killer 'had enticed her into a car, strangled her, stripped her, kept her out of sight for 24 hours, part of the time near a paint spray operation ... reloaded the body into his car, chose a quiet place, drove off the Great

---

50. McConnell, *op. cit.* 23, p.97; Seabrook, *op. cit.* 24, pp.167–168.
51. McConnell, *op. cit.* 23, p.105; Seabrook, *op. cit.* 24, pp.187–189.
52. Seabrook, *op. cit.* 24, pp.191–192.
53. McConnell, *op. cit.* 23, pp.104–105.
54. Du Rose, *op. cit.* 22, p.108.
55. *Ibid*, p.105.

West Road, north in Boston Manor Road, right into Swincombe Avenue …'
where he dumped the normally clean body which was by now 'indescrib-
ably filthy'. Evidence obtained from the body suggested that Barthelemy, in
death, had lain 'close to a point where both primary and secondary colours,
priming undercoating and finished paintwork was performed by spray'.[56]

At this point 'the target for the officers engaged in the "field" investigations' were places 'where men who used their cars for kerb crawling'. Each
night checks were made on such cars in Notting Hill and girls soliciting in
that area were warned of the dangers. This included Barthelemy who had
been warned only a few days before she was killed.[57]

There were no more murders for three months. This was subsequently put
down to a number factors. Firstly, police sought the help of girls soliciting in
the Notting Hill area, and continually warned them of the dangers; secondly,
the girls were obviously cautious about who they went with, particularly
men who used their cars for kerb-crawling; and thirdly, at the same time,
there was considerable press interest and this probably led to the murderer
staying away from the area.[58]

The sixth victim was Mary Fleming whose naked body was discovered
sometime between 5 a.m. and 5.30 a.m. on the morning of 14 July 1964 at
the entrance to the garage of No. 48 Berrymede Road, Brentford. Fleming also lived on Notting Hill's ground, although not initially. Arriving in
London in 1955, she was arrested for soliciting prostitution in Commercial
Road, Stepney, in London's East End, in October 1956. Further convictions
for offences associated with prostitution and theft followed before she began
living with a recently demobilised soldier, Michael Turner, in Pembridge
Gardens. She continued soliciting but in April 1962, she gave birth to a
daughter, Veronica. By now they had moved to flat in Powis Gardens, but
Turner left soon afterwards to avoid arrest for living on her immoral earnings. However, Turner continued to visit her occasionally until February
1963 when he ended the relationship altogether. Nevertheless, the following
month, he visited the flat in Powis Gardens to see Veronica but discovered

---

56. McConnell, *op. cit.* 23, p.105.

57. Du Rose, *op. cit.* 22, p.109.

58. *Ibid*, p.109.

that, not yet one-year-old, she had been left alone. Turner then described what happened next:

> "'I went to a nigger club in Westbourne Park Road (the Jazz Club) and found her drunk and dancing with coloured men. I was furious and went and dragged her outside and a coloured bloke followed, a fight started between the three of us, police were called and I knocked a copper's helmet off.'[59]

About a year after this incident, Fleming met an unemployed painter and decorator, Harry Greenwood, at Pete's Café in Blenheim Crescent and they discussed the possibility of opening a drinking club but it came to nothing. However, she vacated the flat in Powis Gardens at the beginning of April 1964 and moved with Greenwood into a house in Chiswick. The house was occupied by three other people, including a convicted prostitute, Gloria Swanson, and her ponce, Anthony Black. However, on 9 April 1964, the police raided a brothel at 202 Kensington Park Road, arresting Margaret Malik, a young housewife, for keeping a brothel. Also present were six other women, including Fleming and Swanson, and Greenwood, who was apparently present to 'roll the punters'. Malik was sentenced to three months' imprisonment but the others escaped punishment.[60]

Fearing the worse, for he already had six convictions for theft and similar offences, Greenwood immediately left the house in Chiswick. Unable to pay the rent, Fleming soon followed and moved into a ground floor, front room at 44 Lancaster Road, W11. She was regularly seen in the Warwick Castle public house and the Kensington Park Hotel, the cliental of which tended to be 'whores and ponces' and, at which, there were 'frequent disturbances.' On 10 July, Fleming was seen at the unlicensed drinking club at 32a Powis Square, run by Roy Stewart, who, at the time, already had four convictions for selling liquor without a licence. She left at about 5 a.m. and was not seen alive, other than by her killer, again.[61]

The seventh victim was Francis Brown. Born in Scotland, she also went under a number of aliases as well as using the surname of the man she was

---

59. Seabrook, *op. cit.* 24, p.201.
60. *Ibid*, p.202.
61. *Ibid*, pp.207–208.

living with, Frances Quinn. Brown had already been in trouble with the authorities before she left Glasgow for London in 1961 where she started soliciting for the purposes of prostitution almost immediately — she was first convicted on 21 October 1961 but others soon followed. In the summer of 1962 she was living in a flat in Westbourne Park Road when she met an Irish scaffolder, Paul Quinn, who had already been married once and had a string of convictions for theft and shopbreaking. She moved to Shepherds Bush to live with Quinn.[62]

Brown had a number of brushes with the law between September 1962 and August 1964, spent time in a mental hospital and had a second child — she already had one which she left behind in Scotland. During this period, she also spent some time with Quinn back in Scotland with her parents. However, in August 1964, she moved back to London with Quinn, living in Southerton Road, W6. In common with Mary Fleming, she drank in the Kensington Park Hotel and the Warwick Castle. Quinn last saw her alive on Thursday 22 October, when, according to him' 'she left in high spirits.'[63] She was known to be alive for a further 24 hours at least because on Friday, 23 October 1964, she was drinking for most of the evening in the Warwick Castle with another prostitute, Kim Taylor, more commonly known as Blonde Beryl.[64]

Upon leaving the public house at about 11 p.m., they apparently walked 'towards two men in separate cars waiting at the traffic lights at the junction of Portobello Road and Westbourne Park Road.'[65] Before separating, and getting into the two cars, the two girls agreed to meet up outside the Jazz Club in Westbourne Park Road. But Francis Brown was not seen again for 33 days until her naked body was discovered behind the Civil Defence control building just off Kensington High Street at about 1.30 p.m. on Wednesday 25 November 1964. Covered by a dustbin lid and debris, the body was naked and badly decomposed. The post mortem revealed that she had been

---

62. *Ibid*, p.220.
63. McConnell, *op. cit.* 23, p.124.
64. Du Rose, *op. cit.* 22, pp.112–113.
65. Seabrook, *op. cit.* 24, p.228; McConnell, *op. cit.* 23, pp.128–129; Du Rose, *op. cit* 22, pp.112–113.

asphyxiated 'due to pressure on the neck.'[66] A murder squad under Detective Superintendent William Marchant was set up at Kensington Police Station.

The eighth and final victim, Bridget O'Hara was found on the Heron Trading Estate in Acton only yards from the underground line on 12 February 1965. She too was naked and again death was caused by 'asphyxia due to pressure on the face and neck',[67] but the body had only recently been dumped. Born in Dublin as Bridget Moore, she came to England in 1954. Within four years she had accumulated eleven convictions for soliciting for prostitution, primarily on the streets of Bayswater, Holland Park, Notting Hill and Shepherds Bush. In 1962, she married Michael O'Hara and lived with him at a rented flat in Acton.[68]

At the time of her death, Michael O'Hara had eleven convictions for offences such as theft, shopbreaking, robbery and assault and so, in his spare time 'he ponced on his wife.'[69] She was last seen on 11 January when she told someone she was going to see a friend in Brook Green. According to Du Rose 'a curious feature of this murder' was the fact that the body appeared to have been 'kept in some kind of storage and was partly mummified.'[70] Again, spray marks similar to those found on Barthelemy's body were found.[71] A murder squad was set up at Shepherds Bush Police Station under the command of Detective Superintendent William Baldock.

The investigation

Following the discovery of the eighth body, Detective Chief Superintendent John du Rose was appointed to take charge of the investigation into the nude murders. As already mentioned, Du Rose claimed that Jack the Stripper killed six women, Tailford, Lockwood, Barthelemy, Fleming, McGowan and O'Hara, between January 1964 and January 1965. At least one of the investigating officers, Detective Superintendent Baldock, some years later,

---

66. Seabrook, *op. cit.* 24, p.235.
67. *Ibid*, p.305.
68. McConnell, *op. cit.* 23, claimed she had a flat in Agate Road, Hammersmith (p.141).
69. Seabrook, *op. cit.* 24, p.306.
70. Du Rose, *op. cit.* 22, p.114.
71. *Ibid*, p.115.

claimed that Du Rose should never have been called in suggesting that if he couldn't solve a murder in four days he wasn't interested.[72]

The enquiry to find the killer—the police were, by this time, fairly sure that they were looking for one killer—was extensive and far reaching. Early on, Du Rose formed the view it was a man in his forties 'of some strength and virility' who was not 'satisfied with normal intercourse' because, in all cases, the victim 'had slight marks on the neck apparently made by finger-nails, either by the murderer or by the victim in an attempt at self-defence.' In addition, 'some had injuries and very slight bruising as though pressure had been directed in the region of the nose and mouth'. Therefore, suggested Du Rose, 'at the moment of organism, he became utterly frenzied' and the girls died extremely quickly. Then to make identification more difficult, he got rid of their clothing.[73]

On 8 March, three teams of officers began house-to-house enquiries throughout parts of Kensington and the whole of Paddington, Hammer-smith, Fulham, Ealing and Hounslow. When the daytime enquiries ended, the night shift clocked on. Fifty-eight aids to CID,[74] working in pairs and using their own cars, toured an area stretching from Marble Arch westwards, through Notting Hill, to Hounslow and north to south from Harrow Road, through Notting Hill, to Bayswater Road. Their job was to record the details of all vehicles and their occupants seen between the hours of midnight and 8 a.m. Some non-descript vans[75] were also used. A team of police women, eventually numbering eleven, were also checking all motor vehicle records held by the London County Council and Middlesex County Council looking

---

72. Seabrook, *op. cit.* 24, p.350.
73. Du Rose, *op. cit.* 22, p.115.
74. Aids to CID eventually became known as temporary detective constables. They were officers who had applied to join the CID but were temporally attached to it for a period of time to see if they were suitable.
75. Vans with slits in the sides through which police officers inside the vehicle could observe what was happening around them. To all intense and purposes the vans looked as though they were empty.

for the owners of all Hillman Huskies and Commer Cob light vans.[76] This, in itself, was a massive enquiry which was never completed.[77]

The man who had picked up Francis Brown just after she left the Warwick Castle remained a strong suspect for some time. Identikit pictures of both drivers, the one who picked up Brown and the one who picked up Taylor, were produced on the basis of the latter's descriptions, but despite publication in the newspapers, neither came forward and neither were ever traced.[78]

Already the enquiry involved approximately 200 detectives supported by about 100 uniformed personnel. But Du Rose still needed more and the Commissioner, Sir John Waldron, agreed to second the recently-formed Special Patrol Group to him.[79] In the areas of Notting Hill where the prostitutes operated, Du Rose had policewomen, dressed in a similar way to prostitutes, walking the streets after dark in an effort to trap the killer. Pointing out that 'it was a dangerous mission for these girls, despite the plainclothes officers posing as ponces near at hand' Du Rose described how 'each girl was equipped with a small tape recorder, the microphone being concealed in their cuffs or scarves, so that a recording of any conversation from the many men who stopped beside the girls was obtained.' This stage of the operation required considerable care and sensitivity, particularly during the follow-up enquiries when officers interviewed the 'kerb-crawlers' caught in the operation. With a few exceptions, the men were contacted, using business lines, and then interviewed at police stations. Only occasionally, when this could not be arranged, were men visited, albeit discretely, at their homes.[80]

Much effort was put into identifying the premises where some of the bodies had lain close to a paint-spraying operation. Twenty-four miles of West London was identified and broken into three sectors. Each sector was allocated to a detective sergeant who was given 12 officers to assist him. This was a hugely time-consuming task. Eventually the site where some of the

---

76. Three decorators working throughout the night in a nearby restaurant thought they saw the driver of a Hillman Husky type vehicle, which could have been a small van, take something from his vehicle in the middle of the night very close to where the body of Barthelemy was found. See Seabrook, *op. cit.* 24, pp.321- 324.
77. Seabrook, *op. cit.* 24, p.324.
78. Du Rose, *op. cit.* 22, p.112.
79. *Ibid*, p.118.
80. *Ibid*, p.119.

bodies had lain was traced to a transformer at the rear of a factory on the Heron Factory Estate in Acton W4. The transformer faced a paint spray shop from which the right proportions of globules of paint and other substances matched those found on O'Hara's body. Still this did not lead to the identification of the killer. There were 7,000 people working on the Estate and although, technically private property, anyone else could access it, although it was felt that the killer must have had lawful access.[81]

Du Rose published his autobiography in 1971. According to him, as police inquiries narrowed down to the final few suspects, the murderer, a security guard, committed suicide within one month of the murder of Bridie O'Hara. However, because he was never arrested and charged and stood trial, Du Rose declined to name the killer in his book. But McConnell claimed that the only proof against this man was that the deaths and subsequent discovery of the nude bodies of prostitutes ceased after his death.[82]

But, in February 1972, Owen Summers wrote a series of articles about the nude murders in *The Sun*. He suggested that Du Rose was wrong in his identification of the dead security guard as the murderer because he was in Scotland on the occasion of at least one of the murders.[83] Then Summers dropped a bombshell by suggesting that the killer may have been a police officer who had been dismissed from the force after being found guilty of a number of burglaries. Summers suggested that this person had joined the Metropolitan Police in October 1956 and served at Fulham and Notting Hill as a uniformed constable. In March 1961, he was appointed a detective constable and was posted to Kensington. Eleven months later he was transferred to Hammersmith. He then served at Acton and Brentford Police Stations before being charged with five offences of office breaking and suspended from duty on 17 September 1962.

On his release from prison having served a short sentence, he moved to Leigh-on-Sea in Essex, first getting a job with Continental Cars and then with Bright and Marshall of Hadleigh. Summers' theory was taken up by both McConnell and Seabrook. Whilst he did not give as many details as Summers, McConnell goes into great detail about the advantages a former

---

81. *Ibid*, p.118.
82. McConnell, *op. cit.* 23, p.171.
83. Seabrook, *op. cit.* 24, pp.352–353.

or serving police officer would have in, firstly attracting the girls to him, and, secondly, in disposing of their bodies.[84] Seabrook went further, suggesting that each of the bodies had been discovered on a sub-division of the Metropolitan Police at which the former officer had served. Tailford was found on Hammersmith Sub-division (FD), Barthelemy on Brentford Sub-division (TB), Fleming and O'Hara on Acton Sub-division (TA) and Brown on Kensington Sub-division (FK) and that a police officer or a former police officer would know that it was likely that a different investigating officer would be appointed for each. It was possibly, suggested Seabrook, an attempt to gain revenge on the Metropolitan Police for the way he had been treated.[85]

According to Seabrooke, the unidentified officer was interviewed by Du Rose and Baldock on 4 August but they were unable to build a case against him.[86] The only real lead that the police had against him was that he bore a resemblance to the Identikit picture of the man seen to pick up Frances Brown on the night of the 23 October 1964, but, unfortunately, when shown a photograph of the suspect, Kim Taylor, who had been with Brown at the time, failed to identify him.[87]

So the suggestion is that the killer did not commit suicide. But, why did the murders stop? Seabrook's theory is that on 1 April 1965, there was a reorganization of the divisional and sub-divisional boundaries of the Metropolitan Police to conform to the new local authority boundaries introduced when the Greater London Council was formed. So, suggested Seabrook, 'the suspects elaborate taunts would have lost their significance' because the places where the bodies were found no longer coincided with where the suspect had served. For example, 'Bridget O'Hara's body may have been discovered on TA Sub-division but it was now XA sub-division' and the former police officer had never served on X Division at all.[88] Neither had he served on B Division, of which both Kensington and Notting Hill were now a part under the re-organization. McConnell also raised the possibility that there

---

84. McConnell, *op. cit.* 23, pp.171–172.
85. Seabrook, *op. cit.* 24, pp.354–363.
86. *Ibid,* p.363.
87. *Ibid,* p.363.
88. *Ibid,* p.363.

was more than one killer. Indeed, as already explained, Du Rose did not link the first two murders to Jack the Stripper at all.[89]

Whether the identity of Jack the Stripper will become as big a mystery as the identify of Jack the Ripper remains to be seen. Already two books have been written about it and chapters appear in a number of other texts, including that of Du Rose. Suffice to say that there are those who do not accept the version put forward by Du Rose and therefore the debate is still ongoing.

---

89. McConnell, *op. cit.* 23, pp.178–179.

CHAPTER 6

RISE OF THE MANGROVE

Flower Power and Drugs

The late-1960s and early-1970s was the age of so-called 'flower power'[1] and it has been suggested that one of the legacies of the 1960s was the consolidation of Notting Hill 'as a new bohemia for white and black intellectuals where there "were lots of communal houses where you could always drop in and get a joint or a cup of tea, or companionship, conversation and music".'[2] Between 1967 and 1969, Jock Young, then a Reader in Sociology at Middlesex Polytechnic (now Middlesex University) carried out 'a participant observation of drug-taking in Notting Hill.'[3] This was, of course, before Notting Hill, and particularly All Saints Road, gained such a ferocious reputation as one of the main drug centres in London, if not the whole of the United Kingdom; rather it was the period of the 'bohemian marihuana smoker' but, even then, Young claimed that drug-taking in Notting Hill was widespread.[4]

Because of their isolated position in the community, he suggested police officers held stereotypical views about drug-takers, claiming that when arrests were made, 'because of his position of power', the individual police officer negotiated 'the evidence… to fit these preconceived stereotypes.'[5] Clearly, the more people who took illegal drugs, the more demand there was for regular supplies. Therefore, as drug-taking within a particular area increased, the danger was that the buying and selling of it became 'unashamedly overt' and

---

1. Linked with the hippy movement of the same period, 'flower power' originated in the USA at a time when the Vietnam War was ongoing. The movement was associated with communal living, artistic expression and the widespread use of illegal drugs, particularly cannabis.

2. White, Jerry (2008). *London in the Twentieth Century: A City and Its People.* London: Random House, pp.349–350.

3. Young, Jock (1982). 'The Role of the Police as Amplifiers of Deviancy, Negotiators of Reality and Translators of Fantasy'. In *Images of Deviance* (Stanley Cohen ed.). Harmonsworth, Middlesex: Penguin Education, p.27.

4. *Ibid*, p.29.

5. *Ibid*, p.27.

pressure was put on the police by the media and public opinion to the extent that they felt they had to do something about it. However, to the police, 'marihuana smokers' were 'a criminal group' which provided 'a regular source of fairly easy apprehendable villains.'[6] He was, of course, writing about a time far different from the late-1970s, the whole of the 1980s and the early 1990s, a period which saw Notting Hill change from a source of 'soft' drugs to 'hard' drugs. Far from finding a source of 'fairly easy apprehendable villains', the police officer on the beat, as will be seen in later chapters, found that such arrests were likely to be a cause of aggravation, with accusations of 'assault', 'planting' and 'victimisation' levelled against him or her, and, on some occasions, suffering serious injuries whilst patrolling the areas where drug-dealing was taking place.

Opening of the Mangrove

The period was also one in which a number of well-known socialites and other white middle-class people were attracted to the area. In 1969, Frank Crichlow closed down the Rio Coffee Bar, which, as explained in *Chapter 4*, had already attracted such people as Christine Keeler and Colin MacInnes, and moved to All Saints Road where he opened the Mangrove Restaurant. Originally, he was granted an all-night licence, serving 'up market soul food' and it was this that attracted people such as Lord Gifford, Sammy Davis Jr, Nina Simone, Vanessa Redgrave and the writer, C L R James to it during the evenings.[7] However, continuing the Defence concept that Crichlow had, with others, started whilst he was at the Rio, during the day a black barrister was present at the Mangrove to deploy as required to represent any black person who was arrested by the police and taken to Notting Hill, Notting Dale or Harrow Road Police Stations. Darcus Howe claimed that the ready availability of a barrister was 'a major disruption to the well-rehearsed procedures for dealing with black suspects at these police stations,' because it severely reduced 'the time and space within which beatings could take place'

---

6. *Ibid*, p.29.

7. Phillips, Mike and Trevor Phillips (1998*). Windrush: The Irresistible Rise of Multi-Racial Britain.* London: HarperCollins, p.279.

and the opportunity for the police to obtain statements of admission.[8] However, whilst there is no doubt that the police would take any opportunity to obtain a statement of admission, the extent to which beatings occurred was debatable.[9]

Whilst the majority of the population went about their lawful businesses, a minority—by no means all of them resident in the Notting Hill area—were engaged in the buying and selling of cannabis and continuing to run shebeens and illegal gambling clubs. These activities amongst certain sections of the black community, although not reaching the serious level they did in the 1980s, had the effect of focusing police attention on the Mangrove Restaurant. Local officers claimed it was a place where cannabis was often in evidence and the local council saw it as an establishment which refused to conform to the conditions of the licence it had been granted.

Consequently, when the all-night licence came up for renewal in December 1969, this was refused; subsequently an appeal against the refusal was dismissed. However, the restaurant continued to operate, this time with a total disregard of the licensing laws. As a result, both the police and the council pursued policies of enforcement which were naturally resented by the African-Caribbean community. This caused considerable friction and added to the seeds of discord which already existed.

The police supported the council in their efforts to limit the opening times of the Mangrove, either by accompanying council officials, or inviting them to accompany the police, on five occasions during the first seven months of 1970. The most significant of these five raids occurred on 30 May when Inspector Biddle led police officers into the premises. He was in possession of a search warrant issued under the Dangerous Drugs Act and accompanied by a public health inspector. Twelve people were eating meals in the restaurant. During the visit, the police alleged that Frank Crichlow and his brother, Victor, both assaulted police officers and they were arrested and

---

8.   Howe, Darcus (1988). *From Bobby to Babylon: Blacks and the British Police*. London: Race Today Publications, p.41.

9.   From the author's own experience, arrested persons where sometimes 'roughed up' if a police officer had been injured during the course of an arrest. Additionally, some prisoners would be assaulted if they were particularly truculent or abusive. But the extent to which prisoners were beaten as a matter of practice tended to be exaggerated by those arrested to evoke general sympathy and give their defence counsel something to 'beat' the police with in court.

subsequently charged. No drugs were found, commencing a pattern which was to continue, on and off, over the ensuing years and certainly giving Frank Crichlow grounds for complaint. Although both denied the assault charges brought against them when they appeared at Lambeth Magistrates' Court in October, they were both found guilty. Frank Crichlow was sentenced to four months' imprisonment, which was suspended pending an appeal; on appeal, this was reduced to a £25 fine. Victor was fined £20 on the assault charge and given a conditional discharge for two years on an obstruction charge.[10]

Similarly, although he denied the charges brought by the Kensington and Chelsea Council, Frank Crichlow was fined a total of £175 and ordered to pay £50 costs, at West London Petty Sessional Court, for using the Mangrove as a 'night' cafe without a licence; Roy Hemmings, who had been in charge of the restaurant on three occasions whilst Crichlow was absent, was fined a total of £60 and ordered to pay £30 costs; and Jean Cabussel was fined £20 and ordered to pay £10 costs after he was found guilty of being in charge of the restaurant on one occasion. During the course of those proceedings, the barrister representing Kensington and Chelsea Council, suggested there was 'a feeling among some misguided people that this prosecution has been motivated by prejudice against the people who run the cafe and the people who use it.' But, he told the court, this was not the case. 'The only reason for the prosecution' he said, was that there had 'been a breach of the law.'[11]

Tensions Rise

Meanwhile various black organizations were becoming more prominent in Notting Hill. On 1 June 1970, the Black Panther Movement,[12] supported by the Black People's Alliance,[13] organized a demonstration in Notting

---

10. *Kensington Post*, 23 October 1970.

11. *Daily Telegraph*, 12 September 1970; *Kensington Post*, 18 September 1970.

12. A group of African-Caribbean immigrants claimed to have formed the British Black Power Movement in September 1967 (but see comments later in the chapter) but re-named themselves the British Black Panther Movement in 1968. The British Black Panthers appropriated the US Black Panther's revolutionary vision as a model for protest, necessary violence, and engaging the state. The organization folded in 1972. See *Radical History Review*, 2009, Volume 2009, Number 103, pp.17–35.

13. The Black People's Alliance consisted of at least 15 different groups, including the Black Liberation Front, West Indian Standing Conference, Movement for Colonial Freedom and the Anti-Apartheid Movement.

Hill against mass murder, imprisonment and exploitation of black people throughout the world'. The demonstration passed off without incident.[14] During the same month leaflets, headed 'Face the Facts' were circulated in Notting Hill. The leaflet suggested that 'If you desire a coloured for your neighbour, vote Labour" but "If you are already burdened with one, vote Tory.' Both the Tory Candidate, future Home Secretary and European Union Commissioner, Sir Leon Brittan, and the sitting member, Labour's Bruce Douglas-Mann, denied any knowledge of the leaflet.[15]

In July, in an event which was described as being of both national and local importance, the North Kensington Neighbourhood Law Centre, the first of its kind in Britain, was opened by the Mayor of Kensington. Run from a disused butcher's shop at 74 Goldborne Road it was in effect a 'legal surgery' with barristers giving voluntary advice and law students helping with research.[16] Over the ensuing years it was to issue a number of reports and statements that were critical of the police in Notting Hill.

Meanwhile, the police paid increasing attention to the Mangrove Restaurant. In an attempt to curtail what they claimed was criminal activity, their role was directed towards stopping and searching people going to and coming from the restaurant who they believed were in possession of drugs. An extension of this was frequent visits to the restaurant itself, both with and without search warrants. These efforts to inhibit what the police saw as criminal behaviour were unwelcome, and notices criticising the activity of the police appeared in the window of the Mangrove and on the surrounding walls and billboards.

The actions of one particular officer 'epitomised' this activity. During this period Police Constable Frank Pulley 'emerged as a symbol of white oppression in the eyes of those black people who found themselves on the receiving end of the enforcement tactics.'[17] Posted to Notting Hill in 1959, he first came to prominence in 1968 when he was on patrol in a plainclothes police car (known as a 'Q' Car) with two colleagues. Two men were spotted

---

14. *Kensington Post*, 5 June 1970.
15. *Kensington Post*, 19 June 1970.
16. *Kensington Post*, 24 July 1970.
17. Innes, Commander; Chief Superintendent Whitfield and Chief Inspector Aitchison (1983). 'All Saints Road, London, W11: A Definitive Document'. London: Metropolitan Police (typescript), p.8, para. 5.10.

loitering in Westbourne Park Road. Leaving the car, Pulley approached the two men. As he went to question them he was kneed in the groin by one of the men who then produced a revolver and threatened to shoot him if he did not let them go. Pulley sent the revolver flying and, on being joined by his two colleagues, the men were overpowered and arrested. The man was later sent to prison for eight years, whilst his accomplice received a seven year sentence. PC Pulley was awarded the British Empire Medal for his bravery.[18] The other two officers, PCs Thomas Allen and William Cunliffe both received Queen's Commendations for Bravery.[19]

In 1983, the police issued 'a definitive document' on All Saints Road which outlined 'the conflict with the Police', pointing out that it had 'ebbed and flowed for 15 years' and was 'personified in the continuing difficulties between Notting Hill Police Station and the Mangrove Community Association, once the Mangrove Restaurant'.[20] The document, hereinafter referred to as 'The Innes Report', identified the various stages of police activity in relation to The Mangrove.

The Innes Report suggested that 'Crichlow, being a charismatic personality, and the Mangrove, being a focal point,' were particularly associated with PC Pulley and 'the many peripheral issues in Notting Hill between the police and black people were ideologically related to the conflict which had developed between them.'[21] This manifested itself in a demonstration protesting about the victimisation of black people on Sunday 9 August 1970.

Black Power

The demonstrators assembled outside the Mangrove Restaurant in All Saints Road where they heard speeches from Althea Jones-Lecointe and Darcus Howe. Jones-Lecointe, it was subsequently alleged, suggested that they had got to get rid of the pigs whilst Howe was reported to have said:

> 'We have complained to the police about the police and nothing was done. We
> have complained to the council about the council and nothing was done. We

18. *Kensington Post*, 7 March 1969.
19. *Kensington Post*, 21 March 1969.
20. Innes, *op. cit.* 17, p.7, para. 5.1.
21. *Ibid*, p.9, para.5.11.

complained to the politicians about the politicians and nothing was done. The time has come when we have got to do something ourselves.'[22]

As part of the police arrangements for the march, a nondescript van was sent to the assembly area. Inside the van were four police constables, Pulley, Rogers, Lewis and Reid. Their purpose was to 'identify people who were involved in the demonstration.'[23] Describing how 'in every police station responsible for policing [a] black community [there were] a group of policemen who impressed their superiors and colleagues that they were most proficient at handling blacks', one of the demonstrators, Rhodan Gordon, subsequently claimed that this particular group at Notting Hill was known as 'the heavy mob'.[24]

The march started at around 2.30 p.m. by which time there were about 130 people present. At the front of the procession were people carrying a Black Panther banner and a dead pig's head on a stick; also at the front were Frank Crichlow, Rupert Boyce, Gordon and Howe. The placards carried by the demonstrators consisted of 'Hands of the Mangrove', 'Kill the Pigs', 'Fire this Time', 'Slavery is still alive', 'Hands off us, pigs', and 'Black Power is going to get your mama'.[25]

Initially the march was orderly although there was much chanting and some singing with Barbara Beese amongst the chant leaders. Howe claimed that 'a menacing force of hundreds of uniformed officers, outnumbering the demonstrators two-to-one, hovered in the background' and that when the march set off in the mid-afternoon, it was 'hemmed in by hundreds of police officers'.[26] Indeed, Crichlow's obituary notice published in *The Independent* at the time of his death in September 2010, suggested that 'the 150 protestors' were 'flanked by more than 700 police.'[27] Both are gross exaggerations. The march was initially accompanied by about 25 officers from B Division, under the command of Commander Maggs and Chief Superintendent Donnelly, as it wound its way through the streets of North Kensington. Behind

---

22. *Kensington Post*, 15 October 1971.
23. *Ibid.*
24. *Kensington Post*, 17 December 1971.
25. *Kensington Post*, 15 October 1971.
26. Howe, *op. cit.* 8, p.44.
27. *The Independent*, 23 September 2010.

the march in a green police coach were another 25 officers from H Division. Outside Notting Hill Police Station, Howe told demonstrators that it was a place 'where police set out to plant drugs on black people and where black people were beaten up.' Outside Notting Dale Police Station, which was cordoned off by a line of police officers standing shoulder to shoulder, there were shouts of 'We want Pulley', 'Hands off the Metro' and 'Hands off the Mangrove'. Howe tore up a petition which was to have been handed in.[28]

The procession finally turned north along Portnell Road. Between Shirland Road and Marban Road, Chief Superintendent Donnelly arranged for the 25 officers from H Division in the coach to replace those from B Division, who had been policing the demonstration from the start. The procession was orderly at this time. Once the H Division officers had quickly organized themselves, with ten officers along each side of the march and four bringing up the rear, the B Division officers withdrew to the coach. At the junction with Marben Road there was a builder's skip full of rubbish. As the demonstrators drew level with the skip some of the demonstrators grabbed bricks and sticks from the skip, and milk bottles from the doorstep of a nearby house and began to hurl them at the accompanying police officers. An eye-witness claimed that it appeared that 'the police were trying to slow the marchers to a gradual halt' but 'the marchers at the back kept moving, the procession bunched up, and suddenly there was total confusion, with bottles and bricks being thrown from near the back.'[29] Another eye-witness claimed that 'the police went in with their truncheons' while some demonstrators used 'their banners as weapons.' Others went to the skip and took out pieces of wood, and there were claims that one of the demonstrators was 'whirling round' a 'piece of wood about six feet long.'[30] A third eye-witness claimed that 'the demonstrators acted like savages', laying 'into the police with bricks and bottles and anything else they could lay their hands on.'[31]

Eventually the demonstrators re-grouped at the junction with Shirland Road and Ashmore Road but violence quickly broke out again. Howe claimed

---

28. *Kensington Post*, 15 October 1971.
29. *Kensington Post*, 12 November 1971.
30. *Ibid.*
31. *Daily Telegraph*, 10 August 1971; *Daily Sketch*, 10 August 1971; *Daily Mirror*, 10 August 1970.

that the violence was inevitable and his subsequent description of the events makes interesting reading:

> 'The violence was ferocious, as the combatants continued, for 15 minutes to batter, to wound and to maim each other. The police were moved to an orgy of violence and abuse. It was a street fight. Not a single officer entertained that much-touted skill of crowd control. It was pure, unadulterated, unlicensed brutality. We gave as good as we got. Bricks, stones, bottles, any ammunition at hand, we threw at the police. Whole building skips were emptied at them.'[32]

At the time the violence first broke out the police officers on foot with the march, i.e. the H Division contingent, were outnumbered at least five to one and the B Division officers de-bussed from the following coach to assist their beleaguered colleagues. A number of police officers were injured in the ensuing violence.[33] Nineteen people were arrested. Most were charged with possessing offensive weapons, assault and threatening behaviour. All those arrested appeared at Marylebone Magistrates' Court on 10 August. The actress Vanessa Redgrave and her brother, Corrine, were present prepared to stand as sureties for the accused should they be needed.[34]

In the immediate aftermath of the disorder, the chairman of the Black Panthers Party, Roy Sawh, called for a top level inquiry into claims by many black people that there had been constant harassment of them by the police. Jeff Crawford, secretary of the 10,000 strong West Indian Standing Conference, accused magistrates' courts of being 'protection rackets for the police' and warned that policemen will 'almost certainly be killed' if there were any more clashes between police and black people. He claimed that the black community had lost all hope and were hitting back in 'desperation and fear'.[35] However, Ernest Huie, organiser of the School Bus for Jamaica Campaign, an organization based in Notting Hill dedicated to raising money to improve conditions in the Caribbean, claimed that 'demonstrators were "recruited"

---

32. Howe, *op. cit.* 8, p.44.
33. The number of police officers injured tends to vary depending on which newspaper report is examined. Most say 17, e.g. the *Evening Standard* on 10 August but the *Kensington Post*, dated 14 August suggested it was 24.
34. See also *Evening News*, 10 August 1970; *Daily Sketch*, 11 August 1970.
35. *Kensington Post*, 14 August 1970.

by Black Power organizers and "hustlers"'. Although Huie agreed with the purpose of the demonstration in deploring police brutality, he accused the organizers of 'destroying the efforts of people who have some semblance of an idea of how to make things better.'[36]

In the ensuing press coverage, the Mangrove was credited with inspiring a Black Power protest. The *Kensington Post* suggested that only 'a completely independent inquiry' could restore public confidence in the police amongst both black and white members of the Notting Hill community. Anti-police feeling had tended to centre on certain individual police officers, suggested the report, who 'have figured so regularly in cases involving immigrants that they now have only to be involved in a charge against a coloured man for the innocence of that man to be assumed, whatever the evidence.'

Whilst the newspaper was quick to point out that it was unable to say whether there was any truth in the accusations made against these officers, it suggested that they should have been transferred from the area many months previously, not because they had performed any guilty act, but 'because they are like red rags to a bull.' The newspaper also condemned the local authorities and, to a lesser extent, the leaders of local immigrant communities 'for allowing the machinery for discussion of coloured people's problems with police, welfare workers and council representatives to fall into decay.'[37]

There was no independent inquiry. Instead, the Metropolitan Police launched its own investigation into the causes of the violence on the day and a file was sent to the Director of Public Prosecutions. Eleven weeks later, seven men Boyce, Crichlow, Gordon, Howe, Anthony Innis, Rothwell Kentish and Godfrey Millet, and two women, Beese and Jones-Lecointe, were all charged with riotous assembly and affray.

A further demonstration, this time organized by the Black Defence Committee supported by the Notting Hill People's Association, was held on Saturday 31 October. On this occasion, more than 300 people, mostly white students, assembled in Ladbroke Grove. Flanked by police officers on both sides, the demonstrators marched through North Kensington, passing three police stations, Notting Hill, Notting Dale and Harrow Road, and the

---

36. *Ibid.*
37. *Ibid.*

Mangrove Restaurant. A statement by the Black People's Information Centre handed out during the march read:

'We believe that the police are deeply prejudiced against black, the young, the poor, anyone who is different. We believe they try to close down places where black people meet.'

At Notting Dale Police Station, a cordon of police officers again stretched across the front of the building. As the march approached there were shouts of 'Pulley — we want you — dead'. The march ended without incident in Powis Square where a short meeting was held.[38]

Metro Youth Club

Intermittently throughout the following year there were a number of incidents between black people and the police which reinforced the latent antagonism that was becoming increasingly apparent. Two such incidents concerned the Metro Youth Club, which was in St Luke's Road right on the boundary of Notting Hill Division with Harrow Road Division. In January 1971, police entered and searched the club for drugs; nothing was found and no charges were brought. However, four months later, a major confrontation occurred at the club, when, one evening, two police officers saw a youth being chased by another youth in the vicinity of St Luke's Road. The second youth was brandishing a piece of wood and he was detained by the policemen but he broke free and ran into the Metro Club. As he entered the doors were bolted behind him. Shortly afterwards, Sean Baine, the chairman of the Metro Club Management Committee, arrived. Police reinforcements were quickly on the scene and the club was surrounded. There were about 70 people in the club at the time and a stand-off occurred for about two hours during which time police officers tried to persuade those inside to allow them to enter to re-arrest the youth.

According to the police version, a senior officer arrived with a warrant about two hours after the stand-off began but Baine claimed the youths had, by then, decided to leave of their own accord. As the youth who had originally

---

38. *Ibid.*

been arrested emerged from the club he was re-arrested. A series of running fights then occurred during which hammers, bricks and bottles were thrown at the police officers. According to the police, the youths shouted 'Kill the pigs', 'Kill the fuzz' and 'Black Power' during 'the battle' but Peter Kandler, senior solicitor at the North Kensington Neighbourhood Law Centre, who subsequently defended a number of the arrested youths, and Baine denied such shouts were made. Twelve police officers were injured of whom nine were taken to hospital, including two with stab wounds and two with head injuries. Eleven people, including three white youths and one white girl, were arrested at the time. Four youths were injured.[39] Another person was arrested subsequently.[40]

On the morning of 26 May, the front of Marylebone Magistrates' Court was guarded by police officers for the first court appearance of the eleven arrested youths. A small demonstration took place on the pavement outside the court. Presumably, in a reference not only to the incident two days previously but to the charges faced by the so-called Mangrove Nine, one of the demonstrators carried a placard which read, 'The police are guilty of incitement to riot and affray.' In a nearby street, two vans, full of police officers, waited on stand-by in case of disorder. Plainclothes officers were reported to have been mingling with the press representatives that were present.

Once the court opened about 50 people crowded into the public gallery, leaving a number standing in the narrow hallway at the entrance to the court. The magistrate, Anthony Babington, ordered police to clear the hallway of everyone except relatives and those standing as sureties and there were 'ugly scenes' as police officers 'pushed the crowd out of the narrow passageway and down the steps in front of the court.' Another four people were arrested. Present was Lord Gifford, a barrister, who some years later chaired an 'independent' inquiry into the 1985 riot in Tottenham, and Bruce Douglas-Mann, the Member of Parliament for North Kensington.[41] The four people arrested that day, eventually appeared before the court in December. Three were convicted of assaulting police and obstructing police officers; two were fined

---

39. *Kensington Post*, 6 November 1970.
40. *Kensington Post*, 28 May 1971.
41. *Kensington Post*, 4 June 1981.

£15 each and the other £25. The fourth youth was acquitted.[42] Four of those arrested in the original incident outside the Metro Youth Club were eventually charged with affray but 'all were acquitted after the jury had considered its verdict for a mere thirty minutes.'[43]

Trial of the Mangrove Nine

The climax of these and many other incidents, which had divided police and a section of the ethnic community into two distinct camps, arrived amidst a blaze of publicity with the trial of the 'Mangrove Nine'. It opened in somewhat controversial circumstances at the Old Bailey on 5 October 1971. On the first morning, 50 supporters of the nine, some carrying placards, crowded into the corridor leading to the public gallery of No.2 Court where the case was to be heard. The public gallery only held about 20 people and once it had filled up the remainder were turned away by court officers. They responded by sitting down in the passageway in protest at not being allowed to hear the proceedings and were ejected from the court by City of London police officers. As a further protest, they spent the remainder of the morning parading on the pavement outside the court.[44]

Before the court were nine people. A relatively new but increasingly successful ploy where several accused were in the dock together was for one or more to represent themselves because judges tended to give a person, defending himself or herself, far more leeway than they would to a practising barrister. Howe and Jones-Lecointe chose to represent themselves; the remainder were represented by barristers for the duration of the trial except Gordon who dismissed his counsel shortly after the start. As a result, the jury in this trial heard the views of Howe, Jones-Lecointe and Gordon about 'police methods and race relations'. Humphrey, who devoted part of his book to the trial, claimed that 'the brilliance with which the three defended themselves' showed that barristers were 'not indispensable and that much

---

42. *Kensington Post*, 10 December 1971.
43. Kettle, Martin and Lucy Hodge (1982). *Uprising! The Police, the People and the Riots in Britain's Cities*. London: Pan Books, p.81.
44. *Kensington Post*, 8 October 1971.

court procedure' was 'mere dogma, unnecessary good manners or a naked blocking device.'[45]

On Day Two of the trial, one of the defending barristers, Ian MacDonald made an impassioned plea for an all-black jury. Claiming that a 'decision to grant the application would be hailed throughout the world as a mighty blow for liberty', he told Judge Clarke that an all-black jury was needed because it was 'only an all-black jury who can have that sense of community which our law has always demanded'. Judge Clarke refused the application. Eventually, on Day Three after various defendants and, on at least one occasion, the prosecution, had successfully challenged and eliminated 63 potential jurors, the final jury of 12, including two black men and two black women, was sworn in.[46]

The charges of riotous assembly where re-introduced despite the fact that the magistrate, David Wacher, had thrown them out following an interesting exchange with prosecuting counsel at the committal hearings. Part of the prosecution case was that the chant 'Kill the pigs' was evidence of violence. However, in an exchange with prosecuting counsel, Wacher queried this:

> *Magistrate:* 'Where is the evidence of force?'
> *Prosecution Counsel:* '"Kill the Pigs" is the evidence.'
> *Magistrate:* 'It is highly provocative but — forgive my language — if they shouted "Fuck the Pigs" or "Bugger the Pigs" the police would not have taken that literally would they?'
> *Prosecution Counsel:* 'No. But the word "kill" embodies some sort of violence.'
> *Magistrate:* 'So do the other two.'
> *Prosecuting Counsel:* 'One man said, "We are going to mash up the Pig House".'
> *Magistrate:* 'But they passed at least one Pig House and nothing happened.'[47]

The prosecution's case was that, in addition to committing a number of individual criminal offences for which they were individually charged, all nine together had deliberately fanned 'what they knew to be an emotional situation' and had 'egged on the violence and some deliberately joined in'.

---

45. Humphry, Derek (1972). *Police Power and Black People*. London: Granada, p.164.
46. *Kensington Post*, 22 October 1971.
47. Quoted in Humphry, *op. cit.* 44, p.127.

Police Constable Pulley was one of the key witnesses, giving his evidence of Day Nine of the trial. Under cross-examination, Pulley described the Mangrove Restaurant as 'a den of iniquity' alleging that it was 'a haunt of criminals, prostitutes, ponces and the like'. Pointing out that the notices displayed inside were 'sometimes violent, sometimes obscene', Pulley claimed they were such that they were 'unacceptable to most people who go out for an evening meal.'[48] Having completed his evidence, PC Pulley was sitting at the back of the court on Day Eleven when he was accused by two of the defendants of signalling to PC Rogers when the latter was giving his evidence. Judge Clarke immediately ordered Pulley to leave the court and he was told not to return until the other three officers who had been in the van with him had completed their evidence.[49]

The trial highlighted the growing tendency amongst police officers of saying, 'I don't remember' in answer to a question, more often than not, put by defending counsel. Defending himself, Darcus Howe suggested to Constable Lewis, one of the four occupants of the nondescript van, that 'any consistent lack of memory hinders the process of getting at the truth' before pointing out that:

> 'PC Pulley said 33 times that he did not remember. PC Rogers said so 28 times. So far you have been unable to remember 13 times. About 70 times the three of you "can't remember". You were put in the van to observe and record [the demonstration] from beginning to end in order to provide information that would give the truth as to what took place.'[50]

Another area of controversy centred round the use of the words Black Power and Black Panthers. The police claimed in their evidence that the defendants, or, at least some of them, were members of Black Power and were questioned on a number of occasions, both at the committal proceedings and during the trial as to what Black Power was and what the differences were between the Black Power Movement and the Black Panthers. Right at the beginning of the trial proceedings, a chief superintendent had said that

48. *Kensington Post*, 22 October 1971.
49. *Ibid*.
50. Quoted in Humphry, *op. cit.* 44, p.157.

he saw two people 'known to me as being connected with the Black Power movement.' Thus, it was the police that introduced Black Power. Defence lawyers seized on this and the police realised that 'they had chosen to walk into a minefield.' There was confusion, with some officers suggesting there was little difference, others, trying to explain the differences and yet others saying they did not know.[51] But, Black Power then was very similar to al-Qaeda now, not in its aims but in its concept. It was not a physical body or movement but 'a political philosophy' As Humphry explained: it was what, as a result of their common experiences, 'the collective consciousness of black people working together, made it.'[52]

On Day 20, Judge Clarke heard allegations that prosecution witnesses had been intimated. In the absence of the jury, the judge said:

'Such dangerous acts cannot possibly be laid at the door of any of the defendants. Some of their stupid sympathisers may have done this. It is not only an outrage of justice, but all the defendants realise that it cannot do their case any good at all, and have dissociated themselves from it.'[53]

On Day 28, after the lunchtime recess, there was yet more controversy when Howe told Judge Clarke that at the beginning of the recess a prison officer had prevented him from speaking to his solicitor, and had hustled him physically to the top of the dock stairs before slamming him down to the bottom on his 'backside'. Howe's allegation was supported by one of the defending barristers, who said he had been standing by the dock at the time. David Croft, appearing for Crichlow, said his client had also been pushed down the stairs. As a result, the judge ordered that all prison officers manning the dock should be replaced.[54]

The trial finished on 16 December, with all nine defendants being acquitted of riotous assembly. In addition, all except two were acquitted of affray. The two who were convicted were Rhodan Gordon and Althea Jones-Lecointe and both were given 15 month prison sentences suspended for two years.

---

51. *Ibid*, p.95.
52. *Ibid*, pp.103/104.
53. *Kensington Post*, 5 November 1971.
54. *Kensington Post*, 19 November 1971.

In addition, three of the defendants were found guilty of lesser offences. Innes was found guilty of one case of assault causing actual bodily harm and received a nine months sentence suspended for two years. Boyce was found guilty of two offences, one of assault occasioning actual bodily harm and possessing an offensive weapon for which he was sentences in both cases to nine months' imprisonment suspended for two years, the sentences to run concurrently. Jones-Lecointe was found guilty of two cases of assault for which she was sentenced to 15 months' imprisonment on each suspended for two years, the sentences to run concurrently with that which had been imposed on her for affray.[55]

Howe subsequently claimed that some weeks after the conclusion of the court case "Eleven jurors dined at the Mangrove Restaurant to celebrate our victory"[56] After his acquittal, Crichlow 'became a prominent figure', particularly in Notting Hill, a position he was to hold for something like the next 25 years, and 'the Mangrove Restaurant acquired a symbolic status disproportionate to its origins.'[57] Nevertheless, within a few months Crichlow was claiming that the trial had ruined him and there were appeals in the press for donations to support the Mangrove.

Although this particular case arose from an outbreak of public disorder, the police, 'were left frustrated, feeling that their efforts to inhibit criminality had been rejected as inept.'[58] The action taken by them to deal with crime had been based on the traditional assumption that people, including those involved in crime, would reasonably accede to such action. However, a section of the black community took the view that there was no need to abide by the law, particularly if it did not harm anybody. This clash of views resulted increasingly in resentment at police action. As a result, 'feelings of bitterness and hostility were fostered and reinforced.'[59]

The Innes Report suggested that, by this time, PC Pulley was 'a powerful symbol of collective hatred' amongst a section of the black community.[60] Howe recalled how the mere mention of his name 'would strike terror in

---

55. *Kensington Post*, 24 December 1971.
56. Howe, *op. cit.* 8, p.48.
57. Innes, *op. cit.* 17, para.5.15.
58. *Ibid*, p.7, para.5.1.
59. *Ibid*, p.11, para.5.18.
60. *Ibid.*

the hearts of blacks in Notting Hill' and accused Pulley of 'being the colonial governor reincarnate [strutting] through the streets … administering sharp doses of capitalist discipline, abjuring all legal procedure.'[61] But it is doubtful whether senior officers fully appreciated the strength and effect of these feelings.[62]

One week after the march, the front page of the *Sunday People* carried a sensational story exploring the underlying causes of the tensions and difficulties in Notting Hill during the course of which it recommended that Pulley should be transferred away from the area. Pulley eventually sued Odhams Group of Newspapers for libel and defamation of character in relation to the article and was awarded £5,000 for what was subsequently described as 'baseless and wicked propaganda.'[63] At his own request, Pulley was appointed to a new post in June 1971 at New Scotland Yard and he completed his service in the criminal intelligence section. After his retirement he became a consultant to the journalist Martin Short whilst the latter was making a series under the title 'Crime Incorporated', about the Mafia in the United States, which was eventually seen on the Independent Television Network in 1984.

Two of the most senior police officers in the Metropolitan Police have since defended Pulley. Writing in 1986, Gilbert Kelland described Pulley as 'one of the most outstanding operational officers the force has ever known [who] became something of a legend at the station.'[64] Former Commissioner, Sir Robert Mark, pointed out in his autobiography written in 1978, that PC Pulley 'thought it proper to enforce the law impartially against black and white alike.'[65]

Nevertheless, whatever the cause, increased hostility had been aroused and the bad feelings created during these years, all too often, spilled over into violence. The seeds had germinated and, so it could be argued, things were about to get worse.

---

61. Howe, *op. cit.* 8, p.41.
62. Innes, *op. cit.* 17, p.11, para. 5.18.
63. Mark, Sir Robert (1978). *In the Office of Constable*. London: Collins, p.287.
64. Kelland, Gilbert (1989). *Crime in London*. London: Grafton Books, p.84.
65. Mark, Robert, *op. cit.* 62, p.287.

The Angry Brigade

At the same time as the Mangrove Nine were appearing in Court No.1 at the Old Bailey another trial with Notting Hill connections was taking place in Court No.2. A group known as the Angry Brigade, had conducted a bombing campaign in London commencing with the blowing up of a BBC outside broadcast van due to cover the Miss World Contest at the Royal Albert Hall in November 1970. There then followed a series of explosions, mainly directed at government buildings or the homes of prominent government Ministers. In January 1971, the Bomb Squad[66] was set up, initially for the sole purpose of catching the gang. It quickly achieved results, although initially partly by accident.

On 19 January, Jake Prescott, was arrested in Talbot Road, suspected of being in possession of drugs. Prescott, 'a burglar and heroin addict', was only on the fringes of the brigade but had agreed to address three envelopes in which claims for the bombing of Robert Carr MP's home were to be sent. This led them to other addresses in Notting Hill including the basement of 25 Powis Square where officers discovered a copy of Guy Debrod's book, *The Society of the Spectacle*[67] in which a prominent member of the Angry Brigade, John Barker, had made a number of notes. Although the remainder of the group were not arrested until August 1971 in Stoke Newington, and their trial did not take place until the following year, Prescott pleaded guilty to conspiracy to cause explosions at the trial in November 1971 and was sentenced to 15 years' imprisonment, subsequently reduced, on appeal, to ten years.[68]

Postscript

Music was important part of life in Notting Hill because, at various times, a number of prominent people associated with it either resided or worked there. But, in 1970, tragedy struck with the death of a legendry black musician, Jimi Hendrix. On 16 September, he played his last performance at Ronnie Scott's in Oxford Street. What happened between finishing this

---

66. The Bomb Squad was the precursor to the Anti-terrorist Branch.
67. Originally published in France in 1967 the book puts forward a number of radical proposals about capitalism and was regarded as an influential work for revolutionary movements in the late-1960s and early-1970s.
68. Bright, Martin (2002). 'Look back in anger'. In *The Observer*, 3 February.

concert and his death two days later is uncertain. There were suggestions that he 'smoked pot at various pads' around Notting Hill, went to Kensington Market in the High Street where Freddie Mercury of Queen had a stall, followed by a bottle party given by Mike Nesmith of the Monkees. There were also suggestions that he was last seen, with his German girl-friend, ice-skater Monika Danneman, in the Globe Bar at 103 Talbot Road and the Mangrove Restaurant.

What is certain is that on 18 September, Hendrix ended up, with Monika, in the basement of the Samarkand Hotel at 22 Landsdowne Crescent where, having earlier taken barbiturates, followed by a quantity of sleeping pills, he vomited whilst sleeping. When Monika realised something was wrong she buried her illegal drugs in the garden and telephoned a few rock personalities before calling an ambulance.

The police report claimed he was alive when the ambulance arrived but died whilst being conveyed to hospital. The actual cause of death was announced initially as 'inhalation of vomit due to barbiturate intoxication.' It was subsequently described as 'a pharmaceutical miscalculation, rather than a deliberate overdose' and an open verdict was recorded.[69]

---

69. Notting Hill Time Line, 12: One Foot in the Grove 1970/71. Monika Dannermann eventually became a recluse and committed suicide in 1996.

CHAPTER 7

THE EARLY YEARS OF THE CARNIVAL AND RACE RELATIONS

Each year the August Bank Holiday weekend sees the culmination of a year's work by organizers, musicians, costume makers and the police. The Notting Hill Carnival is now nearing its 50th year. It is a triumph for members of the black community, particularly those, who, during the early years, overcame stiff opposition, which included calls for it to be banned altogether and suggestions that it should be removed from the streets, either to Hyde Park, Battersea Park or to one of two nearby stadiums, the White City or Stamford Bridge.

There are some doubts as to how and when the Carnival originated.[1] What is clear is that, with the assistance of Jamaican Prime Minister Norman Manley, Claudia Jones, Trinidad-born, a USA civil rights activist who had been deported for being a Communist, set up a fund to help pay the fines of those black people who had been arrested during the 1958 riots. As part of the fund-raising activities, she organized an event at St Pancras Town Hall on 30 January 1959, which was called the West Indian Gazette Caribbean Carnival, in recognition of her role as founder and editor of the *West Indian Gazette*. For the next five years, up to and including 1964, the venue of the Carnival was a similar hall in West London.[2] Unfortunately, Jones died on Christmas Eve 1964 of chronic heart disease.[3]

---

1. Writing in *West Indian World* in September 1981, Alfred Chow suggested that the Carnival replaced the old Shepherd Rag Fair, which had survived as a yearly festival from the last century, and during its early days was more of an Elizabethan pageant.

2. Cohen, Abner (1980). *Drama and Politics in the Development of a London Carnival.* Man (N.S.) 15, 1980, p.67; La Rose, Michael (2004). 'Forty Years of the Notting Hill Carnival: An Assessment of the History and the Future'. Typescript, p.3.

3. La Rose, *op. cit.* 2, p.3.

Following her death, a white social worker, Rhaune Laslett, announced, in May 1965[4], that she intended to organize a carnival on the streets of Notting Hill. Born in London, although her father was Russian and her mother, American Indian, she founded the London Free School earlier in the year.[5] It was essentially a neighbourhood community centre, the purpose of which was 'to promote cooperation and understanding between people of various races and creeds through education and through working together.'[6] The purpose of such a carnival would be 'to familiarise the various culture groups with each other's customs, to bring some colour, warmth and happiness to a grim and depressed neighbourhood and to correct the image of the Notting Hill, which had been unjustly castigated by the national media as a den of prostitution, drug addiction, crime and potential extremism.'[7] The venture was initially supported by the Conservative-dominated Chelsea and Kensington Council who, like Laslett, saw it as a positive move towards ridding Notting Hill of its unwelcome reputation and, at the same time, improving racial harmony. A grant of £100 was promised, together with the provision of trucks 'to carry the groups taking part in the street procession.'[8] However, shortly before the carnival Laslett received a letter from the Mayor

---

4. La Rose, *op. cit.* 3, p.4. claims that the first Notting Hill Carnival was in 1965. But then La Rose also states that the first *West Indian Gazette* Caribbean Carnival was held in 1958 (see p.3) whereas everyone else, so far as I can tell, agrees that it was in January 1959. A website history of the Carnival states in was 1965 (http://www.nottinghillcarnival.eu/history) and Gary Younge, in his article in *The Guardian* on 17 August 2002, 'The politics of partying' also suggests it was 1965. The fact that in 1986, it was purported to be the 21st Carnival (*The Job*, 8 August 1986; *Caribbean Times*, 22 August 1986; *The Guardian*, 25 August 1986) would suggest that it started in 1965. But Cohen, who arguably wrote the definitive history of Carnival in his book, *Masquerade Politics* (see footnote 5 below) claims it was 1966, p.10. Cohen also suggests that Jones died two years before the first Notting Hill Carnival, p.77. As she died in December 1964, this would make it 1966. However, in an earlier publication, see Cohen, *op. cit.* 2, Cohen states it was 1965 (p.67). Cecil Gutzmore, too, suggested that it commenced in 1966 ('Carnival, the State and the Black Masses in the United Kingdom', in *Inside Babylon: The Caribbean Diaspora in Britain* (Winston James and Clive Harris eds.) (1993). London : Verso, p.215) The blue plaques that have been unveiled to four of the most influential people in the introduction and growth of Carnival, Jones, Laslett, Henderson and Palmer say it was 1965. Therefore despite the existence of some evidence to the contrary, 1965 is taken as the first year on which the Carnival was held in Notting Hill.
5. Cohen, Abner (1993). *Masquerade Politics*. London: Berg, p.10.
6. *Kensington News and Post*, 23 July 1966.
7. Cohen, *op. cit.* 5, p.11.
8. *Ibid*, p.11/12.

withdrawing the offer of assistance on the grounds that 'certain information' regarding the London Free School had come into his possession. Although the Mayor refused to divulge what that information was it is believed that he had been told 'the London Free School was a subversive organization associated with Communists, Fascists, black Muslims and provos,'[9] a truly remarkable mix if it had been true. In the event the carnival went ahead in September and a small number of people, including dancers from Cyprus, India and Ukraine, and a steel band, led by Russell Henderson, performed in the area immediately around Acklam Road.[10]

In 1967, the London Free School changed its name to Notting Hill Neighbourhood Services in which Mrs Laslett again had a leading role.[11] It was, said the *Kensington News*, 'an organization run on entirely selfless and voluntary lines by dedicated men and women who have turned a part-time aid programme into a full-time social mission.' The carnival programme consisted of a week of 'cultural' events opened by a procession of motor and horse-drawn vehicles, two steel bands and about 800 followers parading through the streets of Notting Hill.[12]

The following year, despite torrential rain, a procession, led by a white goat and a steel band, and containing floats depicting Henry VIII and his wives and the Pied Piper of Hamelin, together with a number of West Indians in their national costume, formed up in Tavistock Crescent and meandered through the streets of Notting Hill for three hours. In the evening, there was a barbecue at the Adventure Playground in Telford Road and a dance at All Saints Church Hall with music provided by two pop groups and a steel band. Organizer, Mrs Laslett was full of praise for the police saying that 'they were so friendly towards everyone and went out of their way to be helpful.'[13]

In 1969, the numbers attracted to the event had increased to about three and a half thousand and four steel bands, including the Selwyn Baptiste Adventure Steel Band, took part. Starting in Tavistock Crescent, the procession meandered its way around the nearby streets. The local newspaper

---

9. *Ibid*, p.13.
10. Cohen, *op. cit.* 3, p.67.
11. Cohen, *op. cit.* 5, p.17.
12. *Kensington News and Post*, 8 September 1967.
13. *Kensington News and Post*, 20 September 1968.

described the police as being good humoured, with a few playing 'cards in one of the two green vans that followed the procession.' There 'seemed little need for supervision', most of the 'policing' being done by the organizers.[14]

In 1970, it was touch and go whether there would be a Carnival. In the aftermath of the demonstration, protesting at police action against the Mangrove Restaurant, which ended in violence, described in the previous chapter, Mrs Laslett decided to call off a festival procession, planned for the last Sunday in August, because of the risk of children being hurt in further clashes between the black community and the police. However, some local people were not prepared to allow the event to be dropped and quickly got together to make alternative arrangements. Called 'The People's Carnival', a name that was to stick for the next three years, it was not a great success. Around 800 people took part and the only 'music' was provided by a group of drummers. Nevertheless, it ensured that the growing tradition of a festival on the streets of Notting Hill in late summer was maintained. In the evening, an open-air dance, described as 'a late summer's night dream with bands, free toffee apples, soft drinks and rolls' was held in Powis Square continuing 'until well into the early hours of the following morning'.[15]

Similarly, in 1971, it was not particularly well organized and was poorly attended.[16] In 1972 it was different, with the local newspaper reporting that the crowds were substantially larger. By mid-afternoon, hundreds of people were dancing in the Westway Theatre and on Portobello Green as the bands played. When finally, the procession took to the streets, there were so many people that the floats carrying the bands could not follow the planned route. Instead, they paraded through the streets of Notting Hill at random for over three hours. An un-named police source said 'it was a bit of a shambles, but everything went off well,' stressing 'there was no trouble and it was a great day.' Principal organizer Merle Major claimed that the police had been very co-operative and had let the people go their own way.[17]

It was then that 'a gifted young Trinidadian, Leslie Palmer, came onto the scene and in the next four years he completely revolutionised the event,

---

14. *Kensington News and Post*, 5 September 1969.
15. *Kensington News and Post*, 4 September 1970.
16. Cohen, *op. cit.* 3, p.69.
17. *Kensington News and Post*, 1 September 1972.

transforming its structure and content almost beyond recognition.'[18] In 1973, for the first time, the carnival was held over two days and Palmer and his committee, the Carnival Development Committee, attempted to involve people from all the different West Indian islands. The local council leased six trucks for the floats and there were amplified sound systems playing from underneath the Westway and in Acklam Road. Police estimated the crowd at between 6,000 and 8,000 on the Sunday and at 10,000 on the Monday, although some other estimates put it as high as 30,000. The local newspaper suggested that:

'August Bank Holiday 1973 may go down with the summer of 1958 as a turning point in the history of race relations in Notting Hill. Fifteen years after the low point marked the famous 'race riots', policemen and black West Indians were last week-end literally dancing together in the streets.'[19]

Good relations between the police and the Carnival organizers continued. Speaking on behalf of all black people who took part, Leslie Palmer thanked the police, pointing out that 'they were not out in force, and it made all the difference.' He continued, 'Carnival time for West Indians is a time for joy and love, not fighting.' The Divisional Commander, Chief Superintendent Jim Hargadon, said:

'The whole thing was an outstanding success from everybody's point of view. There was a real carnival spirit in the air and any Jeremiah who suggests that there was a lack of co-operation between Notting Hill police and the local community ought to have been there on Sunday and Monday…'[20]

But by 1974, it had ceased to be a local event. Nationwide publicity drew an estimated crowd of 150,000 spectators on the Bank Holiday Monday and disruption to traffic was extensive. There were 17 bands, more than twice as many as there had been in 1973. Again, there were amplified sound systems under the bays of the Westway and in Acklam Road. Clearly, with such

---

18. Cohen, *op. cit.* 2, p.70.
19. *Kensington News and Post*, 31 August 1973.
20. *Ibid.*

large numbers of people attending, there was a need to improve arrangements and in 1975 the organizers and police agreed that an area of Notting
Hill should be set aside for the event. Parking was banned for the first time
and the bands were allowed to move freely throughout the designated area.
Palmer had managed to persuade Capital Radio, a commercial radio station
listened to by many of Britain's black youth, to become a patron; as a result
of this and the amplified sound systems, 'large groups of black youth' were
attracted to the event for the first time.[21] It had now become a mass activity but 'the local authorities hadn't anticipated the numbers' and 'made no
extra provision at all for sanitary arrangements, even of the most basic kind.'
Consequently, revellers were urinating in people's gardens and their porches
much to the displeasure of local residents.[22]

Afterwards the local police commander expressed his concern, claiming
it had been difficult to maintain control and this had only been achieved by
adopting a low-key policing strategy which involved ignoring many minor
breaches of the law, such as the illegal sale of alcohol and various bye-laws
relating to the many unlicensed street traders attracted into the area. Of
more concern was the pick-pockets, who had operated with immunity in the
dense crowds and over 180 crimes, mostly theft from the person, had been
reported. In addition, it had been difficult to move through the area — two
people had almost been crushed to death in separate incidents — and many
people had seen little of the bands and costume dancers because of the difficulties of moving about.[23] But it wasn't just the police who were, by this time,
expressing concern. There had been 'serious neglect of the event's administrative requirements' and there was mounting opposition from local white
residents and the Kensington and Chelsea Council about holding the 1976
Carnival in the same way. Chief amongst the complaints was the noise from
the amplified sound systems and the lack of toilet facilities.[24]

In summing up the first decade of the Carnival's existence, Owusu, suggested that 'despite the meagre resources of the community', it 'developed
an infrastructure which it slowly consolidated, as more steel bands and

21. La Rose, *op. cit.* 3, p.6.
22. Gutzmore, *op. cit.* 4, p.218.
23. Metropolitan Police (1976). 'Notting Hill 1976'. Typescript. Unpublished, pp.7–8.
24. La Rose, *op. cit.* 3, p.6.

revellers joined the celebrations.' Individual ingenuity enabled the various Mas camps to appear in elaborate costumes but Carnival also came 'to reflect the black working-class experience.' For example, in 1974, some revellers 'appeared on the streets wearing prison outfits' to the accompaniment of 'Rebels on Remand.'[25]

Race Relations

Despite all its shortcomings, the period, between 1965 and 1970, was described as being 'characterised by co-operation across ethnic lines, notably between West Indian immigrants and British working-class natives.'[26] In comparison, the next period, between 1971 and 1975, 'saw a dramatic change'. The economic boom that had dominated the 1960s suddenly came to an end and there was increasing unemployment. Those of African-Caribbean origin 'were particularly hard hit' because, firstly, 'they were relative newcomers'; secondly, 'many were semi-skilled' and thirdly, and perhaps, more importantly, 'they were victims of racial discrimination.' Therefore, 'the relationships of activity' that had, to some extent, grown up between them and the working-class Londoners following the 1958 riots 'gave way to tensions over employment.'[27] The situation was not helped nationally when a member of the Conservative Party's shadow cabinet, Enoch Powell, warned the public in April 1968, of 'the likelihood of violence developing as a consequence of coloured settlement in Britain, and the creation of ghettoes in the main cities.' Using particularly colourful language he declared:

'As I look ahead, I am filled with foreboding. Like the Romans, I seem to see the River Tiber foaming with much blood.'

Powell received a great deal of support from blue-collar workers in Britain but the authorities and the left-wing regarded his speech as alarmist

---

25. Owusu, Kwesi (1986). 'Notting Hill Carnival: "De Road is de Stage de Stage is de Road" In Proctor, James (ed.)(2000). *Writing Black Britain 1948–1998*. Manchester: Manchester University Press, p.159.
26. Cohen, *op. cit.* 2, p.68.
27. *Ibid*, pp.68–69.

and racist. He was immediately dismissed from the shadow cabinet by the opposition leader, Ted Heath.[28]

In 1968, it was suggested that, amongst the half-a-million immigrants then residing in Britain, there was 'a small minority of agitators and extremists' who sought 'to promote discord' and who saw and searched for 'evidence of discrimination at every turn.'[29] Claiming that the 'mistrust and misunderstanding' that resulted, needed to be dispelled, the Metropolitan Police set up a Community Relations Branch, known as A7(1). The first officer in charge, Commander Merricks suggested that it represented 'one of the most difficult and challenging tasks in the field of police/community relations' that the Metropolitan Police had 'ever had to face.'[30] Initially, in July 1969, eight chief inspectors were appointed as full-time community liaison officers, primarily on inner divisions; similar appointments were made to the remaining divisions over the following year.[31] However, Whitfield was critical of its purpose which was articulated as the development of 'closer ties with immigrant communities'; rather, he claimed, 'it was predominantly established to forestall criticism of the Met's relations with immigrant communities and to further the Met's own priorities.'[32]

Three Significant Reports

Meanwhile, three significant events occurred in the early 1970s. The first, in September 1970, was the appointment by the Notting Hill Social Council of a panel, consisting of Alderman Donald Chesworth, the Director of the Social Council, and two barristers, Louis Blom-Cooper, QC, and Rudy Narayan to enquire into Police/Community Relations in the area.[33] Whilst

---

28. Leeds, Sir Christopher (1982). 'Conflict Theories, Government Policies and the Urban Riots of the Early 1980s'. In *Community Disorders and Policing: Conflict Management in Action* (Tony Marshall (ed.)). London: Whiting and Birch, pp.28–29.
29. Pryce, Everton A (1985). 'The Notting Hill Gate Carnival—Black Politics, Resistance, and Leadership 1976–1978'. *Caribbean Quarterly* 31:2, 9 June, p.36.
30. Merrick, F.R. (1970). 'The Development of Community Relations in the Metropolitan Police'. *Police Journal*, Vol. 43, January, p.30.
31. *Ibid*, pp.32–33.
32. Whitfield, James (2004). *Unhappy Dialogue: The Metropolitan Police and Black Londoners in Post-war Britain*. Willan: Cullompton, p.3.
33. *Kensington Post*, 29 January 1971.

the announcement of the setting up of the panel was well-publicised, there is no evidence that it actually produced a report.

The second arose when, in 1972, the House of Commons Select Committee on Race Relations and Immigration inquired into Police/Immigrant Relations. Whilst the Committee looked at the relationships with Asian communities in Sheffield, Rotherham, Keighley, Bradford and Preston and at both Asian and West Indian communities in Manchester, its main concern, insofar as London was concerned was Notting Hill, where it spent a long day in the area hearing evidence. Amongst a number who gave evidence was the Community Relations Adviser for the Borough of Kensington and Chelsea, T. M. Ottevanger, and Darcus Howe, on behalf of the Mangrove. Whilst, a West Indian member of the Race Relations Board, Louise Chase, suggested that 'relations between the police and the community were unlikely to be good in an area of social deprivation' because 'people tended to make scapegoats of the police', most people in Notting Hill, black and white alike, believed that police/immigrant relations were 'very bad or non-existent.'[34] The officer then in charge of the Metropolitan Police's Race Relations Branch (A.7), Commander Rignall, and the officer in charge of B Division, Commander Maggs, submitted memoranda to the committee. In his memorandum, Rignall reported that, in Notting Hill, 'the number of coloured persons arrested, stopped in the street or brought to a police station' was in proportion with the size of the total 'coloured community to the indigenous population in the area.' He went on to suggest that 'if the allegations of victimisation, harassment and the like were true one would expect a much higher proportion of the immigrant population to have come to the notice of police in the manner described.'[35]

In his written evidence to the Committee, Maggs suggested that one of the failings of the area was the lack of a Community Relations Council, although the Royal Borough of Kensington and Chelsea had recently appointed a Community Relations Adviser.[36] Another problem which gave

---

34. House of Commons Select Committee on Race Relations and Immigration (1972). Session 1971–72. 'Police/Immigrant Relations', Volume 1. London: Her Majesty's Stationery Office, p.5, para. 22.

35. *Ibid*, Volume. 2, Evidence, p.44.

36. *Ibid*, p.212.

cause for concern was the number 'of black youths with no ties' who were 'living rough.' Pointing out that events at the Mangrove Restaurant and the Metro Youth Club had caught the headlines, Maggs explained:

'These young men, many of whose educational standards are minimal, leave home, which is usually an overcrowded furnished room, either because the family consider at 15 he ought to be self-supporting and, therefore, making more room available for those too young to leave home, or because he wants the privacy home cannot give him. Or perhaps, in roaming the streets he has, almost inevitably, come up against the law and the stigma of this has caused his parents (more usually a single parent) to reject him for bringing disgrace on the family. These young men quite often spend their nights sleeping in a playground, hall or a friend's room and their days in local cafés where they come in contact with people who suggest easy ways of making money. These youngsters cannot get Social Service benefits because they have no fixed address and so "hustling", i.e. living on their wits, becomes a pattern of life.'[37]

Maggs claimed that the content of any report which contained the 'emotive place name' Notting Hill, immediately took on 'a different slant' because it conjured up in people's minds, the 'vision of riot, racial trouble and suspect policemen.' Instead, he suggested 'what should predominate is the more truthful picture of an area of social deprivation, bad housing and lack of job opportunity,' all problems the police had neither caused nor could resolve, but 'for which the police, usually the only visible sign of authority in the area,' were 'made to feel responsible.' He then issued a warning which, unfortunately, went unheeded for the next 18 years:

'A vital issue that must not be avoided is the need to ensure that in dealing with the militant minority whether they be black or white, police must not, because of pressure groups, allow to develop a situation where these elements become privileged because of non-enforcement of the law through a fear of constant criticism and harassment.'

---

37. *Ibid*, p.213.

Maggs suggested it was 'prejudice in reverse' pointing out that 'policemen like anyone else are sensitive, some more than others, and if through constant criticism and complaint a policeman feels that he is in a hopeless situation, then the grass roots of anarchy are set.'[38]

Following the inner-city riots of 1981 and the subsequent Scarman Report, there was an element of non-enforcement of the law through a fear of criticism and constant accusations of harassment, which grew stronger as the 1980s progressed. Not until 1987, when Chief Superintendent Havard, with strong support from his Commander and Deputy Assistant Commissioner launched Operation Trident, did the tide begin to turn in Notting Hill.

The third significant report arose around the use of the word 'mugging' which has now been a headline-grabbing crime for 40 years. There is, of course, no such offence in law and never has been. It was first introduced to the United Kingdom by the *Daily Mirror* in 1972, having originated in the black ghettos of the USA. At that time, it referred to robbery of individuals on the street in which violence or the threat of violence was used. However, the use of the word quickly became distorted so that, in many cases, it not only referred to these types of robberies but came to include 'pick-pocketing'. Again, there is and never has been any such offence in law. Black youths quickly became associated with 'mugging' for two reasons. Firstly, because, according to the police, many of the victims described the perpetrators as black. Secondly, the media laid stress on those areas where such crimes were committed as being 'inner city areas where black people live', such as Notting Hill.[39]

The Newman Paper

Following the Report by the House of Commons Select Committee, in 1973, Commander Kenneth Newman, by then in charge of the Metropolitan Police's Race Relations Branch, but who was later to become successively Chief Constable of the Royal Ulster Constabulary, Commandant of the Police Staff College and Commissioner of the Metropolitan Police, wrote a paper entitled 'The Policing of Racially Sensitive Areas'. The purpose of the

---

38. *Ibid*, p.215.
39. Benyon, John (1986). 'A Tale of Failure: Race and Policing'. Policy Papers in Ethnic Relations No.3. Warwick: Centre for Research in Ethnic Relations, University of Warwick, p.26.

paper, consisting of 14 closely typed pages, 'was to consider the causes and the implications of the potentially dangerous tension' which had 'developed between police and West Indian youths in some racially sensitive divisions.'[40] It started by analysing 'the nature and causes of tension' and they make interesting reading, particularly in the context of the inner-city riots of 1980, 1981 and 1985. There were eight:

(a) *Internal Stresses in West Indian Families.* Newman claimed that many first generation West Indian families treated their children with a 'Victorian severity' which was 'in marked contrast to the more permissive upbringing of white children and to the atmosphere experienced at school.'

(b) *Homelessness.* He claimed that these family stresses led to a growing number of black youths leaving home and living in hostels.

(c) *Education.* The report highlighted the fact that West Indian children had a poor record at school.

(d) *Unemployment.* Among West Indian youths unemployment was above average, often because their ambitions exceeded their 'capacity and qualifications'. Newman suggested that they were not prepared to 'lower their sights and would rather be unemployed than engage in what they consider to be menial work.'

(e) *History.* He claimed that 'history and the tradition of subjection to white supremacy' meant that many older West Indians had an inferiority complex. Therefore, 'in an effort to free themselves of this psychological hang-up, the idea that "black is beautiful" was promulgated for good and worthy motives.' Unfortunately, 'pursuit of this concept' by black youths often took 'an aggressive form.'

---

40. Newman, K L, Commander (1973). 'The Policing of Racially Sensitive Divisions. Metropolitan Police', Typescript, Unpublished, p.1.

(f) *Political indoctrination.* By exploiting the frustrations implicit in some of the early factors and using 'lies and distortions about police activities', black militants 'actively promoted hostility to the police service.'

(g) *Police symbolism.* Because they were a symbol of authority in a 'white society', the police were a target for all the grievances by black people 'about deprivation, unemployment, prejudice, discrimination and general disadvantage.'

(h) *Involvement in crime.* According to Newman, the statistical evidence supported the view that young black people were disproportionately involved in crime.[41]

Much of what Newman said in this first part of his paper has been repeated by various writers since. For instance, in 1980, Cohen described how, in 1976, a new generation of West Indian teenagers, born and educated in Britain, suddenly appeared on the streets of Notting Hill. He described it as 'a generation of alienated, disillusioned, demoralised and rebellious youth', many of whom had been 'under-achievers in school', and who were unemployed because of 'a scarcity of jobs compounded by discrimination.' Consequently, many spent 'their time hanging around the streets in neighbourhood gangs' which inevitably brought them into conflict with the police.[42] Some seven years later, Ramdin echoed similar thoughts:

'Gradually, during the late-1960s and early-1970s it was realised that the education system had been failing the black second generation "achievement wise". If education was a "major problem" among black youth, then the high and disproportionate incidence of unemployment amongst black school-leavers in conjunction with the "alarming levels'" of homelessness among West Indians were also cause for concern ..... '[43]

---

41. *Ibid*, pp.1–4.
42. Cohen, *op. cit.* 2, p.74.
43. Ramdin, Ron (1987). *The Making of the Black Working Class in Britain.* Aldershot: Wildwood House, p.457.

Newman took the view that factors (a) to (f) could not be dealt with by the police but, at the same time, the majority of police officers had little knowledge of these 'underlying tensions that existed in immigrant areas.' He pointed out that such knowledge was 'vital' if the officer was 'to decide correctly what control measures to use' when dealing with 'an incident involving black youths,' because the measures 'to defuse a tense situation in areas of dense immigrant population [were] in direct conflict with the measures traditionally adopted to contain and prevent serious crime' on the streets, i.e.

Measures to defuse tension	Measures to contain crime
Decrease stops and searches	Increase stops and searches
Go easy on youths loitering	Break up youth groups in streets
Reduce surveillance of suspects	Increase surveillance

Therefore, Newman explained, there was 'a need for clearly understood command policies and carefully drawn guidelines or, in other words, a strategy for policing racially sensitive divisions.'[44] There were, suggested Newman, two key elements to any strategy for policing sensitive areas.

Firstly, management and command policies should: (a) carefully balance the advantages of short term, immediate crime fighting measures against possible disadvantages in terms of civil disorder (an interesting observation in the light of what was to occur in Brixton in 1981); and (b) provide policy guidelines for predictably difficult situations with a view to reducing the number of abrasive police/public contacts.

Secondly, there should be an integrated community relations programme, which sought to enlist the support of the more responsible elements in the immigrant community, for law enforcement which would counteract rumour and suspicion and generally create an atmosphere in which operational

---

44. Newman, *op. cit.* 40, pp.4–5, paras. 3–6.

activities could be conducted with maximum effectiveness.[45] Here Newman may have been a little naïve in his comments because, in the author's experience of policing a 'racially sensitive division' some seven years later, the more responsible elements in the immigrant community had little control over the youths mentioned by Cohen, a number of which formed the criminal elements within that community.

Newman then went on to suggest that, although there was 'very little foundation' for such beliefs, 'young blacks' believed that 'police brutality and harassment was widespread in immigrant neighbourhoods' and that this situation was 'condoned by senior officers' turning a blind-eye to such activities. Pointing out that an allegation of police misconduct in one area could reinforce this widely held belief amongst young black people in other areas, such as Notting Hill, Newman suggested that it was vital to impress on police officers in these areas the need for 'exemplary behaviour' in all contacts with young black people. In particular, he mentioned Crime Squads and the Special Patrol Group and the dangers of what he referred to as 'vigorous patrolling practices' which themselves created 'tension and hostility.'

He concluded this part of the report by suggesting that senior officers 'should carefully consider the law enforcement philosophy behind the employment of vigorous patrolling techniques', pointing out that although there were 'law enforcement gains' from such techniques there were also 'liabilities'[46] as was found in Brixton during Operation Swamp in 1981.

Newman concluded the paper by suggesting some of the areas to be included in the guidelines:

(a) *Arrests in Immigrant Areas.* Pointing out that it takes little to attract a crowd in such areas, Newman stated that 'the crowd can be quick to misunderstand, quick to perceive the police action as discriminatory and quick to exchange curiosity for anger.' In summary he suggested that there needed to be 'more elaborate guidelines for making arrests in immigrant areas, not for the point of view of going soft' in those areas, 'but simply to make police action more effective.'

---

45. *Ibid*, pp.5–6, para. 7.
46. *Ibid*, pp.7–8, paras. 8–16.

(b) *Black Youth Clubs.* Far too often there had been occasions when police units had been confronted with 'upwards of 200 hostile black youths', with its ensuing potential for serious public disorder, following an incident at or in the vicinity of black youth clubs. Should police action be necessary in relation to incidents occurring in the vicinity of black youth clubs it needed to be quick, effective and adequately supervised claimed Newman.

(c) *Breaking up Youth Groups.* Pointing out that West Indians looked upon 'social gatherings in the street as normal and unobjectionable' Newman suggested that such groups could 'appear menacing to ordinary citizens.' Therefore, he claimed a balance needed to be struck between what West Indians would call harassment and the preservation of reasonable order on the streets.

(d) *Searching Premises.* Newman pointed out that West Indians were 'ultra-sensitive about police officers entering their homes'. It followed that even if a warrant was not strictly necessary, police hands were strengthened by the possession of one, 'if, as so often happens, the occupants are violent and obstructive and there is an aftermath of complaints.'

(e) *Domestic Incidents.* Newman suggested there had been many cases where police officers attending domestic disputes involving immigrant families had 'been assaulted and even seriously injured'. Too often, Newman suggested, officers told immigrants that 'there is nothing they can do' when there were various counselling services and welfare agencies to which they could be referred.

(f) *Fairgrounds and Places of Public Entertainment.* Because of their liking for festive occasions, black youths regularly attended fairs and similar occasions in large numbers, often gathering around and dominating a particular aspect of the occasion. This could cause friction with white groups, giving a high potential for civil disorder.[47]

---

47. *Ibid*, pp.8–11, paras. 17–18.

In each of the above cases, Newman suggested that the situation demanded good command and control, maximum discipline and suitable restraint by the police officers dealing with them. If not, suggested Newman, extremist organizations were 'not slow to misrepresent the situation as one of over-reaction and brutality' on the part of the police.

In summary, Newman pointed out that, at that time, 1973, there was a tendency within the Metropolitan Police Force to regard 'community relations programmes as somewhat peripheral to the main operational activities of the Force.' However, he suggested that they were 'an integral part of law enforcement' for four reasons:

- They increased communication and decreased hostility between operational officers and immigrants.
- The officers involved in community relations sought to enlist the understanding and support of West Indian leaders and other community residents.
- Community relations personnel could mitigate hostility and reduce operational difficulties by preventing the spread of unjustified rumour and suspicion.
- Finally, the relations they had with the community often enabled community relations officers to collect, evaluate and disseminate information essential to operational decision-making in immigrant areas.[48]

Newman recommended the setting up of a working party to consider what command and control policies and procedures should be put in place to reduce the number of confrontations between police officers and black youths and to consider how community relations activities could be integrated more effectively with operational needs.[49]

Little, if anything, changed as a result of Kenneth Newman's paper. Although serving as a chief inspector in Islington at the time, the author was unaware of the existence of the paper until he joined the staff at the Police Staff College, Bramshill, in 1982. Indeed, James Whitfield makes no

---

48. *Ibid*, pp.12–13, paras. 19–23.
49. *Ibid*, pp.13–14, paras. 25–26.

mention of it in his book, *Unhappy Dialogue*.[50] Insofar as the author is aware no such working party was set up. Consequently, no force-wide strategy was drawn up for policing racially sensitive divisions, no command and control policies and procedures were put in place to reduce the number of confrontations between police officers and black youths, no guidelines were drawn up for making arrests in immigrant areas, and neither were any issued relating to the breaking up of groups of black youths on the streets.

As will be seen later in the book, not until the 1980s, following the Scarman Report into the 1981 Brixton riot, did individual senior officers introduce strategies in an attempt to pre-empt outbreaks of disorder. Instead, the police continued to use the 'sus' law as a major part of their armoury for dealing with street crime. Ramdin described how it worked in general:

'[T]wo or three youths are walking down the street or standing at a bus stop. The police swoop and arrest them. The charges are loitering with intent to steal or attempting to steal from person or persons unknown. There is, in most cases, some resistance which leads to an additional charge of assault on police.'[51]

'Sus' was a favourite 'arrest' for many of those attempting to get into the Criminal Investigation Department, aids to CID or temporary detective constables as they were successively known. It would be wrong to say that Ramdin's description of events applied in every case. Some youths, both black and white, were no doubt loitering with the intention of stealing whatever they could lay their hands on but there is little doubt that, in some cases, those arrested were innocent of the charges brought against them.

Whitfield is particularly critical of the Metropolitan Police at this point, claiming that its failings towards 'race and diversity matters' from the 1970s onwards 'stemmed policies and attitudes' that were prevalent throughout the 1950s and 1960s, including 'a desire to always put its own interests first, a reluctance to accept criticism from outside its own organization, and an inability to accept that community and race relations was anything more than the preserve of social workers.' Thus, as time passed, West Indians saw police officers as 'biased, uncaring, prone to use excessive force and willing to

---

50. Whitfield, *op. cit.* 32.
51. Ramdin, *op. cit.* 43, p.479.

lie on oath to obtain convictions.' On the other hand, police officers found West Indians to be 'truculent, likely to make unwarranted and unfounded complaints, and to be possessed of violent criminal tendencies and low moral standards.'[52] Thus the fermenting of poor relations between the police and the black community in Notting Hill persisted and there were sporadic outbursts of trouble.

52. Whitfield, *op. cit.* 32, pp.141–142.

CHAPTER 8

THE 1976 RIOT [1]

Introduction

What happened on August Bank Holiday Monday in 1976 has been described as 'a full scale battle on the streets of Notting Hill, waged for four solid hours by black youth against the police.'[2] It has also been described as 'a watershed in modern day public order policing'.[3] The serious disorder that occurred, during which 413 police officers were injured, was, up until that time, 'one of the worst outbreaks of public disorder in London since the second world war'[4] and led directly to the acquisition of protective shields by police forces throughout Great Britain.[5] It was the beginning of the end for the traditional police image in dealing with hostile crowds, which had been in existence for nearly 150 years.

Disagreements

The lead up to the 1976 Carnival was marred by accusations and counter-accusations between the police and local council on the one side and the Carnival organizers on the other. After what they saw as the chaos of the previous year, senior police officers suggested that the Carnival was no longer an appropriate event to be held on the streets and attempts were made to get the Carnival Development Committee (CDC), to hold it at an alternative venue such as the White City Stadium, Battersea Park or Stamford

1. Details of the police response to the riot have been taken from the official police report, viz: Metropolitan Police (1976), 'Notting Hill Carnival 1976'. Unpublished; from interviews and correspondence with some of the senior officers involved, and other sources as indicated.
2. Howe, D (1977). *The Road Make to Walk on Carnival Day*, p.11. London: Race Today Collective.
3. Moore, Tony (1986). 'The Carnival Comes of Age'. In *Police Review*, 22 August 1986, p.1729.
4. 'Report of the Commissioner of Police of the Metropolis for the Year 1976'. Her Majesty's Stationery Office, London, 1977, p.10.
5. Protective shields were already being used to respond to civil disorder in Northern Ireland by the military and the Royal Ulster Constabulary.

Bridge, the home of Chelsea Football Club. Not surprisingly, perhaps, the CDC opposed the suggestion, at the same time making a counter-proposal that the area in which the Carnival was held should be extended as a means of relieving congestion in the centre. The CDC then disbanded, only to reform under the same name with different people in the leading roles and all attempts to change to venue of the Carnival came to nothing.[6] Relationships between the carnival organizers and the police were not improved when a photograph of a local chief superintendent, holding a lengthy petition from local residents calling for the Carnival to be banned, was published in the *Kensington News and Post*.

As the date of the Carnival drew near it became apparent that it would be held on the streets of Notting Hill as usual, but the carnival organizers were unable to reach agreement amongst themselves as to how best to reduce the chaos of the previous year; for example, some wanted the bands to follow specified routes but the majority felt they ought to be allowed to wander about at will. This had caused problems in 1975 when two bands going in opposite directions had met in the same street but neither would give way to the other. Finally, at a very late stage, the CDC agreed to a plan, proposed by the police, which would, hopefully, allow the free movement of the various attractions through the area.

Briefly the plan entailed dividing the area into six sectors. The bands would be divided into six groups, each group initially being allocated to a particular sector; each band would spend an hour in their initial sector before moving anti-clockwise into the next sector. In this way it was hoped to avoid the congestion of the previous year. It also meant that the attractions of the Carnival would be spread over a wider area.

Police Arrangements

Deputy Assistant Commissioner Gibson was to be in overall command of the operation, assisted by Commander Charles Jackaman, who would effectively be the ground commander. Each of the six sectors would be commanded by a chief superintendent, assisted by, with one exception a superintendent or

---

6. In an interview with Superintendent Patterson on 14 February 1989.

a chief inspector.[7] The number of serials[8] allocated to each sector depended on its location, its size, the anticipated density of the crowd and the number of bands and processions starting within its boundaries.

Whilst all the serials had a duty to preserve order, some were given the specific task of assisting the bands and processions to move along the agreed routes within the Carnival area; some were to prevent unauthorised street trading; others were to be deployed at places where particular difficulties could be expected, e.g. Ladbroke Grove Underground Station to assist pedestrians, Ladbroke Grove and Great Western Road to assist traffic at junctions, and in the vicinity of Acklam Hall, to preserve order.

Five serials were to be kept in reserve from 12 noon onwards, two based at Notting Hill Police Station, two at Harrow Road Police Station and one at Notting Dale.[9] Ninety-six detective officers, operating in plain clothes in groups of four[10] under the overall command of Detective Superintendent Small, were warned for duty to watch for, and if necessary arrest, the expectant gangs of pick-pockets. Half were to commence duty at 11 a.m., the other half at 4 p.m.

In addition, four units of the Special Patrol Group, under the command of Superintendent Jim Dickinson, were on stand-by in London in the event of trouble at any one of a number of football matches being played that day.[11] They could be deployed to the Carnival on the specific directions of Deputy Assistant Commissioner Gibson.

The main police control room, known as GT, was located about five miles away in the Operations Room at New Scotland Yard but there would be a police control van in Portobello Road just north of Portobello Green for the

---

7. The one exception was Chief Superintendent Perrett in command of potentially the busiest area, Sector A, who had two chief inspectors to assist him.
8. A serial generally consisted of one inspector, two sergeants and 20 constables. If mobile in a police or private coach, it would also include a woman constable as radio-operator.
9. Each of the reserve serials was divided into two units of one sergeant and ten constables; each unit had its own personnel carrier. An inspector generally travelled in the lead carrier.
10. Each group consisted of a detective sergeant and three detective constables.
11. The units were No. 2 Unit, No. 3 Unit, No. 4 Unit and No. 6 Unit. Each normally consisted of an inspector, three sergeants and 28 constables. Transport consisted of three personnel carriers and the inspector normally had a police car, with driver, for his use.

use of the ground commander. In all, nearly 1,600 officers, operating in two shifts, were scheduled to police this event on the Monday.[12]

Sunday 29 August

It was estimated that about 70,000 people attended the Carnival on the first day. Numerous stalls, together with static sound systems, were set up, particularly in Portobello Road, Acklam Road and on Portobello Green. Whilst not keeping to the timetable of events, the agreed plan under which the steel bands moved anti-clockwise from one sector to another, worked fairly well.

However, police fears about crime were realised and a total of 123 offences were alleged to have been committed, generally by gangs of youths operating in groups of 12 or more.[13] One detective constable was attacked and stabbed in All Saints Road as he attempted to arrest a youth who was caught trying to steal a woman's purse. Fortunately, there were a number of uniformed officers in the vicinity who, despite themselves being attacked by a large crowd of youths, went to the detective's assistance and both the original thief and the person who stabbed the officer were arrested. Elsewhere, at Portobello Green, a sergeant, also attempting to make an arrested, received an injury to his arm which subsequently required 30 stitches.

About 50 of the stalls 'licensed' by the Carnival Development Committee and premises such as the Mangrove Restaurant in All Saints Road were illegally selling alcohol. The people running them were warned by the police that they were breaking the law but few heeded the advice. Realising that any attempt to take positive action was likely to precipitate serious disorder, the police, in the main, turned a 'blind-eye' to these activities and the illegal sales continued.[14]

At the end of the first day, 19 people had been arrested, mostly for minor offences, and six police officers had been injured. More significantly, perhaps, 13 members of the public had been injured in separate incidents when groups of predominantly black youths attacked them during the course of stealing

---

12. On the Sunday, the total number of officers available for policing the Carnival was less than 900 in total, operating in two shifts, because, traditionally, it was a quieter day.

13. The total was made up of 28 robberies, 92 thefts from the person and three miscellaneous crimes.

14. Prosecutions were brought against five people as a result of the illegal sale of intoxicating liquor on the Sunday.

property; of these, ten were women. In his report written at the conclusion of the two day festival, Commander Jackaman summed up the situation at the end of the first day as one in which large numbers of people attending the carnival were affable, cheerful, law-abiding and intent only on enjoying the pleasures offered by the occasion. However, he went on to say:

'[T]here were, interspersed amongst them…groups of black youths who were committing serious crimes and were prepared to use violence against the Police to ensure their immunity from the law. This dichotomy of attitudes created an extremely difficult atmosphere in which Police had to work. On the one hand being relieved that the majority of people, if not exactly on their side were not liable to offer physical obstruction towards their presence and on the other never being sure as to whether close at hand, in the dense crowds there might not be a substantial gang of youths whose attitude would at least be uncooperative and in the event of them taking action would be distinctly and violently hostile. Added to this was the fear that the surrounding, up to then happy crowd, might be caught up in the hysteria of the disorder if it should start and join in…'[15]

Nevertheless, the general feeling amongst the senior officers at the end of the first day was that the event had gone fairly well and only minor changes were made to the original plan. It was against this backcloth that the Bank Holiday Monday dawned.

Monday 30 August

By 2 p.m. on Monday 30 August, large crowds had already gathered in the area of Acklam Road, Portobello Green and Cambridge Gardens and additional police resources had been deployed in the area. Whilst the general mood was one of a genuine carnival with most people enjoying the sunshine and music, at least six people had either been robbed or had property stolen from them. From about 3.45 p.m., police officers attempting to arrest people committing or attempting to commit crime, came under attack, and, at about 4 p.m., Commander Jackaman voiced his growing concern at the deteriorating situation to Deputy Assistant Commissioner Gibson who was

---

15. Metropolitan Police, *op. cit.* 1, pp.33–34.

in the Force Operations Room at New Scotland Yard. As a result, Gibson agreed to meet him at Notting Hill Police Station.

Within a relatively short time the situation worsened quite dramatically. Two hundred crimes had been committed,[16] most of them in the area in and around Portobello Green, by groups of black youths numbering as many as 20. Individual policemen witnessing these crimes were generally quite powerless to stop them in the densely packed crowds.

Trouble in Acklam Road

The one occasion on which the police were in a position to intervene, arguably triggered the riot. At about 4.40 p.m., a woman was robbed of her handbag in Acklam Road. When she tried to chase the black youth who had snatched it, some dozen youths surrounded her, and she was punched and kicked. Two policemen, quickly followed by another six, rushed to her aid but were attacked by the crowd. Chief Superintendent Perrett arrived with yet more officers but they too were attacked. As more officers arrived, the youths ran away, forcing a route through the dense crowds. Almost immediately, a barrage of beer cans, stones, rubble and bricks began to rain down on the police officers in an attack, launched not by the youths who had been involved in the original incident, but by others who had decided to join the 'festivities'.[17]

There were between 60 and 70 police officers present, but, without any means of protection, they were powerless to act against the continual barrage of missiles which intensified the longer it went on. Some of the youths were on the overhead motorway from where they were able to rain down

---

16. Two-hundred-and-one to be exact, made up of 25 robberies, 89 thefts from the person, 65 assaults, two attempted robberies and 16 cases of criminal damage.

17. This version of the start of the rioting is at variance with Owusu's description of how it all began. He claimed that 'revellers' had 'moved back into a tight space in front of Acklam Hall' when the police 'formed up around them' and blocked 'all possible exits' before charging into 'the besieged crowd' to arrest pickpockets, hitting out 'indiscriminately' with their truncheons. But 'some of the cornered youths broke through the rain of batons and broke the siege', before regrouping and launching 'an offensive which surprised the police by its effectiveness'. Owusu, Kwesi (1986). 'Notting Hill Carnival: De Road is de Stage de Stage is de Road'. In *Writing Black Britain* 1948–1998: an interdisciplinary anthology (James Procter (ed.)). Manchester: Manchester University Press, 200, p.156.

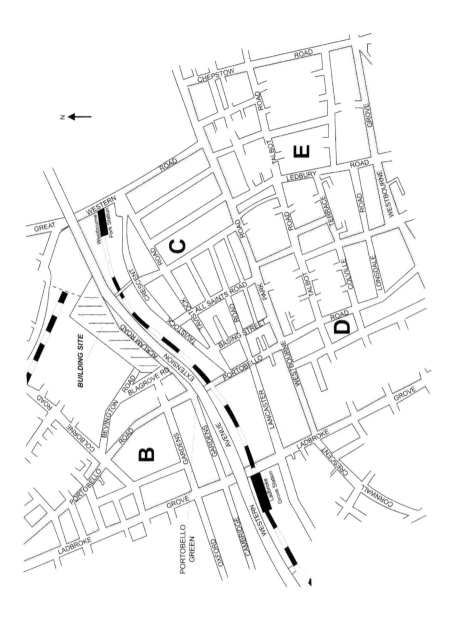

Main area of the 1976 Carnival riot.

Map drawn and © Kate Whittingham.

yet more missiles on the unprotected officers. One witness described the scene as Bedlam:

> 'Stalls were being turned over and the blacks began hurling fruit and tins at the police. Even legs were being torn off stalls and thrown at them. The police were defending themselves with whatever they could lay their hands on.'[18]

The police officers retreated in some disarray eastwards along Acklam Road until they reached a position just past Blagrove Road where a corrugated iron fence afforded them some protection from the missiles.

The missile-throwing youths found an ample supply of ammunition on the huge building site behind the corrugated iron fence, parts of which were soon torn down. One newspaper reporter referred to it as 'a fortress of bricks and rubble manned by rioters.'[19] By this time, many of the officers had equipped themselves with pieces of wood, empty milk crates and dustbin lids to use as shields and, with truncheons drawn, made a number of baton charges in an attempt to disperse the rioters. On each occasion, the police would advance and the crowd, having temporarily run out of missiles, would disperse only to reform once they had re-armed themselves. Caught in the open, the police would be forced to retreat 'amidst a blanket of hurled weapons'[20] until they found cover. Once they had regrouped the same process would be repeated.

The sheer density of the crowd at this point prevented those who did not want to get caught up in the violence from leaving the area immediately. People 'screamed' and attempted to run

> 'for their lives. Many were hit, others trampled on the ground as it became impossible to escape the seething masses — pushed in a see-saw fashion from one end of Acklam Road to the other.'[21]

---

18. Davies, Tom and John Smalldon. 'Gang of 12 Sparked Notting Hill Riot'. *Sunday Telegraph*, 5 September 1976.
19. *Kensington News and Post*, 3 September 1976.
20. *Ibid.*
21. *Ibid.*

The one radio channel in use by the police was swamped with calls for assistance from officers either in trying to contain the disorder or deal with the growing number of criminal attacks by gangs of youths on innocent people. The inadequate communication system meant that it was impossible for senior officers to discuss any strategy to deal with the disorder—and the necessary tactics to implement the strategy—by radio.

A personnel carrier attempting to go along Acklam Road had only gone 40 yards when it was attacked by a large group of youths throwing missiles, including bricks, bottles of mineral water and full beer cans. The wind-screen of the personnel carrier was shattered and it was ordered out of the area. By now it was 5.20 p.m. The disorder was restricted to Acklam Road in the vicinity of Blagrove Road and Bevington Road, the groups of youths involved being either in or around the building site or in the arches underneath the motorway flyover.

The Police Response

Meanwhile Deputy Assistant Commissioner Gibson arranged for all units finishing duty at London football matches and additional units of the Special Patrol Group to be sent to Notting Hill after which he followed Commander Jackaman to the north end of Portobello Road. By now the disorder was spreading and Gibson was forced to abandon his car and, with his staff officer, walk the last 50 yards or so to the police control van. As he came in sight of Acklam Road he saw a 'seething mass' of people and policemen

'and it seemed to be raining bricks on them—the whole lot—the police, the black people and the white people that were there. And they were coming towards me, civilians and policemen alike, with blood streaming down their faces.'[22]

Almost immediately, Gibson was besieged by community representatives. One, Councillor Paul Stevenson, later gave an interview to television reporters in which he said he had asked Gibson to make a 'strategic' withdrawal of police officers from the area as a response to the worsening situation.[23]

22. In an interview the author had with Wilfred Gibson on 22 October 1988.
23. British Broadcasting Corporation. 'Summer of '76'. A 50-minute television programme broadcast on BBC 2 in September 1976.

Gibson refused on the grounds that gangs of youths would be even freer to commit crime and innocent members of the public caught up in the disorder would be in even greater danger.

Eventually, more police officers arrived in Acklam Road and, whilst they engaged the rioters on the building site, a small contingent of police stormed the 'rubble fortress' from the rear, forcing the rioters to flee. The police quickly cordoned off Blagrove Road but it was obvious that the whole area would have to be cleared if the police were to stand any chance of restoring order. At the same time, it was essential to try and stop the disorder spreading.

The principle strategy used by the Metropolitan Police to deal with violent crowds had been built up over a number of years. It consisted of increasing the number of police officers present, containing the disorderly crowd within a controlled area and then dispersing the people through police lines in an orderly fashion. On this occasion, however, the violence in Acklam Road seemed to increase for a while in proportion to the number of police drafted into the area.

At 5.30 p.m., the police attempted a strategy of containment and dispersal. Serials under the command of Chief Superintendent Perrett and Superintendent Dickinson, who had by now arrived with Special Patrol Group units, advanced west along Acklam Road driving both the rioters and the few innocent people still remaining before them towards Portobello Road. At one stage, it was estimated that about 800 youths confronted the police and they continued to bombard the advancing police officers with a hail of missiles, bringing them to a stop. An offer to mediate between the police and the disorderly crowd by an unknown black man was abandoned when he was struck by a missile and forced to retire to safety.

As a result it became an uncontrolled attempt at dispersal and once the youths had been driven back to Portobello Road, they split, moving in three different directions. One group ran towards Cambridge Gardens; a second group turned south down Portobello Road, whilst a third group made its way under the Westway and over an un-policed footbridge across the railway line to Tavistock Crescent. The police succeeded in their initial objective of dispersing the crowd away from the large stock of ammunition in Acklam Road but had effectively made the situation worse. The crowd had now split into smaller groups but each still contained a significant number; others, who had not been involved in the initial incident, joined them as the evening progressed. At least 100 police officers had been injured by this time and many were receiving treatment at first aid posts or had been taken to hospital.

Cordons are Established in Portobello Road

The police in and around Portobello Green now came under increasingly heavy attack from a large group of between 400 and 500 youths from underneath the Westway in Portobello Road. Whilst some started to erect a barricade, using abandoned stalls and similar material, others threw missiles. As well as causing injuries to police officers, innocent members of the public attempting to leave the area were caught up in the onslaught. About 100 police officers formed a cordon, three deep, across Portobello Road just south of the junction with Acklam Road. As they did so, some of the youths ran forward throwing 'bottles, beer cans and other missiles.'[24]

As they had done in Blagrove Road earlier, the officers armed themselves with makeshift shields — dustbin lids, traffic 'no parking' cones and bottle crates; anything which could afford them some protection from the missiles. Suddenly, they charged with truncheons drawn. No order was given; it was purely spontaneous. The charge 'ran out of steam around Lancaster Road and the youths followed it back to the flyover.'[25] Twice more the police charged before establishing a cordon across Portobello Road underneath the Westway. The youths had by now retreated to Tavistock Crescent, putting a fairly large orderly crowd of mainly black people between themselves and the police cordon. From there they continued to throw missiles at the police officers but many landed amongst the orderly crowd, which, again, because of its density, meant that those within it were finding it difficult to the leave the area. Some were injured as a result; many were frightened.

Unaware of what was happening around the northern end of Portobello Road, vehicles were still entering at the Notting Hill Gate end and coming under attack from the missile throwing youths. As a result a police cordon was set up in Portobello Road at the junction with Westbourne Park Road to stop vehicles travelling north, and to prevent pedestrians coming into the troubled area. At about 6.20 p.m., the cordon in Portobello Road was

---

24. *Kensington News and Post*, 3 September 1976.
25. *Ibid.*

bombarded with missiles from a group of about 150 youths who approached southwards down Portobello Road from the direction of Tavistock Crescent. During the next 30 minutes, the officers making up the cordon made a series of baton charges, clearing the crowd from Portobello Road and creating a sterile area by retaining the original cordon just north of Westbourne Park Road and closing off the two entrances to Lancaster Road and the one entrance to Tavistock Road.

Trouble Erupts in Ladbroke Grove
In the meantime, a group of youths launched a ferocious attack on about 50 police officers grouped in Ladbroke Grove at the junction with Oxford Gardens. Urged on by bystanders, the youths threw 'bricks, cans, bottles and stones' as the police searched for 'dustbin lids, yellow marker cones, empty milk-crates—anything they could lay their hands on to act as shields.'[26] Eventually, the police forced the youths to move south towards Ladbroke Grove Underground Station.

At about this time, a car bringing Chief Superintendent Collie[27] arrived to find between 600 and 800 people, at the underground station all wanting to leave the area by train. But some of the trains had already been stoned and drivers were refusing to stop and pick-up passengers; the station staff had therefore closed the station. After pleas from the police over a loud hailer most of the crowd dispersed on foot. But those intent on disorder were increasing rapidly. Vehicles travelling north along Ladbroke Grove ran the gauntlet of an army of missile throwers on either side of the road whilst others attacked them from the roof of a small block of flats.

Due to the spread of disorder, Deputy Assistant Commissioner Gibson left the area at about 7 p.m. to return to the main Police Control Room at New Scotland Yard from where he considered he was better able to exercise

---

26. *Kensington News and Post*, 3 September 1976.
27. Each district in the Metropolitan Police was required to have a senior officer on duty from four p.m. to 12 midnight. Chief Superintendent Collie was the late senior duty officer for 'B' District which included Chelsea, Kensington and Notting Hill Divisions. According to an interview the author had with Chief Superintendent Patterson, Collie had come to the scene on his own initiative to have a look.

effective command and control.[28] Before leaving he gave instructions that each chief superintendent was to have command of five serials, approximately 115 men including supervisors, to ensure that available manpower was used effectively.

Disorder Increases in Ladbroke Grove

Meanwhile, the British Transport Police officers on duty at Ladbroke Grove Underground Station had requested assistance from their own Force Control Room. At 7.10 p.m., two British Transport police officers drove north along Ladbroke Grove in a marked police car, but seeing the road was completely blocked by the crowd as they approached, turned left into Cornwell Crescent where they were confronted by another crowd of about 150 youths. The crowd quickly surrounded the car, making it impossible for the driver to go forward or reverse, and attacked it from all sides; fortunately, the two officers managed to escape into a nearby house leaving the crowd to turn the police car on its side and set fire to it.

On seeing the smoke from the fire, Chief Superintendent Perrett,[29] who had by this time had reached Ladbroke Grove by way of Cambridge Gardens, led about 100 men south, driving the crowd before them towards Cornwall Crescent. Meanwhile, a group of youths

'broke into a derelict house and started to fling bricks out into the street. Others broke them in half to use as ammunition.'[30]

Under heavy attack from the missile throwing youths, the police made a number of baton charges to disperse them. Eventually they reached the burning police car. To the east, a barricade, consisting of two motor cars,

---

28. Gibson told the author that his return to the main control room coincided with information being received that youths from the Carnival area had gone to Brixton to encourage others to come to Notting Hill. Immediately on receipt of this information, traffic units were deployed to the three main bridges over the River Thames to intercept and turn back any people trying to reach the Carnival area.

29. Details of the events in Ladbroke Grove were described to the author in an interview with Chief Superintendent Perrett on 23 January 1989.

30. *Kensington News and Post*, 3 September 1976.

tables and sundry items of rubbish had been erected in Westbourne Park Road about 50 yards from the junction with Ladbroke Grove.

Perrett quickly realised he had three main priorities at this time:

(a) To protect the burning police car and prevent it from becoming a symbol of the crowd's success. At the same time he wanted to rescue the two police officers from the house in which they had taken refuge;

(b) To prevent the crowd from going south down Ladbroke Grove towards the police station, the smart residential property and the shops in Holland Park Avenue; and

(c) To remove the barricade in Westbourne Park Road and disperse the crowd of missile-throwing youths from behind it, who were, at this time, beginning to inflict injuries on the largely unprotected officers.

But he was now presented with another problem, the youths who had climbed onto the roof of a two-storey block of flats on the south-east corner of the junction and were bombarding everything that moved with cans, bricks and small pieces of concrete.

Having dispersed the crowd from around the burning police car, Perrett sent a squad of 30 officers, under the command of an inspector, to remove the youths from the roof of the flats. This was no easy task without protective equipment. It was eventually achieved but only after a number of injuries had been inflicted on both sides during hand-to-hand fighting.

Regaining Control in Ladbroke Grove

Perrett then led a series of baton charges along Westbourne Park Road towards the barricade. At one stage, one of the motor cars in the barricade was pushed driverless towards the advancing police officers. Fortunately, it mounted the footway and crashed into some garden railings before it was able to do any serious damage. As had occurred earlier in Acklam Road, each police charge was greeted by a hail of missiles from the rioters. When the crowd ran out of missiles they would disperse only to reform and attack the police again once they had found further stocks of ammunition. The police, caught out in the open without adequate protection, would be forced to retreat to their original position because it afforded them better cover.

Eventually the crowd in Westbourne Park Road was dispersed and Perrett was able to turn his attention to the crowd in Ladbroke Grove. For the next hour or so, police mounted a series of baton charges in attempts to disperse the crowd. It was 8 p.m. before the police managed to disperse them altogether. During the three hour period between 5 p.m. and 8 p.m., over 70 police officers were injured.

The Area to the East of Portobello Road

Numerous calls for assistance from the area to the east of Portobello Road were now flooding into the Police Operations Room but it was unable to respond for two reasons. Firstly, because the system of recording where units were located had completely broken down, it was unable to differentiate between those that had already been deployed and those that were uncommitted; secondly, the sheer volume of traffic over the communication system still prevented any co-ordinated plan being developed or articulated.

Throughout the whole of this period, Chief Superintendent Hunt, who was in charge of an area well to the east of Portobello Road, centred on Powis Square, had had little to do. However, when he heard a radio message suggesting that there was serious disorder outside Westbourne Park Underground Station, in Great Western Road, he was able to converge on the location with four serials in two 40 seater private-hire coaches.[31] A large number of youths were rampaging about, banging on car roofs and generally creating mayhem when the police arrived but the sight of some 80 officers leaping from the two coaches was sufficient to restore calm. Although some missiles were thrown, most of the youths dispersed rapidly, many of them running through side streets, towards All Saints Road.

Following this, he was directed take his men to the junction of Westbourne Road and Portobello Road but en route they were attacked by a mob throwing missiles, shattering windows in each of the coaches forcing the vehicles

---

31. Details of the dispersal of the crowd from Westbourne Park Road and All Saints Road were described to the author during an interview with Chief Superintendent Hunt on 16 February 1989.

to come to a standstill; some of the police officers leapt off the coaches to chase the missile throwers who quickly disappeared.

Having regrouped his resources, Chief Superintendent Hunt moved westwards again, but they had only travelled a short distance when they came under attack for a second time. On this occasion, he ordered all officers off the two coaches and lined them up on both sides of the vehicles in an effort to prevent further attack, and moved forward again.[32]

By now many of the youths who had been causing trouble earlier in Acklam Road and Ladbroke Grove had made their way towards All Saints Road. Consequently, as Hunt's contingent neared the mouth of All Saints Road, they were bombarded with missiles for a third time. At the same time, a radio message reported that the Co-operative store on the corner of All Saints Road and Westbourne Park Road was being ransacked.

In fact, the steel netting covering the windows had been ripped down and all the windows had been smashed. The inside of the shop 'had been torn out and brushed aside like paper.' Some people in the large crowd which gathered 'on the glass littered pavement' entered the shop and threw

> 'bottles of wine, whisky, gin and vodka and cans of beer into the hands of the crowd outside. Some missed their mark and shattered onto the pavement, adding to the litter of glass which extended right across the road.'[33]

Ordering his officers to draw their truncheons, Hunt gave instructions for the main body of police to charge towards the crowd but, on this occasion, he told them not to pursue individuals randomly but to stick together and to only follow them about 15 yards into the side streets before regrouping. The crowd fled in all directions as the police charged but many still had time to throw missiles. A number of people were arrested and some police officers were injured. The extent of these two actions effectively meant that Hunt had lost about one-third of his men so he formed a loose cordon across the junction of Westbourne Park Road and All Saints Road. Many of his officers had by now acquired dustbin lids, 'supermarket baskets, plastic

---

32. In the interview with the author on 16 February 1989, former Superintendent Hunt likened it unto a wagon train being escorted through hostile territory in an old western movie.

33. *Kensington News and Post*, 3 September 1976.

milk crates, saucepan lids, wooden box-crate lids and trays'[34] with which to protect themselves against further missile attack.

Although the area in the vicinity of Westbourne Park Road at the junction of All Saints Road was clear. There was now a large disorderly group between Hunt's position and the positions held by Chief Superintendents Dovey and Starns in Portobello Road. The original plan to clear the area was to enlarge the sterile area from Portobello Road, with the police moving outwards but the presence of Hunt and his men at the entrance to All Saints Road meant that the large group of youths was trapped between the two bodies of police. Mindful, no doubt, of the recommendations made by Lord Scarman two years earlier that the police should, wherever possible, ensure that 'a crowd has sufficient means of moving away before taking action to disperse or disrupt it',[35] Commander Jackaman instructed Hunt to bring his men to the junction of Portobello Road and Westbourne Park Road where he was joined by Chief Superintendent Cree.

By now the crowd to the south of the Westway but to the east of Portobello Road was increasing. Missiles were thrown at any police officers on foot or police vehicles that happened to come within sight but the missile throwing did not have the same ferocity as had been the case in Acklam Road and Ladbroke Grove. Instead the rioters turned to another activity, the looting of shops.

The Area is Cleared

Looting continued whilst the police planned their re-deployment from the sterile area in Portobello Road. The plan was for Collie, with about 115 men, to advance eastwards along Tavistock Road and then into All Saints Road whilst Hunt, supported by Cree, with approximately 140 men between them, were to advance eastwards along Westbourne Park Road, meeting Collie's contingent in All Saints Road.

Hunt set off with his men but Collie's contingent was pinned down by missile throwing youths in Tavistock Crescent. However, the aggressiveness of Hunt's advance was such that the missile throwers at the mouth of All

---

34. *Ibid.*
35. Scarman, Rt. Hon. The Lord (1975). 'The Red Lion Square Disorders of 15 June 1974: Report of an Inquiry' (Cmnd 5919). London: Her Majesty's Stationery Office, p.40.

Saints Road dispersed, many of them mingling with an orderly crowd of between 500 and 600 assembled around an open-air static-sound system, still pumping out reggae, in Lancaster Road. After being approached by Cree, the disc jockey appealed to the crowd to behave, turned up the music and everyone joined in the dancing that followed. Meanwhile, Collie had succeeded in reaching the northern end of All Saints Road. With police keeping a watchful eye, dancing continued until 10 p.m.

There were a number of isolated incidents of disorder in the carnival area after this; some were deliberately engineered by groups of youths who threw missiles at both officers on foot and vehicles but they quickly dispersed when confronted by police contingents of reasonable numbers.

The Final Toll

During the period of serious disorder, i.e. between 4.45 p.m. and midnight, at least 89 people were robbed and a further 154 had property stolen from them. The total number of crimes reported to the police during the two days of the Carnival, including assaults on police officers, was in excess of 1,000. The degree of violence used in the robberies was, in some cases, considerable. One woman had a finger broken as her assailants ripped the rings from her hand, another woman in a car was forced to stop by a crowd of youths who smashed the windows, dragged her out of the vehicle and stole her handbag whilst in another case ten youths kicked two girls to the ground and stole £50 from them.

In all 84 people were arrested but only 20 of these were for what could be genuinely classified as crimes. Well over 50 were connected directly with the disorder, being arrested for such offences as possessing offensive weapons — in the majority of cases these were bricks and other missiles — using threatening behaviour and assaulting the police. The total number of police officers injured was 413 which included seven officers from the British Transport Police and five civilian drivers employed by the police.[36] At least 188

---

36. Whilst this figure was unacceptably high it should be put into perspective. The majority of these injuries were cuts, sprains and bruises of the type many officers throughout the country receive during the normal course of their duties, e.g. arresting disorderly drunks on a Friday or Saturday night.

members of the public were either conveyed to hospital or treated for injuries at First Aid Posts within the Carnival area.[37]

---

37. Again, many of the injuries were of a minor nature.

CHAPTER 9

WORSENING RELATIONS

Analysis of the 1976 Carnival

Black people were generally scathing in their criticism of the police. Chairman of the Carnival Development Committee, Selwyn Baptiste 'put the blame firmly on the shoulders of the police', alleging that on the Monday, in particular, 'there had been over-policing of the Carnival floats and the processions.'[1] Gutzmore described how black youth fought 'a defensive battle' against the police; later he referred to it as 'a pitched battle'.[2] The Race Today Collective Association, led by Darcus Howe, described how 'several hundred young blacks inflicted a military defeat on a military organization' suggesting that 'the police came prepared for confrontation and got it.'[3] Owuso wrote in a similar vein some time later. Pointing out that the youths 'knew the terrain intimately' and using 'bricks from nearby building sites, cans and bottles', for 'four hours, these untrained youths waged a guerrilla battle with the police on the streets of Notting Hill, and won'. Calling the youths who took part 'young warriors,' he pointed out that they had a notable history being the descendants of those who had opposed the suppression of the 'drum dance' in Trinidad in the 1880s.[4] Subsequently, Kettle and Hodge, looking back at police/black relations in the aftermath of the subsequent 1980 St Paul's riot in Bristol, also blamed the police, claiming that, given a force of 1,600 police officers were deployed, 'confrontation was inevitable.'[5]

1. *Kensington News and Post*, 3 September 1976.
2. Gutzmore, Cecil (1983). 'Capital, "Black Youth" and Crime'. In *Race and Class*, XXV, 2, pp.21 and 25.
3. *Race Today*, Vol. 8, No. 9, September 1976, p.171.
4. Owusu, Kwesi (2000). 'Notting Hill Carnival: "De Road is de Stage de Stage is de Road"'. In *Writing Black Britain* 1948–1998 (James Proctor (ed.)). Manchester: Manchester University Press, p.157.
5. Kettle, Martin andLucy Hodge (1982). Uprising! *The Police, the People and the Riots in Britain's Cities*. London: Pan Books, p.79.

From some quarters there were calls for the Home Secretary to set up a judicial inquiry similar to the one held two years previously by Lord Scarman into the disorders in Red Lion Square.[6] In supporting these calls *The Times* asked:

'why, even though there has been tension for some while between the black community and the police in that part of London, there was an explosion at this particular time. Was it because there were too many police around to accord with the festive spirit of the Caribbean Carnival?'[7]

In the event, no such inquiry followed. Given the 'limited scale of the disorder', the Home Secretary, then Roy Jenkins, was probably correct. However, in looking back on what happened in the 1980s, Timothy Brain suggested, given the perilous state of police/ethnic relations, either Mark or Jenkins or their successors—both were due to leave office—could have instigated a review of the way that such areas were being policed in London, and it may have been a missed opportunity.[8]

It is estimated that there were about 150,000 revellers on the streets on the Monday. By 4 p.m., the late shift having joined the early shift, there were nearly 1,600 police officers in the area. But, as the *Sunday Times* pointed out, this was 'fewer than are on duty to control only 100,000 fans in the relative order of a Wembley Cup Final.'[9] And, in case the impression was given that the whole of the Carnival area was affected by rioting, most of the bands were blissfully unaware of the disorder. Acklam Road was not on any of the band's routes and by the time the trouble erupted in Ladbroke Grove, those bands due to pass through had already done so.

Nevertheless, things did go horribly wrong; the reasons for this were many and varied. Commissioner Sir Robert Mark 'blamed a hard core of about 800 young black hooligans who had deliberately attended the Caribbean

---

6. Scarman, Rt. Hon. The Lord (1975). 'The Red Lion Square Disorders of 15 June 1974'. Cmnd 5915. London: Her Majesty's Stationery Office.
7. *The Times*, 1 September 1976.
8. Brain, Timothy (2010). *A History of Policing in England and Wales from 1974: A Turbulent Journey*. Oxford: Oxford University Press, p.33.
9. Blundy, David *et al* (1976). 'Carnival Riot: The Sunday Times Inquiry'. *Sunday Times*, 5 September 1976.

Carnival to mug and rob, secure in the knowledge that other 'revellers' would go to their aid if police intervened.'[10]

The organizers showed an irresponsibility bordering on negligence in their failure to make proper arrangements for an event which was fast becoming the biggest street festival in Europe. Despite repeated requests by the police, the organizers failed to provide any stewards to assist in making the carnival self-regulating,[11] and they refused to accept that the event was likely to attract people whose sole purpose was to steal even though it 'already had a bad history of poor organization and crime, in the form of robbery and theft.'[12]

Black writer, Everton A Price, suggested that the police, in increasing their numbers, 'seemed well-informed, for a grotesque battle ensued in the streets of Notting Hill.'[13] In reality, the police were totally unprepared for a confrontation. Once the disorder started, they had only two options, either:

(a) Withdraw from the area; or
(b) Attempt to re-establish control.

The first option was rejected by Deputy Assistant Commissioner Gibson for the reasons stated in the previous chapter. Talking some years after the event, he described how the level of violence forced the police to 'change gear to a different form of policing' actually while the disorder 'was happening'. He explained further that, prior to August 1976, the Metropolitan Police had used a system with disorderly crowds of

'containing and dispersing as gradually and smoothly as you could, picking out the ringleaders.... Suddenly it no longer worked. We had to improvise a solution to the problem literally on the day when it happened. We had all sorts of contingency

---

10. *Daily Telegraph*, 1 September 1976.
11. At a meeting with the police four months before the Carnival, the organizers had promised to recruit 300 stewards.
12. Stead, P. J. (1985) *The Police of Britain*. Basingstoke: Macmillan.
13. Pryce, Everton (1985). 'The Notting Hill Gate Carnival—Black Politics, Resistance and Leadership 1976–1978'. *Caribbean Quarterly* 31:2: 9 June, p.38.

plans for dealing with any ordinary disorder that we could have anticipated but we suddenly found ourselves batting in a totally different league.'[14]

The *Sunday Times*, in comparing the situation with events in Northern Ireland at that time, described it as a routine disturbance which the Royal Ulster Constabulary and the British Army would have dealt with quite easily.[15] But police forces on the mainland lacked the standard riot equipment. Indeed, it was as a direct consequence of this riot that police forces began to acquire the long protective shields.[16] They also 'lacked practical experience' of policing riots on this scale, believing that 'the very presence of more police would quell it.'[17] Training in crowd control techniques was minimal, confined in the main to forming cordons, pushing against a crowd and forming wedges to divide it up before dispersing it. None worked against crowds of youths who were fit and moved quickly from one area to another and these mobile running groups out-manoeuvred the police time-and-again. Even when the police mounted a baton charge it was invariably a ragged affair, running out of steam after a short distance or coming to a halt due to the ferocity of the missile attack directed at them, rather than coming to a controlled stop having achieved its objective. But this was not surprising. Although it was a tactic the police had used spasmodically for over 140 years, it was not one in which they had undergone any training.[18]

A further problem was the police's totally inadequate system of communication for an event of this kind. As Deputy Assistant Commissioner Gibson pointed out, 'Initially the chaos was so great that the commanders couldn't even hear their own instructions.'[19] Consequently, they were forced

---

14. In an interview with former Deputy Assistant Commissioner Wilf Gibson on 22 October 1988.

15. The Royal Ulster Constabulary, supported by the British Army, had been involved in a number of violent confrontations with the local population since 1969. Many books have been written about the troubles.

16. At a meeting with the deputy commissioner of the Metropolitan Police after the Carnival, chief superintendents made it clear that police officers should never again be expected to face such a barrage of missiles without protective shields.

17. Blundy, *op. cit.* 9.

18. Gibson, *op. cit.* 14, told the author that he had never before ordered a baton (truncheon) charge.

19. Interview with Gibson, *op. cit.* 14.

to withdraw from the front line to hear messages being passed to them. Every police officer of the rank of inspector and above had a personal radio; in some cases sergeants were issued with one as well.[20] As the disorder increased there were just too many officers on foot trying to use the one radio channel available for this event. This overload on the communication system meant that although the overall Commander, Gibson, and the ground commander, Jackaman, knew, in general terms, what the situation was they were unable to play a significant role in the formulation of any kind of strategy; neither were they able to advise on the tactics to be used.

In assessing his own role subsequently, Gibson readily admitted that, as the overall commander, the ideal place for him to have been when the disorder broke out was in the Force Operations Room. Despite the inadequate communication system he would have had a better overall view of the situation. But he had responded to fears expressed by the senior officer on the ground, Commander Jackaman, immediately prior to the disorder and was at Notting Hill Police Station when it broke out. At this point, he had two alternatives, either:

(a) To go to the scene and liaise with Jackaman; or
(b) Return to the Force Control Room about three miles away.

He chose the former and it wasn't until three hours later that he felt able to stand back:

'from what I had been doing—which I shouldn't possibly have been doing in the first place—which was really acting as a commander on the ground, because there was no way I could go away once I got there. It was so violent that it was obviously the only place I could be. I felt that if baton charges were going to be ordered I was the man to do it...'[21]

---

20. Those who had access to a police vehicle equipped with radio had access to a second channel but this tended to be used for administrative matters, such as booking on and off, refreshment times, etc. In any event, very few policemen were deployed in vehicles within the Carnival area because it was impossible to drive through the densely packed crowds.
21. *Ibid.*

With the exception of some of the earlier problems, where those from whom property had been stolen had been assaulted, most of the violence was directed against the police. But, as *The Times* pointed out:

> 'Police have a double responsibility on an occasion of this kind; to avoid provocation by too ostentatious a presence but also to maintain general order and protect innocent people from molestation on the streets. It would be quite wrong to criticise the police for seeking to perform their second task, but a balance does have to be struck'[22]

The question is, did the police get the balance right on this occasion? In deploying a somewhat larger body of police, when compared with the previous year, the aim was to allow people to move freely and safely through and within the area, and to prevent crime. But, as a leader in *The Observer* pointed, whilst 'the press photographs of a heap of empty stolen purses at Notting Hill Police Station were intended to illustrate the scale of pick-pocketing and mugging the police had to deal with' what they actually showed was 'how unsuccessful the massive presence of uniformed policemen was in averting crime.'[23] Also, whilst it was clear that they were apprehensive about the possibility of disorder, the police failed to anticipate the level of violence and had no real plan for dealing with it once it occurred. It could be argued therefore that they failed to live up to their responsibilities in all respects. Waddington subsequently described how 'the scale of the assault upon the police ... showed the police to be impotent in their primary responsibility of maintaining "the peace".'[24]

It was, without doubt, a turning point in public order policing. Up until that time, the police escalated their tactics only in response to the change in public attitudes towards the increasing violence of any crowd. From then on, it would be different. Slowly the Police Service forced the Home Office into approving the acquisition of new equipment. Training in the skills necessary to deal with these increasingly violent confrontations soon followed. Within ten years the British Police had become indistinguishable, in their

---

22. *The Times*, 1 September 1976.
23. *The Observer*, 5 September 1976.
24. Waddington, P. A. J. (1991). *The Strong Arm of the Law*. Oxford: Clarenden Press, p.22.

dress, in responding to serious disorder, from many of their counterparts in Europe and elsewhere.

But, leaving the rioting to one side for a moment and looking to the future, an *Observer* leader suggested Britain was 'failing to solve the problems created by large immigrant populations in the inner-cities' and warned that 'this amalgam of the crisis over employment, education and housing, could easily swell into a racial explosion of the kind, though not on the scale, that the USA suffered during the sixties.'[25] Four years later, Bristol exploded; the following year it was the turn of London, Manchester and Liverpool.

Trials of Those Arrested

Most of those arrested were tried summarily at magistrates' courts. Eighteen, however, were sent for trial charged with more serious offences. The trial, before a jury made up of seven white people and five black people, was finally concluded in August 1977. The jury took 170 hours to reach its verdict on a total of 51 charges. In only eight cases did they return guilty verdicts; in 28 cases they were unable to agree a verdict and in the remaining 15 cases they found the defendants not guilty. Two years previously, Sir Robert Mark was critical of the way the judicial system had dealt with those arrested during the Red Lion Square disorders of June 1974.[26] In his autobiography, which was published in 1978, he returned to this theme, describing how, in such cases,

> 'the prosecution suffers every kind of handicap. The difficulty in gathering evidence, the delay in proceedings, the fact that only a small number of mass offenders can be caught and charged, the scope for the defence lawyers to accuse the police of racial or political prejudice, even before a competent judge, as in the Notting Hill trial, the case is almost hopeless from the start. The inevitable failure then opens the way to a spate of retaliatory allegations against the police.'[27]

---

25. *The Observer*, 5 September 1976. Between 1963 and 1967 there was major disorder in a large numbers of cities and towns in the USA, arising primarily between African-Americans and the police. See Kerner, Otto (Chairman)(1968). *Report of the National Advisory Commission on Civil Disorders*. New York: Bantam.
26. Mark, Sir Robert (1978). *In the Office of Constable*. London: Collins, pp.167–169.
27. *Ibid*, p.223.

He claimed that the system of justice in England was 'not fitted to deal with political or racial violence on a large scale' and suggested that,

'the police wind up bewildered and resentful. They are faced from time to time with a deliberate breakdown of law and order and can do little about it unless they take the law into their own hands which might win the immediate battle but involve them in a war they must inevitably lose.'[28]

This was to happen again in various parts of England in the 1980s and most notably in Notting Hill in 1982.[29]

Effects on the Organization of future Carnivals

In the aftermath of the 1976 Carnival a 'serious rift in Carnival leadership' occurred which led to the existence of two rival organizing committees, the Carnival Development Committee (CDC) and the Carnival Arts Committee (CAC) for the 1977 Carnival. In an open letter to the Carnival Development Committee, the Race Today Collective, led by Darcus Howe from its headquarters in Brixton, accused that committee of abdicating its responsibilities to the black community and called on it to report 'to a general meeting of those who had a direct interest in the carnival.'[30] The letter went on to suggest that the meeting should 'elect a committee which will be responsible for organizing next year's Carnival.'[31] With mounting criticism also from other sections within the black community, Selwyn Baptiste broke away from the existing CDC, taking the name with him, and, interestingly, together with Darcus Howe and others set up the CDC 1977 with its headquarters in the Mangrove. Those left behind, the majority, waited until January 1977 to see if such a meeting would take place, before renaming themselves the CAC.

There was considerable antagonism between the two groups over the next few years which did little to enhance the prospect of the Carnival becoming a well-organized event. In assessing the future of the Carnival at its

---

28. *Ibid*, pp.223–224.

29. See *Chapter 12*.

30. This included 'mas men and women, steelbands men and women, stall holders, local businessmen and women, sounds men and women and interested individuals.' *Race Today*, September 1976, pp.178–179. Mas is a Caribbean short form of masquerade.

31. *Ibid*.

40th anniversary in 2004, Michael La Rose, who had been vice-chairman of the CDC, summed up the late-1970s as being a period when there was 'civil war in the Carnival movement'.[32] According to Cohen 'many issues were involved—financial, personal, island-of-origin loyalties, neighbourhood—but by far the most basic was whether Carnival was essentially a political or a cultural movement to be promoted as a tourist attraction.'[33]

The CAC combined both streams. Louise Chase, the first chair, supported by at least four others on the new committee, argued that the Carnival 'should be used as a political lever to press for reforms and concessions'. The remaining members of the committee said it was a cultural event which held 'immense economic possibilities for West Indians' in the sale of a variety of products associated with it.[34] The CDC 1977, on the other hand, saw the Carnival as 'essentially an artistic, creative event'. It was therefore 'first and foremost…a cultural event' and if it became 'politicised', its 'nature' would 'change' to the extent that the masses would 'cease to participate, leaving…only political activists who would inevitably transform it into a political demonstration.'[35]

Raid on The Mangrove

The Innes Report suggested that, following the violence at the 1976 Notting Hill Carnival, 'the Mangrove re-emerged as a shelter for the disaffected and whilst Police were trying to re-establish the status-quo, the criminal fraternity took advantage of the situation' as a result of which 'drug-dealing increased.'[36]

Consequently, in July 1977, a substantial raid was made on the Mangrove by some 60 police officers, in possession of a warrant, issued under the Misuse of Drugs Act 1971. A number of people, including Frank Crichlow, were arrested. Crichlow was subsequently indicted for permitting the premises

---

32. La Rose, Michael (2004). 'Forty Years of the Notting Hill Carnival: An Assessment of the History and the Future'. Typescript (pages not numbered). Copy in the possession of the author.
33. Cohen, Abner (1980). 'Drama and Politics in the Development of a London Carnival'. In *MAN* 15, p.81.
34. *Ibid.*
35. *Ibid*, p.82: see also Pryce, *op. cit.* 13, pp.40–42.
36. Innes, Commander; Chief Superintendent Whitfield and Chief Inspector Aitchison (1983). 'All Saints Road, London, W11: A Definitive Document'. London: Metropolitan Police (typescript), p.13, para. 5.26.

to be used for the smoking of cannabis and for allowing the premises to be used with intent to supply cannabis. Five others were also indicted—Roy Hemmings, Lee Webber and Ashford Longdon, for possessing cannabis with intent to supply and for simple possession; Norman Morris and Claudius Francis merely for the latter. The case—the Trial of the Mangrove Six as it became known—opened at Knightsbridge Crown Court, before Judge Stephen Tumin, nearly two years later, on 17 May 1979 in a blaze of publicity; it lasted 44 days. The prosecution's evidence was riddled with inconsistencies, added to which £560 found on Hemmings at the time of his arrest had disappeared whilst being held by the police as an exhibit. Defending barristers claimed that the drugs had been planted on their clients. Indeed, at the insistence of his counsel, a packet of drugs alleged to have been thrown away by Webber was sent for fingerprinting whilst the trial was in progress, but the only prints found on the packet were those of the detective sergeant who had allegedly recovered them.

The defence called some prominent witnesses, including local Member of Parliament, Sir Brandon Rhys-Williams, who, under cross-examination, denied suggestions made by some senior police officers earlier in the trial that he had told them 'that drugs and illegal liquor' were to be found at the Mangrove Restaurant. Another defence witness, Richard Wells, who had been the police community liaison officer from October 1973 to March 1977,[37] agreed under cross-examination that there had been 'a real tension between some parts of the black community and some local police.'

During the trial, it had been suggested that, ever since 1971, the police had had looked upon the Mangrove as being one nil up and the raid in 1977, described as a vendetta during the hearings, had been an attempt to even the score. When Wells was specifically asked whether, because of the acquittal of the Mangrove Nine in 1971, the police held the view that the West Indian Community was one up, he answered, 'Yes, I think some police thought that.'

In his summing up, Judge Tumin, pointed out that 'much of the police evidence was contradictory,' but suggested that this might have indicated

37. Richard Wells was a chief inspector when he was the police community relations officer. He eventually rose to the rank of deputy assistant commissioner in the Metropolitan Police before being appointed as chief constable of the South Yorkshire Police soon after the Hillsborough Stadium disaster in 1989.

'sloppiness and incompetence, rather than dishonesty or conspiratorial wick-edness.' It took the jury little more than two hours to unanimously find Crichlow and Webber not guilty. However, it took them a further six hours to find Hemmings and Langdon not guilty of possessing cannabis with intent to supply but both were guilty of simple possession and each was fined £50; Francis was also found guilty of possession and fined £25. At the conclusion of the trial, Sir Brandon Rhys-Williams, said, 'I hope that relations between the police and ethnic minorities in the borough will improve.'[38]

Lead-up to the 1977 Carnival

In the meantime, the lead-up to the 1977 Carnival was marred by serious outbreaks of disorder at two demonstrations involving the National Front, firstly at Ladywell in Birmingham and then at Lewisham in south London. In both cases it appeared the police were protecting the members of a far right-wing organization, the membership of which expressed views abhor-rent to the black communities, against left-wing demonstrators, many of whom threw missiles. In both cases officers, with the new shields acquired after the 1976 Carnival, were deployed. At Lewisham, a number of officers had received head and facial injuries from bricks, glass and ammonia spray and, consequently, there were calls for the police to have available to them, the NATO-style helmets, with visors, for the Carnival instead of the rein-forced traditional helmet.[39]

The police did hold 'constructive' talks with the CAC in an attempt to ensure a 'positive and peaceful Carnival'. However, CDC 1977 declined to attend the meeting, because, it was claimed it would be 'a waste of time'.[40] The police announced that they would keep a low profile but, at the same time, made it clear that they would be prepared to deal with any disturbances should they arise'.[41] Arrangements included the deployment of over 6,000 officers over the two days, clearing the streets of anything that could be used as missiles and ensuring building sites were securely protected to prevent

---

38. The story of the trial has been compiled from the various weekly reports in the *Kensington News and Post*, commencing on 18 May 1979 and concluding on 29 June 1979.
39. *Evening Standard*, 24 August 1977; *Evening News*, 24 August 1977; *Daily Telegraph*, 25 August 1977.
40. *Daily Telegraph*, 23 August 1977.
41. *Evening Standard*, 23 August 1977.

potential rioters from accessing ammunition. They also secured several covert observation posts overlooking areas where crime was prevalent in 1976, from which officers would provide feedback information on crimes being committed and, hopefully, direct officers to arrest the culprits.

Arrangements were also made for extra staff to be on duty at St Mary's Hospital, Paddington, St Charles Hospital, Ladbroke Grove, Hammersmith Hospital and at the Western Ophthalmic Hospital, where several police officers and civilians with eye injuries had been treated in 1976.[42] St Johns Ambulance Brigade provided five 'field hospitals' with its staff moving around the Carnival route. Lawyers were on stand-by at the North Kensington Law Centre, the Grassroots office and the Black People's Information Centre to give instant advice to those arrested. Many shops and public houses in the area boarded up their windows.[43]

Not surprisingly, given what had occurred in 1976, there was an expectation of disorder. On the Sunday 'pickpockets were active and, in the evening, groups of black youths ran through the crowds stealing.' As a result 'a total of 165 crimes were reported and 20 members of the public were taken to hospital suffering from injuries'[44] but there was no disorder. However, the prophecy of violence was fulfilled on the Monday. The proceedings began relatively peacefully with the police presence being kept to a minimum. But by 6 p.m., 'roving groups of black youths' were committing assaults, robberies and thefts to such an extent that 'large numbers of police had to be deployed.' In an article in *Race Today*, which was edited by the chair of the CDC, Darcus Howe, two black reporters described the activities of some of those who were committing such crimes and how black stewards, provided by the CAC, attempted to deal with them. They claimed that 'at first there was support' for the stewards but this quickly diminished as they increased in numbers and began beating people 'wildly and viciously' with the sticks they were carrying.[45] However, in a response which showed the gulf between the CDC and the CAC, black writer, Cecil Gutzmore, after accusing the CDC

---

42. *Daily Telegraph*, 27 August 1977.

43. *The Sunday Times*, 28 August.

44. McNee, Sir David (1979). 'Report of the Commissioner of Police for the Metropolis for 1978'. Cmnd 7580. London: Her Majesty's Stationery Office, p.24.

45. *Race Today*, September/October 1977, p.130.

of providing no stewards, defended the role of the CAC stewards, describing how, when they tried to intervene when pickpocketing was occurring, they were faced with 'ruthless young black men' who 'pulled knives' and it was only then that they 'went in with the sticks.'[46]

Later, as they attempted to close down the static sound systems at around 8 p.m., the stewards were attacked by some of the crowd throwing missiles. When the police intervened, the attack switched to them. Shield serials were deployed and the police 'made several charges, some with truncheons drawn' eventually succeeding 'in splitting the crowd into smaller groups and dispersing them.' The statistics for the two days make interesting reading. A total of 945 crimes were reported to the police, of which 86 per cent were robbery, attempted robbery, theft from the person, burglary, assault on police, causing criminal damage or possessing offensive weapons. One hundred and three members of the public required hospital treatment, some as a result of stab wounds. A total of 192 police officers were injured, 33 of whom were taken to hospital for treatment. Eight of them were detained overnight, one with a stab wound to the stomach.[47]

Gutzmore suggested that, unlike 1976, in 1977 'the youths launched a direct frontal attack' on the police, who 'moved in' and 'swept all before them', claiming that this was 'significant and should be talked about' because 'the police didn't attack the youths in the first instance in 1977.'[48] However, the actions of the police in preserving public tranquillity did not meet with approval within the Mangrove community and, in consequence, a public meeting was held in All Saints Road on 7 September 1977, at which a resolution was passed which strongly deplored 'the brutal and unprovoked attack on black and white people at the Mangrove Restaurant on Monday 29 August 1977', and directed 'that a letter be written to Mr Merlyn Rees the Home Secretary, describing that attack and demanding that he institute an immediate and thorough enquiry (into that attack), with a view to bringing criminal prosecutions against those members of the Metropolitan Police Force responsible for that attack.' The meeting also called 'upon

---

46. Gutzmore, *op. cit.* 2, p.229.
47. McNee, *op. cit.* 44, p.24.
48. Gutzmore, *op. cit.* 2, p.228.

concerned individuals and organizations to write in similar terms to the Home Secretary.'[49]

The resolution received little publicity and was ignored by the Home Office. Nevertheless, suggested the Innes Report, 'the issues drifted into the folklore of the black consciousness.' More importantly, perhaps, Crichlow had been 'restored in the public eye as the promoter of the black person's disenchantment with authority.'[50]

Reviewing the Period 1972 to 1977

In its critique of the period 1972 to 1977, the Innes Report suggested that within the police:

(a) There existed a mood of frustration because enforcement tactics were exploited as harassment;

(b) The deployment of dedicated officers invested responsibility for the area around All Saints Road (or Colville Ward to give it its proper name) in them and inhibited encroachment by other officers, less sensitive to the need for discretion;

(c) Drug-dealing and unlicensed drinkers still demanded concentrated enforcement policies throughout the division, but it required a more structured approach to be developed to bring about enforcement without stimulating hostility;

(d) The rise to prominence of the Notting Hill Carnival occupied the minds of senior officers and became the overriding issue of policing concern; and

(e) Carnival 76 disrupted much of what had been achieved and re-opened old wounds between the police and black people.

On the contrary, within the black community:

(a) The policing methods to deal with public disorder by the use of force invoked cries of harassment and calls for public inquiry;

---

49. Innes, *op. cit.* 36, p.13, para. 5.28.
50. *Ibid*, p.14, paras. 5.29 and 5.30.

(b) Other policing methods which arrested criminals, kept the peace or prevented crime was met with silence, not approval;

(c) There was no apparent public condemnation of drug-dealers; and

(d) Criticism of the police was part of the Mangrove's *raison d'etre* by this
time.[51]

The Carnival Continues

In the lead-up to the 1978 Carnival, the police once again reported that
arrangements were 'hampered by conflicts between the separate organizing
committees.' More than 9,000 police officers were deployed over the two
days.[52] From the organizers' point of view, they reported 'more mas bands on
the streets … than any previous year, more steel bands paraded and the quality
of the costumed presentations stood head and shoulders over anything that
had gone before.'[53] There was only limited disorder on the Monday evening between 8 p.m. and 9 p.m. when, following a missile attack on police
officers, shield units were deployed and order was quickly restored.[54] The
Commissioner, Sir David McNee, who visited the area on the Monday, got
the impression that the work and co-operation of the Carnival organizers,
allied to the careful deployment of police, resulted in less tension than in
1977 and helped to capture the spirit of Carnival.' This resulted in 'a noticeable reduction in the number of reported crimes and injuries.'[55]

In response to much of the negative publicity that had occurred since
1976, and in a warning to all those agencies and organizations that had a
role to play, McNee wrote in his report:

'The carnival at Notting Hill is now an annual feature of London life. If it is to
be fully enjoyed by all it is time for positive initiatives: and they need to be taken
by all the relevant authorities jointly with the carnival organizers.'[56]

---

51. *Ibid*, p.15, para. 5.31.
52. McNee, *op. cit.* 44, pp.8 and 27.
53. *Race Today*, September/October, p.123.
54. McNee, *op. cit.* 44, p.27.
55. *Ibid*, p.8.
56. *Ibid*.

Crichlow Arrested Again

As the 1978 Carnival approached, Crichlow had put himself forward as one of the organizers for the All Saints Road area, although he never associated directly with either of the official committees. However, in the week after the Carnival, he was arrested for using threatening words and behaviour as he remonstrated with police officers about an incident outside the Mangrove. On 5 September, three officers from the Thames Valley Police had come to Notting Hill to keep observation on a taxi firm in All Saints Road because they had received information that a woman, described as 'extremely attractive' and 'white' wanted for questioning by them, was likely to visit it. They were joined by Detective Constable Quinn from Notting Hill; all the officers were in plain clothes.

As the officers approached the woman she ran into the Mangrove. Immediately six black men came out and stopped the officers from entering. Detective Constable Quinn said they were police officers and the woman was wanted for questioning but as he did so another 30 black men emerged from the Apollo public house. Quinn called for assistance and when it arrived, Crichlow, who, it was claimed, was holding a screwdriver at the time, is alleged to have said 'Let's do what we should have done last week and kill these f.....g pigs'. He was arrested and subsequently charged with inciting others to assault police, and using threatening words.[57]

So the dust had hardly settled from the trial of the Mangrove Six, which finished at the end of June 1979, when, in December, Crichlow was again before the courts as a result of his arrest in September 1978. The police once again found themselves on the defensive when it became known to the court that Crichlow's photograph was on display inside Notting Hill Police Station, because, according to the evidence of one officer, he was a known criminal. Although this was subsequently denied by Sergeant Mann, who gave evidence to the effect that the photographs were of prominent local residents for the information of officers, and included local councillors and a judge, the damage had been done. Half way through the trial, the magistrate stopped it, criticising the police and questioning the credibility of some of

---

57. *Kensington News and Post*, 21 and 28 December 1979.

the prosecution witnesses. At the same time he directed that a senior police officer be informed of what he called 'the most unfortunate state of affairs.'[58]

The 1979 Carnival

Led it seemed by the London evening newspapers, there were still those who wished to either denigrate or restrict the Carnival or, indeed remove it from the streets altogether. In the run-up to the August Bank Holiday weekend, articles appeared under provocative headlines such as:

> 'Curb the Carnival' (*Evening News*, 18 June 1979)
> 'Ban the Carnival' (*Evening Standard*, 18 June 1979)
> 'Notting Hill Carnival Fear' (*Evening Standard*, 19 July 1979)

Even some of the national daily papers emphasised planning problems as the Carnival approached.[59] In the event, the Commissioner's Annual Report for that year merely reported that 'detailed and careful planning was successful in reducing the incidence of crime and injury.'[60]

Change of Policy at the Mangrove

As the decade drew to a close, it was clear that the tensions between the police and the frequenters of All Saints Road were as serious as they had ever been, but a new development was taking place which perhaps acted as a restraining influence on the more extreme elements. Crichlow was making the transition from restaurant owner to community leader. The declining business between 1972 and 1977, together with the adverse publicity, prompted a change of policy at the Mangrove, and various agencies during late-1977 and early-1978, including the police, were approached to see if they would give support to a proposal to form a Mangrove Community Association. Meetings were attended by the police community liaison officer, Chief Inspector Ray Tanner, and by February 1980, a document setting out the aim and objectives of such an association, with a request for council funding, was laid before the

---

58. *Ibid.*
59. *Daily Telegraph*, 16 July 1979.
60. McNee, Sir David (1980). 'Report of the Commissioner of Police for the Metropolis for 1979'. Cmnd 7932. London: Her Majesty's Stationery Office, p.8.

Kensington Borough Community Relations Committee. However, although the proposals were endorsed by the committee, the request was turned down by a higher council committee. The result was that Crichlow had to go to other agencies for funding. According to a letter, he also provided funding from what he called 'his private investment'.[61]

This apparent desire to be of public service and to secure the co-operation and support of the police was indicated by his defence at the trial for drug-dealing in the summer of 1979 at the end of which he made the following statement to the press:

> 'Although the people convicted still protest their innocence, everyone is relieved that the trial is over at last. We hope we can go ahead with the plans for turning the Mangrove into a Community Centre. We would like to have a better working relationship with the Police — and I think I speak for all black people of the area — not just "the boys from the Mangrove" as we have been described.'[62]

Excluding the occasion when he was prosecuted by Kensington and Chelsea Council, Crichlow had now been before the courts four times in a decade. On each occasion there had been intense media interest. The net result was a £25 fine. Kettle and Hodges described the raids on the Mangrove and other similar establishments as being 'inept and insensitive'. In fact, they triggered a far more serious problem in that it instilled in the youths who frequented such premises a sense that they were 'under collective attack by the police,' and it was suggested that whatever else was involved, the raids had become 'tactically disastrous for the police.'[63]

Review of the Period 1978 to 1979

In its critique of the period 1978 and 1979, the Innes Report suggested that:

(a) It was a period of uncertainty for the police because they faced criticisms of provoking public disorder by their very presence;

---

61. Innes, *op. cit.* 36, p.17, paras. 5.38–5.43.
62. *Ibid*, p.18, para. 5.45.
63. Kettle and Hodge, op. cit. 5, p.82.

(b) The raid on the Mangrove had been executed to enforce the law and to be seen to be so doing;

(c) The need to establish a presence and suppress an increasing drug trade was compelling;

(d) The prevention of crime was paramount and there was little conceptual analysis that the efforts of the police in this field should be subordinated to the preservation of public tranquillity; and

(e) There were frustrations at having again been exposed to criticism of their efforts to enforce the law.

On the other hand, within the black community:

(a) Crichlow's arrest whilst awaiting trial for other charges was taken as a signal of outright victimisation;

(b) Passion was aroused by small incidents and pressure was put on the new Member of Parliament to support their grievances as they had been by his predecessor;

(c) Those arrested were mainly acquitted of criminal behaviour by the courts thus vindicating their actions and divesting them of blame; and

(d) The corollary to their established innocence was that police were therefore guilty.[64]

Black Youths Increasingly Linked with Criminality

But there was a more general problem by this time. With some justification, it was suggested that young black people 'were increasingly being linked with criminality' throughout the 1970s. The police, particularly in London, claimed that black youths 'were usually found to be over represented in every main category of crime,' and the word 'mugging' 'was liberally used' in connection with the criminality of those 'living in the multi-deprived, inner city areas' of which Notting Hill was one.[65] According to Benyon, by 1976–1977, 'race was firmly on the agenda under the general headings of crime, law and order and policing, largely placed there by the media and

---

64. Innes, *op. cit.* 36, p.19, para.5.47.
65. Ramdin, Ron (1987). *The Making of the Black Working Class in Britain*. Aldershot: Wilwood House, p.457.

the "moral panic" over "mugging" and by the police themselves in releasing crime statistics.'[66] In London, particularly, black youths 'were regarded with suspicion' and consequently 'sus' and stop and search legislation were increasingly used against them.[67]

Throughout the 1970s, there was a growing resentment about the use of the so-called 'sus' law by the police. A report by the Runnymede Trust claimed that of the 2,112 people charged with this offence[68] in 1976, 42 per cent were black.[69] Further research carried out by the Home Office reported that a black person was 15 times more likely to be arrested for this offence than a white person.[70] The House of Commons Home Affairs Select Committee therefore examined the use of the 'sus' law and the effect it was having on race relations during the 1979–1980 parliamentary session and, as a result of its recommendation to repeal the law,[71] this was done by virtue of the Criminal Attempts Act 1981. But, arguably, it was too little, too late. The damage had already been done and a number of deprived inner-city areas, inhabited by large ethnic communities, were about to explode in orgies of violence over the next two years.

As for Notting Hill, former Commissioner Ian Blair, who was a detective sergeant there in 1979, claimed that 'the sense of being almost a garrison was very strong' and suggested that, even by then, All Saints Road 'was virtually a no-go area.'[72] Another officer who was there at the time was Detective Inspector John Grieve, who later, in his career was successively in charge of

---

66. Benyon, John (1986). 'A Tale of Failure: Race and Policing'. Policy Papers in Ethnic Relations No. 3. Warwick: Centre for Research in Ethnic Relations' University of Warwick, p.32.

67. *Ibid*, p.33.

68. The Vagrancy Act was originally introduced in 1824 as a measure to deal with specific problems in England following the discharge of large numbers of soldiers who had no accommodation and no jobs at the end of the Napoleonic Wars. Section 4 mainly dealt with vagrancy and begging but there was a provision for the arrest of any suspected person frequenting any street with intent to commit a felony. The Criminal Law Act 1967 substituted the term 'arrestable offence' for 'felony'.

69. Demuth, Clare (1978). "'Sus": A Report on the Vagrancy Act'. London: Runnymede Trust.

70. Stevens, Phillip and Carole Willis (1979). 'Race, Crime and Arrests'.. Home Office Research Study No. 58. London: Her Majesty's Stationery Office, pp.31–33.

71. House of Commons. 'Race Relations and the "Sus" Law: Second Report from the Home Affairs Select Committee, Session 1979–1980, HC 559. London: Her Majesty's Stationery Office.

72. Blair, Ian (2009). *Policing Controversy*. London: Profile Books, p.68.

counter-terrorism, led the Metropolitan Police's response to the McPherson Inquiry[73] and set up its new Race and Violent Crime Task Force.

---

73. McPherson, Sir W (1999). 'The Stephen Lawrence Inquiry'. London: Her Majesty's Stationery Office.

CHAPTER 10

I ARRIVE AT NOTTING HILL

The Bristol Riot

In June 1980 I was promoted Chief Superintendent and posted to Notting Hill as the Divisional Commander. Shortly before I took up command a hugely significant event occurred in the west of England which could have had serious implications for the job I was about to undertake.

St Paul's, a small district in Bristol had come to be regarded by some as 'a place of vice and shame with a high potential for trouble.'[1] The previous year, police statistics showed that 'offences such as robbery, drugs and selling alcohol on unlicensed premises [were] rife'.[2] Although not nearly as well-known as Notting Hill nationally, the circumstances were similar. Like Notting Hill, St Paul's had a Front Line, Grosvenor Road and one of the premises in that road was the Black and White Café.[3] Shortly after 3 p.m. on April 2, police officers from the Avon and Somerset Constabulary, in possession of search warrants for drugs and the illegal sale of alcohol, raided the premises.

Everyone on the premises was searched and the owner, Bertram Wilks, was taken away in handcuffs to be charged with possessing cannabis and allowing it to be smoked on his premises. The police also seized large quantities of alcohol, so much, in fact, that it filled a police van. By the time the police left the premises, a crowd had gathered and missiles were thrown at the departing officers. The violence quickly spread and by 5.30 p.m. a full-scale riot was in progress to the extent that the police were unable to regain control of the area for some seven hours. Buildings, including a branch

---

1. Kettle, Martin and Lucy Hodge (1982). *Uprising: The Police, The People and The Riots in Britain's Cities.* London, Pan Books, p.24.
2. *Ibid*, p.24.
3. Timothy Brain (2010), a constable at the time in the Avon and Somerset Police, who rose to be Chief Constable of Gloucestershire, referred to it as an 'iconic location' in his book, *A History of Policing in England and Wales from 1974: A Turbulent Journey.* Oxford: Oxford University Press, p.55.

of Lloyds Bank, were destroyed or severely damaged. The police made 134 arrests (88 black and 46 white). Of these, 75 were charged with offences such as assault, burglary, criminal damage, theft, handling stolen goods and public order offences, and were dealt with relatively quickly at magistrates' courts. However, on the advice of the Director of Public Prosecutions, 16 were charged with riotous assembly.

In retrospect, the Avon and Somerset Police had been extremely complacent in their planning for the raid on the Black and White Café. They had remained at the scene for far too long and had failed to have a 'public order' back-up, something I was always conscious of in my time at Notting Hill.

My Arrival at Notting Hill

It was against this background that I arrived at 'The Hill', as it was affectionately known, on 30 June 1980. Ramdin suggested that 'relations between the police and black youth and, in general, the black community had deteriorated considerably throughout the 1960s and 1970s, so that by the beginning of the 1980s the situation had become one of serious concern' with frequent 'incidents of police harassment.'[4] Whilst I agree that the situation had become one of serious concern, Ramdin appeared to lay it all at the door of police harassment but there was a failure by the black community to even recognise, let alone condemn, the criminal element in its midst.

My two years in command of Notting Hill Division was, without doubt, the most difficult, but, at the same time, challenging period of my police career. I found a mixture of experience and inexperience amongst all the ranks. There was only one black officer there, Detective Constable David Michael, who went on to become an inspector and chair of the Black Police Officers Association. But, too many of the uniformed constables who interfaced with the public, sometimes in very difficult circumstances, were young and inexperienced. A few were racist. Of that there was no doubt. But it was very difficult to prove. In many cases, officers accused of racism were those who actually believed that everyone was equal before the law and dealt with them accordingly. Nevertheless, I had an excellent command team. For most of my time there this consisted of Superintendent Gwen Symonds as my

---

4. Ramdin, Ron (1987). *The Making of the Black Working Class in Britain*. Aldershot: Wilwood House, p.458.

deputy, and three chief inspectors, David Cooke, in charge of operations, Bob Morrow, in charge of administration and Ezra Pritchard, in charge of criminal investigations.

In my first interview with the press I was asked about a story they ran shortly before I arrived. Three black men had been arrested for robbing a man and a woman of their bags near All Saints Road and it had been necessary to hold an identification parade to see whether the victim and witnesses could identify them. However, a lack of co-operation from the African-Caribbean community meant that it had been impossible to hold a conventional identity parade at Notting Hill Police Station. With their agreement, therefore, the three suspects had been taken to the bottom of the escalator at Notting Hill Underground Station and told to go up, in their own time, whilst the witnesses waited at the top. Two out of the three were identified in this way.[5]

The 1980 Carnival

I had three main priorities when I arrived — to reduce crime, particularly the drug-dealing and street robberies, to improve relationships between the black community and the police and, finally, to ensure that the annual Carnival passed off peacefully. The immediate priority was planning for the Notting Hill Carnival which was only two months away and it was this which took up much of my time during the early stages. Although the actual policing arrangements were made by the Public Order Department at New Scotland Yard, there was much liaison work and planning to be done locally.

In a statement to the local newspaper at the beginning of July, the chairman of the Carnival Arts Committee, Vijay Ramlal, expressed his concern about the public image of Carnival, complaining bitterly, 'we've had a lot of bad Press against us, especially the Nationals whose photographers just stand around all day, near large groups of police, waiting for the trouble.'[6] As the Carnival approached I was interviewed on BBC 2's 'Newsnight' and was specifically asked whether I thought the events at Bristol earlier in the year would have any repercussions for the forthcoming Carnival. Of course, I said 'No', based on the grounds that the Carnival was a festive occasion

---

5.   *West London Observer*, 2 July 1980.
6.   *Kensington News and Post*, 4 July 1980.

for the vast majority of people who attended and did not reflect what was necessarily happening in other parts of the country.

During the Carnival itself, one potentially serious incident was averted by a quick thinking constable when a scuffle, involving reggae bandsmen broke out on the stage at Portobello Green at a time when nearly 6,000 people were packed into the area. Police Constable Sid Scott, who had served at Notting Hill for a number of years and who was standing at the rear of the stage when the dispute arose, quickly grabbed the microphone and told the crowd that it was an argument between the entertainers and the police were in no way involved. This was accepted by the crowd and no trouble ensued.

There was some minor disorder at dusk on both days. Former Metropolitan Police Commissioner, Sir Ian Blair, then a uniformed inspector, described how his unit 'faced stone throwing black youths' underneath the raised motorway, known as the Westway.[7] But the disorder was 'quickly quelled with the minimum use of manpower.'[8] The Commissioner, Sir David McNee, paid a visit to the Carnival as it was drawing to a close on the Monday evening and, in a statement to the media, made it clear that he had no intention of trying to move the festivities away from the streets of Notting Hill, and he did not think that Carnival was a 'barometer' of race relations. He added that things would be better if they were left up to the police and public without interference from political troublemakers. In my post-Carnival statement, I expressed my delight at the way things had gone, pointing out that both the police and organizers 'worked hard to make it a successful event and for the first time since 1975 it had passed off without serious incident.' I suggested 'that black people and the police' could 'work together towards bringing racial harmony to this country.'[9]

However, an incident shortly after the Carnival showed just how transient the success was in terms of police/black relationships in the area. Two police constables, Trevor Prager and David Harland, were approached in Portobello Road at about 11.15 p.m. one night and told that there was an injured woman in a nearby building. On entering the building, the two officers were

---

7. Blair, Ian (2009). *Policing Controversy*. London: Profile Books, p.68.
8. McNee, Sir David (1981). 'Report of the Commissioner of Police for the Metropolis for 1980'. Cmnd 8254. London: Her Majesty's Stationery Office, p.26.
9. *The Job*, 29 August 1980, *Kensington News and Post*, 29 August 1980.

met by a large group of black youths who threw bottles and other missiles at them. One of the bottles hit PC Prager in the face, splitting his bottom lip; the injury required eight stitches.

Crime and Drugs

In her book, *Notting Hill Girl*, which was first published in 2001, Denise Watson described how, around this period, at the age of eleven years, she used to hang around All Saints Road and claimed people could get whatever they wanted, provided they knew the right man to approach.[10] Suggesting that, in those days, the 'whole community' was 'high on a mixed cocktail of various types of drugs,' she regarded it as 'a nice place to be'. It was here she said that she carried out her 'apprenticeship in drug dealing'.[11]

'There were a total of about one hundred runners, all boys aged between 12 to 30. In the beginning I was the only girl. We were basically all independent runners and dealers, and at that time there didn't seem to be a big boss ... We traded our weed in a very professional way. We cut up half an ounce of hash into ten sticks, which would fit into an empty Swan Vesta matchbox. It became like our own miniature showcase, but instead of gems, it was hash. A half-ounce cost me £45, and selling ten sticks at £10 each, I would make a £55 profit.'[12]

She further described how 'customers, mainly white, would come back regularly on the same day each week and park in the same spot.'[13] She also described some of the other crimes that were committed in the area. Girls were generally either 'shoplifters' or 'kiters'. The former stole small items such as clothes and jewellery whilst the latter, using stolen chequebooks and credit cards bought large items such as fridges, televisions and the like. Often they would be stolen or 'bought' to order.[14]

In addition, she pointed out, rightly in my experience, that none of the dealers 'took his or her drugs home for fear of being arrested'. Instead it

---

10. Watson, Denise (2001). *Notting Hill Girl*. London: Westworld International Ltd, p.36.
11. *Ibid*, p.86.
12. *Ibid*, p.87.
13. *Ibid*, p.89.
14. *Ibid*, pp.89/90.

was left somewhere in All Saints Road. During the day, the centres for such activity tended to be the betting shop, E W Kensington Limited at No.14 and the Apollo public house at No.18 All Saints Road.[15]

In the months before and after the 1980 Carnival, information filtering back into police circles suggested that drug-dealing was on the increase and a slow but structured build-up of police activity resulted in 30 arrests during the month of October. In November, drugs warrants were executed at both the above premises and a carefully planned operation ensured that the street was sectioned off and the Mangrove kept out of the action. The use of police dogs and a Special Patrol Group unit in a supportive role ensured that no violence occurred. However, to the frequenters of All Saints Road, it was an affront, resulting in an outbreak of indignation and resentment which was expressed by Frank Crichlow in allegations of harassment.[16]

There was little return for this operation. Indeed, in hindsight, it was the kind of operation that Scarman was to suggest, some months later, 'caused a crisis of confidence between the police and certain community leaders.'[17] Crichlow was a community leader, not officially appointed, but the reality was he was looked upon as such by a large section of the black community that lived in and frequented the area. One can argue that the gulf between Crichlow and the police had been steadily increasing ever since he opened the Mangrove in 1969. He had, after all faced serious criminal charges on two occasions in 1971 and 1978 and been acquitted. With each acquittal, his status, as a leader within the black community, had grown.

Shebeens

There were at least three shebeens still operating regularly in Notting Hill at this time, one at 26 All Saints Road, Fathers in Aklam Road and the notorious Graveyard Shebeen which operated from a private house adjacent to the cemetery, known as Kensal Rise off Harrow Road, from whence the shebeen took its name. Watson described how 'many drug-dealers would come in

15. *Ibid*, p.88.
16. Innes, Commander, Chief Superintendent Whitfield and Chief Inspector Aitchison (1983). 'All Saints Road, London, W11: A Definitive Document'. Typeset: Metropolitan Police, p.21, para. 5.55.
17. Scarman, Rt. Hon. The Lord (1981). 'The Brixton Disorders 10–12 April 1981: Report of an Inquiry' (Cmnd. 8427). London: Her Majesty's Stationery Office, p.52, para. 4.22.

the shebeen when the pubs closed, and would carry on selling their weed …'[18] Whilst the police would raid them regularly, those running the shebeens had learnt only to stock sufficient alcohol to last for the next hour or so and they would keep re-stocking it throughout the night from supplies that were kept elsewhere. Thus, when the police raided a shebeen, as they did quite frequently, those running it did not have all their stocks confiscated and were able to recommence operations virtually as soon as the police had left. Nevertheless, the raids were a way of keeping things under reasonable control and ensuring that things did not get out of hand, without expending inordinate amounts of police time in lengthy observations.

Relationships Between the Police and the Black Community

In October, the committal proceedings involving the 16 persons charged with riotous assembly arising from the riot on 2 April opened in Bristol. They lasted for six weeks, during which time there were clashes between the charged youths and their supporters, and the police both inside and outside the court building. Amongst those supporting the 16 before the court were some 70 people from Notting Hill, displaying a large banner 'Mangrove supports the Bristol 16', who had travelled to Bristol for the occasion.[19] At the end of the six weeks, the magistrates found that 12 of the 16 had a case to answer and committed them for trial at the Crown Court. All were black except for one.

The case finally opened at Bristol Crown Court on 3 February 1981. The result was similar to those experienced over the years at Notting Hill in relation to bringing serious charges against people involved in disorder. By using all but one of the three challenges each defendant had towards potential jurors, the defence was able to form a jury of which five of the 12 were non-whites and eight in total were women. In the fifth week, the judge directed the jury to find three of the accused not guilty for lack of evidence and at the end of the trial, which lasted seven weeks, the jury acquitted a further five.

---

18. Watson, *op. cit.* 12, p.94.

19. In an interview he gave to Hassan Mahamdallie in 1995, Frank Crichlow claimed that he was asked to assist those who had been arrested and he and others went to Bristol 'and started taking statements'. He also claimed that the police had objected to bail between the committal proceedings and the trial and 'they got bail for them'. http://socialreview.org.uk/article.php?articlenumber=11443 accessed 14 October 2012.

They were unable to agree a verdict on the remaining four and the Director of Public Prosecutions, acting on the advice of the local Chief Constable in the interests of racial harmony in Bristol, decided it would not be in the public interest to apply for a re-trial. Thus, when everything was finally over on 20 March 1981, there were celebrations in the public house opposite the court and later at the Black and White Café; three of the non-white jurors joined in these celebrations.[20]

Meanwhile, back in Notting Hill, a small incident two days after the drug raid in November, occurred when officers arrested a person in the Mangrove which turned out to be a case of mistaken identity. This precipitated a meeting during which the local Member of Parliament was urged to speak to the Home Secretary about police methods. One significant development in parallel with these incidents was the change of tactics adopted by the Mangrove Community Association in that they now began to commit in writing to the MP and the police, all their generalised complaints about policing which had previously been articulated through the press, at court hearings and at public meetings.[21]

In November 1980, one of the UKs Fascist organizations, the British Movement, held a march through an adjoining district, Paddington, using, as its principal slogan, 'Equal rights for whites'. Black unemployment in Paddington at that time was four times higher than white unemployment and the area was unofficially described by a Westminster City Council spokesman as 'a potential racial fireball.'[22] Predictably, there had been calls from nearly 50 community and church groups, including the Conservative controlled Westminster City Council, the Commission for Racial Equality and the All-party Joint Committee Against Racism, for the Commissioner to seek the Home Secretary's approval to ban the march by the British Movement, but these were refused on the grounds that the Commissioner felt there was no serious threat to public tranquillity.

The Anti-Nazi League mustered approximately 2,500 people in opposition from a variety of organizations including Communist, Labour and Socialist Workers Parties, and formed up outside Notting Hill Police Station; the

---

20. Kettle, *op. cit.* 1, pp.36–38.
21. Innes, *op. cit.* 18, paras. 5.55–5.56.
22. *The Times*, 23 November 1980.

British Movement, totalling some 600, formed up in Hyde Park. Police officers on foot and mounted, escorted the rival marches along different routes and, for the main part, were able to keep them apart. However, some Anti-Nazi League supporters did circumvent the police cordons and clashed with members of the British Movement at the foot of the Marylebone flyover in Harrow Road, resulting in 73 people being arrested.

Two Events that Could have had Serious Implications for Notting Hill

In addition to the trial of the St. Paul's rioters, two other events during the early part of 1981 had potentially serious implications for the policing of Notting Hill. The first was a fire during a party at a house in Deptford on 18 January 1981, which killed 13 young black people. Despite lengthy police investigations and two inquests,[23] the events surrounding the fire remain contested, even to this day, with the police believing that it started accidently in the house, which was only attended by black people, but many black people claiming it was started by 'white racists'. However, the fire led to a Black People's Action Day on March 2, which saw about 6,000 people[24] march between Deptford and Hyde Park, via Fleet Street, the home of most of the national newspapers at that time, and Downing Street, to protest at what they saw as the police's mishandling of the investigation into the fire.

The day started peacefully enough with a floral tribute being laid at the site of the fire before the march set off. Despite strenuous efforts by the police and stewards to control an unruly element on the march, two jewellers' shops in Fleet Street were looted, and there were scuffles between police and demonstrators towards the end of the march during which several journalists were punched and kicked. The police made 23 arrests. Seventeen police officers were injured and although none of the injuries turned out to be serious, six were detained in hospital overnight.[25] *The Daily Telegraph* was critical of the reasons for the march, claiming that there was ample evidence to suggest

---

23. One in 1983; one in 2004.
24. Estimates vary; the police estimated 3,000 and 4,000; most newspapers suggest around 6,000 but the *Daily Express*, 3 March 1981, suggest up to 10,000.
25. *The Times*, 3 March 1981; *Daily Telegraph*, 3 March 1981; *Daily Express*, 3 March 1981; *Morning Star*, 3 March, 1981; *The Sun*, 3 March 1981; *Daily Star*, 3 March 1981; *Daily Mail*, 3 March 1981; *Evening Standard*, 3 March 1981.

that the police were investigating the fire with exceptional thoroughness', but prejudice against the police, within the black community, was widespread.[26]

But far worse was to come and, as it turned out, 1981 proved to be a particularly difficult year for the Police Service in England. On this occasion, the complacency that had been displayed in Bristol the previous year was displayed by a number of Police Forces much larger than the Avon and Somerset Police Force, including the Metropolitan Police.

Three days of rioting in Brixton, from 10 to 12 April, during which there was widespread damage to property, left more than 450 people, many of them police officers, injured, 207 motor vehicles destroyed or damaged beyond repair and resulted in 354 people being arrested.[27] The most serious rioting occurred on the Saturday night when a contingent of Notting Hill officers, under the command of Inspector Maurice Smith, was sent to assist their south London colleagues. Inspector Smith was quite seriously injured during the disorder and was off work for some weeks. So, too, was a colleague of mine, Chief Superintendent John Robinson, who was in charge of the adjoining Kensington Division.[28] The rioting led to the setting up of the Scarman Inquiry which was to have major implications as to how areas with ethnic black populations were policed in the future.

Four Days of Skirmishes

Three months later, in July, rioters took to the streets again, firstly in Southall, in London, then in Toxteth, Liverpool, followed by Moss Side in Manchester and Brixton again. These were by far the most serious areas of rioting but there were outbreaks of violence in many towns and cities in England and Wales. Because of its history, Notting Hill was expected to be a major flashpoint. In fact, it was relatively quiet although there were minor skirmishes

---

26. *Daily Telegraph*, 3 March 1981.
27. Scarman, *op. cit.* 19, p.20, para. 3.17; p.36, para. 3.74; p.41, para. 3.91.
28. Chief Superintendent Robinson was the late senior duty officer that weekend for the whole District, which meant that he was on duty between four pm and 12 midnight. His role during the Brixton riot can be found in Scarman's report on Brixton, *op. cit.* 19 at pp 33/34, paras. 3.63 to 3.67.

over four days.[29] On Thursday, 9 July, at about midnight, a mob of about 100 youths rampaged along Portobello Road, breaking four shop windows and taking part in some minor looting. When police units responded, the youths ran off towards All Saints Road. The duty officer happened to be Inspector Maurice Smith, now fully recovered from the events of Brixton and when he drove along Westbourne Park Road, passing the entrance to All Saints Road, there were about one hundred people in the street. Fearing that the youths might seek to damage and loot property again, Inspector Smith requested assistance from the Public Order Branch at New Scotland Yard, which was, at that time, on full alert. Seven serials, about 140 officers, were sent and Inspector Smith assigned them to specific areas on the Division to ensure no further damage or disorder occurred.

Late the following evening, a car was turned over and set on fire in Clydesdale Road; another car was turned over in Lansdowne Road and a shop window was broken in Westbourne Grove. More ominously, small groups of youths threw missiles at patrolling police vehicles. Four police vans and one police car were damaged and three people were arrested.

Saturday is by tradition market day in Portobello Road. In addition to the normal type of goods found in most street markets such as clothes, china, foodstuff and toys, it is famous for its antiques. During the early part of the afternoon, a jewellers shop was attacked by between 40 and 60 teenagers in front of hundreds of shoppers. The gang seized trays of rings, gold chains, brooches and watches, worth nearly £50,000, after kicking in the windows.

Two of the gang were subsequently arrested and convicted. During their trial at the Old Bailey in September 1982, it was alleged that 'the robbery was planned by about half a dozen youths at the Mangrove in All Saints Road' and, following the raid, 'most of the stolen jewellery was…taken to the club and disposed of there.' It was claimed that one of the defendants 'sold a gold bracelet to another club guest for £100.'[30] From then on, tension in the area increased and the division was placed on full alert. Anticipating pos-

---

29. Michael Keith describes the events of these four days in Notting Hill in his book, *Race, Riots and Policing: Lore and Disorder in a Multi-racist Society*, published by UCL Press, London, in 1993. However, his version contains a number of inaccuracies and he makes no mention of the events that occurred on 12 July.

30. *The Observer*, 12 July 1981; *Kensington News and Post*, 17 September 1982.

sible serious disorder as the Saturday progressed, my deputy, Superintendent Gwen Symonds took charge at Notting Hill Police Station, where a control room and a charge centre was set up, whilst, together with Inspector Martin Murray, I took control of everything that was happening on the ground. All uniformed officers were made available for ground operations and detective sergeants, who had recently performed duty in uniform as part of their career progression, were drafted into the charge room.

By 10 p.m. that night, a mob of about 200, predominantly black youths — but there were some white youths present — had gathered in the All Saints Road area. At about 11.20 p.m., I visited the area in a police car driven by Police Constable Bob Taylor. Both of us were in uniform. As we turned from Westbourne Park Road into All Saints Road, Bob Taylor suddenly remarked that there were no parked vehicles in the street which was extremely abnormal for that time of night. No sooner had he said this than a brick smashed through the windscreen. Bob slammed the car into reverse and we quickly got out of the street. Fortunately, the brick passed between us and was lying on the back seat of the car.

Almost immediately a car was turned over and set alight in Westbourne Park Road. Police reinforcements were called in and, just before midnight, were drawn up in a line in Westbourne Park Road just east of Lancaster Road. Led by Martin Murray and Inspector John Stevens, who, with two sergeants and 20 constables, had been sent from the adjoining Kensington Division to assist, the officers drew their truncheons, and without protective equipment, charged the crowd who threw bottles, bricks and a few petrol bombs. The charge was determined and the youths quickly fled. Seven people were arrested..

A complaint arising from one of the seven arrested prisoners was typical of many that were made against officers who served at Notting Hill. A black youth, aged 18 years, who had been one of those throwing missiles at the advancing officers, was extremely violent at the time of his arrest and sustained a cut to his head. The following morning, his mother made a formal complaint by telephone to the Complaints Investigation Bureau at New Scotland Yard, alleging that he had been arrested at 11 p.m. but had not been taken to St Charles Hospital until 6.45 a.m., despite suffering from a fractured skull and broken fingers. In fact he had been arrested shortly before midnight, and had been seen by a police doctor about an hour later who advised that he be taken to hospital to have the cut stitched. An ambulance crew refused to take him because of his violent nature and he was taken to hospital by the first available police transport at about 4 a.m. He was kept in hospital for 36 hours observation due to the head injury and returned to police custody at 5 p.m. on 13 July; his skull had not been fractured, neither had his fingers been broken. Incidentally, he was wanted on warrant for other offences at another police station at the time of his arrest. But the upshot of it was that five police officers were the subject of a formal disciplinary investigation, the arresting officer, an officer who had been with him, two sergeants who were on duty in the police station that night and the duty inspector. The complaint was eventually found to be unsubstantiated, primarily because the original complainant, the mother, declined to assist with the investigation. Even had she, there was no substance in the complaint.

The following evening, i.e. 12 July, just before midnight, two fire engines responding to an emergency call were attacked by a stone-throwing mob as they drove along Westbourne Park Road. Again, police with batons drawn but without protective equipment, charged the crowd of about 200 missile-throwing youths. On this occasion eight arrests were made. Unfortunately, an incident on this particular evening, involving the Unity Association, a hostel for black youths in Lancaster Road, was added to the list of events that have allegedly marred police/community relations. The accusation first appeared in a local newspaper under the headline 'Police run riot in hostel' as a result of a statement apparently issued by the management of the association:

'The staff and residents were terrorised when approximately 100 police officers kicked in the front door, smashing the glass in the process. They ran through the building, breaking down several doors, while abusing and threatening staff and residents. The unexplained intrusion by the police lasted for about 20 minutes—during which time various rooms were entered as scores of officers rampaged through every part of the building.'[31]

---

31. *Kensington News and Post*, 17 July 1981.

The incident arose when police received reports of looting in the area and, as officers approached, a number of youths ran down Lancaster Road and into the Unity Association building, slamming and locking the door behind them. Officers forced the door to get in. I was in the building approximately 30 seconds after the officers had forced the front door. There were never more than 15 officers inside the building with perhaps another 15 outside scouring the streets for the location of the alleged looting. It turned out that the initial report was one of a number of false calls received by police that night and, as soon as this was apparent, I ordered the officers from the building.

I apologised to the warden on duty and invited him to write to me for compensation for the damage. Whilst I accept that, over the years, there were occasions at Notting Hill when the behaviour of officers was less than satisfactory, many of the myths relating to police action in black communities arose because of the way the incident was reported in the first place, and then repeated by others without verifying whether the initial report was correct. This was one such case. The myth, started by the report which appeared in the local newspaper, has been perpetuated over the years. In one case, an author suggested that resentment by junior officers because of what they saw as a surrender of control to the local black community was vested in the carrying out of 'a police search that ... succeeded only in causing a lot of damage to the Unity Association in Lancaster Road.'[32] In another case, a writer, using as his source the *Caribbean Times*, which itself was drawing on the initial report in the local newspaper, described how '100 police officers raided a hostel for black youths' running 'through the building breaking down doors' but 'no arrests were made' and neither was 'any explanation forthcoming.'[33]

The disturbances in Notting Hill in 1981 were certainly not racial as they had been in 1958; neither were they a case of black youths against the police as they had been in 1976. Of the 28 arrests during the four days, 15 were white and 13 black. Eight police officers were slightly injured. Ten premises and six motor vehicles were damaged to varying degrees.

---

32. Keith, Michael, *op. cit.* 31, p.150.
33. Gordon, Paul (1983). *White Law: Racism in the Police, Courts and Prisons*. London: Pluto Press, p.31.

The 1981 Carnival

In the aftermath of these relatively minor incidents and in particular the serious rioting that had occurred in other parts of England and Wales, predictions for the 1981 Carnival were ominous. The previous November, a story had appeared in the *West London Observer* suggesting that 'after two years of peace, violence could break out again' if it was not given sufficient financial support to allow them to pay community workers to mingle with the crowd at traditional trouble spots.[34] This was a reference to the constant difficulties in recruiting sufficient stewards to try to make the activities more self-regulated. Added to that, a disturbing story appeared on the front page of the *Daily Mirror* under the headlines, 'Carnival Bomb Plot' about a month before it was due to take place.[35] That same evening, it was reported that Shadow Home Secretary Roy Hattersley had been in touch with the Commissioner about 'a plot to provoke a race riot' at the Carnival under the headlines 'Carnival Riot Plot'.[36]

The story behind this headline involved a former member of the British Movement, Ray Hill. He had joined the British Movement in the mid-1960s and, for a few years, was quite active. He emigrated to South Africa in late-1969, where he spent the next eleven years undergoing 'a dramatic change of heart.' Returning to the UK in 1979, he became a mole inside the far right, at the same time feeding information to *Searchlight*, an anti-Fascist magazine. The far right scene had changed quite dramatically since the days when they had been so active in Notting Hill following the 1958 riot. In 1981, a man called Tony Malski had left the British Movement to set up his own organization, the National Socialist Action Party. Described as 'uncontrollable and extremely violent',[37] Malski boasted to Hill that he was going to 'give them a f....g carnival to remember', claiming that he already had 'the geli' but they needed 'the detonators.' He then went on to describe how 'he planned to put two snipers in position on the roofs of buildings overlooking the Carnival' who would 'open fire after the bomb exploded so that the

---

34. *West London Observer*, 26 November 1980.
35. *Daily Mirror*, 21 July 1981.
36. *New Standard*, 21 July 1981.
37. Hill, Ray (1988). *The Other Face of Terror: Inside Europe's Neo-Nazi Network*. London: Grafton Books, p.207.

black people would believe the police were shooting at them and respond violently.'[38] Hill passed the information to one of his *Searchlight* contacts who informed Special Branch. However, it appeared that Special Branch did not take the threat seriously and Hill therefore told the *Daily Mirror*.

Despite these stories, just over a month later, at the 16th Notting Hill Carnival 'a policy of relative policing' ensured that it passed off peacefully, spoilt only by one isolated outbreak of disorder late on the Monday evening. The newspaper, *West Indian World*, claimed it was 'one of the most peaceful in recent times,'[39] whilst the *Kensington News and Post* described it as the 'happiest ever.'[40]

Conclusions

The Innes Report described 1981 as 'one of the most difficult years in Police memory,' but, despite this, 'All Saints Road had remained fairly calm.' In its critique for the years 1980 and 1981 the report suggested that, insofar as the police were concerned:

- Given the country-wide disorder, the policing of Carnival in 1980 and 1981 was highly successful, in public order terms.
- An increasing build up of political pressure criticising the police had an impact on routine daily functions and influenced decisions.
- Despite this, they were able to execute warrants and enforce the law by arrest throughout all the problems of St. Paul's and Brixton.
- Apart from relatively minor outbreaks of disorder in July, the peace was maintained.

Insofar as the community was concerned, although the potential for political capital to be made out of Notting Hill was a stimulus to certain minority factions, the escalating political tone used in criticising the police did not find favour because:

---

38. *Ibid*, p.216.
39. *West Indian World*, 4 September 1981.
40. *Kensington News and Post*, 4 September 1981.

- There was a determination to ensure a peaceful Carnival and this was a strong influence in promoting co-operation with the Police.
- This mood was reflected in other aspects of policing.[41]

However, in its summary of this period, the Innes Report did not give an accurate picture, particularly when it claimed that the police were able to enforce the law by arrest throughout the period. A newly-promoted inspector summed up the situation, insofar as All Saints Road was concerned, when he arrived in the summer of 1981:

> '[I]t was virtually a no go area for police. Senior officers would tell you that it was not and that an officer could walk down the road at any time. Well that is probably true provided the officer was prepared to ignore blatant law breaking in front of his nose and put up with a tirade of abuse, because any attempt to deal with an offence would result in the officer literally being run out of the road. Arrests required "snatch squads" complete with massive back up and literally only about 60 seconds could be allowed to "complete the mission".'[42]

Michael Keith, who, shortly afterwards undertook academic research relating to Notting Hill and two other areas of London, suggested that during this period 'there existed a remarkable consensus about the importance of symbolism, posing the question "Who controlled All Saints Road?"' According to him, this question 'could be couched in either of the mutually exclusive idioms of community resistance or policing strategies.' But, in defining it thus, he ignored the criminal elements that were slowly taking a hold on All Saints Road, under the name of community resistance. Describing it as 'a deeply rooted historical struggle', Keith suggested that 'the uneasy peace that ... prevailed from 1981 onwards [was] no more than a compromise answer to this question — it [was] not an authentic resolution of the conflict.'[43] In this he was correct. An uneasy peace existed for most of the time but, given what was happening in the rest of the country, it is

---

41. Innes, *op. cit.* 16, p.23, para. 5.61.
42. Correspondence received from Graham Sharp, dated 18 January 2011.
43. Keith, Michael, *op. cit.* 31, p.129.

a measure of the police's success that, with a few minor exceptions, the lid was kept on All Saints Road.

CHAPTER 11

INCREASING TENSIONS — THE LEAD UP TO THE 1982 RIOT

The Scarman Report and its Aftermath

The publication, in November 1981, of the Scarman Report into the Brixton riots of the preceding April, gave the police, and particularly those of us who were responsible for policing areas similar to Brixton, plenty to think about. Scarman described how 'many of the young people of Brixton' were 'born and raised in insecure social and economic conditions and in an impoverished physical environment.' Because many of them failed to gain any educational qualifications at school, they found it extremely difficult to find employment when they left. Such difficulties applied equally to many young white youths but, in addition, young black people faced 'discrimination, much of it hidden and some of it unconscious and unintended.' So, Scarman suggested, it was inevitable that many of these largely, disaffected young black people tended to live their lives on the streets and in the 'seedy commercially run clubs' where they met criminals, who appeared 'to have no difficulty in obtaining the benefits of a materialist society'.[1] He could just as easily have been referring to Notting Hill.

Whilst he was quick to claim that nothing could 'excuse the unlawful behaviour of the rioters' Scarman found that the police had to 'carry some responsibility for the outbreak of disorder.' Firstly, they were partly to blame for the breakdown in community relations. My District Commander, Bob Innes, and I were acutely aware that there was no community relations forum in the Royal Borough of Kensington and Chelsea. Secondly, whilst Scarman found there had been 'instances of harassment and racial prejudice among junior officers', he found that 'the direction and policies of the Metropolitan Police' were 'not racist'. Again, although I trusted the vast majority of officers under my command at Notting Hill, I was not naïve enough to

---

1. Scarman, Rt. Hon. The Lord (1981). 'The Brixton Disorders 10–12 April 1981: Report of an Inquiry' (Cmnd. 8427). London: Her Majesty's Stationery Office, p.11, para. 2.23.

believe that there were no instances of harassment or racial prejudice during my period there. As I have already indicated, the difficulty was identifying those officers whose behaviour might occasionally fall short of the standards demanded of them given that they were extremely unlikely to show such tendencies in front of supervising officers. Thirdly, there was a 'failure to adjust policies and methods to meet the needs of policing a multi-racial society'.[2] Scarman claimed that the emphasis placed on the prevention of crime as the primary function of the police by Sir Richard Mayne in 1829[3] was no longer applicable. Instead, suggested Scarman, the primary function of the police was to maintain 'the Queen's Peace' and they should have this in mind when enforcing the law.[4] This particularly applied to a multi-racial society in which a section of it already had a deep mistrust of the police and I was always mindful that a relatively small incident, particularly in All Saints Road, could blow up into a major confrontation. I had, therefore, issued an instruction that all calls for police to attend All Saints Road and its vicinity must be attended by the duty inspector or some other more senior officer.

Rastafarians

It is impossible to write about Notting Hill without mentioning the Rastafarians. Lord Scarman exonerated them from any role in the Brixton riots, suggesting that they 'deserved more understanding and more sympathy' from people in Britain. Despite the desire by Rastafarians to be allowed to smoke cannabis, Scarman described the 'true Rastafarian' as a 'deeply religious, essentially humble' person whose 'aspiration — the return to Africa from exile in Babylon' — was 'embodied in a religious and peaceful discipline.'[5] Shortly after the Scarman Report came out another report, this time by the Catholic Commission for Racial Justice, suggested that Rastafarians should be allowed to hold services in Christian Churches.[6]

---

2. *Ibid*, p.73, para.4.97.
3. When the Metropolitan Police was formed in 1829, Sir Richard Mayne declared that 'It should be understood at the outset that the principal object to be attained is the Prevention of Crime. To this great end every effort of the Police is to be directed.'
4. *Ibid*, pp.62–63, paras. 4.56–4.58.
5. Scarman, *op. cit.* 1, p.44, para. 3.106.
6. *Daily Telegraph*, 19 January 1982.

The problem the police had with the so-called Rastafarian community in Notting Hill was that a number of youngsters engaged in crime wore the 'crown' and had dreadlocks but could not be regarded as 'true Rastafarians'; rather they were criminals who posed as Rastafarians. That having been said, one of the most famous Rastafarians in London was Gladstone Robinson who went under the name of 'Sledge' or 'Glady'. He had come to Britain from Jamaica in 1958. During his early years he was involved in musical and artistic collaborations with a number of different musicians, including Bob Marley and he had appeared on television in early episodes of 'Z Cars' and 'The Professionals'.[7] Partly because of his appearance — with his huge build and long dreadlocks — he was easily identifiable as a result, and his sense of what was right and what was wrong occasionally brought him into conflict with the police at Notting Hill.

Christmas Eve 1981

Whilst the Scarman Report was likely to influence the way policing was carried out at Notting Hill, in hindsight, the lead up to the outbreak of disorder on 20 April 1982 arguably started on the preceding Christmas Eve. It is perhaps worth reiterating what occurred in some detail because it was typical of the kind of incidents faced by patrolling officers from Notting Hill on a weekly, if not a daily basis. At about 4.40 p.m., Police Constables Martins and Dimmock, the latter a female officer, stopped a youth they believed was in possession of cannabis in Lancaster Road, very close to the junction with All Saints Road. Both officers were in uniform. Almost immediately they were surrounded by a group of between ten and 12 black youths. One of the youths threw the liquid contents of a polystyrene cup into the face of Constable Martins and the original youth ran off. The two officers pursued the youth who had thrown the liquid, into All Saints Road. He went down into the basement of No.12, the Mangrove. In response to a call for urgent assistance from PC Dimmock, two patrol cars responded.[8]

---

7. www.fulhamchronicle.co.uk/2008/12/24/London-obituaries-gladstone-robinson-113489—225460. Accessed on 12 November 2012.

8. The details described here are taken from the internal police report prepared immediately the incident was over.

But, before the patrol cars arrived, PCs Martins and Dimmock had entered the basement, which was used for gaming and other recreational activities, to be confronted by between 40 and 50 black men. Recognising the youth who had thrown the liquid into PC Martins' face, the officers went to arrest him but several of the black occupants pushed a card table against the officers in an attempt to trap them against the wall. The youth was arrested but some of the occupants started to smash the overhead lights with snooker cues, plunging the basement into darkness. By this time the patrol cars had arrived and additional officers entered the basement, only to be attacked by some of the occupants who threw snooker balls and cues. With the aid of 'seek and search' lamps carried on the patrol cars, the officers managed to leave the premises with the arrested youth, who was placed in a police van which had arrived in All Saints Road.

By now the duty inspector, Dick Stephens, had also arrived to be immediately confronted by a hostile crowd numbering between 100 and 150. Two Immediate Response Units (IRUs) and a dog van also arrived to be met by a hail of missiles, including bricks, pieces of paving stone, cans and bottles. Inspector Stephens ordered the crews of the IRUs to deploy with shields to protect the officers who were exiting from the basement of the Mangrove with their prisoner. Once the police van had left with the prisoner, the missiles stopped and Inspector Stephens ordered all police units to leave.[9]

Writing after the riots in Birmingham and London in the autumn of 1985, Professor John Benyon, who was, at the time, Director of the Scarman Centre for Public Order at the University of Leicester, pointed out that 'the succession of raids' on the Mangrove since 1969 had 'led to resentment and anger' as a result of which there had been considerable unrest in the area. He then went on to describe the events on Christmas Eve as 'a particularly notable operation, involving a large number of officers' as though it was planned.[10] But, as already explained, it was not a 'notable operation' but a spontaneous event precipitated by a crowd releasing a prisoner, who had been lawfully arrested, with one of the main role-players taking refuge in the basement of the Mangrove.

---

9. Internal police report, *op. cit.* 8.
10. Benyon, John (1986). 'A Tale of Failure: Race and Policing'. Policy papers in Ethnic Relations No. 3. Warwick: Centre for Research in Ethnic Relations, University of Warwick, p.41.

Less than a week later, following a march from All Saints Road, about 100 people, led by Frank Crichlow, demonstrated outside Notting Hill Police Station to protest about the incident on Christmas Eve. In a lengthy statement to the media, Crichlow suggested that

> 'If the first two officers had gone in alone, and if their approach was right, they could have arrested their man unhindered. Instead they called for the back-up force before they went inside the club.'

This statement was, at the very least, misleading. The so-called 'back-up force' had not arrived when the officers first ventured into the basement but immediately they did they were confronted by people who clearly would have done everything to prevent an arrest being made. Crichlow continued:

> 'We were having a Christmas Eve party — it came at a particularly upsetting time. It was quite peaceful in the club — it always is. It's ironic that the police should do this at the time the club's proprietor was out doing his bit for the community spirit by giving a party for the local pensioners.'[11]

Crichlow also accused 'the police of looking for confrontation' claiming that senior officers at Notting Hill Police Station had 'no control over those on patrol.'[12]

Increasing Tension

On 4th January 1982, I was sitting in my office at about 8 p.m. when I received a telephone call from Gareth Peirce, a solicitor who often represented Frank Crichlow. She told me that someone had telephoned her from the Mangrove and claimed that police officers in a car had just driven down All Saints Road, photographing people as they went. I told her that this was extremely unlikely and promised to investigate. On-one at Notting Hill Police Station had been issued with equipment to take photographs under such conditions — it was dark — and, knowing police officers, they were extremely unlikely to use their own cameras.

---

11. *Evening Standard*, 31 December 1981.
12. *Kensington News and Post*, 8 January 1982.

The truth of the matter was this. Two officers had driven slowly down All Saints Road in a marked police car. As they did so, a youth dashed out in front of the car and nearly got himself run over. The police officer sitting in the passenger seat had flashed his torch at him a couple of times as a way of saying 'that was a silly thing to do'. I rang Ms Pearce back and explained what had happened. Despite this, the story appeared in the *Kensington News and Post* under the headline 'Youths claim they were photographed by police-man', but not until eleven days later.[13] Clearly, someone from All Saints Road had telephoned the newspaper despite my denial.

At the local elections held the previous May, Labour gained control of the Greater London Council (GLC). Ken Livingstone became leader and 'wasted no time in creating a GLC police committee' putting 'as its chair-man a prominent civil and minority rights lawyer, Paul Boateng, the newly elected member for Walthamstow.' The committee had no statutory function and was, therefore, purely political. Boateng was quick to deny that he was involved in a 'police-bashing exercise' but, with his encouragement, borough monitoring committees were established in a number of areas.[14] In North Kensington it was set up by the North Kensington Labour Group 'to pre-vent' what was announced as 'a serious breakdown in relations between the police and local black people'. However, in what was termed as an exclusive interview with the newspaper, Frank Crichlow suggested that such a body was 'doomed from the start', partly because relations between black peo-ple and the police were at their worst ever and partly because, although he thought there should be a monitoring group it was 'difficult to trust anyone to do a good job of it.'[15]

In a letter to the *West London Observer* in February, the aims of what became known as the North Kensington Police Monitoring Group were set out:

- To work to improve relations between the police and the local community.

---

13. *Kensington News and Post*, 15 January 1982.
14. Brain, Timothy (2010). *A History of Policing in England and Wales from 1974: A Turbulent Jour-ney*. Oxford: Oxford University Press, p.71.
15. *Kensington News and Post*, 8 January 1982.

- To assist in the development of a police service which serves the community effectively and sensitively.
- To monitor police activity in the area.
- To work towards the Metropolitan Police becoming accountable to the appropriate elected authority and the community.
- To work towards an independent police complaints procedure.
- To work with similar groups which may be established in neighbouring areas.[16]

It was, perhaps, significant that the police were not invited to the first meeting!

Meanwhile, progress had finally been made on closing down one of the shebeens within the division when it was announced that the Graveyard Club had lost an appeal to the Department of the Environment against a move by Kensington and Chelsea Council to close it. The club had been raided by the police on at least ten occasions in the previous year. However, other shebeens remained, and during the early hours of 22 January, police officers raided an unlicensed drinking club on the ground floor of No.26 All Saints Road. Four people were arrested and a quantity of liquor was seized.

But it wasn't just the shebeens that needed to be kept under control. On the evening of 29 January shortly after 10.30 p.m., several missiles were thrown at police vehicles and patrolling officers were verbally abused after a youth had been arrested for being in possession of drugs. Drug-dealers were operating extensively in All Saints Road, both from within premises and on the street and clearly something needed to be done.

Operation Michael

The mounting of a large scale operation to arrest both the main dealers and their 'runners' was considered but, in the climate that prevailed post-Scarman, it was felt that it would be seen by some as insensitive and provocative for the following reasons:

---

16. *West London Observer*, dated 17 February, 1982.

- To have any chance of success, All Saints Road would have to be blocked off by police at its junction with both Lancaster Road and Westbourne Park Road.
- Such an operation would result in a large number of officers, both in uniform and plain clothes, being in the street.
- There would inevitably be a certain amount of indiscriminate stopping and searching of people.
- It was likely that premises abutting onto the street would be entered by police officers in immediate pursuit of fleeing drug-dealers and their 'runners'.
- The opportunities to dispose of drugs by dealers and 'runners' were considerable.

The idea was therefore rejected; instead, it was decided to set up an undercover operation, under the codename Operation Michael, to identify key targets and obtain evidence to justify a subsequent raid on the street.[17] From a covert observation post, officers observed and filmed the drug activity in the street. It was very much as Denise Watson had described in the previous chapter. The main dealers stayed close to buildings on the east side of All Saints Road at a point midway between Westbourne Park Road and Lancaster Road. Runners, carrying one or two small packets of drugs would stop people at the two junctions, sell them the drugs and then return to their respective dealers and give them the money. In return, they would be given another one or two packets and the process would be repeated.

In the meantime, once a sale had been seen to be made, a message, describing the person who had bought the drugs and the direction in which he or she was walking, would be sent from the observation post to officers patrolling on the periphery of the area. The person would then be stopped and searched well away from All Saints Road and, if in possession of drugs, would be arrested. During the operation, 62 people were arrested in this way for possessing drugs.

In order to allay any suspicion of the undercover operation, normal policing and police activity generally were maintained in the area. On 3 February,

---

17. Details of Operation Michael are from memory refreshed by the internal police report prepared immediately on its conclusion.

at about 9.30 p.m., two home beat officers left All Saints Road after being confronted by a large group of black youths. Although the youths did not physically assault them, their demeanour and the verbal abuse directed at the officers was such that they considered discretion to be better than valour. Five days later, at about 4.30 p.m., bricks and missiles were thrown at a police car as it left All Saints Road. Later that evening, shortly after 11 p.m. two officers on foot patrol were verbally abused by a gang of black youths in All Saints Road; a bottle was thrown at the officers but it missed its target.

By the beginning of the third week, six people had been identified as being the principal drug-dealers operating in the area and plans were made for their arrest. The operation continued until the end of the week by which time, in the three weeks it had been running, two people had been arrested for conspiracy to rob, one had been arrested for assault with intent to rob, two for handling stolen property and three for possession of drugs with intent to supply, in addition to the 62 for possessing drugs. It was decided to conclude the operation on Saturday 20 February.

The Drugs Raid on 20 February

The raid was simple. Two enclosed, rented vans were driven to the area. One was parked on the corner of Lancaster Road and All Saints Road; the other in St Luke's Mews at its junction with All Saints Road. The drivers left the vehicles as though they had parked there but, hidden in the backs of each of the two vans, were nine officers in plain clothes, making 18 in all. Divided into six teams of three, each had a main drug-dealer as its target. When it appeared that the six targets were all in All Saints Road, at a given signal from the observation post, the officers left the vans and arrested five of the six people. At the same time, two police vans, each with a driver and a sergeant, in uniform, were driven to the junctions of Westbourne Park Road and All Saints Road and Lancaster Road and All Saints Road, and the officers quickly placed their prisoners on the vans and leapt in themselves. From the time police leapt from the rented vans to the time the police vans left with the prisoners and officers this was timed at one minute 53 seconds. With the exception of the Apollo public house, no premises were entered and, with the exception of the crew of the police vans, no uniformed officer was seen in All Saints Road. Four of the five persons arrested had sufficient drugs in their possession to warrant a charge of possession with intent to supply; three of them also had substantial sums of money. The fifth man was charged with possessing an offensive weapon and possession of drugs. The sixth target was arrested a short while later in a basement in Lancaster Road. He, too, had a sufficient quantity of drugs and money in his possession to warrant a charge of possessing with intent to supply.

The Innes Report described how 'a very professional and skilful execution of a prepared plan resulted in the arrest of five dealers from the street simultaneously.' The effect was to remove 'the main criminals at street level ... from the heart of their operational base under the noses of their compatriots and associates without most people being aware of what was going on.' Once again, the report identified both positive and negative factors. The positive factors were that large numbers of officers had not been deployed in the street; people, particularly those not connected with the drug trade had not been stopped and searched which meant that there was no danger that the raid would be likely to give rise to hostility; and, with one exception, no premises had been entered in pursuit of the identified dealers.

There were two negative factors. Firstly, through no fault of the police, the dealers were released on bail to continue their activities; secondly, it was argued that the vacuum that was created should have been filled by the police but it was not.[18] The effect of the drug arrests was significant, but only for a short period. For over three weeks there were no incidents involving missile throwing or verbal use. However, on 14th March, officers were again verbally abused and a bottle was thrown at a passing police car.

More importantly, following this operation, some of the key people in a Web of Affiliation identified in the Innes Report,[19] were invited to a meeting at the B District Headquarters in Kensington on 5 March. These were:

---

18. Innes, Commander; Chief Superintendent Whitfield and Chief Inspector Aitchison (1983). 'All Saints Road, London, W11: A Definitive Document'. Typeset: Metropolitan Police, p.42.

19. The Web of Affiliation consisted of a number of community and pressure groups that had grown up in Notting Hill. As a result there existed a network which frequently articulated their views about the police, some more rationally and objectively than others. If the community were to be persuaded that police action was both appropriate and necessary, then, arguably, the members of the Web of Affiliation had to be convinced first. Innes, *op. cit.* 13, pp.27/28, paras. 7.1. to 7.5. The Groups that were initially identified as part of the Web of Affiliation are detailed in *Chapter 13*.

- Sir Brandon Rhys-Williams, the Member of Parliament for North Kensington;
- The Community Relations Advisor for the Royal Borough of Kensington and Chelsea;
- The Councillor of Colville Ward within which All Saints Road is located;
- Notting Hill Social Council;
- The Carnival Arts Committee; and
- Mr Frank Crichlow of the Mangrove Community Association.

Frank Crichlow declined to attend, giving, as his reason, the incident that occurred on Christmas Eve. A solicitor from the North Kensington Law Centre asked to attend but this was refused on the grounds that 'he had no client representation to make.' The Innes Report suggested that 'a forthright and constructive meeting took place where opinions were freely expressed and the foundation laid upon which avenues could be opened and common purposes identified.'[20]

Release of the Crime Figures

In January, in a widely publicised statement, chairman of the Police Federation of England and Wales, James Jardine, who was a Metropolitan Police officer, suggested that 'in certain inner-city areas' the situation had been reached where people regarded 'the income' they got 'from mugging as a form of unofficial supplementary benefit.' As a result 'many old people [were] afraid to go out and about in the areas in which they were born and bred' and had spent their whole lives. Pointing out that 'saturation policing' had been put forward as one of the causes of the Brixton riot, he inferred that a police commander 'faced with an upsurge of muggings in his area' had little option in the short term.[21]

On 10 March, the Metropolitan Police revealed its crime figures for 1981 at a press conference at New Scotland Yard. However, well before that, with the assistance of selected newspapers, the police launched what could only be described as a coordinated media offensive against black crime. A number of the reports focused on the Home Secretary, then William Whitelaw,

---

20. *Ibid*, p.43.
21. *Daily Telegraph*, 21 January 1982.

accusing him of being weak on law and order.[22] Towards the end of January, an article from its chief crime correspondent, Peter Burden, under the heading 'More and More Muggings But The Yard Fights Back', appeared in the *Daily Mail*. The report pointed out that although crime figures did not normally identify the race of muggers, there were areas in London where most of the attacks were carried out by young black people.[23]

A string of articles followed. Under the headline, 'Muggings of Women Double', the *Daily Telegraph* told its readers that 'the number of women mugged by roaming groups of black youths' had 'almost doubled' in many parts of London since last April's Brixton riots.[24] The following day, an editorial in *The Sun* referred to Britain's 'Danger Street'[25] and on 18 February, the same paper ran a two-page feature under the heading 'The Menace of the Muggers'.[26] The following day, the *Daily Mirror* claimed that mugging was Britain's top crime[27] and a few days later, *The Evening Standard* reported that the figures to be released on 10 March would reveal a 96 per cent increase in muggings.[28] An article in the *Sunday Telegraph* was headed 'Muggings in London Now Top 50 A Day'[29] and, two days before the press conference was due, an article in *The Times* claimed there were at least 56 crimes an hour in London.[30] The same day, the *Daily Mail*, published a feature article by Andrew Alexander, claiming that street crime under the present Home Secretary had risen from 13,000 reported offences in 1980 to 18,000 in 1981.[31] All the articles appeared before the official press conference was held at New Scotland Yard.

Chaired by the Assistant Commissioner (Crime), Gilbert Kelland, a breakdown of street crimes by non-whites and whites was given for the first time at the press conference. Of the 18,763 offences of robbery and other

22. Sim, Joe (1982). 'Scarman: The Police Counter-Attack' in *Social Register*, Vol. 19. See: http://socialregister.com/index.php/srv/article/view/5475/2374. Accessed 29 December 2010.

23. *Daily Mail*, 21 January 1982.

24. *Daily Telegraph*, 4 February 1982.

25. *The Sun*, 5 February, 1982.

26. *The Sun*, 18 February 1982. Cited in the *Runnymede Trust Bulletin*, No. 143, May, p.6.

27. *Daily Mirror*, 19 February 1982. Cited in op. cit. 27.

28. *Evening Standard*, 4 March 1982.

29. *Sunday Telegraph*, 7 March 1982.

30. *The Times*, 8 March 1982.

31. *Daily Mail*, 8 March 1982.

violent theft, it was alleged that 10,399 had been carried out by 'non-whites'. Although the broadsheets, such as *The Guardian*, the *Sunday Times* and the *Observer* attempted to analyse the figures in a constructive way, the tabloid media leapt on the figures almost with a sense of glee. 'Black Crime: Alarming Figures' screamed the *Daily Mail* the following day.[32]

On the disclosure of the racial breakdown of crime, Kelland claimed that the police felt there had been a demand 'for this information from the public and the media'; it had therefore been given 'to prevent gossip, rumour, and miscalculations and to set the record straight'. However, there is some suggestion 'that the demand from the media had been instigated by the police themselves' as part of their fight-back to the criticisms and some of the recommendations in the Scarman Report.[33]

Five years later, writing in his autobiography, Kelland gave two reasons for the decision to announce the figures in this way. Firstly, were reports that some of the 'younger male relatives of some of the elderly street robbery victims' would 'take revenge by attacking black youths.' Secondly, 'the great majority of operational policemen felt there was a conspiracy of silence which was causing resentment in the community about the known disproportionate involvement in these crimes of a minority of black youths.'[34] Despite the adverse publicity the released figures received from some quarters, Kelland, in hindsight, still thought it the right thing to have done.[35] However, there was a suggestion that it might have been considered by some as 'wilful' and 'arrogant' behaviour on Kelland's part.[36]

That is as maybe, but Kelland overlooked an extremely important point here. The strategy adopted by the hierarchy of the Metropolitan Police had not been discussed with those who were physically responsible for policing the racially sensitive areas in London on a day-to-day basis. Consequently, here was an example of senior management at New Scotland Yard instigating a pattern of events which, despite Kelland's claim that the majority of operational officers resented what he called the conspiracy of silence around

---

32. *Daily Mail*, 11 March 1982.
33. Sim, *op. cit.* 23; see also Kelland, Gilbert (1987*). Crime in London*. London: Grafton Books, p.284.
34. Kelland, *op. cit.* 34, p.283.
35. *Ibid*, p.285.
36. Benyon, *op. cit.* 11.

street crime, made the job of those on the front line that bit more difficult. Certainly, black people in Notting Hill were extremely angry and this did nothing towards assisting in the reduction of tension in the area which had been one of the primary aims of the meeting five days earlier. Indeed the Innes Report goes so far as to suggest that the release of the crime figures in this way 'created a problem' because the black people in attendance at the meeting 'who had been exhorted to act as intermediaries between Police and black youth felt betrayed and used', thus putting future cooperation at serious risk.[37]

Law Centre Report

On 14 March, the North Kensington Law Centre made public a report that had been completed in January. It was in two parts. The first part was a summary of the experiences of 70 people from community groups and advice centres working in the Notting Hill area. It was suggested that a black man was almost four times more likely to be stopped as a white man 'in circumstances where he could see no legitimate reason for being stopped.' More disturbingly, perhaps, insofar as the relationship between the police and black people was concerned, the report found that a black man would be 30 times more likely to be stopped as a white man 'in circumstances which he perceived as police harassment.'

Part two highlighted 30 cases in which black defendants had been taken to either Notting Hill or Harrow Road Police Stations. In 28 of these cases, the defendant had made allegations of what the report described as 'disturbingly bad policing'. The allegations included assault, police harassment, detention in police custody for an unnecessary length of time, unnecessary humiliation by strip searches and not being allowed to make a telephone call. In 14 of the 30 cases, the report alleged the only evidence against the defendant was from police officers and in nine of the 14 cases the defendant was acquitted.[38] The problem with the report was that it was so sparse on detail my staff were only able to identify one case that related to officers from Notting Hill Police Station.

---

37. Innes, *op. cit.* 19, p.44.
38. North Kensington Law Centre (1982). *Police and the Notting Hill Community.* London: North Kensington Law Centre. The pages of the report are not numbered.

Many of the allegations were, in my view, spurious. Where the allegation was supported by any evidence at all, vigorous action was taken, sometimes to the detriment of an individual officer. In April 1981, Lloyd Anthony Reid, who lived in Clarenden Road in Notting Hill, was arrested by three officers for allegedly using threatening words and behaviour. He was later acquitted but claimed that, as he was about to step into the police van, he received a kick or a punch as a result of which he fell face down on the floor of the van. He was picked up, thrown up against the inside of the van and punched in the mouth. As a result of an internal investigation, PC David Slavinskas, was charged with the criminal offence of assault causing actual bodily harm. Pending the trial, which did not take place until March 1983, the officer was suspended from duty. When he did eventually appear at Knightsbridge Crown Court, a jury took just over two hours to acquit him in a unanimous verdict.[39]

Serious Escalation Averted

On Thursday, 8 April, which was close to the first anniversary of the Brixton riot, an incident occurred which was all too familiar in the area during this period.[40] Shortly before 9 p.m., Information Room at New Scotland Yard received a telephone call from a woman who lived on the ground floor of 241 Westbourne Park Road to the effect that someone had tried to gain entry to her flat but, having failed to do so, had gone upstairs and she believed had entered a flat on the first floor. Three police cars were assigned by Information Room to deal with the call, which was commonly known in police parlance as 'suspect on premises'. Immediately on their arrival two officers from the first police car spoke to the woman who recounted her story. On the arrival of the second police car, the two officers from the first car went to the second floor flat where they found a 20-year-old youth. The youth claimed that he was in the flat with the permission of the occupier, a woman whom he had recently met in the Mangrove in All Saints Road. He readily admitted that he had tried the door of the ground floor flat, explaining that although he had the key to the second floor flat, he had not realised which

---

39. *Daily Telegraph*, 22 March 1983, *The Times*, 23 and 26 March 1983.
40. The details of this incident are taken from the police report completed the following day.

flat it fitted. When the key didn't unlock the door to the ground floor flat he realised his mistake.

At this moment, Reginald Davis and Frank Crichlow, accompanied by two women, arrived and immediately demanded that the police officers leave. Shortly afterwards, the owner of the flat arrived to verify that the youth was there with her permission. However, by now, one of the officers had found a container on the table that contained what was subsequently identified as a mixture of cocaine and cannabis. Before the officers could question her about the contents of the container, Crichlow despatched Davis to the Mangrove to obtain assistance.

Meanwhile, the owner of the flat was questioned about the substances and arrested. One of the police officers returned to the ground floor and, on looking into the street, saw that a crowd was beginning to gather. Using his personal radio, he called for further assistance. As the flat owner was escorted from the building into the street, a mob of about 50 people came running from the direction of All Saints Road, indiscriminately throwing bricks and bottles. Other police units arrived. Amongst them was Inspector Peter King who instructed all police personnel to withdraw from the area, taking the arrested woman with them, to give them an opportunity to re-group should it become necessary to return. Although no police officer had been injured in the incident, four police vehicles suffered damage, ranging from dents to broken windscreens.

There were, by this time, between 50 and 60 youths present — predominantly black — and Inspector King described the situation as being 'highly charged'. Superintendent Gwen Symonds, the deputy divisional commander, who was at Notting Hill Police Station when she heard of the disturbance, immediately instructed all police units to return to Notting Hill Police Station. The situation was left in the hope that it would defuse itself but, by 9.40 p.m., Superintendent Symonds began to receive reports suggesting that cars were being overturned to form make-shift barricades in All Saints Road and St. Lukes' Mews. Together with Inspector King she therefore decided to visit the scene.

Parking their car well away from All Saints Road to avoid it coming under missile attack, the two officers walked the remainder of the way to All Saints Road where they found in excess of 50 youths milling about at its junction with Westbourne Park Road. A derelict car, without front wheels, had been dragged into the centre of All Saints Road to prevent vehicular access. Two old mattresses and a quantity of wood, doused in petrol, had been placed around and on top of the car.

Superintendent Symonds, who was in plain clothes, attempted to engage Davis and Crichlow in conversation but found both of them agitated. Inspector King, who was in uniform, was subjected to a continuous stream of verbal abuse from the crowd to such an extent that Superintendent Symonds sent him back to the parked police car.

Superintendent Symonds remained at the scene, trying to influence the older members in the crowd to calm the situation down. Eventually she discovered that Davis's hostility towards her was mainly due to the fact that the arrested woman was his common-law wife. As the situation became a little calmer, Superintendent Symonds was able to walk into All Saints Road where she saw two vehicles blocking the western side of St Lukes' Mews. There were about 30 youths around them. After about 15 minutes, Superintendent Symonds agreed to take a woman who identified herself as a solicitor's clerk to Notting Hill Police Station to see Davis's common-law wife but, before leaving, she warned some of the older members of the crowd, including Crichlow, that unless the street was back to normal within 30 minutes, she would instruct police units to move in to clear the street.

Having returned to Notting Hill, Superintendent Symonds received a telephone call from someone in All Saints Road to the effect that the road had been cleared. Superintendent Symonds returned to All Saints Road and saw that the vehicles had been removed. By this time Paul Boateng had arrived and was talking to Crichlow opposite the Mangrove. She approached them and, after a brief exchange of words, invited them to accompany her in a walk round the area to speak with people on the streets in an effort to defuse the situation. This they did.

Foot patrols were resumed in the area but a mobile reserve of officers was retained at Notting Hill Police Station until 2 a.m. the next morning in case there should be a repetition of the events. At 12 midnight, accompanied by District Commander Innes, Superintendent Symonds walked through All Saints Road where they discussed the events with people who were still on the street at this time. Superintendent Symonds showed considerable courage, firstly in going to the scene of potential disorder with Inspector King, but more particularly, in remaining after she had sent Inspector King away.

Again, the Innes Report identified positive and negative factors. The positive factors were that a possible serious escalation had been averted and no members of the public or police officers had been injured. Police action was even praised by some interested onlookers and the difficulties faced by the police precipitated the first rumblings about residents' associations being formed. However, there were also a number of negative factors. Police officers being threatened and attacked when making arrests was becoming the norm and there appeared to be a feeling in All Saints Road that they could take the police on and 'win'. Hostility within the Mangrove was not assuaged by the peaceful end to the incident and there remained a residual tension in the street which was menacing. Finally, there was discord amongst police ranks about negotiating with those who erected barricades.[41]

Twelve days later, the first of the four negative factors came to the fore when a number of those who frequented All Saints Road on a regular basis attempted to take the police on.

---

41. Innes, *op. cit.* 19, p.48, para. 12.10.

CHAPTER 12

THE 1982 RIOT AND AFTERMATH

The Incident on 20 April

The build-up on the evening of 20 April 1982 which led to the riot has already been described in some detail elsewhere.[1] Suffice to say here that the trigger, as so often in the 1980s, was a confrontation between police officers and black people which, on this occasion, resulted in a prisoner being released from police custody and fleeing to All Saints Road.

In response to a call for urgent assistance, missiles were thrown at police cars by a large group of youths who had assembled at the entrance to All Saints Road. I happened to be at Notting Hill Police Station that evening and went to the scene in a police car, driven by Sergeant Hole. I was sitting in the front passenger seat. Behind me, in a rear seat, was Inspector Graham Sharp, the duty inspector. My intention was twofold, to assess the situation at first-hand, and to search out one of the local 'street leaders' to discuss with him how we could, together, defuse the situation, as Superintendent Symonds had done 12 days earlier.

Unbeknown to me, one of my detectives, John Kearney, was on a roof-top overlooking All Saints Road with a pair of binoculars. Unfortunately, on that day a number of personal radios were defective and one had not been available for his use when he decided to undertake the observation. On reaching his vantage point, he saw about 120 people in the street. Some were excitedly running up and down; some, at the corners of Lancaster Road and Westbourne Park Road, were digging up tarmac from the road. When he had first taken up his position, the road was lined with motor vehicles but now there was a mass exodus. Shortly after that he saw the people, many of them carrying lumps of tarmac and bottles, run towards the Westbourne

1.   See Moore, Tony (2002). 'Public Order Command'. Chapter 5 in *Incident Command: Tales from the Hot Seat*. Rhona Flin and Kevin Arbuthnot (eds.), Aldershot: Ashgate. Metropolitan Police (1982). Internal report on the disorder that occurred on 20 April 1982.

Park Road end of All Saints Road—someone was blowing a whistle—and they threw the missiles westwards from the junction.

The object of their attack was the car I was travelling in. We approached All Saints Road by driving in an easterly direction along Westbourne Park Road. That was a mistake because when we reached a point approximately 30 yards west of the junction we were suddenly confronted by a crowd of about 50 people who immediately attacked the car with missiles. I had been too pre-occupied thinking about how I was going to deal with the situation and what I was going to say to any of the 'street leaders' to notice the route Sergeant Hole was taking. Because the events of that evening were totally unexpected, my normal driver, Rod Brown, was not available. I had visited All Saints Road on a number of previous occasions when tension was high. From experience, I knew that when trouble did erupt, it did so in the southern half of All Saints Road, between Lancaster Road and Westbourne Park Road. On these occasions, Rod would invariably skirt the area and come in from the northern end of All Saints Road, i.e. from Tavistock Road.

Two pieces of tarmac crashed through the front windscreen of the car. One hit Sergeant Hole on the shoulder; the other flew between us and landed on the back seat next to Inspector Sharp. Despite being slightly injured, Sergeant Hole immediately threw the car into reverse and we speedily backed down as far as Portobello Road. At the same time I ordered those Immediate Response Units (IRUs) that were in the vicinity into All Saints Road, with instructions to disperse the crowd which they did. Some missiles were thrown but the crowd rapidly melted away with many of them running into the terraced houses on either side of the street.

Withdrawal

Mindful of the sensitivity of any police operation in a mainly ethnic area at that time—Scarman had criticised the police for "errors of judgement" and "a lack of imagination and flexibility" at Brixton[2]—I was anxious not to

---

2. Scarman, *op. cit.* 1, p.64, para. 4.62. Whilst I was not conscious of thinking specifically about the Scarman Report during this time, in the five months between its publication and the these events, i.e. 20 April 1982, I had given a great deal of thought to what I would do if faced with serious disorder in Notting Hill. Additionally, I had discussed the subject with senior staff, i.e. the superintendent, chief inspectors and inspectors at the normal monthly management meetings.

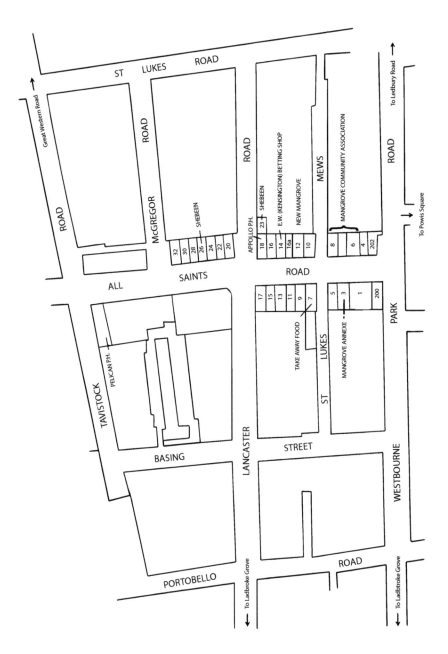

Area in which the 1982 riot occurred.

Map drawn and © Kate Whittingham.

draw unnecessary criticism on the Metropolitan Police. On learning that the crowd had dispersed, I ordered all the police units to leave All Saints Road and return to Notting Hill. My purpose in doing this was twofold — to, hopefully, allow the situation to cool down, and, at the same time, re-group my resources and be in a position to redeploy in a more orderly fashion than had been the case previously.

I was conscious of the comments that had been made in 1980 when the Avon and Somerset Chief Constable had withdrawn police from St Paul's, Bristol, in the hope that, as they appeared to be the object of the violence, it would quieten the crowd and "help the return to order."[3] However, at the subsequent trial of some of the rioters, the judge called it "a period of re-arming, not a prelude to normality."[4]

At the police station, I recognised time was short if this was to be resolved speedily. I gave the officers-in-charge of the IRUs — some were inspectors and some were sergeants — a brief outline of what had occurred and what I expected of them should the situation worsen. This meant putting on flame retardant overalls, which were currently being evaluated, and wearing protective helmets. They were also in possession of the new, small, round protective shields introduced following Scarman's claim that long shields encouraged 'officers to adopt a largely defensive posture' which only served 'to attract missiles from a crowd,' resulting in 'lines of police officers behind the shields effectively become "Aunt Sallies" for the crowd to aim at.'[5]

I was joined by Chief Inspector Jim Beaton, who was the late senior duty officer for the whole of B District. Jim was a former Royalty Protection Officer, who had been awarded the George Cross in saving Princess Anne from an armed kidnap attempt in The Mall in 1974, but had little experience of public order policing. I therefore left him to organize things at Notting Hill Police Station that were sure to be needed if arrests were made. I also

---

3. The Report to the Home Secretary by the Chief Constable of Avon and Somerset, as reported in *Police*, the Journal of the Police Federation of England and Wales, May 1980, p.11.
4. Joshua, Harris; Tina Wallace and Heather Booth. *To Ride the Storm: The 1980 Bristol 'Riot' and the State*. Heinemann, London, 1983.
5. Scarman, *op. cit.* 2, p.97, para. 5.73.

received an offer of assistance from Chief Superintendent David Kendrick,[6] who was the late senior duty officer on E District, a little distance away but did not feel that I needed him at that stage.

Re-deployment

Fourteen telephone calls were received in the Metropolitan Police Control Room at New Scotland Yard, between 9.45 p.m. and 10.10 p.m., from members of the public, claiming youths were arming themselves with bricks, barricades were being erected and petrol bombs were being prepared. One caller estimated the number of people in the street to be about 500; others estimated it at slightly less. I had no reason to doubt the general accuracy of the information because I was aware that some of the calls came from residents who overlooked the area but were not part of the group that normally frequented All Saints Road. In fact, the information turned out to be remarkably accurate.

As soon as it was clear that the situation was not going to quieten down, I deployed the IRUs and units of the Special Patrol Group that were beginning to arrive, to stand-by positions in the vicinity of All Saints Road but well out of sight of the crowd in the street itself. An operational plan, by my chief inspector (operations), David Cooke, existed for such an eventuality, and I deployed units as follows:

Lancaster Road, 50 yards west of Ladbroke Grove	B30, F30
Westbourne Park Road, 50 yards west of Ladbroke Grove	C30, G30, G31
Great Western Road junction with Tavistock Road	D30, H30
Ledbury Road 50 yards south of Westbourne Park Road	E30, BH2, N30
Powis Square (south side)	No.6 Unit SPG.[7]

This effectively meant about 130 officers

---

6. David Kendrick and I had been constables together in the early-1960s at Commercial Street in the East End of London. He went on to become the officer in charge of the Public Order Training Centre at Hounslow.

7. A Special Patrol Group Unit then consisted of an inspector, three sergeants and 30 constables with appropriate protected transport.

By 10 p.m., I had taken up a position in a police car at the northern-most end of All Saints Road—just to the north of the junction with Tavistock Road. Under cover of darkness, with the exception of some fairly dim street lights, this was far enough away not to be seen by the crowd. I had a map of the area on my lap; a police constable was acting as my driver and another constable as my radio operator. Later I learned from John Kearney what had been happening in All Saints Road. Immediately the IRUs left on the second occasion, people began erecting barriers and collecting lumps of tarmac and bottles which were stored close to the barriers. It was quite noticeable that a few were organizing the many at this time. He saw petrol being siphoned from motor vehicles in two separate places, one into bottles which were in a crate by the vehicle; the other was being collected in a petrol can. During this time, Frank Crichlow was seen standing on the corner outside the Apollo public house.

As more information was passed to me from the Central Control Room, I moved some of the units closer to the scene at 10.05 p.m. B30 and F30 were moved forward in Lancaster Road to a position approximately 50 yards west of Portobello Road. The stand-by position at their original location was filled by No 8 Unit of the Special Patrol Group, under the command of Inspector James Barnham, who had only recently left Notting Hill. C30, G30 and G31 were moved forward along Westbourne Park Road to a position approximately 50 yards west of Portobello Road. Their original stand-by location was filled by No.5 Unit of the Special Patrol Group, under the command of Inspector Colin Fisher.[8] The arrival of the two Special Patrol Group units added about 60 officers to the original 130.

Shortly after that, I gave instructions that, on my word of command, units were to move from their stand-by positions to the following locations:

All Saints Road junction with Lancaster Road	H30, D30, B30, F30
All Saints Road junction with Westbourne Park Road	
	No.6 Unit SPG, E30, G30, G31
St Lukes Mews junction with Basing Street	C30
St Lukes Mews junction with St Lukes Road	BH22

8. Colin Fisher had been a station sergeant at Caledonian Road for a period when I was there as a chief inspector in the early 1970s.

By 10.10 p.m., I was able to tell units that there appeared to be barricades across All Saints Road in two places and in both sides of St Lukes Mews. Satisfied that all units were in position, at 10.14 p.m., I instructed them to move in, demolish the barricades and to make as many arrests as possible. All units immediately moved in quickly and silently, taking the crowd in All Saints Road totally by surprise. At All Saints Road junction with West-bourne Park Road, a car had been placed at right angles across the street and doused in petrol. In St Lukes Mews (west), C30, under Inspector Peter Connor, found a van turned on its side with old doors and other pieces of wood and galvanised steel placed around it to make a barricade. In St Lukes Mews (east) a second car had been parked at right angles across the mews. In Lancaster Road, about 20 yards west of All Saints Road, F30, under Inspec-tor Rowe, found a builder's skip and a third car, both placed at right angles across the road. Interestingly, John Kearney had seen this vehicle driven into this position; the driver had carefully wiped the steering wheel when he got out. Two caches of petrol bombs were found, one at the junction of All Saints Road and Lancaster Road and one in All Saints Road at the junc-tion with St Lukes Mews; these totalled 25. The bottles of what had been a third cache in All Saints Road at the junction with Westbourne Park Road were quickly broken as the police approached.

I remained where I was in case further deployments were necessary, but after about five minutes, one of the IRUs reported the road to be all clear. I then moved forward to take charge of the clear-up operations where I was quickly joined by John Kearney, who told me briefly where he had been, what he had seen and that he could provide evidence against a number of people who had committed criminal offences. I therefore assigned a unit to John and, as a result, four people were arrested.

In all, 27 people were arrested that evening; another nine were arrested subsequently. They were charged with a variety of offences including the possession of offensive weapons, threatening behaviour, assault on police and using insulting or threatening words. It is relevant to note that only three of those arrested resided in the vicinity of All Saints Road and only eight on Notting Hill police division. Damage to property was minimal. Two small window panes were broken in the door of No.7 All Saints Road by police officers in immediate pursuit of persons seen committing criminal offences when the officers entered the street. Two large windows and one smaller window were broken in the Mangrove under similar circumstances.

The Aftermath

The Home Secretary, William Whitelaw, subsequently described it in the House of Commons as 'an example of the sort of action which has to be taken quickly and decisively.'[9] Subsequently, my actions were queried on three counts. Firstly, I gave no warning to the crowd to disperse before ordering the police units in with instructions to 'demolish the barricades and make as many arrests as possible.' The second related to my instruction to make as many arrests as possible. Thirdly, I left no escape routes.

I was well aware that, in a previous report, Scarman had said that warnings should generally be given before the police took offensive action in order to allow those "without violent intent" to leave.[10] As a result, police commanders were advised to give warnings before taking any offensive action, but Scarman had also suggested that 'there will be some occasions where the police need to keep the element of surprise in order to secure the success of their operation.'[11] Had a warning been given on this occasion, I am convinced that at least one of the barriers erected across the street, which had already been doused in petrol, would have been set alight and petrol bombs and other missiles would have been thrown at the advancing police officers.

As to the criticism of my instruction to arrest as many people as possible, the units had come from all over London in response to a worsening situation and there had been insufficient time to give a detailed briefing. I was therefore concerned that excessive force might be used. By focusing the minds of the officers on arrests I hoped to prevent this. When I was aware that arrests had been made, I sent an instruction by radio to Notting Hill Police Station to the effect that all those arrested must be seen by a doctor as soon as possible. Twenty-four of those arrested were subsequently seen by the doctor at the police station. Some had superficial cuts and bruises consistent with struggling whilst being arrested; one was taken to hospital where he

---

9. *Hansard*, 26 April 1982, p.107, col.1.
10. Scarman, Rt. Hon. Lord Justice. 'The Red Lion Square Disorders of 15 June 1974: Report of an Inquiry' (Cmnd. 5919). Her Majesty's Stationery Office, London, 1975, p.40, para. 142.
11. *Ibid.*

was detained for observation because he claimed he had been unconscious for a short while although no apparent injuries were found. He was released from hospital the following day. Three of those arrested refused to allow the doctor to examine them other than visually. The examinations failed to reveal any evidence of excessive violence and neither was any complaint made at the time that unnecessary force had been used.

Finally, in relation to the failure to leave any escape route, Scarman had criticised the police in an earlier report for not leaving an escape route when they were deployed to disperse the crowd, saying "it is important for the officer in charge to ensure, wherever possible, that a crowd has sufficient means of moving away before taking action to disperse or disrupt it."[12] I took the view that the circumstances on this occasion were different. Scarman was referring to a political demonstration where many peaceful protestors had been caught up in a crowd boxed in by the police. At Notting Hill, however, anyone who wanted had an opportunity to leave the area following the withdrawal of police units on the first occasion they entered All Saints Road. People seeing the activity that followed — the barricades being erected and people arming themselves with bricks and petrol bombs — must have been aware that the police were likely to take some positive action and therefore had an opportunity to leave the area right up until the time the police were ordered in.

What the Newspapers Said

Needless to say, the incident of 20 April brought forward a plethora of articles in the national and local media, despite the fact that this coincided with British Forces engaging the Argentineans in the South Atlantic. The headlines the following day read:

Police arrest 30 as troubles flares (*The Guardian*)
Police hurt in Notting Hill battle (*Daily Express*)
22 held in Notting Hill clash (*The Times*)
Notting Hill mob battles (*Daily Mail*)
Notting Hill riot — 24 held (*The Standard*)

---

12. *Ibid.*

30 held in Notting Hill clashes (*Daily Telegraph*)

Police seize 22 as blacks riot at Notting Hill (*The Sun*)

Two days after the event, some more measured comments appeared. Those from people such as Paul Boateng, chairman of the Great London Council's police committee, who had arrived in All Saints Road very quickly after the event, were predictable. He claimed that 'undue force would appear to have been used against both people and property.'[13]

The gulf that existed in Notting Hill was amply demonstrated in an article in the *Daily Mail* written by the crime correspondent, Tim Miles, in which he interviewed two people, one a white clergyman and the other a local black leader. Praising the two home beat officers, Paul Cardew and Harry Bedford, who regularly patrolled All Saints Road, the Reverend Peter Myles, then the vicar of St Peter's in Kensington Park Road, said:

'There was no major violence last summer which, in itself, is a major tribute to the way the police have handled the situation. But now the black youngsters are being used by the criminal element to put on pressure to get the police removed from the area so that they can continue unhindered and rake in the money. The men behind these rackets are the godfathers.'[14]

From the other side, Frank Crichlow was full of rhetoric:

'This was a very serious incident. I would say to all my brothers: Arm yourselves. Whitelaw and the police used All Saints Road as a training ground for their riot measures. It's not going to be a bad summer—it's going to be a bad 20 years. Notting Hill is riddled with racism. We have been harassed for years. The hatred is heavy, man. The black kids are not going to lie down and give up like their mothers and fathers did in the Fifties. There's no turning back.'[15]

---

13. *Daily Mail*, 22 April 1982; see also *The Guardian*, 23 April 1982 and *Daily Telegraph*, 26 April 1982.
14. *Daily Telegraph*, 26 April 1982.
15. *Ibid.*

During the following two weeks, two intrepid reporters ventured into All Saints Road and reported on what they found. First was James Allan. In a lengthy report under the title, 'Children push drugs in Notting Hill', he described how, on the Saturday following the riot, he 'ran the gauntlet of drug pushers interspersed with offers of a visit to a gambling session in a seedy-looking unlit basement at the bottom of a rickety staircase' in All Saints Road 'before reaching the Apollo public house.' Once there, 'the air was blue with smoke and thick with the pungent smell of cannabis.' One pusher told him that 'he tried to keep out of the way of the police but if he was taken to court it would mean a fine which he could recover in a couple of hours once back on the street.'[16] A week later, Michael Parry from the *Daily Express* reported he had been 'offered "hash", "grass" and "red leb" by drug pushers, some of whom looked no more than ten-years-old'. He was also 'asked by a pimp brandishing a knife' why he did not want a prostitute and was then 'offered a stolen radio still bearing the owner's name for a knockdown £10.'[17]

The Times, Guardian and *Daily Telegraph* each included a piece on Notting Hill in their respective editorials. *The Times* suggested that the police in Notting Hill had worked 'especially hard to improve relations over many years.'[18] *The Guardian*, predictably, perhaps, 'posed a number of difficult questions':

- Did the police over-react and thus escalate the problem, or did they react in the best way they could in those circumstances?
- How far was the flashpoint the result of a protracted period of bad community relations between the police and local people?
- How far could this have been avoided by a different approach to the local drug problem?

It went on to suggest that, in dealing with drugs, a more sensible way to the 'stop and search', an approach that 'is a guaranteed source of problems', was to use 'less visible, forensic techniques of detection' and go 'after the suppliers and "godfathers" of the syndicate that appears to be operating a

---

16. *Daily Mail*, 27 April 1982.
17. *Daily Express*, 4 May 1982.
18. *The Times*, 22 April 1982.

fully-fledged business in Notting Hill.'[19] Using video cameras in a covert observation post that is precisely what had taken place in the period up to and including 12 February, when six of the pushers were arrested, all of them quickly back on the streets after being fined at the magistrates' court.

The Guardian leader also suggested that urgent action needed to be taken to improve the relations between the police and the black community, claiming that the efforts of senior officers to improve those relations were being 'seriously undermined by the behaviour of some officers on the streets'. The leader concluded by suggesting that, if the police believed that there was the makings of a riot 'they had to do something to nip it in the bud [but] that would not explain or excuse the kind of behaviour' that was alleged on that night if it was true — 'that they charged into local restaurants and laid about them wildly and brutally.'[20] Such allegations were a gross exaggeration of what happened. The fact that none of those arrested were seriously injured belies the use of the words 'wildly' and 'brutally'. However, it was the leader in the *Daily Telegraph*, under the title Notting Hill Dilemma, which summed up the difficulties facing the police in such areas. Dilemmas arise, it said:

> 'when the police are placed by their respective obligations to enforce both the law of the land and yet to uphold it in such a manner that they keep the peace in areas of racial tension. The police know better than their critics that if their stop-and-search operations appear to be arbitrary racial harassment and not quite proper enforcement of the laws pertaining to drug abuse, they may trigger off street rioting. Yet, on the other hand, if they observe a policy of "benign" neglect when crimes are seen to be multiplying they are open to accusations of dereliction of duty and of setting up one law for blacks and the other for whites. It is a curious cast of mind, indeed, which would advocate racial equality without the corollary of that equality — equality before the law.'

The leader concluded by stating that 'it is easy to criticise' the actions of the police from 'the outside [but] in the present climate [they] have to play

---

19. *The Guardian*, 23 April 1982.
20. *Ibid.*

each operation with great care [and] that demands speedy judgements that only the man on the spot can make.'[21]

Ken Hyder claimed that 'the potential for conflict between the police and the public' in 1982 'had shifted from Brixton to Notting Hill following a series of clashes' in previous weeks and he accused the police of adopting 'overly aggressive tactics' which had 'destroyed community relations.'[22] Duncan Campbell claimed that 'heads were cracked, arrests were made and another chapter was added to the street's stormy history.'[23] Police Community Relations Officer, Bert Aitchison, summed up the problem succinctly when he told Campbell, 'the problem of All Saints Road is basically one of criminality... which has acquired a racial connotation.'[24]

Unfortunately, immediately following the riot, a particularly nasty allegation of police misconduct elsewhere in London received widespread publicity on 23 and 24 April, although the actual incident had occurred nearly six years earlier. Two weeks after the 1976 Carnival riot, on 15 September to be exact, some 17 police officers 'illegally' entered the home of an elderly black couple, David and Lucile White, in Stoke Newington, allegedly to search for stolen goods. None were found but both Mr and Mrs White, despite their ages and the fact that David White was frail, were arrested and charged with assault on police; they were subsequently acquitted and sued the Commissioner for damages. They were eventually awarded £51,392 on 23 April 1982. In making the award, Mr Justice Mars-Jones said that the police officers had been guilty of 'monstrous, wicked and shameful conduct' and had assaulted Mr White, a defenceless man, 'in his own home with a weapon and beat him in a brutal, inhuman way...'[25] As the next Commissioner, Sir Kenneth Newman, was to point out some years later, 'one incident of an unnecessary use of force by a police officer gives rise to a dozen rumours and gives colour to a hundred unfounded allegations of the same nature.'[26] Incidents such as

---

21. *Daily Telegraph*, 23 April 1982.
22. *Labour Weekly*, 14 May 1982.
23. *City Limits*, 23 July 1982.
24. *Ibid.*
25. *The Standard*, 23 April 1982; *The Guardian*, 24 April 1982; *Daily Telegraph*, 24 April 1982; *Times Law Report*, 24 April 1982. Quoted in Benyon, pp.38/39.
26. Newman, Sir Kenneth (1987). 'Will "no do" turn to "no go"'. In *Police*, Vol. XIX, No. 7, March 1987, p.10.

that which occurred in Stoke Newington had a distinctly negative impact on the policing of an area such as Notting Hill where rumours, which bear little resemblance to the truth, have become part of the black mythology relating to the area.[27]

Difficulties in Prosecuting Those Who Had Been Arrested

In prosecuting those who had been detained as a result of the events on 20 April, the police experienced many of the problems Sir Robert Mark had identified in the aftermath of the 1976 Carnival riot.[28] Of the 36 people[29] that were finally arrested, 31 were dealt with summarily at Marylebone Magistrates' Court. Initially, 17 were convicted and 12 acquitted and two failed to appear. Four of those who were convicted appealed against the conviction. In two cases, the appeals were upheld; in the other two cases, the appeals were dismissed.

Five people were arrested for allegedly possessing petrol bombs at the time the police entered All Saints Road. They were initially each charged with possessing an offensive weapon but, on the advice of the Director of Public Prosecutions, were charged with conspiracy to cause injuries to police officers and all were committed to the Central Criminal Court for trial. Four of them were acquitted on the directions of the trial judge, Oliver Martin. The fifth, Anthony Francis, was convicted and sentenced to 18 months' imprisonment.[30] Subsequent to their appearance at the Crown Court, in an entirely different case, the Court of Appeal held that a petrol bomb was an 'explosive substance' under the Explosive Substances Act 1883.[31]

The circumstances surrounding these prosecutions and the events that happened that night, highlighted a number of weaknesses in the collation of evidence and in the way that police prosecutions were conducted at that time.

---

27. For instance, the suggestion that 150 protestors were flanked by 700 police officers during the Mangrove protest in 1971 (see *Chapter 6*); the suggestion that approximately 100 police officers 'rampaged' through the Unity Association Hostel in 1981 (see *Chapter 10*); and the so-called raid on The Mangrove in December 1981 when it was merely officers in pursuit of a person, who had been arrested on the street, and who had fled into the premises after escaping from them (see *Chapter 11*).

28. See *Chapter 9*.

29. A further nine people had been arrested as a result of subsequent enquiries.

30. *Kensington News and Post*, 2 September 1983.

31. *Times Law Report, Regina v. Bouch*, 19 July 1982.

As might be expected and even at that early stage, when incidents of public disorder occurred, legal representation was quickly available, particularly from firms of solicitors such as Birnberg and Company, and Saunders and Company, and from the local Neighbourhood Law Centre. Representatives from these bodies were soon on the scene, often having been telephoned by self-appointed, unofficial local community leaders. In the case of Notting Hill, a list of 'call out' telephone numbers was displayed in The Mangrove. It inevitably followed that, even in outbreaks of disorder where a large number of people had been detained, those arrested ended up being represented by one of the two firms of solicitors or the local Law Centre. Thus they had knowledge of all the individual arrests and, by the use of a well-organized team, could carefully piece together what had happened. Even when, for instance, solicitors from different firms were involved, there was a cross-flow of information and an exchange of prosecution statements, served on defendants under the judicial procedures that existed at that time. Sometimes, copies of such statements would be circulated within the community in an effort to encourage witnesses to come forward for the defence. The defence also had an intimate knowledge of the relevant written instructions under which the police were operating, e.g. in the use of truncheons, and would, if necessary, produce photocopies to the court when it would appear that such instructions had not been complied with.

Of the 31 persons dealt with summarily, only one pleaded guilty and the local magistrates' court at Marylebone experienced difficulties in handling the sudden influx of summary trials. This was made more difficult by the delaying tactics employed by the defence, who contrived to have certain cases heard before others in an effort to use the evidence of officers from one case to cast doubt on the credibility of officers in another case. Information giving rise to suggested discrepancies was obtained, not from an officer's evidence-in-chief but from cross-examination. It some of the later cases to be heard at the magistrates' court, up to seven officers would be *subpoenaed* to give evidence by the defence. This was in addition to the arresting officers. Thus, a single case could easily spread over three separate hearings with considerable periods elapsing between each.

In cases were two or more defendants were tried together it was common practice for counsel to be instructed for each defendant. When, as sometimes happened, evidence of the same incident was being given by as many as eight officers, if one included those *subpoenaed* by the defence, it was very easy for defence advocates to 'divide and conquer'. This was especially prevalent on matters which were not recorded by the officer at the time because he was then forced to rely on his memory of an incident which may have happened up to 18 months previously and with which he had not been directly connected. Consequently, in answer to many of the questions posed by the defence, officers merely said, 'I don't remember' or 'I don't know'. This was, of course something that Humphry had identified in his book, published in 1978, arising from the Mangrove case of 1971.[32]

For instance, officers were asked why they had been sent to Notting Hill on the night and what briefing and orders they had received from the senior officer in charge of their vehicle, what form the briefings took and where it was held. A number of what might appear, on the surface, to be trivial points became important during the course of some trials. An officer would be asked where he was sitting in the vehicle and to identify where his colleagues were sitting. They were asked to describe the vehicle they were in, the number of windows and doors it had and the visibility through the glass or Perspex windscreens. Officers were asked to show on a map precisely where there vehicle had stopped, and through what door they exited and in what order. They were asked whether they received any further briefing or orders before exiting the vehicle from the senior officer in charge, and whether they formed up in front or beside the vehicle before being committed against the crowd.

Great attention was paid to the equipment that the officer had on that night. Requests were made for the NATO-style helmet, the flame-retardant overalls, and shields to be produced in court. It should be remembered that this was the first occasion police officers had been deployed with the new round shields developed after Scarman's criticism of the long protective shields. And both the new protective flame retardant overalls and NATO-style helmet were in the process of being evaluated.

Where no identifiable markings were displayed—and, given that they were in the process of being evaluated and officers did not have them as a personal issue—it was suggested by defence counsel that the officer felt a

---

32. See earlier in *Chapter 7* and Humphry, Derek (1972). *Police Power and Black People*. London: Granada, p.157.

sense of protection and immunity should he wish to extent his legal powers because he could not be identified. It was also suggested that, without such markings, the officer would have no way of recognising who a colleague was that came to his assistance in making an arrest. Finally, it is surprising how many officers did not know the length of the truncheon they were then issued with—about 40 centimetres. It was suggested during some of the trials that they were issued with longer truncheons when dealing with incidents of public disorder. This was not so.

A number of the arrests that night were made by officers who were relative strangers to the area. As the prosecutions progressed, it became clear that I should have ensured that a local police officer, with a good knowledge of the area, was present at the police station, with a detailed map of the scene of the riot area, to assist those officers in pinpointing precisely where an incident they had witnessed had occurred.

Despite assurances from the Metropolitan Police Solicitors Department[33] at the outset that efforts would be made to ensure that one or, at the most, two legal assistants would represent the prosecution in all cases arising out of the Notting Hill riot, this did not occur. Following the dismissal of one case in which the police were ordered to pay £400 costs, the magistrate made some highly critical remarks about the fact that three different advocates had represented the prosecution at the three separate hearings and the last two appeared to have little knowledge of what had occurred at the first hearing. Following this, the Solicitors Department did ensure that one advocate represented the prosecution throughout and, interestingly, the conviction rate improved.

The trial of the five who had been arrested for offences in connection with the petrol bombs followed a similar pattern to the summary trails at the magistrates' court. A total of eight police officers were called by the defence. The first was my deputy at that time, Gwen Symonds, who by then had been promoted and was in command of Kingston Police Station, to give character evidence for one of the defendants, whose son was a serving police officer in the Metropolitan Police. As the officer in overall command that night, I had not been present when the arrests were made. I had therefore made a written

---

33. The Crown Prosecution Service did not come into being until 1986.

statement which had been served in accordance with the Attorney-General's Disclosure Rules that were then in force. The prosecution had not thought it necessary to call me because I could offer nothing of evidential value in relation to the specific offences with which the defendants were charged. Nevertheless, I was called on the pretext that I could help the defence with the location of various vehicles and street furniture at the venue. However, once in the witness box, it quickly became apparent that they wanted to know my reasons for taking certain actions on that evening. The remaining six officers were all from D30 IRU which had followed H30 IRU to the corner of Lancaster Road and All Saints Road where the petrol bombs had been found. Some of the D30 officers had also made arrests; others had followed the officers from H30 into the Mangrove to where two of the alleged petrol bombers had fled. Needless to say, in the confusion that must have existed when all the police units entered All Saints Road from different directions, it was not difficult for the defence to highlight discrepancies in the evidence.

In his address to the court at the close of the case, the Judge, Oliver Martin, said this:

> 'I say this because I think it is very frustrating for young officers to have a judge direct to acquit persons whom they have arrested but I am sure they realise that cases like this—ones involving disturbances in the street—do present difficulties with identification. Although it is desirable to arrest those seen to be committing offences, a police officer's most important duty is to contain a disturbance like this, to restore order and to prevent injury to people and damage to property. These duties were, in my opinion, ably and courageously performed and a situation which might have developed into a very serious riot was brought under control and diffused. These police officers did, therefore succeed in their primary objectives and I think they realise that.'[34]

---

34. *Kensington News and Post*, 12 August 1983.

Departure from Notting Hill

Keith described the mood amongst officers following the events of 20 April as 'euphoric' because officers saw it as a 'triumph'.[35] An inspector who was stationed there at the time described it in somewhat more graphic terms, as

> 'an event that was met by universal approval by officers at Notting Hill who saw it as some payback for the crap they'd suffered previously. I have to say after months of tiptoeing around the road and the people in it, it was a jolly nice feeling!'[36]

Police officers are, after all, only human!

I left Notting Hill just over a month after the riot. Some months earlier I had been selected to become the Director of the Junior Command Course at the Police Staff College, Bramshill, a six-month course for inspectors about to be promoted to chief inspector. In an article announcing my departure, Grania Langdon-Down described what I was leaving behind:

> 'Notting Hill Officers police a diverse beat that stretches from the elegant homes of Holland Park to the boarded-up shops and run-down buildings of North Kensington. Burglaries, muggings and drug dealing keep its crime figures high. Combating crime in an area with the highest percentage of foreign-born residents of any London borough calls for sensitive policing. Community police relations can blow up in seconds, destroying hours of painstaking work. One of the major triggers that gets the sparks flying in Notting Hill is cannabis.'[37]

In an interview with her, I elaborated on what she had written:

> 'The police face a difficult task of enforcing a law which many people feel obsolete. If the community doesn't want the police to uphold the present cannabis laws, then they should get Parliament to change the law. The drug dealing in All Saints Road is fairly extensive. There are large amounts of money to be made. Competition is so great that innocent people are hassled to buy drugs as they pass through the area.

---

35. Keith, Michael (1993). *Race, Riots and Policing: Lore and Disorder in a Multi-racist Society*. London: UCL Press, p.125.
36. In correspondence with the author; from Graham Sharp, 18 January 2011.
37. *Kensington News and Post*, 14 May 1982.

Juveniles are involved both in selling and buying drugs. And then there are the ancillary crimes which go hand-in-hand with drugs, such as burglaries, dishonest handling of stolen goods, to finance the buying of it. When you reflect on it, it is incorrect to say that there is a problem between the police and blacks—rather it is problem between police and criminals.'[38]

Claiming that the so-called 'godfathers' of the drug trade had tried to turn the area into a 'no-go' area because of the financial rewards that were forthcoming, I pointed out that 'the less police activity, the more money they will make.'[39]

This was the situation I was, somewhat reluctantly I might add, leaving behind. Over the next six years or so, whilst tremendous strides were made in getting the local community on board and in involving other agencies, the police officers on the street faced an increasingly difficult task during which time they continued to suffer from verbal abuse and a number suffered injuries, some of which were serious.

---

38. *Ibid.*
39. *Ibid.*

CHAPTER 13

A CHANGE OF APPROACH

Early Baptism for the New Divisional Commander

My successor as Divisional Commander at Notting Hill was Chief Superintendent Jack Whitfield. He had spent a period of time in the Race Relations Branch at New Scotland Yard and it was natural that he should use his training and experience to good effect. He was to receive an early baptism to the problems of Notting Hill when, on May 10, a black man, Michael de Silva, attacked the E W (Kensington) Betting Shop in All Saints Road, spraying the interior walls with water using a hose. The police were called but when they arrived they were met by a threatening crowd and no-one would identify the person who had carried out the attack; therefore they left. Michael de Silva returned, this time with a brother, Nigel, and, armed with hammers, systematically broke all the glass, causing damage amounting to £2,000. A number of police units, in addition to Chief Inspector Bob Morrow, responded to the second call from staff at the betting office.

By now there was a large crowd in All Saints Road. A melee followed during which Chief Inspector Morrow was knocked to the ground by the two de Silva brothers who kicked him a number of times, bruising his back, shoulders and head, before stealing his personal radio. They then ran into an empty house in St Luke's Mews and tried to rouse the crowd to attack the police. The police withdrew for the second time.

Later that day the drama switched to Tooting, in South London, when police were called to Springfield Psychiatric Hospital as some people tried to get Michael de Silva admitted but on their arrival he made his escape in a BMW Car, owned by Frank Crichlow, driven, so the police alleged, by a second brother, Derek. Pursued by police cars, the BMW was then driven back to Notting Hill, sometimes at high speed scattering other cars and, on occasions, mounting the pavement. The car eventually came to a stop in All Saints Road where, again, police officers attempted to arrest the de Silva brothers but were prevented from doing so by a hostile crowd that quickly assembled on their arrival. The police therefore made what was subsequently referred to in the later court hearing as yet another 'tactical withdrawal', but not before two officers had been injured.[1]

All three brothers were arrested a few days later. At Knightsbridge Crown Court, Michael de Silva was found guilty by a jury of three cases of criminal damage and of causing actual bodily harm to Chief Inspector Morrow and sentenced to two years' imprisonment. Nigel was found guilty of two cases of criminal damage and assault and sentenced to six months imprisonment. Derek was acquitted of driving the BMW car without permission—although Crichlow denied he lent him the car—and driving recklessly, in part because there was confusion amongst the police officers involved in the chase as to whether it was a left-hand or right-hand drive vehicle. In his summing up before sentencing the two de Silva brothers, Judge Watts said:

> 'There has been startling evidence in this case, of the frequency with which police officers, trying to carry out their duties in this area, are subject to attack. The message must go out loud and clear in the All Saints Road, that the community will not tolerate attacks on police officers in the execution of their duties.'[2]

A Deteriorating Situation

The same month, the *Kensington News and Post* reported that children were increasingly becoming involved in drug-dealing in Notting Hill. In the 12 months from March 1981, 15 young persons[3] had been arrested. The officer in charge of the Police Juvenile Bureau claimed that unemployment—so often given as a cause as to why people dealt in drugs—was not the problem as the majority of those arrested should have been attending school. He claimed that some of the youngsters had not been to school for months and there appeared to be 'a lack of urgency on the part of the education authorities to deal with ... truancy problems.'[4] As if to emphasise the dangers, the

---

1. *Kensington News and Post*, 14 May 1982.
2. *Kensington News and Post*, 15 October 1982.
3. Under the Children and Young Persons Act, 1963, a young person was a youth under the age of 17 years.
4. *Kensington News and Post*, 14 May 1982.

following week the newspaper reported that at Chelsea Juvenile Court, a 12-year-old had been found guilty of dealing in drugs in February on the corner of All Saints Road and Westbourne Park Road.[5]

By June, people living in the area were becoming increasingly concerned about the amount of drug-dealing in All Saints Road. In an open letter to the Mayor of Kensington and Chelsea, Peter Masson of the McGregor Area Residents Action Group, pointed out that the police had 'a difficult task' before claiming that:

> 'As residents of North Kensington living adjacent to All Saints Road we wish to place on record a situation that is totally intolerable. It currently constitutes a complete travesty of all laws governing social and public conduct in the United Kingdom. We are faced daily with constant noise, open drug peddling and prostitution, and now the possible threat of riots when certain members of the black community meet face to face with the police, attempting to enforce the law.'[6]

Also it was apparent that the events of 20 April would not go away quietly, at least in the short-term. At the end of July, the London Association of Community Relations Councils (LACRC) called for a public inquiry into the disturbances. The association gave three reasons for its demand:

- Referring to the Home Secretary's endorsement of police action,[7] it claimed that because it had been alleged by some members of the community that 'unjustifiable and indiscriminate violence' had been used, his 'uncritical endorsement of the affray was, to say the least, premature.'
- Because those who alleged that they were unjustly and violently attacked by police officers had been told they could not lodge complaints against individual officers because the officers had no numbers or other insignia on their new overalls and were therefore unidentifiable.

---

5. *Kensington News and Post*, 21 May 1982.
6. *Kensington News and Post*, 9 July 1982.
7. See *Chapter 12*.

- Further damage would be done to community relations in Notting Hill if clashes of that kind happened and the accusations arising from them were not investigated.[8]

The wording of the association's demands cannot go without comment. There was no 'unjustifiable and indiscriminate violence'. As has already been described in *Chapter 12*, by focusing the minds of the officers who took part in that operation on arrests, the amount of indiscriminate violence was almost negligible, which was borne out by the doctor's examination of each arrested person shortly after their arrival at the police station and the fact that none of those arrested complained that excessive force had been used at the time.

At a series of conferences between mid-May and mid-June attended by senior police officers from Notting Hill, account was taken of the recommendations in the Scarman Report on Brixton, and, with the Carnival only two months away, it was decided there was a need to balance the three-fold function of preventing crime, protecting life and property and preserving public tranquillity. It was also decided there was a need to engage with those bodies, identified as being part of the Web of Affiliation in the Innes Report, to gain public support. The Web of Affiliation was the term given to a collection of groups that the police believed could assist with the problems associated with All Saints Road. Interestingly, they were split into four groups, viz:

- Community Groups such as the Notting Hill Social Council, the Notting Hill Housing Trust, the Tabernacle Community Association, the Notting Hill Council of Churches and the various Residents Associations;
- Official Bodies. Included in this group was the Member of Parliament, Ward Councillors, the Community Relations Adviser and the North Kensington Law Centre;
- Black Groups included the Mangrove Community Association and the Carnival Arts Committee; and finally

---

8. *Kensington News and Post*, 6 August, 1982.

- Politically Motivated Groups of which there was one — the North Kensington Police Monitoring Group.[9]

By mid-June, a number of conclusions in relation to police action in All Saints Road had been arrived at:

- A prime consideration was the avoidance of public disorder in the lead-up to Carnival;
- The presence of four home beat officers in a traditional preventative role over 24 hours was as much as All Saints Road could stand without precipitating serious incidents;
- Other officers would still respond if it was necessary but an inspector would attend every emergency call or reported incident;
- No new initiatives to arrest drug-dealers would be taken in the current hostile atmosphere but arrests were to continue away from All Saints Road itself;
- The Apollo public house, which had become the centre for drug-dealing, would not be raided by the police but the brewery would be asked to consider closing the premises after Carnival;
- The initiative taken on 5 March of involving the community in discussions should be vigorously re-activated after its disruption by the events of 20 April and the community discord that arose from it;
- A strategy for the deployment of concentrated uniformed patrols would be devised to be introduced immediately after Carnival.
- The local authority, property owners and other agencies would be invited to co-ordinate activities with the police to enforce planning laws and regulate the use of the properties in the street to that which was lawful;
- The research by A7 Race Relations Branch and the Police Foundation to prepare for a 'Neighbourhood Policing Project' for Notting Hill should be given every encouragement.[10]

---

9. Innes, Commander, Chief Superintendent Jack Whitfield and Chief Inspector Bert Aitchison (1983). 'All Saints Road, London, W11: A Definitive Document'. Typeset: Metropolitan Police, pp.27–28, paras 7.1. to 7.5.
10. *Ibid*, p.53, para. 14.2.

Efforts by the Police and Others

As the 1982 Carnival approached, a number of things occurred which emphasised just how much effort both the police and others were putting into trying to sort out the problems associated with All Saints Road. Firstly, Whitfield's availability 24 hours a day was reaping some benefit. A detective constable had been seriously injured when a brick was thrown at him by a 17-year-old youth. At about 10 p.m. on August 14, in order to keep the response low-key, Chief Superintendent Whitfield and two plainclothes detectives went to All Saints Road to arrest the youth. On his arrival in the area, Whitfield told local community leaders why they were there. The youth was arrested in the Apollo public house but as they attempted to leave they were confronted by a number of people who had gathered outside. Attempts were made to release the prisoner but local community leaders intervened and cooled the situation. The youth was subsequently charged with causing grievous bodily harm to the injured detective. Afterwards Whitfield said, 'There is a criminal element there that is a source of constant aggravation. Our policing of the area hasn't changed and there is a police presence there almost all the time.'[11] Secondly, the North Kensington Police Monitoring Group announced that it intended to install video equipment in All Saints Road 'so that if there is another April 20 a proper record of what happens will be made.'[12] There is no evidence this was done at the time.

Thirdly, prompted by an increasing number of 'complaints from the public about the policing of All Saints Road',[13] Commander Innes decided to call another Police Community Meeting on 18 August. The decision was taken to hold it on police premises, so that it would be recognised as a police initiative, and to invite mainly those who had been identified as making up the Web of Affiliation, whether they were supportive or critical of police action. It would not be open to the public but the media would be admitted and, in order to encourage people to be open, no minutes would be taken for circulation, although people were free to take their own.

The meeting was to some extent pre-empted when the North Kensington Police Monitoring Group deliberately called a public meeting the day

---

11. *Kensington News and Post*, 20 August 1982.
12. *Ibid.*
13. Increasing number of complaints.

before at All Saints Hall and, for the first time, the secretary, Tim Midgeley from the North Kensington Law Centre, invited the Police Community Relations Officer, Chief Inspector Aitchison to attend. However, when Aitchison arrived to address the meeting it soon became clear that not all members of the group were in favour. The treasurer, Pat Bolster, claimed that the group's meetings should not be a platform for the police and was adamant that hearing Aitchison was 'pointless and tantamount to collaboration'. Eventually, by a majority vote, he was allowed to put his case. A lively debate followed and on the break-up of the meeting, some participants were interviewed on local radio.[14]

At the Police Community Meeting the following day, held at B District Headquarters adjacent to Kensington Police Station, the following groups were represented:

- The Member of Parliament for Kensington and Chelsea.
- Colville Ward Councillors (All Saints Road was part of Colville Ward).
- The Community Relations Adviser for the Royal Borough of Kensington and Chelsea.
- Notting Hill Social Council.
- The Carnival Arts Committee — joint-organizers of the Notting Hill Carnival.
- The Carnival Development Committee — joint-organizers of the Notting Hill Carnival.
- Notting Hill Council of Churches.
- Powis Youth Project (Tabernacle).
- Lancaster/All Saints Residents' Association
- McGregor Area Residents Action Group.
- St Luke's Mews Residents' Association.
- All Saints Road Businessmen.

A number had attend the meeting the night before but the two main black organizations, the Black People's Information Centre and the Mangrove Community Association, together with the North Kensington Law

---

14. Innes, op. cit. 9, p.60, paras. 16.1 and 16.2.

Centre, declined their invitations to attend.[15] In his letter, Tim Midgeley, representing the North Kensington Law Centre and the North Kensington Police Monitoring Group, claimed that 'previous views and opinions put to the police had not been respected' and suggested that the real reason for calling the meeting was 'to gain some political and apparent community backing for police tactics' which showed 'a lack of sensitivity and regard for individual rights in the future policing of All Saints Road.'[16]

Initially, the atmosphere was tense but Commander Innes was able to put across police concerns by initially posing a question, 'How do I tell a victim of crime that there is no certainty of us finding the guilty person in All Saints Road but there is a certainty that if we try we will be opposed by black youths?' Pointing out that All Saints Road was an area of conflict between the police and black youths, many of whom came from outside the area and were jobless and homeless, Innes continued,

> 'They see us as looking for the least excuse of going to smash them and the Mangrove up. They see us as people they don't like and don't trust and have no feeling for us except for a fairly intense dislike, I don't think that is a healthy situation and it doesn't serve the community. The violence in All Saints Road has increased enormously and has taken a particularly nasty turn. When a guy says to us that he has been offered drugs and on refusing, has been beaten up—that leaves a bad taste in our mouths. The noise is sometimes so bad that people can't get a night's sleep—they can't get peace in their own home. Some say to us that they direct their visitors on special routes so that they avoid All Saints Road. My home beat officers are being subjected to brick throwing, bottle throwing, spitting and verbal abuse and that is becoming more and more frequent. I totally accept the concept of Scarman's "sensitive policing". But when people scream at me—"What about me and my wife and my child feeling safe in this area?"—I feel pretty ashamed.'

All Saints Road was now widely known as a centre for drug-dealing, Commander Innes told the meeting, claiming that he had 'West Indian mothers' complaining to him that they were 'trying to bring their kids up decently'

---

15. *Ibid*, pp.60–61, para. 16.4.
16. *Kensington News and Post*, 27 August 1982.

but they were being 'sucked into All Saints Road'.[17] Chief Superintendent Whitfield told the meeting that Notting Hill was the most difficult area he had ever policed, but the vast majority of the problems arose in the area immediately surrounding All Saints Road. Because of the crimes that were committed and the disturbances that occurred, these two factors coupled with the number of complaints from residents, meant 'a disproportionate amount of police effort' was expended on this one area as a result of which the remainder of Notting Hill suffered.[18]

A lively debate followed in which a succession of speakers claimed there was a lack of faith or trust in the police with a number of contributors suggesting that there was a need to teach 'the policemen on the beat not to harass people and—if they stop them—to speak to them civilly and not as pieces of dirt.'[19] Some reservations were expressed about the breadth of representation at the meeting—this was resolved by allowing each organization present at the meeting to bring one other person to the next meeting. The meeting concluded with the police agreeing that they should not chair the next meeting; neither should it be held on police premises. However, it was also an opportunity for the police to tell the community that immediately after Carnival they intended to implement a strategy which involved high visibility foot patrols in and around All Saints Road.[20]

In July and August, the Police Foundation carried out a survey of public attitudes towards crime and the police in Notting Hill as a prelude to an attempt to introduce Neighbourhood Policing, described in the next chapter. Asked how the police performed, more than two-thirds, 70 per cent said they did a good job, and nearly a quarter, 22 per cent, said they did a very good job. Only one in ten judged police performance poor. The public had particular concerns about two kinds of crime, with 90 per cent saying they were concerned about burglary (65 per cent said they were very concerned) and 89 per cent saying they were concerned about people using violence to steal things from people in the street (with 64 per cent saying they were very concerned). There was a perception by people who saw Notting Hill

---

17. *Ibid.*
18. *Ibid.*
19. *Ibid.*
20. Innes, op. cit. 9, p.61, paras. 16.5 to 16.9.

as suffering more from crime than the surrounding area. In summary, burglary and mugging stood out as the crimes which concerned most people in Notting Hill. Indeed, it was widely seen as a particularly bad area for crime, although few thought it had worsened in recent years. Most people saw the danger as lying in specific areas of Notting Hill, such as All Saints Road, Portobello Road and the Lancaster West Estate. Fifty-eight per cent said they were worried about certain areas and 45 per cent said they actively avoided these places.[21]

The 1982 Carnival

Although trouble flared briefly on the Monday night when gangs of youths ran through the late-night crowds stealing personal property, the 1982 Notting Hill Carnival passed off relatively peacefully. The one situation that did arise was defused without a confrontation between the police and black youths which had been a feature of previous carnivals. In total there were 250 allegations of crime over the two days, with nearly 170 people losing personal items. A large number of these were wallets that were subsequently recovered minus the contents. There were 63 arrests mainly for minor offences, such as drunkenness and possessing drugs; a few were arrested for carrying offensive weapons, pick-pocketing and robbery. Commander Innes claimed he was pleased with the two days but disappointed by the number of reported crimes, particularly on the Monday evening. Chief Superintendent Whitfield said he found the level of crime 'unacceptable.'[22]

A leading article in *The Times* suggested that 'much credit' for the success of Carnival 'must go to the police' because 'over the years' they had 'carefully developed ... tactics of being visible but discreet, of avoiding provocative displays of strength while having forces within call sufficient to cope with any possible outbreak.' The article then went on to suggest that 'the strategy that seems to work at the carnival is one that entails a certain amount of self-denial in overlooking minor infringements of the law' because, as Scarman

---

21. Irving, Barrie L; Cathy Bird: Malcolm Hibbard and Jon Willmore (1989). *Neighbourhood Policing: The Natural History of a Policing Experiment*. London: Police Foundation, pp.42–43.
22. *Kensington News and Post*, 3 and 10 September 1982.

had identified, 'the maintenance of public order can be more important than the arrest of one petty criminal.'[23]

High Profile Patrols

There were two significant events in September, one at the beginning of the month, the other at the end. Immediately Carnival was over, the new strategy of high profile policing was implemented. In order to achieve it, 24 officers—six from each of the four reliefs at Notting Hill—had been selected for their experience and general demeanour. Every time they were on duty these officers would be posted to All Saints Road and its surrounds. The instructions issued by Whitfield specified:

- There would be a 24-hour presence of uniformed officers in All Saints Road.
- The presence would be relevant to the need but there would be a minimum of two officers visible at all times.
- The remaining four officers would patrol the vicinity and be available to enhance the presence as and when required.
- Whenever possible, arrests would be made by following suspects and arresting them away from All Saints Road to avoid confrontations.
- Due to a history of missiles being thrown at police vehicles, mobile police patrols in All Saints Road would be confined to responding to emergency calls for assistance only.
- Every incident likely to develop into serious disorder would be attended by the duty inspector.[24]

Initially, the officers conducting the foot patrols were met with hostility and abuse and Keith described how 'on several occasions pairs of policemen were bundled off the road by large crowds of people who resented what they saw as an "army of occupation".'[25] Indeed Innes and Whitfield became so concerned with the hostility towards these patrols that the police called for

23. *The Times*, 1 September 1982.
24. Innes Report, op. cit. 9, p.62, para. 17.3.
25. Keith, Michael (1993). *Race, Riots and Policing: Lore and Disorder in a Multi-racist Society*. London, UCL Press, p.127.

the next meeting of the Police Consultative Committee to be brought forward from October to September. The meeting, chaired by the Father Michael Hollings of the Notting Hill Council of Churches, was held at the Westway Information Centre in Ladbroke Grove. Once again, the police came in for criticism about their tactics; some invitees to the meeting picketed it and others staged a pre-planned walkout. However, several black people were at the meeting throughout and the debate was described as both constructive and positive. Again, the public was not invited but the media was. The success of the police strategy for All Saints Road was seen to be in the absence of disorder and in the claim by the police that they were able to maintain a balance in their three-fold function.[26]

It was a particularly difficult time for the inspectors who were expected to keep the 'lid' on All Saints Road and one inspector, who served there at the time, saw things differently. Claiming the drugs-dealers 'showed a degree of shrewdness by mostly dealing out of sight of the police' there were nevertheless occasions when officers would stumble across a deal being made. There followed 'a short period of excitement' and a call for 'urgent assistance' over the police radio system as the officers tried to make an arrest and a crowd gathered. He went on to suggest that for the duty inspector, 'there wasn't a worse shout to hear.' Controlling the total number of officers who attended and what they did individually when they got there was difficult, made the more so when officers came from other divisions, intending 'to show' their Notting Hill colleagues 'how to police the road "properly".' Eventually, the Commissioner decided he wanted a written report of all incidents in All Saints Road, 'which occasionally required' the duty inspector to use 'imaginative writing skills.'[27]

The second significant event in September was the closure of the Apollo public house. After over 50 years of trading, the owners, Whitbreads, finally called time 'because its reputation was giving the brewery a bad name' as a result of which its licence was at risk. Whilst a representative from the Lancaster and All Saints Resident Association expressed the Association's delight at its closure, an unnamed black resident told the local newspaper that 'it

---

26. Innes, op. cit. 9, p.62, paras 17.4 to 17.7.
27. In correspondence to the author from Graham Sharp, dated 18 January 2011.

was just another form of harassment' claiming that the pub had been 'a part of the community' and 'somewhere for us to focus'.[28]

Anniversary of the Publication of the Scarman Report

As the first anniversary of the publication of the Scarman Report on Brixton approached, there was a flurry of activity and comment. Conservative Party Councillor on the Greater London Council (GLC), Robert Hughes, claimed that the North Kensington Police Monitoring Group was 'souring relations between the police and the community' and criticised the GLC for funding a body which appeared 'to stand in the way of co-operation between the public and the police.' In response, the chairman of the GLC's Police Committee, Paul Boateng replied:

> 'The main objectives of a monitoring group are to monitor police activity in its particular area, to work towards the establishment of an independent and effective complaints procedure and towards the Metropolitan Police becoming account-able to an appropriate elected authority and the community as a whole. ... While contact with the police can be valuable in certain circumstances, it should be stressed that monitoring groups are not liaison committees, so that the question of what, if any contact there should be will always be the subject of individual decisions by the group.'[29]

Those representing the rank-and-file police officers in London felt there had been little progress during the year. Whilst recognising the importance of the Scarman Report to the police service, Leslie Curtis, chairman of the Police Federation, claimed that 'many individual policemen' were 'against the idea of "soft" policing in areas such as Brixton and Notting Hill' point-ing out that the views of the officers he represented were 'that no matter what colour or creed lives in the areas, police should wage an all-out "war" on crimes such as muggings and burglaries'.[30] To this, the chairman of the London Branch of the Police Federation, John Newman, added, 'We now treat ethnic minorities in a different manner than we do the white population

---

28. *Kensington News and Post*, 1 October 1982.
29. *Kensington News and Post*, 22 October 1982.
30. *The Daily Telegraph*, 25 October 1982.

in London.' He went on, 'to arrest coloured people in areas of high ethnic minority groupings leads to trouble, so we don't and the crime figures soar.'[31]

The Commissioner Enters the Fray

It coincided with the new Commissioner of the Metropolitan Police, Sir Kenneth Newman, visiting two police stations in so-called sensitive areas, Brixton and Notting Hill, after which he spoke to the media. He promised a crackdown on 'muggings and street crime' and 'a more efficient system of gathering intelligence'. Whilst he did 'not rule out largescale operations', he said 'they would have to be efficiently and professionally organized.' Despite the fact that officers were 'being spat at', 'gratuitously abused', 'having things thrown at them for no reason at all', and, in some cases 'enticed into ambushes', he said 'we are going to police these areas and will enforce the law.' Referring specifically to All Saints Road, the Commissioner suggested that progress 'was being made with cooperation from the public' although there were complaints from some residents about the increased foot patrols. Pointing out that what was required was 'a brand of policing where the police do what the majority of the public, both black and white, want them to do' he said the patrols were having 'a beneficial effect' and other local residents had written to say how pleased they were.[32] A year later, in a memorial lecture, the Commissioner returned to the difficulties faced by the police in such areas, suggesting that 'the strategy of balancing law enforcement and tranquillity raised difficult moral, legal and political dilemmas for police.'[33]

Towards the end of the year, Whitfield re-activated a covert operation, similar that undertaken in February, only this time various resources from Police Headquarters at New Scotland Yard were utilised. Working with local detectives, eight out of eleven main drug-dealers then operating on All Saints Road were arrested.[34] Although there were no significant incidents during the latter months of 1982 and the early part of 1983, patrolling officers were

31. *Ibid.*
32. *Daily Express,* 27 October 1982; *Daily Mail,* 27 October 1982; *Daily Mirror,* 27 October 1982; *Daily Telegraph* 27 October 1982; *Guardian,* 27 October 1982; *Morning Star,* 27 October 1982; *The Times,* 27 October 1972; *Kensington News and Post,* 29 October 1982.
33. In the Sir George Bean memorial Lecture, 'Policing London Post Scarman.' Reported in *The Daily Telegraph* and the *Daily Express,* 31 October 1983.
34. Innes, op. cit. 9, p.64, para.18.6.

still subject to abuse and the threat of violence remained high. More fuel was added when a spokesman for the Home Office-funded North Kensington Law Centre claimed they were;

> 'growing increasingly concerned at reports of people being beaten up in Notting Hill Police Station. Until recently we always felt there was less chance of such behaviour at Notting Hill Police Station than some others around here. But in the past two months several such incidents have been reported to us.'[35]

Attempts to Reduce Tension

In an attempt to reduce tension, in February, 1983, Commander Innes and local MP, Sir Brandon Rhys-Williams, met with black community leaders, who claimed that police officers in Notting Hill were 'too young' and 'too pushy'. Frank Crichlow was particularly critical, claiming that repeated complaints about police harassment and behaviour had been ignored. Suggesting that young black people were 'at boiling point', Crichlow warned that they could start taking the law into their own hands.[36]

However, the meeting was told that a new scheme to make local policing more effective and responsive to community needs would come into operation over the coming months. A product of research carried out by New Scotland Yard's Community Relations Branch, the independent Police Foundation and Notting Hill Police themselves, it gave inspectors responsibility for policing special geographical areas. A special squad of 24 older policemen, aged between 35 and 40 years, was being drafted into Notting Hill in an attempt to defuse clashes between the black community and young officers. The Criminal Investigation Branch at Notting Hill would also be part of the new scheme, with two detective inspectors being given specific responsibilities for the west and east sides of Ladbroke Grove respectively. But the meeting ended in uproar when Crichlow announced that he would 'refuse any invitation to discuss with police their policy for the area.'[37]

---

35. *The Standard*, 1 February 1983.
36. *Ibid.*
37. *Ibid.* The attempt to introduce Neighbourhood Policing is referred to in more detail in the next chapter.

Scarman devoted some 34 paragraphs of his report to recruitment, training, supervision and monitoring within the police service.[38] A number of complaints had been made to him about 'the deployment of young police officers in sensitive areas.'[39] However, he pointed out that they have an advantage over older officers when dealing with young people on the streets in that 'no generation gap separates them.' He felt that young officers should not be removed from sensitive areas but it was necessary to ensure that they received 'proper guidance and supervision in discharging their difficult, delicate, and indispensable function.'[40] So, in effect, the setting up of this special squad of older police officers to some extent went against Scarman's recommendations. He stressed the importance of sergeants and inspectors exercising supervision but suggested insufficient attention had been given to their training in this respect.[41] Pointing out that he had heard that, in some cases, black people were treated 'without respect' and the police officers were 'deliberately provocative and insulting' which was all 'designed to strip the individual of whatever dignity he may possess',[42] Scarman claimed that close supervision was particularly important in those operations that involved 'stop and search'.[43]

In a statement to the media following the meeting, Sir Brandon Rhys-Williams suggested that 'a year or so ago' the area round All Saints Road was almost regarded as a 'no-go' area. He claimed 'the situation' had 'improved since then' and whilst there would be 'conflict' he believed they were 'on the right road.' He then went on to suggest that black people in the area:

> 'don't like to be given the idea that they are lawless, that humiliates them. The police have to win their confidence, and I think Mr Whitelaw has got it right now

---

38. Scarman, Rt. Hon. The Lord (1981). 'The Brixton Disorders 10–12 April 1981: Report of an Inquiry' (Cmnd 8427). London: Her Majesty's Stationery Office, Part V, pp.76–87, paras. 5.6 to 5.40.
39. *Ibid*, p.84, para. 5.34.
40. *Ibid*, p.85, paras. 5.34–5.35.
41. *Ibid*, p.85, para. 5.36.
42. *Ibid*, p.85, para. 5.37.
43. *Ibid*, p.86, para. 5.37.

with his formula for complaints.[44] It's now a matter of convincing people. If they feel that it is being dealt with by a totally independent element, and that nothing is being covered up, then I think things will improve as well.'

A police spokesman took a similar line. Pointing out that there had been demands for the police to take action in relation to crime, disorder and general anti-social behaviour in the area, he claimed that the situation in All Saints Road had improved 'greatly in recent months' and 'there has been a lot of co-operation from the community, both black and white.'[45]

News of the meeting brought forth a major article about Notting Hill written by the Editor of London's only evening newspaper. In an interview with Max Hastings, the Police Community Liaison Officer, Chief Inspector Aitchison, summed up the situation:

'We recognise that this area is symbolic, because of Carnival, because of its history, because of the memory of the 1950s, it has special significance. And there is one particular 150 yard stretch in this division which symbolises the difficulties for West Indians living in this country. This is an area on the classic Scarman model: the crime exists in certain parts of it and the police operations to inhibit this pose a threat to public order, which occasionally results in confrontations.'[46]

Max Hasting himself pointed out that it was unreasonable to expect 'the police alone to do other than enforce the law as it stands,' before going on to suggest that 'if minority communities are to be policed by different standards to those of the rest of the country, this seems to be a decision that politicians and society must make.'[47]

In March 1983, the *Caribbean Times* once again highlighted the dilemma of all police commanders responsible for policing areas such as Notting Hill,

---

44. A Bill had been introduced in the House of Commons by the then Home Secretary, William Whitelaw which eventually became law as the Police and Criminal Evidence Act 1984. The Act created the Police Complaints Authority, established in 1985, which introduced an independent element into the investigation of complaints made against police officers.
45. *The Standard*, 2 February 1983.
46. Hastings, Max. Suspicion and the Sinners of All Saints Road. In *The Standard*, 7 February 1983.
47. *Ibid.*

when it reported that Kensington and Chelsea Residents' Association had 'collected over 400 signatures from local people ... calling on Home Secretary, Douglas Hurd, to put more police on the streets to stop ... violent robberies, particularly at knifepoint, occurring in North Kensington.' Although the call was supported by two existing Labour councillors, a black prospective Labour councillor for a ward which bordered onto All Saints Road, Maxwell Worrell suggested it was 'misguided hysteria' and that 'bringing more police on the streets' was 'a recipe for riots'.[48] Once again, the dilemma for the police was exposed. Local politicians could not agree how an area should be policed.

On 29 March, Kensington Council finally won a battle to close an illegal drinking club at No. 26 All Saints Road. Following widespread complaints that music, shouting fighting, and the slamming of car doors often went on all night, the Council had served enforcement and stop notices on the club in October 1982, but the owner had appealed and it went before a public inquiry where the appeal was eventually turned down. As the club continued to operate, police raided the club three times in the week following the refusal to allow the appeal and commenced prosecutions against the owner, Newton Fitzroy Clarke, for selling intoxicating liquor without a licence.[49] However, even this failed to deter Clarke and the premises continued to operate as a shebeen for another two years until, finally, he was given a three months suspended prison sentence by the High Court for breach of an earlier injunction ordering him to cease operating the property as a café, a disco and recreational centre and to conform to planning permission.[50]

Release of the Crime Figures

As it did in 1982, the release of crime figures for London in April 1983 created a furore and resulted in a wave of condemnation by various black groups and the Commission for Racial Equality. The Shadow Home Secretary, Roy Hattersley, went so far as to describe them as 'statistical garbage'. However, on this occasion, the police were not wholly to blame. The figures were released by the Home Office in response to a parliamentary question by the Conservative MP for Basildon, Harvey Proctor. The reason for the furore

---

48. *The Caribbean Times,* 14 March 1983.
49. *Kensington News and Post,* 5 April 1983.
50. *Kensington News and Post,* 5 July 1985.

was a three per cent rise in muggings, i.e. theft where violence or the threat of violence has been used, over 1981. In addition, the figures revealed that in 10,960 (56 per cent) of the 19,258 incidents, the victims identified the assailants as 'coloured', and only in 5,262 incidents (27 per cent) were the assailants identified as 'white'. The remainder of the muggings were either committed by mixed groups (534) or, race wise, were unknown (2,502).[51]

Peter Newsam, chairman of the Commission for Racial Equality 'condemned the selective manner in which the figures had been released', claiming that nothing appeared 'to have been learnt in the past year' about 'the consequences' of releasing crime figures in this way. He went on to suggest that their publication had 'destroyed a year of efforts to restore good relations between the black community and the police.' The Metropolitan Police Commissioner, Sir Kenneth Newman, whilst defending the collection of such statistics in an attempt to 'try to identify the causes of various types of crime and the people involved' said that 'he would not have released them' thus suggesting that at least the police had learnt something from the previous year. However, a number of newspapers asked what the police were supposed to do, given that the figures were based on the description of the attackers given by the victims.[52]

---

51. *The Daily Telegraph* 23.3.83; *The Standard* 23.3.83; *The Times*, 24.3.83; *The Daily Telegraph*, 24.3.83; *Daily Mail* 24.3.83; *Daily Mirror* 24.3.83; *The Sun* 24.3.83; *Daily Express* 24.3.83; *Morning Star* 24.3.83; *The Caribbean Times* 1.4.83; *The Voice*, week ending 9.4.83; *City Limits* 1.4.83; *Labour Weekly* 25.3.83; The media muggings by Martyn Harris in *New Society* 31.3.83.
52. *Ibid.*

CHAPTER 14

THE DEFINITIVE DOCUMENT ON ALL SAINTS ROAD

Police Consultative Committee Meetings

From its inception, the monthly Police Consultative Committee meeting called to discuss the problems of All Saints Road and chaired by Father Michael Hollings, had only been attended by local ward councillors all of whom were from the Labour Party, the minority group within the Kensington and Chelsea Council. In an effort to get representatives of the ruling Conservative Party to attend, the venue of the meeting for April 1983 was changed to Kensington Town Hall and invitations were sent. These were rejected and, because the meeting was not initiated by the council, Father Hollings was asked to pay the booking fee for the room. The meeting went ahead after the police had promised to reimburse him.

At the meeting, Chief Superintendent Whitfield said the police were 'cautiously optimistic' about the situation in All Saints Road. Pointing out that the concentration of uniformed officers patrolling the area was part of an effort to stop the street being used as a drug market. He said: 'We are half-way through that operation but there is still a fair amount of drug-dealing going on in and around the area.' The dealers were being targeted, he claimed, but a continuing problem existed, because, when they were caught, charged and taken to court the following morning, they would plead not guilty, be given bail and where back on the street that afternoon.[1] Even when one was taken out of circulation by, for instance, being sentenced to a term of imprisonment, there were others to take his place.

More Incidents in All Saints Road

However, the cautious optimism expressed by Whitfield was arguably premature. Immediately after the meeting an organization, calling itself Workers

---

1. *Kensington News and Post*, 22 April 1983.

Against Racism, launched a campaign under the title 'West London Police put in the dock for attempted murder'. The allegation was that a 13-year-old boy, had been stabbed by a police officer on March 10. The circumstances were, however, somewhat different. The boy was seen by a patrolling police officer in All Saints Road at 4 a.m. As he was approached, the boy, pursued by the officer, ran into the basement of the illegal drinking club at No.26. The officer tripped and tumbled down the steps, landing on top of the boy. People from inside the drinking club emerged, assaulted the police officer and dragged the boy inside where he was found to have a stab wound. However, when interviewed subsequently, Baron Baker, a respected black representative on the newly-formed All Saints Road Positive Action Committee, expressed the view that it was likely that the boy was in possession of the knife and had drawn it to use against the police officer.[2]

Over the next three months, further incidents suggested that the situation, rather than improving, was deteriorating. On May 7, police officers, attempting to arrest a man suspected of a drug offence in All Saints Road, were again met by a hostile crowd and reinforcements, including dog handlers, were deployed to the area. In all, about 40 officers, under the overall command of the duty inspector, Peter King, sealed the street off for a short while. Two people were arrested.[3] Accusations of over-reaction by the police followed, during which specific emphasis was placed on the use of police dogs. People were quick to point out that, in his report on the Brixton disturbances in April 1981, Lord Scarman had stated that 'all police officers who gave evidence to the inquiry recognised that dogs were not an appropriate instrument for dispersing crowds in sensitive situations.'[4]

Similar incidents were to occur on two other occasions within the space of the next three months. On 20 June, at least 100 people quickly gathered in All Saints Road after a man had been arrested for an earlier assault on an

---

2. *Ibid.*
3. *Kensington News and Post*, 13 May 1983.
4. Scarman, Rt. Hon. The Lord. 'The Brixton Disorders 10–12 April 1981: Report of an Inquiry' (Cmnd. 8427). Her Majesty's Stationery Office, London, 1981, p.69, para.4.84. Scarman made two other references to the use of police dogs in his report. Firstly, he wrote: 'Arrangements must be introduced to prevent the deployment of dogs in handling major crowd disorders in future' (p.70, para.4.84). A little later he suggested that his report re-affirmed the 'importance of avoiding the use of police dogs in dispersing a disorderly crowd' (p.97, para.5.73).

officer. Inspector Martin Jaul had been hit on the head with a billiard ball causing a cut which required seven stitches. A second man was also detained. Police reinforcements, including dogs, were called in to control the situation and the road was again closed for a time. In addition to the inspector, five police officers were slightly injured.[5]

Then, on August 1, police dogs were again used in All Saints Road to clear crowds who had gathered round a police van after officers had called for assistance during the arrest of a man who was eventually charged with possessing drugs and assault on police. Frank Crichlow took this opportunity to criticise the police for its use of stop and search tactics claiming they were provocative and caused bad relations with the community. Chief Superintendent Whitfield responded by claiming that the police were only doing their job as law enforcers, and, whilst incidents such as these did not 'improve relations', at the same time, they did not 'detract from them either.'[6]

Internal Publication of the Definitive Document

The month of May did see a major initiative on the part of the police to get to grips with the situation when the Definitive Document, referred to in a number of previous chapters as the Innes Report, was published internally within the Metropolitan Police Service. As has already been seen in those earlier references, the document provided a brief historical analysis and critique of the policing of All Saints Road since 1968. It started by outlining the political interest, both from central and local governments, before describing police activities and providing a critique of each major confrontation. More importantly, perhaps, the document described how conflict with the police was 'personified in the continuing difficulties between Notting Hill Police Station and the Mangrove Community Association.'[7]

In summarising the history of All Saints Road between 1968 and 1983, the report claimed that it was and had been 'a haven for wrongdoers' for some years. However, over the same period, there was recognition that the police

---

5. *The Guardian*, 22 June 1983; also *Hansard*, 30 June 1983.
6. *Kensington News and Post*, 5 August 1983.
7. Innes, Commander; Chief Superintendent Whitfield and Chief Inspector Aitchison (1983). 'All Saints Road, London, W11: A Definitive Document'. Typeset: Metropolitan Police, p.7, para.5.1.

had used the same or similar methods in reacting to the problems without having regard to the implications of their actions. Thus the use of stop and search on a regular basis, the execution of search warrants and 'some insensitive behaviour' at street level, 'had incurred the hostility of black people in the area and to some extent alienated a wide section of the community who viewed these methods as heavy handed and discriminatory'. But, at the same time, there had been little noticeable effect on the criminal activity that took place, particularly in relation to the availability of drugs. It could therefore be argued that all the police had achieved over the years was to prevent the 'market' from getting out of control—some would say it was already out-of-control at this stage[8]—before going on to describe what it termed as the spiral effect. As criminality and anti-social behaviour increased, law enforcement activities became greater which, in an area such as All Saints Road, led to an increase in the number of unsavoury incidents, as a result of which there was reduced support for the police and thus the ability of the police to influence the criminality and anti-social behaviour decreased.[9]

The effect of this on both the police and the community was summarised as follows:

- Either directly or by association, police operations had played a prominent part in the lives of many local people;
- Unwilling to abide by the law, sections of the black community interpreted those operations as a personal bias against them because of their colour, not because of their criminality;
- Police officers who had become involved in vigorous pursuit of their powers inevitably incurred the wrath and hostility of those black people and their supporters, most of whom were closely associated with the Mangrove environment;
- Old wounds never healed; as a consequence each new crisis was related to the past, thereby prolonging bitter feelings on both sides;
- The police frequently felt themselves to be on the receiving end of unjust criticism because their efforts to enforce the law were so often called into question;

---

8. *Ibid*, p.24, paras.6.1 to 6.5.
9. *Ibid*, p.25, para.6.6.

- The police point of view was difficult to articulate at times of crises, when they were most often publicly challenged, and therefore they tended to respond defensively;
- The concentration of public attention on the police brought both positive and negative effects, but in All Saints Road, the sustaining impression militated against the police;
- All the expressions and actions of good intent by officers of all ranks were constantly held hostage to chance and circumstances.[10]

The document also described how the Web of Affiliation, referred to in previous chapters, provided swift communication and a means of distributing material in Notting Hill. Public and community meetings were frequently used to express both positive and negative views about the police. However, when police operations involved the use of force, as for instance, it did on 20 April 1982, those critical of police action tended to smother elements who were supportive of the police, simply by expressing their views more forcefully and louder.[11]

Taking into account the comments by Lord Scarman about the policing of such areas in his report on Brixton, the document concluded by giving a broad overview of the problem as it then was before setting out, what it described as, a strategy for the future. It is worth looking at these two sections of the document because very few attempts had been made by the police anywhere in the country at that time to examine, in detail, what could have been done in such problem areas.

Dealing firstly with the overview, the guarded optimism that emerged from the meeting of senior police officers and Sir Brandon Rhys-Williams with black community leaders in February, and the police/community liaison meeting in April, meant that, tactically, the police were very much on the back foot. The recurring disturbances — the examples given here of the incidents on May 7, June 20 and August 1 were merely three of a number — together with the rising tension meant that the police were inhibited from developing the initiatives that came from the two meetings. However, it was clear that whenever the police carried out carefully planned

---

10. *Ibid*, pp.25/26, para.6.7.
11. *Ibid*, p.27, para. 7.4.

operations—such as that which took place at the culmination of Operation Michael on 20 February 1982—the likelihood of disorder breaking out was considerably reduced. There were also many occasions when it was not necessary to arrest people at the time but they would be targeted and action taken, without the risk of confrontation, away from All Saints Road. The report continued:

> '[T]he outrageous behaviour of some black youths in seeking to challenge the police deliberately drawing them step-by-step from normality to conflict, precipitated a spontaneous response to restore order, and when that escalated to full scale deployment it carried a risk of an individual officer's emotional involvement prejudicing his judgement and influencing his action to the detriment of the objective. In consequence, isolated instances of over-reaction provoked criticisms disproportionate to their effect because the critics chose to ignore the cause.'[12]

However, the document pointed out that, in cases when there was a victim or people were at risk, the police were duty-bound to act immediately but 'were held hostage to the threat of public disorder resulting from their actions because the black man endeavoured to protect his own kind and defend his assumed territory.'[13] The document then listed what it termed 'important markers' for future strategy:

- The most likely cause of public disorder was a stop in the street to search for drugs or stolen property;
- When a prisoner or suspect thwarted police by running for sanctuary, the initial police reaction was crucial in determining the level of escalation;
- The response to anything that occurred in All Saints Road was initially, almost certainly, going to be from someone at constable rank. His or her perception of the situation and the reaction was generally single-minded in pursuit of law enforcement;
- The constable was the most likely recipient of abuse and attack and therefore less likely to see the need to exercise discretion in responding to it;

---

12. *Ibid*, p.51, para.13.4.
13. *Ibid*, p.52, para.13.5.

- The controlling influence of supervising officers was an important moderator of police behaviour.[14]

Attempt to Introduce Neighbourhood Policing

In addition to all the difficulties associated with policing Notting Hill at that time, the division was chosen in 1982 as one of the places in which neighbourhood policing would be introduced. The whole concept of such a system was born out of a joint BSc thesis submitted to City University in London by two inspectors, Ian Beckett and Jim Hart in May 1981[15] which was taken up by the then Chief Constable of Surrey, Sir Peter Mathews and the Police Foundation, which had opened for business on January 1. Brought to the attention of the Metropolitan Police Commissioner, Sir David McNee, the Metropolitan Police saw it as a 'response to some of the criticisms contained in Lord Scarman's report on the Brixton riot.'[16]

The Police Foundation Report on 'Neighbourhood Policing' is an account of how attempts were made to introduce it in Notting Hill. It was chosen because it was 'a politically attractive "worst case" site', it was the location of 'the famous carnival [and had] a unique demographic mix' of people.[17] However, it was beset with difficulties once the project was initiated in January 1983.[18] The basic idea was to divide the division up into four geographical areas and each of the four reliefs that were then operating at Notting Hill would have responsibility for policing one of these areas.[19] However, one of the obstacles was the chief superintendent's insistence that All Saints Road must be 'manned by six officers 24 hours a day, regardless of innovations.'[20] The Report suggested that, to Notting Hill officers, All Saints Road was special for a number of reasons. It was:

---

14. *Ibid*, p.52, para.13.6.
15. James Hart went on to eventually become the Commissioner of the City of London Police; Ian Beckett rose to the rank of Deputy Chief Constable of the Surrey Police.
16. Irving, Barrie L; Cathy Bird: Malcolm Hibbard and Jon Willmore (1989). *Neighbourhood Policing: The Natural History of a Policing Experiment*. London: Police Foundation, p. ix.
17. *Ibid*, p.25.
18. *Ibid*, pp.11–15 and 24–30.
19. *Ibid*, pp.59–69.
20. *Ibid*, p.59.

- an illicit drug market;
- a centre for clubs in which known dealers, their clients and known criminals were regulars;
- an epicentre for civil disturbance;
- a potential no-go area; and
- a symbolic piece of 'ethnic' territory where West Indians in particular had
  stamped some sort of cultural identify on a small piece of London.[21]

The report described how the differences of opinion between senior management and those who were required to police All Saints Road on an
everyday basis had become a major problem. Many officers 'saw duty in
All Saints Road as something to be avoided at all costs [because] there was
no management will to grapple with the problem.' Matters came to a head
at a meeting of the Notting Hill Working Party set up at the outset of the
project which was observed by representatives from the Police Foundation
when it was clear that 'the station did not support the Chief Superintendent's All Saints Road policy although it recognised why there was a need
for caution in dealing with West Indians in this particular location.' Constables and sergeants

> 'were opposed to treating it differently from any other part of the ground. More
> specifically they objected to providing a passive police presence divorced from
> traditional law enforcement activity to guard against the risk of serious public
> disorder. They did not favour turning a blind-eye to trivial crime, and they believed
> the wholesale closing of clubs with unsavoury reputations could pave the way for
> returning the road to normality.'[22]

The project eventually failed. Waddington referred to it as an 'ill-fated
attempt to involve the police in Notting Hill's social problems' although he
suggested 'there was much to be learned' from reading the report and 'far

---

21. *Ibid*, p.77.
22. *Ibid*, pp.78/79.

from being dismissed as yet another failure to be shunned [it] should become compulsory reading for all police managers.'[23]

There was, however, no let up. On July 31, three police officers were stabbed, one in the back, one in the leg and one in the arm during an incident in St Luke's Road. A man was arrested and subsequently charged with maliciously wounding the three officers. Later that day, 30 black youths attempted to gatecrash a private disco in Acklam Hall which had been organized by the Spanish Community in Notting Hill. Two people were taken to hospital.[24] Meanwhile, the police continued to arrest and prosecute people for drug offences. In August, at Marylebone Magistrates' Court, a further seven people, amongst them a 15-year-old boy who had been caught supplying drugs, were fined varying amounts.[25] Shortly before the Carnival, it was announced that the police had smashed a drugs ring which was planning to flood the Carnival with cannabis. Twenty kilos of cannabis resin and 20 of cannabis oil, with a street value of over £1 million, had been discovered in lock-up garages in West London along with two heavy presses which it was believed the gang would have used to make blocks of cannabis from the oil and resin.[26]

The 1983 Carnival

Although it was an entirely peaceful event in public order terms, 333 crimes were reported to the police during the two days of the 1983 Carnival. In 79 per cent of cases, the victims had purses, jewellery or handbags stolen. One interesting thing to come out of the Carnival on this occasion was the results of a survey undertaken by the Management Services Department of the Metropolitan Police, although to those who had some experience of the event there were no surprises. It revealed that the great majority of victims of crime were white, 62 per cent being women. The greater number of crimes (79 per cent) were committed on the Monday with 91 per cent of these occurring between 4 p.m. and midnight, and 64 per cent of the crimes occurred

---

23. Waddington, P. A. (1989). 'Neighbourhood Policing—The Light that Failed'. In *Police*, Vol. XXI, No. 11, July, p.36.
24. *Kensington News and Post*, 5 August 1983.
25. *Kensington News and Post*, 12 August 1983.
26. *Kensington News and Post*, 26 August 1983.

in three roads, Portobello Road, All Saints Road and Ladbroke Grove, areas where congestion was normally at its greatest. The survey found that the presence of uniformed police officers did not appear to be an effective deterrent; in nearly a third of the cases, the victims of crime claimed they were 'near' a police officer when the property was stolen.[27]

The Difficulties Continue

There were any number of minor incidents during the latter part of 1983 and the first half of 1984, and tensions remained. However, the situation began to worsen again from July onwards when, in a particularly nasty incident, a woman was dragged out of the Mangrove by two Notting Hill men, forced inside a taxi and taken to a nearby flat where she was held prisoner for 16 hours during which time she was raped and indecently assaulted. Eventually, the two men were traced and arrested, and, in March 1985, were sent to prison for ten years having been found guilty of kidnapping, false imprisonment and assault. In his defence, one of the defendants claimed that 'she was a white girl in a black man's club [and] that she was there to get us into trouble.'[28]

Meanwhile, a report on the front page of the *Kensington News and Post* in July claimed that 'sacks of pot' were for sale in All Saints Road, with one resident claiming that he personally saw between 20 and 30 drug-dealings taking place outside his door every day. A meeting of the All Saints Police Liaison Group was told that there had been 500 arrests in All Saints Road in the previous six months. Chief Superintendent Whitfield claimed that, although the situation fluctuated from time-to-time, arrests would continue to be made. Chief Inspector Bert Aitchison, Community Liaison Officer, said the mood and temper of the area was now less threatening and less difficult, claiming that 'a great deal of work' had 'been done by many people other than the police to inhibit the anti-social behaviour.'[29] Shortly after the report appeared in the newspaper, more than 100 police officers descended on All Saints Road in early August, sealing the street off before entering Nos.26 and 28. Seven people were arrested; six were subsequently charged

---

27. Metropolitan Police Management Services Department (1984). 'A Survey of the Victims of Crime at the 1982 Notting Hill Carnival'. MSD Report Number 17/83. January, 1984.

28. *Kensington News and Post*, 1 March 1985.

29. *Kensington News and Post*, 6 July 1984.

with drug-related offences. Crichlow suggested that it was 'very bad strategy on the part of the police with just a few weeks to go before carnival.'[30]

In August, the police again claimed that 'the problems of crime' could not be solved by the police alone. Pointing out that 'other agencies [had] responsibilities', Superintendent Aitchison, who had, by now, been promoted and appointed as deputy divisional commander at Notting Hill, claimed that the police were hopeful that the gradual development of All Saints Road would act as 'a crime-busting measure' in that new businesses in North Kensington's 'front line' street could help to put an end to the drug trade there. He felt that a thriving commercial community, on the right side of the law, would 'cold-shoulder' drug traffickers.[31] However, that stage had not yet been reached because when a man was stabbed in All Saints Road on August 18, the police, not for the first time, ran up against a wall of silence, despite the seriousness of the incident. The blade touched the edge of the man's heart; half-an-inch further over and he would have been dead.[32]

The 1984 Carnival

Following the 1983 Carnival, complaints had been made about the obstructions caused by stalls in heavily congested streets and, with ever-increasing numbers of people attending, there were serious concerns about public safety. Only 18 months previously, two women had been crushed to death at the New Year's Eve celebrations in Trafalgar Square. In an effort to improve safety the police suggested to Kensington and Chelsea Council that all stalls operating during the event should be licensed; this would be the first occasion that this had been done. However, the council refused, suggesting that such a plan would be unworkable. Superintendent Aitchison, expressed his disappointment at the decision, commenting, 'I pressed them hard to have street trading legitimised.'[33]

However, in an effort to reverse the trend of rising crime at previous carnivals, not for the first time it must be said, a vigorous crime prevention campaign was mounted. But, in a major difference to previous years, on

---

30. *Kensington News and Post*, 10 August 1984.
31. *Kensington News and Post*, 17 August 1984.
32. *Kensington News and Post*, 24 August 1984.
33. *Kensington News and Post*, 10 August 1984.

this occasion the pre-carnival press conference was a joint one, attended by both carnival organizers and senior police officers. During the event itself the police used three news scanners to flash messages, including warnings of the likelihood of pick-pockets operating, to the crowd. Despite these efforts, reported crime increased for the second successive year, rising by something like 30 per cent on 1983, to the highest figure since 1976, nearly 600.[34]

In the aftermath, a fierce disagreement broke out between police officers locally and those at Scotland Yard. Initial statements by senior officers suggested that it had been a peaceful event but, after some junior officers had contacted the *Kensington News and Post*, the newspaper published a front-page article under the headlines, 'Five hours of rape, violence and a killing; Carnival's Secret Timetable of Terror'. Describing how Scotland Yard had announced at the conclusion of the Carnival, that 11 officers had been injured and 288 people had had their pockets picked, the article reported that this figure had since been revised by Notting Hill Police who claimed that 22 officers had been injured and nearly 600 crimes had been committed. The article went on to suggest that at about 9 p.m. on the Bank Holiday Monday, two policemen were injured, one seriously when he was slashed with a knife causing a wound which required 20 stitches. Two-and-a-half hours later, a man was murdered on the border of the Carnival area; at just before midnight, two dozen passengers were robbed at knifepoint on an underground train travelling between Westbourne Park and Edgware Road stations, taking passengers away from the Carnival, and three women were raped, one in Notting Hill and two in Kensington as they walked home from the Carnival. In a subsequent interview, B District Commander, John Perrett, suggested that a 'nasty theme of violence ran through the crimes reported to police.'[35]

Setting up of a Formal Police Consultative Committee

Kensington and Chelsea Council finally agreed to the setting up of a Police Consultative Committee in September but a leading black councillor, Ben Bousquet, refused to take part, claiming that it would be a 'cosmetic exercise', dominated by the white middle-class, in which black people would be outvoted and would merely be included to look good. In an effort to allay

34. *Daily Telegraph*, 29 August 1984; *Kensington News and Post*, 31 August 1984.
35. *Kensington News and Post*, 14 September 1984.

such criticisms, it was announced that the election of the 12 members, half of whom would be black, to serve on the Committee would be conducted by an impartial body, the Notting Hill Social Council.[36]

The Departure of Chief Superintendent Whitfield

In a letter to *The Standard* in mid-January 1985, a local resident claimed that drugs were 'available 24 hours a day in Notting Hill's All Saints Road.' Accusing the police of taking the view that 'softly-softly tactics' would 'reduce racial tension', the writer suggested that 'this form of discrimination does not benefit the community except the pushers themselves.'[37]

As Chief Superintendent Jack Whitfield relinquished his job as the Commander of Notting Hill Division in January, he received praise from Frank Crichlow for 'doing a good job' in improving relations between black people and the police. In summing up Whitfield's time at Notting Hill, Keith described how he made a conscious attempt 'to take away the symbolism of All Saints Road' by, firstly, changing the style of policing in introducing a special squad of 24 constables 'for the express purpose of recovering All Saints Road' and 'dramatically' curtailing 'mass raids', and secondly, in attempting to involve other agencies in 'policing' the area. He also 'embarked on an extensive PR campaign, making himself available to all community leaders 24 hours a day, a move' suggests Keith 'that won him grudging respect from some of the most hostile local people.' Finally, he claimed that he was one of the 'very few chief superintendents on speaking terms with Frank Crichlow'.

So, Keith claimed, when he left Notting Hill, Whitfield was optimistic that he had started down a road which would lead to All Saints Road losing its symbolism. However, Keith claimed that 'it became increasingly evident [that his] reforms [were] extremely unpopular [with] many of his junior officers'[38] [and] in spite of the permanent police presence, the drugs trade continued.[39]

---

36. *Kensington News and Post*, 21 September 1984.
37. *The Standard*, 17 January 1985.
38. Keith, Michael (1993). *Race, Riots and Policing: Lore and Disorder in a Multi-racist Society*. London: UCL Press, p.127.
39. *Ibid*, p.128.

An alternative view was expressed by Chief Superintendent Denis O'Connor, who became the divisional commander at Notting Hill in 1990. In a presentation to the Association of Chief Police Officers National Drug Conference in 1992, he alleged that, by the mid-1980s, drugs had become 'a focus of difficulty' by pointing out that All Saints Road had 'gained a reputation as a street market' for drugs, and 'open trading' in cannabis and cocaine was accompanied 'by disorder, abuse, assault on local police officers and street robberies, all of which engendered fear in the local community.' Any significant police action, he claimed, ran the risk of generating 'large scale disorder [and] organizing an effective response presented difficulties for police management.'[40]

Within days of replacing Whitfield and having toured All Saints Road twice, Chief Superintendent Albert McKew was warned by Critchlow that good relations between the police and the black community were 'still a long way off.' McKew's response was to pledge 'to tackle crime on the street using the softly, softly tactics suggested by Lord Scarman's report on the 1981 riots.' But, at the same time he pointed out that, 'with 1,000 arrests annually in the All Saints Road area the visible police presence' would remain;[41] so, too, did the strong feeling of resentment about the police within the black community.

April saw the departure of another senior police officer from B District. The retirement of Commander John Perrett, who had taken over from Bob Innes, and the announcement by the Metropolitan Police that, due to reorganization, he would not be replaced, received a hostile reception from the local Police Consultative Committee, resulting in the chairman writing a letter of protest to the Commissioner.[42] In fact, the policing of the Metropolitan Police area was being reorganized to bring it more in line with local government boundaries. As a result, the 24 districts were being done away with; in their place, were eight areas, each under the command of a Deputy

---

40. O'Connor, Chief Superintendent Denis (1992). 'Notting Hill—Developing a Local Strategy'. In the proceedings of the 11th National Drug Conference. Association of Chief Police Officers, p.34.
41. *Kensington News and Post*, 1 February 1985.
42. *Kensington News and Post*, 12 April 1985.

Assistant Commissioner, assisted by two Commanders. Henceforth, Divisional Commanders would report direct to Area Headquarters.

Perritt's departure coincided with the issue by the Metropolitan Police of new instructions relating to professional behaviour. These instructions, contained in a handbook, issued to each officer and to top members of the civil staff, reminded them of the Policing Principles dating back to 1829 before going on to emphasise the vital importance of the role of the constable in a free society. Pointing out that 'the attitude to the police of black youngsters—particularly those of West Indian origin [had] given much cause for concern' the handbook described how some incidents were 'capable of rational explanation' but others gave 'some grounds for apprehension and police over-zealousness and misbehaviour.'

The handbook suggested it should be acknowledged that there was 'an uncritical readiness' in some police officers 'to think poorly of the black community.' It also pointed out that there was 'an over-generalised assumption,' on occasions, of black involvement 'in violent crime, deceit and collaboration in avoiding detection and rescuing lawfully detained prisoners, lack of intelligence and the ability to articulate, and absence of the motivation to work.' On the other hand, comments coming from black communities included 'allegations of racial prejudice, harassment and abuse, use of excessive force, falsification of evidence, and indifference to the problems of black people.' Claiming that 'allegations of this nature coming from both "sides" fed off each other,' the handbook pointed out that the police would 'need to work hard and patiently to increase their understanding of minority ethnic groups, especially the young blacks'.[43]

Worsening Situation in All Saints Road

Meanwhile, little had changed in the vicinity of All Saints Road. If anything the situation was getting worse. In one week at the beginning of April, three separate attacks within a few hours left one man with a fractured skull, and two others the victim of robberies, one at knifepoint. Firstly, a man was knocked unconscious in Tavistock Road. When he recovered, he found his watch, a quantity of money, his keys and his shoes had been stolen. Then

---

43. Newman, Sir Kenneth (1985). *The Principles of Policing and Guidance for Professional Behaviour.* London: Metropolitan Police, p.40

a motorist and his passenger were robbed at knifepoint in McGregor Road when they refused an offer to buy drugs. Finally, the man who had his skull fractured was set upon by a group of men in the vicinity of All Saints Road and hit over the head with a paving stone. Meanwhile his companion was beaten to the ground with a piece of wood.[44]

Following these incidents, the police were accused by the black community of being 'too tough' and by other residents of All Saints Road of being 'too soft'. The former claimed there had been an increase of police activity following the departure of Whitfield which had led to an increase in tension. Labour Councillor Ben Bousquet claimed there had been 'a deliberate policy by Notting Hill Police to attack North Kensington's black community' alleging that 'the goodwill created by senior officers' over the previous two years had gone. A meeting was held with local Member of Parliament, Sir Brandon Rhys-Williams, at which they asked him to raise the policing of Notting Hill in the House of Commons but he refused, saying he would make their views known to senior police officers and the Home Secretary. Meanwhile, other residents claimed they were 'frequently threatened with physical violence' and hard drugs, including heroin and cocaine, were 'openly bought and sold' in All Saints Road, under 'the nose' of police officers who 'turned a blind eye.' As a result they had instructed a solicitor to examine the possibility of going to the High Court to ask for an order 'compelling the police to carry out its legal obligation.'[45] In the event this did not happen.

In June 1985, an article headed 'Scandal of No-Go Cops', claimed that *News of The World* reporters were approached 'five times in 17 minutes' by drug pushers in All Saints Road. Describing how one West Indian offered them 'heroin at £60 a gramme while a policeman stood in a shop doorway ten yards away' the reporters claimed that the drug pusher said of the policeman 'he's no problem, man. They come and go. We're always here.'

When the *News of The World* reported the results of their investigation to New Scotland Yard, a spokesman claimed that the police knew the area to be a 'major drug-dealing' centre. Officers in the area were, he said, 'attempting to combine firmness with sensitivity — to take action against drug-dealing while trying to avoid public disorder.' He claimed that 'with a lot of people

44. *Kensington News and Post*, 12 April 1985.
45. *Kensington News and Post*, 26 April 1985.

hanging around street corners and the summer just beginning, the situation is sensitive.'[46]

In the meantime, the 'All Saints Road Patrol' set up by Whitfield 'became an increasingly unpopular tour of duty, until in 1985 it was effectively separated from the rest of the station'. Within a matter of months it was to become known as the 'Black Watch' with 'the level of antagonism' between the police and the black community remaining 'as high as ever.'[47]

The 1985 Carnival

Two further improvements were made in respect of police arrangements for the 1985 Carnival. Firstly, using a micro-computer, the police attempted to predict likely areas and patterns of crime with a view to cutting their own response times. Secondly, it was publicly announced before the Carnival that the crowd would be filmed, using video cameras, and the tapes would be shown to officers and victims of crime in an attempt to identify offenders. The result, 90 people arrested for criminal offences and a reduction of 23 per cent in the total number of crimes reported. But an article in *The Times*, describing how one of its reporters was robbed and his female companion beaten to the ground, continued to highlight the uglier side of the Carnival.[48]

Widespread Hostility

During September and early October 'relationships between the police and black people were at the centre of the serious disorder which occurred in several English cities'. The most serious of these were in Handsworth, Birmingham, on 9 and 10 September, in Brixton, London on 28 and 29 September and in Tottenham, London, on 6 October. Reporting in November 1985, the Archbishop of Canterbury's Commission on Urban Priority Areas, said, 'we have heard numerous complaints from black people of alleged discrimination against them by the police…'[49] Similarly, in his paper 'A Tale of Failure: Race and Policing', John Benyon claimed the picture that emerged

---

46. *News of the World*, 2 June 1985.
47. Keith, *op. cit.* 31, p.128.
48. *The Times*, 28 August 1985.
49. Archbishop of Canterbury's Commission on Urban Priority Areas (1985). *Faith in the City: A Call for Action by Church and Nation*. London: Church House, p.351, para.14.67.

during his research, was 'a depressing one of widespread hostility towards, and resentment of, the police.'[50] Indeed, each of the incidents of serious disorder that autumn was precipitated by an incident involving police officers and black people. But, Benyon claimed, although there was 'considerable evidence of racial prejudice among police officers' prejudice does not necessarily 'result in discriminatory behaviour.' Rather, he suggested, the contacts between police officers and all young people were generally 'far from satisfactory'. Consequently, 'police behaviour' which was 'interpreted as racial discrimination or harassment of black people' was 'merely "heavy handed" or discourteous conduct' which was 'not prompted by racial motives.'[51]

Whilst Notting Hill was largely unaffected, in terms of disorder that autumn, the evidence tended to suggest that the relationships between the police and the black community at The Hill was little different to those in areas where disorder had occurred. In summing up the events of the first half of the decade, former Commissioner, Sir Ian Blair, claimed 'the best that could be said about the outbreaks of disorder were that,

> 'they placed the relationship between the black community and the police at the
> centre of policing in London, with many community leaders and many senior
> police officers recognising that something had to be done to prevent a total break-
> down in trust between a force that was now policing an increasingly multi-racial
> city. But it would be a long, bitter road. And it was very tough for those on the
> inside …'[52]

The Changing Face of All Saints Road

Eventually, with the help of the other agencies, All Saints Road began to change. By 1986, new buildings were slowly growing up in the surrounding streets and part of All Saints Road itself was undergoing a face lift. The Apollo public house, once described as a 'notorious drug centre', had been sold by its owners, Whitbreads, and there was a plan to turn it into 16 workshops. The Mangrove received a grant for refurbishment. With an optimism

---

50. Benyon, John (1986). 'A Tale of Failure: Race and Policing'. Policy Papers in Ethnic Relations No. 3. Warwick University: Centre for Research in Ethnic Relations, p.2.
51. *Ibid*, pp.57–58.
52. Blair, Ian (2009). *Policing Controversy*. London: Profile Books, p.71.

that proved to be mistaken, Whitfield is alleged to have claimed, 'when the Mangrove re-opens as a decent West Indian restaurant that will be the end of symbolism.'[53] The Mangrove never did re-open as a decent West Indian restaurant. Although the number of people on the street may have been reduced, three shebeens, where alcohol was sold illegally and 'the drugs trade continued', remained. In summing up the situation in 1985, Keith suggested 'the elegant but dilapidated rental properties of the 1950s and 1960s [had] to a great extent ... been lost to "the reclaiming of the inner city" [and] the Residents Association of the newly refurbished St Luke's Mews [had] threatened to sue the police for their failure to enforce the law in the area (particularly drug trafficking)'.[54]

---

53. Keith, *op. cit* 39, p.127.
54. *Ibid*, p.128.

CHAPTER 15

THE LEONARD INCIDENT, OPERATION TRIDENT, THE NOTTING HILL RAPIST AND THE BLACK WATCH

The Leonard Incident[1]

During the early hours of 8 October 1986, three police officers went to the eleventh floor of a block of flats known as Maitland House, in Darfield Way, Notting Hill, after the occupier had telephoned to say she was hiding a woman from a man who had attacked her and her two daughters. On their arrival the officers found Anthony Leonard, a 35-year-old West Indian, in an extremely agitated condition waving two knives. Reinforcements were called, Leonard was disarmed and handcuffed. Struggling, he was carried into a lift, taken to the ground floor, placed in the back of a police van and taken to Kensington Police Station because Notting Hill Police Station was undergoing renovation and there were no charging facilities there.

He continued to struggle and had to be restrained during the journey to Kensington Police Station but had quietened down by the time he arrived. He was taken from the van and laid down on the charge room floor in the police station. It was at this point that it was realised that he was not breathing. An ambulance was called; in the meantime, police officers attempted heart massage and mouth-to-mouth resuscitation without success. When the ambulance arrived, the paramedics too were unable to revive Leonard who was then taken to St Stephen's Hospital in Fulham but was found to be dead on arrival.

The Metropolitan Police immediately took action on two counts. Firstly, even though no formal complaint had been made at the time, the decision was taken to inform the Police Complaints Authority and a senior police

---

1. Except where otherwise noted, the information relating to the Leonard incident was provided to the author by Rod Havard, the chief superintendent in charge of Notting Hill Police Station at the time, in an interview on 1 February 2011.

officer from the West Midlands Police was appointed to investigate the death. Secondly, within four hours of the death, a meeting had been arranged with the Police Consultative Committee and other community representatives to inform them of the full circumstances of the case. Despite this, there was uproar from within the black community, both from the Stonebridge Park Estate in Harlesden, where Leonard lived, and from All Saints Road, where he was a frequent visitor.

Leonard was married but had been separated from his wife for some time. Although she was living in the USA at the time of his death, she quickly returned to London and was seen at all subsequent events

During the evening of October 9, a demonstration formed outside the Mangrove Community Association in All Saints Road and marched to Notting Hill Police Station. Immediately upon its arrival, Leonard's wife, a lawyer representing the family and representatives of the black community were invited into the police station to meet with the Area Deputy Assistant Commissioner, John Newing, and the Divisional Commander, Chief Superintendent Rod Havard. Meanwhile, the demonstrators, some of whom were from Harlesden, were kept behind temporary barriers opposite the police station. Although media reports suggested there were approximately 500 people present, the police put the number at 150 at the most. Some missiles were thrown towards the police station, breaking a couple of windows and damaging a car in the police station yard.[2] Although reserves had been brought in from elsewhere in London, the police officers controlling the crowd were local officers who, bearing in mind that a death had occurred, reportedly whilst in police hands, and friends and relatives were present amongst the demonstrators, had been instructed to deal with the crowd 'sympathetically'. So, no attempt was made to arrest those who threw missiles and the demonstration broke up. In the meantime, in a further effort to defuse the situation, the Coroner, Dr Paul Knapman, after discussing the case with pathologist Dr Ian West, announced that the cause of death did not appear to be due to violence.[3]

---

2. *Caribbean Times*, 17 October 1986.
3. *The Guardian*, 10 October 1986.

The second demonstration took place on Saturday 18 October. It is unclear whether it was organized by community leaders from the Stonebridge Park Estate or All Saints Road. What is certain is that both the Socialist Workers Party and Black Liberation Front, which (despite an office in Portobello Road did not have much of a following amongst the black community) put out leaflets, blaming the police for Leonard's death, encouraging people to join the demonstration.[4]

The Socialist Workers' Party were invariably present at any event affecting the black community in Notting Hill but, being predominantly, if not solely, a white, solidly left-wing organization, it also had little support from the black community in Notting Hill, which had its own leaders, including Frank Crichlow, and attempts from outside to change this situation were generally resisted. Tempers flared outside the police station at the end of the march, which was led, on this occasion, by Leonard's mother carrying a placard accusing the police of killing her son, but it was only attended by about 200 people most of whom seemed to come from outside Notting Hill.[5] Police and stewards eventually managed to persuade the demonstrators to disperse but not before bricks and bottles had been thrown at the building, and several officers were slightly injured. Again, no arrests were made.

At the inquest at the beginning of November, bio-chemist, Dr Patrick Tozland told the court that 'Leonard had inhaled a huge dose of cocaine and smoked cannabis between 20 and 60 minutes before death', in other words shortly before he was arrested. The effect of the drugs, said Tozland, would have made Leonard 'hyperactive and very excited' and he would probably have 'hallucinated'. It could, explained Tozland, have made him 'ill-tempered' if people tried to restrain him but 'it probably had the effect that he could not understand what was happening.'

Tozland also said that Leonard had the highest level of blood cocaine he had seen in England and the level of drugs in the urine was 'one of the highest ever reported from around the world'. Asked by Dr Knapman whether he

---

4. *Police Review*, 14 November 1986, p.2289.
5. *Ibid*; *The Guardian*, 20 October 1986, claimed there were 400 demonstrators.

thought Leonard could have taken 'crack', [6] Dr Tozland replied, 'Yes, it could be, but despite extensive tests I could not find whether Leonard had taken "crack" or cocaine.' If it was crack, Leonard was probably the first person to be killed by the drug in Britain.[7] Pathologist, Dr West, told the inquest that 'cocaine had caused Mr Leonard's death although the mechanism of death was from inhalation of vomit.' He also told the court that 'his post mortem showed no signs of Mr Leonard being either violently restrained or involved in a violent struggle.'[8] Two other pathologists, Professor Bernard Knight, for Leonard's family, and Dr Geoffrey Greaseham, for the police officers, agreed with Dr West's findings.

In returning their verdict, the jury decided that Leonard's death had been caused by non-dependant abuse of drugs, aggravated by lack of care. Shouts of protest from Leonard's family and friends greeted the verdict and one man shouted, 'This verdict is a whitewash, you can't keep on killing black people'.[9] When the coroner, Dr Paul Knapman, asked court officers to detain the man, fighting broke out and police dogs were used to clear the court. The investigation under the supervision of the Police Complaints Authority cleared the officers of using undue force and of negligence.[10]

Drugs Again

At the end of October, an article in the *London Evening Standard* suggested the police in Notting Hill were continuing their softly-softly policy on drug-dealing in All Saints Road.[11] This resulted in a number of critical letters from people living in the area, claiming that they were not being properly protected.[12] Denise Watson saw it from the other side. Although there is some doubt about the precise accuracy of her recollections it does give an insight as to how the front line operated and its feelings about the police.

---

6. Crack is a form of cocaine that can be smoked; it is the most addictive form of cocaine and offers short but intensive highs to those who smoke it.
7. *Today*, 5 November 1986.
8. *The Guardian*, 5 November 1986.
9. *The Guardian*, 8 November 1986.
10. *The Guardian*, 10 November 1986.
11. *London Evening Standard*, 31 October 1986.
12. *London Evening Standard*, 5 and 6 November 1986.

According to her, the area had been taken over by the Yardies who 'were a different breed of hustlers.'[13] Whereas, previously, the people who lived in the area 'knew who was who' and only generally approached those they knew 'who had come to buy a smoke' the new dealers would stop everyone, 'even people who were just going home after a night out, and would try to sell them drugs.' In addition, they were vicious, using guns and 'special ratchet knives on chains that enabled them to slash you without the risk of dropping the knife'.[14]

By now, according to Watson, the police had learned from mistakes made in the past, claiming that they would 'go through a battery of guidelines in order to prevent a possible riot.' But, although the 'runners knew instantly that the police were about to pounce, nobody ever knew who they were after until the police made their move.' Once the word spread that,

> 'the police were coming, everyone guilty of something would act at once. Some rushed for the safety of the hole, others would stash their drugs under cars or in nearby basements.'[15]

Watson described how, on one occasion when the police came to arrest her, the crowd prevented them and she ran into the 'hole', where a man exchanged jackets and hat with her and she was able to walk out unrecognised by the officers who were still outside now dealing with a hostile crowd.[16] The changing of clothes under such circumstances to 'hide' one's appearance or 'change' ones visible identity was a common occurrence in All Saints Road.

In February, in an address to 'Tory lawyers', the Commissioner, Sir Kenneth Newman, 'spelt out the horrors of inner city policing.' Referring to All Saints Road as one of three centres in London 'where crime is at its worst, where drug-dealing is intolerably overt, and where the racial ingredient is at its most potent' he pointed out that 'in such places indiscriminate police action, however proper an enforcement of the law may be, runs a real risk

---

13. Watson, Denise (2001). *Notting Hill Girl*. London: Westworld International, p.125.
14. *Ibid*, pp.125–126.
15. *Ibid*, p.128.
16. *Ibid*, pp.129–130.

of provoking serious public disorder.' Pointing out that 'successful policing' of these areas required 'a complex and carefully judged combination
of tactics' he suggested it was important to build up a cooperative body of
support for a crime-free environment among the law-abiding majority; provide a high level of visible police presence to damp down disorder, and have
police back-up available in the event of disorder occurring; and target those
around whom the crime focused, specifically the drug-dealers and handlers
of stolen property, mounting operations to arrest them.[17]

Sir Kenneth then gave as an example someone deliberately blowing the
smoke from a cannabis cigarette into the face of a patrolling officer in All
Saints Road. The officer knew that if he attempted to arrest the person he
was 'likely to be opposed by heavier numbers' and by the time other officers
arrived to assist him, he would 'probably have lost his prisoner' and, at the
same time, would have run the risk of an outbreak of 'public disorder by taking action over what by any standards [was] a minor offence.' He continued:

> 'But, for any officer, taking immediate action in such circumstances can easily
> become a matter of personal pride. After all, he will reason, if I allow such an
> arrogant display of illegal behaviour to go unchecked, it will only get worse and
> make my job more difficult to do in the future.'

Sir Kenneth then pointed out that, whilst it might be extremely frustrating
and difficult for the individual officer, 'the best means of dealing with such a
situation [was] to allow it to pass, to get to know as many local faces as possible, to mount an observation, and to arrest offenders in a well-organized
and disciplined operation.'[18]

At the beginning of May 1987, Notting Hill police were again in the news
over a drugs arrest. Michael Campbell was arrested shortly after midnight on
May 6 'by six or seven policemen who put him in a van.' Campbell subsequently claimed he had been beaten, both before being put in the van and
whilst in the van on the way to the police station. Complaining of pains

---

17. *Police*, Vol. XIX, No. 7, March 1987, p.10.
18. *Ibid.*

shortly after his arrival at the station, an ambulance was called and he was taken to St Charles Hospital. He was discharged after receiving treatment for a black-eye, an injury to a cheek bone and injuries to both lower arms and wrists.[19]

By June 1987, a number of cases involving Notting Hill officers were the subject of investigations being supervised by the Police Complaints Authority.[20] This, together with the effect that sustained criticism in the media was having on the morale of police officers serving at the station,[21] persuaded Deputy Assistant Commissioner Paul Condon, the officer now in charge of No.6 Area of which Notting Hill was a part, to call a special press conference on June 9 at which he revealed that in a seven-week period earlier that year, 23 officers had been injured on duty in All Saints Road and the surrounding area; amongst these were two women constables. On May 29, all five police officers responsible for policing All Saints Road at that time, ended up in hospital. One of the injured officers, Police Constable John McCormick, described how they were in a police van,

> 'when we got a call about two white men being robbed of a gold watch by a gang of blacks. We went looking for the men responsible and found one who answered the description. We went up to him and immediately he started whooping and fighting. Within seconds the stones and bottles were coming over. There was a huge crowd. They grabbed four of our radios and slashed the tyre of the van. We lost the prisoner, and we all needed treatment.'[22]

In another incident, Police Constable Paul Siddall twice had missiles thrown at him from an unidentified position. As a result of the second incident, he required hospital treatment. Whilst he was away, his partner, Police Constable Peter Hebden was attacked by a group of youths, one of them armed with an iron bar, whilst he stood in a shop doorway answering

---

19. *The Guardian*, 8 May 1987.
20. See later in the chapter for more details.
21. Hasler, Terry (1987). 'Hill Morale Hit by Critics'. *The Job*, 12 June 1987.
22. Judge, Tony (1987). 'Will Trident be the Ultimate Deterrent for Notting Hill's Drug Barons?' *Police*, Vol. XIX, No.12, August, p.10.

a call on his radio. He received a fractured cheekbone and other injuries as a result of which he was on the sick list for some months.[23] The attacks on the officers were in marked contrast to the way the divisional commander, Chief Superintendent Rod Havard, was treated. During much of his time at Notting Hill, Havard made it a practice to walk along All Saints Road, alone and in uniform, at least once a day. On occasions, he would walk unannounced into the Mangrove and speak with Frank Crichlow and his staff. Havard claimed he never felt threatened during these solo sorties.[24] As previous divisional commanders had found, if nothing else, other than the Yardies, the African-Caribbean community that regularly frequented All Saints Road tended to respect rank, particularly if the cap had gold braid across its peak. Nevertheless, at the conference held by Condon, Havard suggested 'drug-dealing in and around All Saints Road' was 'big business' and those involved in it were 'not going to give up easily.' Condon pointed out that the police 'were working with community groups to improve conditions in the area but alongside the community involvement there was also the need to enforce the law.' He concluded, 'All Saints Road is not an easy area to police but it will never become a no-go area.'[25]

Following the conference, there was a proliferation of articles. The *Daily Express*, for instance, referred to it as 'one of the most dangerous areas of Britain', claiming that officers had been drawn into ambushes by taunting youths and that, on other occasions, trouble had deliberately been started elsewhere to lure away police patrols from the scene to enable street drug-dealing in heroin and cocaine to take place uninterrupted.[26] Reference was often made in the media during the 1980s to All Saints Road being a 'no-go' area insofar as the police were concerned but as the Commissioner, Sir Kenneth Newman, had pointed out earlier, far from being 'no-go' areas, in terms of numbers, more police went into such areas than most other places in London, simply because of the special attention they required.[27]

---

23. *Ibid*, pp.9–10.
24. Interview with Rod Havard, *op. cit.* 1.
25. *The Job*, 12 June 1987.
26. *Daily Express*, 10 June 1987.
27. Police, *op. cit.* 17, p.10.

The conference appeared to have little effect. Exactly one week later, three police officers were injured when they were attacked by over 100 youths during a routine drug search in Lancaster Road, just off All Saints Road. Two people had been placed in a van, suspected of being in possession of drugs. A mob attacked the van, breaking its windows, slashing the tyres and stealing the ignition keys. It coincided with one of Chief Superintendent Havard's visits to All Saints Road. The van was badly damaged, the two people who had been detained made good their escape and a stand-off position had developed. The three police officers were in close proximity to the van whilst the crowd of people were in a group a short distance away. Havard approached the scene, ensured that the police officers were not seriously injured, turned towards the group of youths, and saw Frank Crichlow at the rear of the group. He immediately came forward as Havard walked towards the group and, after a short conversation, Crichlow persuaded the group to disperse.[28]

According to Havard, many officers at Notting Hill were, and had been for some time, in a disturbed and confused state as to the apparent lack of effort by senior officers to get to grips with the problems that now beset All Saints Road. People who lived and ran businesses in All Saints Road and its vicinity felt they were under siege.[29] All shops had wire grills over their windows even when open for trading, businesses were unable to get insurance, and people living in the nearby St Luke's Mews, who had bought property in the belief that the area was on the up and up, could not leave their homes via All Saints Road because of the fear of crime. Denise Watson claimed 'the entire area' was 'swimming in crack' and with the Yardies killing each other, 'the police just had to do something.' Additionally, 'after years of putting up with it, the law-abiding residents had had enough' and 'wanted their street back.' As a result, 'they were ready to support the police.'[30]

Operation Trident

With the approval of Deputy Assistant Commissioner Condon and the Commander in charge of operations for the area, Larry Roach, Havard therefore

---

28. Interview with Rod Havard, *op. cit.* 1.
29. *Ibid.*
30. Watson, Denise, *op. cit.* 13, p.236.

decided to mount Operation Trident in the summer of 1987. It was to be a planned operation over a number of weeks, not simply to arrest drug offenders, but also the principal dealers. Having arrested the principal dealers he intended to have a high-profile police presence in the area to prevent them from returning. Then he planned to conduct a high-profile crime prevention campaign to restore the confidence of the local community and persuade them that their businesses would be secure in the hope that new businesses would be attracted into the areas to provide work for local people. Thus the image of All Saints Road would be changed.[31]

However, he had a major problem in mounting Operation Trident, certainly at its commencement. Over the preceding months, the Notting Hill police had conducted a number of raids in the area, all of which had come to nothing and it had become apparent to Havard that information was being leaked from within the Metropolitan Police to those who were being targeted. He therefore used officers from the Territorial Support Group (TSG), based some distance away at Alperton in north-west London, for the preliminary observations and operations. Havard never met the TSG officers at Notting Hill, preferring to travel either to Area Headquarters at Notting Dale or the TSG base at Alperton to brief them. This presented him with an emotional conflict. He wanted to tell local Notting Hill officers that something was being done about the problem because they were the ones who were being attacked and assaulted regularly whilst on patrol.[32]

The operation lasted from 18 May to 21 July. Observation on the area from a number of covert observation posts had revealed that there were 18 principle drug-dealers.[33] The home addresses of a number, but not all, of them were identified. Therefore, whilst some could be arrested at their home addresses, others could only be arrested in All Saints Road or its vicinity. Various 'well-to-do' people were caught up in the operation. One paid £20 for 278 milligrams of cocaine and was eventually fined £125 for possession and £50 for failing to appear at the police station when ordered to do so;

---

31. Interview with Rod Havard, *op. cit.* 1; see also Judge, *op. cit.* 22, p.10; and Grice, Elizabeth (1988). '"Designer policing" beats muggers and pushers'. *The Sunday Times*, 25 September 1988.
32. Interview with Rod Havard, *op. cit.* 1.
33. This compares with only eight when Moore supervised a similar operation in 1982.

another was fined £135 and ordered to pay £25 costs after being found in possession of 699 milligrams of cannabis resin.[34]

The arrest of the principle dealers was arranged for 30 June. The weekend before that, a uniformed police officer had been 'badly beaten up' in All Saints Road, in what was described as a 'brutal and unprovoked' attack. This brought the number of officers who had been injured in the area in the previous two months to 32, including a woman chief inspector struck in the face with a brick.[35]

On 30 June, Havard made a number of significant arrangements in order to arrest the main dealers.[36] Using the command arrangements that had been set up following the Tottenham riot in 1985, he assumed the role of Gold Commander, setting up Gold Control at the TSG base at Alperton. Havard's deputy, Superintendent Clive Pearman, was the Silver Commander, responsible for overseeing what occurred on the ground. Nearly 90 police officers, some from Notting Hill, both uniform and detectives, together with those from the TSG[37] were used; also on hand were specialists with hydraulic door opening equipment and two detective sergeants from the drugs squad at New Scotland Yard. The operation lasted from 8 a.m. to 10 p.m. Raids on the dealers' home addresses were carried out under the authority of search warrants, granted by a magistrate. Each raiding party consisted of Notting Hill and TSG officers. Uniform snatch squads arrested those on the street.

By the end of the day, 15 major dealers had been arrested.[38] At Marylebone Magistrates' Court the next morning, the magistrate, Barrington Black, left the court at one stage following angry scenes in the public gallery when he remanded 12 of the 13 people before him in custody.[39] More arrests were made over the following days.[40] Throughout the period of Operation Trident, over

---

34. *The Guardian*, 29 September 1987; *Daily Express*, 29 September 1987.
35. *Daily Telegraph*, 1 July 1987; *The Times*, 1 July 1987; *Kensington News and Post*, 2 July 1987.
36. Interview with Rod Havard, *op. cit.* 1.
37. The Territorial Support Group consisted of an inspector, three sergeants and 30 constables.
38. *Daily Telegraph*, 1 July 1987; *The Times*, 1 July 1987, reported that it was 14 (eleven men and three women).
39. *Daily Telegraph*, 2 July 1987.
40. *The Independent*, 7 July 1987.

260 people were arrested, 19 for supplying drugs, over 100 for possessing drugs and the remainder for assaults, robberies and other crimes.[41]

Havard then arranged for a survey to be carried out by the police about the police. In hindsight, he suggested this ought to have been done by an independent organization but he wanted to move quickly to gain an insight into public perception in the area and found that 90 per cent of the 300 local residents interviewed approved of the police action. In addition, within a few weeks of the operation, 'more than 250 letters and messages of support arrived at the police station' and 'one-hundred-and-eighty local shopkeepers signed a resolution expressing thanks to the police.'[42] Having gained the initiative, Havard was determined to keep the pressure on the drug-dealers. He commented, 'I intend to pursue the drug-dealers right out of North Kensington altogether so it is no longer tenable for them to do business there.'[43]

Commenting on the operation, Havard said the police 'were faced with an escalating use of Class A drugs and outright defiance of the law.' Because the selling of drugs was so open, an increasing number of drug-dealers were being attracted to the area. In addition, the number of occasions on which knives were being used to commit 'muggings' was on the increase.[44] The weeks following Operation Trident saw a significant reduction in crime on the Notting Hill Division as a whole. In the first three weeks, robberies, which included bag snatches and pickpocketing were down by 56 per cent, compared to an increase of 10 per cent in the six months preceding the operation.[45] Havard then made an outspoken attack on those who claimed to be leaders within the black community:

'The "black community leaders" are always saying that they condemn the drug dealers. But the fact remains, the drug dealers are nearly all black people themselves, and they are sustained by the same community. I wouldn't be surprised to see something of a power struggle for the real leadership of the black community

---

41. *Kensington News and Post*, 30 July 1987.
42. Judge, Tony, *op. cit.* 22, p.9.
43. *Kensington News and Post*, 9 July 1987.
44. Judge, Tony, *op. cit.* 22, p.10.
45. *Kensington News and Post*, 30 July 1987.

develop. So many black people are coming up to us and saying that they have nothing to do with the Mangrove, and Frank Crichlow doesn't speak for them'[46]

But, more importantly, insofar as the officers at Notting Hill were concerned, because the operation was seen as a success, morale improved.

The response from the black community was predictable. Paul Boeteng and Bernie Grant, controversial leader of Haringey Council at the time of the Tottenham riot in 1985,[47] who had both been elected to Parliament at the 1987 general election, called a press conference at the House of Commons, and, although they claimed 'that they approved of police efforts to stamp out drug-dealing' suggested that intensive patrols — Boeteng referred to them as 'swamp tactics'[48] — were harassing the black community in Notting Hill.[49] Speaking on behalf of the Mangrove Community Association, Jebb Johnson suggested that, although 'the group was opposed to hard drugs' they were 'unhappy with the police blitz' because they had hoped 'to clean up the street' in their own way 'without alienating the black community.'[50]

Meanwhile, one of Havard's earlier initiatives was called into question by a stipendiary magistrate whilst Operation Trident was under way. Frank Crichlow and Jebb Johnson appeared before Audrey Jennings at Wells Street Magistrates' Court in June 1987 having been arrested at an incident in All Saints Road earlier. Crichlow was charged with assaulting a police officer and damaging a police van whilst Johnson had been charged with obstructing a police officer in the execution of his duty. At the hearing, the prosecution dropped the charges against both men, but they were bound over by the court to keep the peace for one year.

Jennings was critical of what she heard about the policing arrangements for All Saints Road, suggesting they could have 'implications throughout the

---

46. Judge, Tony, *op. cit.* 22, p.10.
47. A police officer, Constable Keith Blakelock, was brutally attacked and murdered during a riot at the Broadwater Farm Estate in October, 1985. Following Blakelock's death, Bernie Grant, then the leader of Haringey Council, upset a number of people by claiming that the police 'got a bloody good hiding.'
48. *Caribbean Times*, 31 July 1987.
49. *The Guardian*, 21 July 1987; Judge, Tony, *op. cit.* 12, p.9.
50. *Kensington News and Post*, 9 July 1987.

judicial system.' Her comments were directed at an arrangement which had been introduced by Havard whereby, at the discretion of the senior officer at the scene of any incident when arrests were made, community leaders, not necessarily from the Mangrove, were allowed to travel in police transport with the arrested person when he was conveyed to the police station. The arrangement had come about in an attempt to reduce the number of allegations by those arrested that they had been beaten up in police vans.[51] Following Jennings remarks, Havard suggested that, although he doubted such an arrangement would be tolerated anywhere else in the country, it was 'something to be encouraged' because he firmly believed that the police had 'nothing to hide.'[52] Havard also allowed community leaders to visit prisoners in their cells at a time before the lay-visitor scheme was set up. Although these arrangements were not popular with the lower ranks at Notting Hill, it did bring about the desired result by reducing the number of allegations of assault.

Inner-City Task Force

It was about this time that the Government announced the setting up of two Inner-City Task Forces, one in Peckham and the other in Notting Hill. Finance was already in place. In Notting Hill, the North Kensington Task Force was led by a senior civil servant; a black coordinator was appointed and Havard seconded two police officers, Sergeant Hazel Hulse and Constable Brendon Brett, to work with the task force on which there were representatives from a number of agencies including the Royal Borough of Kensington and Chelsea. The task force set about introducing a number of initiatives designed to improve security in the area but, at the same time, to enhance the general appearance. Businesses were persuaded to remove the grills in front of their premises; in return, locksmiths and carpenters fitted a host of crime-proofing devices such as reinforced but attractive doors and frames, new locks, entry-phones to residential property and laminated glass replaced the normal window glass behind the old grilles.

---

51. Interview with Rod Havard, *op. cit.* 1.
52. *Kensington News and Post*, 18 June 1987.

Plans were made to renovate some of the dilapidated buildings, doing away with the recesses in the building lines which allowed drug-dealers and other criminals to hide; and to improve street lighting. And, finally, insurance companies were persuaded to provide cover. An article in the *Sunday Times* was premature in suggesting that these improvements, which cost around £1 million, had beaten the muggers and pushers and 'virtually designed' crime out of All Saints Road. Indeed, as will be seen in the succeeding chapters, there was still plenty of illegality to occupy the police for a few years to come but it was arguably the start of a relatively slow progress towards gentrification.[53]

The Notting Hill Rapist

Between 1982 and 1988, women living alone, particularly in basement or ground-floor apartments in Notting Hill lived in fear of the 'Notting Hill Rapist'. Whilst this had nothing to do with the Front Line it supported the view that, even without it, Notting Hill was a busy division. In all, body-builder Tony McLean attacked seven women, all living within an area bounded by Clarenden Road, Elgin Crescent, Lansdowne Road and Ladbroke Grove. McLean lived in Clarenden Walk, off Clarenden Road. The victims included a television researcher, a solicitor, a personal secretary and the daughter of a peer. Although none of the victims were 'badly hurt physically', McLean would 'inflict the maximum psychological cruelty'. Usually, he would 'tie, blindfold and gag the girl, threaten her with a knife and then assure her he had broken into the flat only to burgle [but] just before leaving, he would rape her'.[54] Five of the attacks took place in 1982 and 1983. This was a particularly difficult period for the police because, at the same time, another rapist was attacking women in South Kensington, and it was not known whether it was the same person. However, insofar as Notting Hill was concerned, there was then a four-year gap before the attacks resumed

---

53. Interview with Rod Havard, *op. cit.* 1. The government had announced a new initiative in February 1986 designed, amongst other things, improve the environment of and reduce the levels of crime in deprived inner-city areas. See also Grice, *op. cit.* 31.
54. Phillips, Caroline. Rapport with the raped. An article which originally appeared in the *London Evening Standard* reproduced in *Police Review*, 5 May 1989, pp.910–911.

on 4 May 1987. It subsequently transpired that McLean had been in custody for violence and burglary offences during those intervening four years.

Following the resumption of the rapes in late-1987, the police at Notting Hill, under the command of Detective Superintendent James Hutchinson, made strenuous efforts to capture McLean by conducting carefully planned surveillance and stake-out operations. This involved 'scores of police lying in wait for him disguised as roadsweepers and tradesmen [and] even moving in and living in homes they thought could be his next target.'[55] On two occasions he narrowly escaped capture. In December 1987, he was seen by an alert neighbour lying in wait under a balcony for another victim. Pursued by police officers, Mclean made his escape by fleeing across back gardens and through a children's play area. Then on 16 February, he was able to dodge through the undergrowth and a communal garden to avoid capture. On another occasion, he was actually caught by a patrolling constable climbing a fence within the 'rape area' but the police officer allowed him to continue on his way when McLean persuaded him he was taking a short-cut home! His skill at adopting what were described in court as 'military-style techniques', both in stalking his victims and in evading capture were learned during 'a 20-month spell with the Territorial Army'. This coupled with his 'extreme fitness and unrivalled knowledge of the area ... enabled him to slip through tight cordons set for him.'[56]

He was eventually caught by an astute uniformed constable, Graham Hamilton. Hamilton 'knew him as a burglar' and had a 'gut reaction' about him. Two simple errors made by computer operators were to have huge consequences and allow McLean to be active for longer than he should. McLean had voluntarily given a blood specimen, along with a number of other men, during the investigation in 1983 but his blood group had been recorded on the computer as an 'O secretor' whereas the rapist's blood group was known to be in the 'zero secretor' category.

Hamilton called at McLean's address in February 1988 to ask him to provide another specimen of blood. McLean was out but he was so confident

---

55. *Daily Telegraph*, 14 April 1989; see also 'The Notting Hill Rapist' in *Real Life Crimes ... and How They Were Solved*, Volume 5, Part 70. London: Midsummer Books, 1994, pp.1544–1548.

56. *Ibid.*

at not being implicated that, a couple of days later, he 'swaggered' into Notting Hill Police Station and provided another sample. When the result came back, it showed McLean to be a 'zero secretor', the same as the rapist. The first computer error had been revealed. A computer operator had pressed the letter 'capital O' instead of the 'zero' in making the entry. The second error concerned his release date from prison which was shown as June 1987, thus giving him a cast-iron alibi for the May 1987 rape. So, Hamilton made enquiries at the Home Office (then the relevant department: now the Ministry of Justice). This revealed that he had actually been released in January 1987; a computer operator had typed 'Jun. 1987' instead of 'Jan. 1987'.[57] Fortunately for the police, but unfortunately for McLean, 'the techniques of DNA genetic profiling had just been developed' and his 1988 blood sample was 'one of the first to be analysed' using this method. It revealed an identical match with the semen taken from his victims. At his subsequent trial, McLean was given three life sentences.[58]

Police Complaints Authority Investigation.

Mention has already been made in *Chapter 13* that the squad of 24 officers set up specifically by Chief Superintendent Whitfield to patrol the area around All Saints Road had become known as the Black Watch. The existence of this squad came to prominence in 1987 as a result of allegations made in two television programmes. This was not particularly surprising because, as was pointed out, one of the features 'of the continuing "war" against the drug-dealers and muggers [was the] frequent allegations of police brutality and corruption [made] against officers at Notting Hill.'[59] But, as a result of the two programmes, which referred to incidents dating back to 1984, the Police Complaints Authority announced that an investigation would be carried out by David Williams, then an Assistant Chief Constable with the Hertfordshire Constabulary. The investigation, code-named Operation Adjacent looked into 19 cases, involving more than a dozen Notting Hill officers, in which

---

57. *Ibid.*
58. *Ibid.*
59. Judge, Tony, *op. cit.* 22, p.10.

it was alleged that drugs had been planted and those arrested, mainly black people, had been mistreated.[60]

The contrary argument was that a number of active police officers — active in the sense that they were continuing to arrest those committing crime in the area — attracted the abuse of the black community. Indeed, Chief Superintendent Havard regularly knew who these officers were because their numbers were scrawled on walls in and around All Saints Road. Involved in a number of the allegations was Police Constable Dave Judd, who some would argue became the Police Constable Pulley of his time. Havard claimed that Judd was one of the most active officers at Notting Hill. He knew many of those who frequented All Saints Road and were associated with crime, by name and made arrests on a regular basis. Consequently, he was hated by the black community to the extent that Frank Crichlow kept asking Havard 'when are you going to move Judd before something happens to him?' Havard took this not as a threat by Crichlow himself but as a warning that, if he did not arrange for his transfer, it was likely that he would suffer serious injury or worse.[61]

Although the Police Complaints Authority gave assurances that it would issue a summary of the findings of the Williams investigation, which it received in late-1988,[62] it never did, other than to issue a statement that none of the officers involved would be subject to criminal prosecution. Consequently, there were claims of a cover-up.[63] A string of awards for damages against the Commissioner of the Metropolitan Police then followed in 1989.

Rupert Taylor had been arrested in December 1984 and was subsequently charged with the possession of a small amount of cannabis. He was acquitted at Knightsbridge Crown Court in 1986, subsequently issued a writ against the Commissioner and was awarded £100,000 damages—£10,000 for false imprisonment; £20,000 for malicious prosecution and £70,000 as exemplary

---

60. In an interview the author had with former Chief Superintendent Ken Diccock on 20 October 2010.
61. Interview with Rod Havard, *op. cit.* 1.
62. *The Guardian*, 16 December 1989.
63. Waterhouse, Rosie. 'Inquiry into police assaults suppressed'. *The Independent on Sunday*, 24 June 1990.

damages—by the High Court. Gareth Peirce, his solicitor, suggested that the exemplary damages reflected 'the jury's disgust at the police's "callous, cold-blooded abuse of power".'[64]

Vincent Lee was awarded £3,500 by a High Court jury after he complained he had been assaulted by police officers and had had cannabis planted on him when he was arrested in July 1985.[65] In February 1986, at Knightsbridge Crown Court, he was acquitted of possessing cannabis with intent to supply and assault with intent to resist arrest.[66] Brothers, Dennis and Michael Hayes, accepted £8,000 and £10,000 respectively in 'out-of-court' settlements for false arrest, assault, malicious prosecution and false imprisonment. They had been arrested in July 1985, and taken to Notting Hill Police Station where Dennis was charged with being drunk and disorderly and Michael with assault on police. Both, it was alleged, were beaten by police officers following their arrest and a subsequent X-ray on Michael revealed 'a broken jaw'. The brothers both pleaded not guilty and, after several adjournments, the cases were dismissed after the arresting officers failed to appear at court.

Finally, Hughgine Wilson, a nephew of the Jamaican High Commissioner, accepted an 'out-of-court' settlement of £20,000. He had been arrested on 15 April 1985 during a raid on the shebeen at No. 28 All Saints Road and charged with the possession of cannabis and two cases of assault with intent to resist arrest. During the course of his arrest it was alleged that 'he suffered severe bruising and a suspected fractured rib'. He was acquitted on all charges at Knightsbridge Crown Court in March 1986 and subsequently issued a writ against the Commissioner, claiming assault, malicious prosecution, false imprisonment and unlawful imprisonment.[67]

In December 1989, it was announced that the Police Complaints Authority would supervise a second inquiry 'into allegations of drug-planting and assault by officers' in the cases of Taylor and Lee, this time to be carried out

---

64. *The Guardian*, 6 December 1989; *The Sun*, 6 December 1989. The police appealed against the amount and Mr Taylor subsequently agreed to a settlement of £65,000.
65. *The Guardian*, 15 November 1989.
66. *Kensington News and Post*, 20 March 1986; *The Guardian*, 6 December 1989.
67. *The Guardian*, 16 December 1989.

by Chief Superintendent Diccocks from the Thames Valley Police.[68] The complaint by Taylor amounted to one of unlawful arrest, malicious prosecution, assault, unlawful detention, wilful damage by police to his motor car and racial abuse, against three officers. Although Taylor had complained of the damage to his car shortly after his arrest in December 1984, the police were unaware of the other allegations until the writ was served in 1987. On the advice of his solicitor, he declined to assist with the Williams inquiry and continued to do so until he had been awarded damages in November 1989. By the time Diccocks had completed his inquiry in May 1990, five-and-a-half years had elapsed. Nevertheless, he found the prosecution's case against Taylor to be seriously flawed, primarily because the arresting officer, PC Judd, could not recall which other officers had been present at the time of Taylor's arrest, and he recommended that his file should be sent to the Director of Public Prosecutions with a view to prosecuting PC Judd.[69]

In the case of Lee, the allegation was one of assault, and a conspiracy by four officers to bring a false prosecution following the planting of drugs on Lee at the time of his arrest; also he alleged that one of the officers had racially abused him. Despite the presence of two independent witnesses to some of the events that took place, the Crown Prosecution Service did not think there was sufficient evidence to support criminal proceedings against the officers. However, the Police Complaints Authority recommended that, in the case of one officer, he should appear before a full disciplinary tribunal but the two independent witnesses categorically refused to attend. Therefore, all four officers were severely admonished by the Director of the Metropolitan Police's Complaints Investigation Bureau for 'their totally unacceptable behaviour'. Whilst he was investigating these two cases, Diccock was also asked to carry out enquiries into the circumstances surrounding the arrest of Hughgine Wilson and his allegations of 'drug planting and assault'. However, the absence of any independent witnesses to the arrest of Wilson meant that there was insufficient evidence to take action against the officers complained of.[70]

---

68. Interview with Ken Diccock, *op. cit.* 60.
69. *Ibid.*
70. *Ibid.*

The two investigations, and subsequent prosecution of PC Judd, highlighted a serious problem encountered by the Police Complaints Authority. The burden of proof required to gain a conviction in a criminal case is somewhat greater than that required in a civil case. In September 1992, PC Judd appeared in the dock of the Old Bailey, charged with conspiracy to pervert the course of justice. The case arose as a result of the prosecution of Rupert Taylor for possessing cannabis in 1984. The jury failed to agree on this occasion and a re-trial was ordered. When he re-appeared, it had been brought to the judge's notice that a month before the re-trial Bernard Levin had written an article in *The Times* in which he posed the question, somewhat sarcastically, '[S]houldn't crooked policemen be sent on some sort of course with such a title as "How to Pick the Right Victim"?' This was, according to Judge Tyrer who was due to preside over the re-trial, prejudicial to PC Judd.[71] For this reason and the suggestion by Judge Tyrer that it had taken far too long to bring the case to court, when PC Judd re-appeared at the Old Bailey for the second time in November 1992, the prosecution decided to offer no evidence and he was formally found not guilty.

Complainants invariably, on the advice of their solicitors, declined to assist with any investigation by the Police Complaints Authority on the grounds that it might prejudice any claim for damages. Because such claims took some time to come before the civil courts, the incidents from which their complaints arose had occurred anything up to five years previously. Added to that was the time it took to undertake a criminal investigation and, if a prosecution was to follow, the delay in getting it before the criminal courts could mean that anything up to eight years had elapsed, as it did in PC Judd's case. Such delays were frowned upon by criminal court judges who claimed that it was prejudicial to the defendant, i.e. in these cases the police officer, to have to wait for so long before the case was heard.

---

71. *The Times*, 24 November 1992.

CHAPTER 16

MORE TROUBLE AT THE CARNIVAL

Introduction

During the next three years, the organization of the Carnival moved from a voluntary, under-staffed body to one that had full-time staff, was more professional in its approach and which was supposed to eventually make the event self-funding. The change was brought about following a damning report by Coopers and Lybrand, which criticised the existing Carnival Arts Committee (CAC) for its alleged amateurism and incompetence. Nevertheless, two of the three carnivals within this period were marred by violence.

The 1987 Carnival

Early in 1987, the team that gave Havard the go-ahead for Operation Trident, Deputy Assistant Commissioner Paul Condon and Commander Lawrence Roach, became responsible at senior level for the policing of the carnival. Roach already had experience of the problems associated with the event because, during the early-1980s, he had been the District Chief Superintendent on B District, a position which effectively made him deputy to then Commander, Bob Innes. The new team saw a need to deal with the 'sinister side' of carnival, 'represented by gangs of youths, predominantly black' who ran through the crowds snatching and stealing 'cameras, wallets and personal jewellery from bystanders.'[1]

This form of street robbery had become known as 'steaming' simply because the youths steamed through the crowd indiscriminately. Cohen described how some gangs 'wove among the crowds in single file like crocodile dancers; they would surround a person and steal a purse or jewellery without making any attempt to hide what they were doing, relying on their force of numbers, openly challenging the police.' Once the offence had been

---

1. Hillyard, Brian. 'Planning for Notting Hill'. In *Police Review*, 25 September 1987, p.1910.

committed, the gang immediately surrounded the person who had done the snatch and, forcing their way through the dense crowds, quickly moved away. If anyone opposed them they were beaten to the ground.

Often the police saw what was happening on closed circuit television (CCTV) but had tended, in the past to 'turn a blind-eye' fearing that any intervention would precipitate a riot.[2] Therefore, plans were made to counter the rising levels of crime that had become a feature of the recent Carnivals and part of the police operation was to target gangs of youths likely to commit crime as they approached the area and turn them away. But, if that failed, eight arrest squads, each consisting of an inspector, two sergeants and 14 constables, would be available to watch them as they moved about within the Carnival area and, if they committed crimes, arrest them. Dressed in conventional uniform, except the inspector wore a helmet instead of the normal flat cap, they wore body armour under their jackets in case they were attacked with knives. Prior to the Carnival, each squad underwent two hours training each week for ten weeks perfecting arrest and restraint techniques.

Not unnaturally, perhaps, 'disorder was confidently anticipated' because, it was suggested, the success of Operation Trident 'had created antagonism and a desire for revenge in some quarters.'[3] Indeed, on the last occasion police had made serious attempts to combat crime, in 1976, serious rioting resulted. Therefore, as had been the case for the previous ten years, 'shield serials' were on stand-by, predominantly in Isaac Newton School. These serials, 16 in all,[4] divided into two contingents of eight—one under the command Chief Superintendent John Purnell; the other under the command of Chief Superintendent George Crawford—had undergone six days intensive training prior to the event. In each contingent there were four serials with long shields and four with the round or short shields. The serials worked in pairs, one with long shields and one with short shields. Each serial was under the command of an inspector and each pair under the command of a chief inspector. The two chief superintendents each had a superintendent to assist them. If disorder did break out, the arrest squads would withdraw immediately, go behind the shield serials and take into custody anyone arrested by

2. Cohn, Abner (1993). *Masquerade Politics*. Oxford: Berg, p.59.
3. Hillyard, *op. cit.* 1, p.
4. Four serials were on stand-by in Bevington School.

the officers from those serials. In this way it was hoped that the shield serials would be kept at maximum strength until the disorder had been curtailed.

But Commander Roach had identified a problem with the command and control system in dealing with fast-moving, public order events. The police relied upon the use of personal radios to deploy units but the system quickly became overloaded when serious disorder occurred; also the noise of Carnival, particularly if officers were close to a moving band or an amplified sound system, made it difficult to hear detailed radio transmissions. Roach suggested that disorder basically presented two options:

- Contain and arrest offenders; or
- Disperse the crowds involved.[5]

Therefore, he devised a new system for the 1987 Carnival, in which each message would basically consist of only four words. Roach explained: 'The first identified the sector, the second the nature of the disorder, the third was the instruction, and the fourth the originating officer.'[6] The carnival area was broken-up into seven sectors with each sector commander having a designated call-sign. The nature of disorder was colour-coded as follows:

- Green—Normal.
- Amber—Situation beyond control of units on ground. Other foot serials being deployed.
- Blue—Shields deployed.
- Red—Firearms deployed.[7]

Predictably, trouble broke out at about 8.50 p.m. on the Monday when 'gangs of youths, both black and white, started hurling missiles, including bottles and beer cans, at police in the Portobello Road under the A40 Westway flyover.' As the police tried to break up the crowds, stalls were overturned

---

5.   Hillyard, *op. cit.* 1, p.1911.
6.   *Ibid.*
7.   Correspondence with former Commander Larry Roach, dated 17 February 1990. Roach retired as a Deputy Assistant Commissioner.

and looted.[8] Similar incidents quickly occurred at two other locations in the vicinity of Portobello Road. In one, a policewoman, Donna Kingsley was stabbed in the back.[9] The shield serials, were deployed from Isaac Newton School, under the command of Purnell and Crawford respectively. In accordance with the plan, they quickly divided those creating disorder and Purnell pushed some to the south and east of the problem area, whilst Crawford dispersed the remainder to the north and west.[10]

But, almost immediately, Purnell's contingent encountered a large 'float' coming towards them. Purnell, who had a hand-held megaphone, announced to the crowd: 'If you stop throwing stones police will withdraw and you can get on with Carnival; if you don't you will be dispersed!' Some stewards meanwhile, attempted to get the stone throwers to cease which, by and large, they did. Purnell then withdrew his serials back to the school and regrouped.[11]

Crawford's serials, meanwhile, had gone north from Isaac Newton School, but were pinned down in Portobello Road, under the Westway by the ferocity of the missile throwing. This gave the crowd sufficient time to push a lorry across the Portobello Road just north of the Westway. Two serials from the Territorial Support Group who were in Blagrove Road, at the northern end of Portobello Road, moved southwards towards the missile throwers. Recognising the danger of becoming trapped between the two advancing contingents of police, the crowd dispersed in two directions, west along Cambridge Gardens, towards Ladbroke Grove, and east along Acklam Road.[12]

More trouble followed in All Saints Road which was quickly dealt with when Purnell redeployed his serials but once order had been restored he withdrew for a second time as a number of foot cordons were put in place to stop people who were dispersing from re-entering the area. It is often said that 'no plan survives first contact with the situation'. It was certainly so in this case. Many of the well-behaved Carnival-goers were 'offended by having their way blocked by a police cordon without any obvious reason for it.'[13]

---

8. *Daily Telegraph*, 1 September 1987.
9. *Daily Telegraph*, 2 September 1987;; *Daily Mail*, 2 September 1987.
10. Interview with former Chief Superintendent John Purnell, G.M., on 9 May 1990. Purnell retired as a Commander.
11. *Ibid.*
12. *Ibid.*
13. Hillyard, *op. cit.* 1, p.1911.

'Tank' Waddington,[14] who was officially observing the policing arrangements for the Carnival that year, described how:

'Strategic options had been devised: for example, the direction of dispersal was determined in advance and a pattern of cordons to facilitate this had been prearranged. When disorder broke out, the plan swung impressively into operation and met with considerable success, despite inevitable unforeseen difficulties.'[15]

The unforeseen difficulties referred to by Waddington occurred in All Saints Road at its junction with Westbourne Park Road where a cordon had been established in accordance with the dispersal plan. Again, Waddington explained:

'After the violence had subsided, but with the dispersal of carnival-goers still continuing in line with the strategic plan, it was clear that this cordon was coming under considerable pressure from a large crowd of people attempting to regain access to All Saints Road. The Bronze Commander at the scene decided to allow people to pass through the cordon at a controlled rate so as to avoid what was developing into an ugly scene.'

His judgement was 'that the majority of people were trying to access All Saints Road ... in order to make their way northwards [but] the dispersal plan [had not allowed] for this.' So, the initial strategy had to be over-ridden in order to prevent a potential outbreak of further disorder.[16]

The following day, 1 September, the newspapers were full of sensational headlines:

Riot Terror at Carnival (*Daily Mail*)

Carnival terror as riot police charge stone-hurling mob (*Daily Express*)

---

14. P A J (Tank) Waddington, himself a police officer for a short time before becoming a full-time academic at the University of Reading, had been given unprecedented access by the then commissioner, Peter Imbert, to look at the policing of armed incidents and public order policing in the Metropolitan Police.

15. Waddington, P. A. J. (1991). *The Strong Arm of the Law: Armed and Public Order Policing.* Oxford: Clarendon, p.145.

16. *Ibid.*

Carnival riot cops storm in (*Daily Mirror*)

Rioting erupts at end of carnival (*The Independent*)

Rioting breaks out as night falls on Notting Hill (*The Times*)

Riot police battle with mobs in Notting Hill (*Daily Telegraph*)

Some even carried similar headlines on 2 September:

Face-to-face at the riot carnival (*Daily Mail*)

The Battle of Portobello Road (*The Independent*)

The disorder lasted only for about 45 minutes. However, the black media was not slow to blame 'heavy-handed police behaviour' as the cause of the 'violent confrontations' that occurred.[17] Other media outlets took a different view. On 2 September, the *Daily Express* and *The Sun* called for it to be the last Carnival in its present form unless the organizers could better regulate it and guarantee law and order. One conservative Member of Parliament, Terry Dicks, claimed he would urge the Home Secretary to ban the Carnival, whilst one of the two local MPs, John Wheeler, merely said he would discuss what had taken place with the Home Secretary.[18]

In its editorial, *The Guardian* suggested that, 'whilst it was unpleasant and unwelcome', it was not a riot, merely 'a certain amount of street disorder' which the police quickly brought to an end by putting 'into operation a carefully prepared plan.'[19] *The Times* suggested in its editorial that the organizers bore 'much responsibility.' They provided 'too few marshals' and 'their carping ... at necessary police action [was] too common.' They would 'not accept that one of the defining characteristics of a community [was] an ability to police its boundaries,' suggesting that 'if the lawless element' did 'not belong' at the Carnival, 'then community leaders' owed it to their fellow black people 'to co-operate much more positively with the police in expelling them.' In conclusion, it said it was 'an unfortunate fact that leaders of the African-Caribbean population in London' were 'ambiguous about the

---

17. *Caribbean Times*, 4–10 September 1987.

18. *Daily Telegraph*, 2 September 1987.

19. *The Guardian*, 2 September 1987.

police and in their ambiguity' they laid 'themselves open to exploitation by young black men living a life of crime.'[20]

Despite the outward peacefulness for much of the 1987 Carnival, a total of 1,161 crimes were reported to police of which nearly 400 were theft from the person or robbery. Many of these had been committed by the 'loosely organized gangs' steaming through the crowd. A number of the victims 'suffered serious injuries, including knife wounds and broken bones.'[21] One such victim was Paul McKinley who was left permanently blind in one eye and with a partially paralysed right arm.[22] Worse, a 23-year-old man, Michael Galvin, had been stabbed to death on the Sunday, in an argument over a 40p can of soft drink.[23] For the first time after a Carnival, a 25-minute video, backed-up by some 600 photographs, showing robberies, handbag and jewellery snatches, pick-pockets, drug-dealing and public order offences, was shown at all London police stations in an effort to identify people responsible for unsolved crimes.[24]

Summing up the 1987 Carnival, Deputy Assistant Commissioner Condon, said:

> 'I think that society as a whole must decide whether the criminal side of the carnival is too high a price to pay for the fun side. The paradox is that the atmosphere can be super, friendly and marvellous, but within a few minutes, totally hostile in the same location. The catalyst is always criminal action with police trying to intervene and that is when the mood turns nasty.'[25]

---

20. *The Times*, 2 September 1987.
21. *Daily Express*, 5 November 1987.
22. *Ibid.*
23. Alban Turner was eventually convicted of his murder at Aylesbury Crown Court after a retrial and sentenced to life imprisonment. However, after two-and-a-half years in prison, Turner was freed by the Court of Appeal when the only eye-witness to give evidence against him admitted that he had lied, accusing investigating officers of putting pressure on him. The three police officers involved in the investigation, Detective Inspector Arwyn Hughes, Detective Inspector Christopher Simpson, and Detective Sergeant Peter Fitzpatrick all denied the allegation. The *Caribbean Times*, 3 April 1990; *Evening Standard*, 7 March 1990; *The Guardian*, 21 and 22 March 1990.
24. *Kensington News and Post*, 5 November 1987.
25. *Daily Mail*, 1 September 1987.

The 1988 Carnival

Condon and Roach had learnt from their experiences the previous year and decided that the police would adopt the theme of 'safety for the public' for the 1988 Carnival.[26] They decided that 'any attempt to remove the Carnival from the streets, or to allow it to degenerate into regular riot, would be tantamount to an admission that it was impossible for Londoners and their police to achieve the goal of maintaining public order and safety while allowing the majority to go about their lawful and traditional celebration.' They therefore 'concluded that the task for police and the community was to ensure that the Carnival took place without undue danger to the local people or the visiting revellers — either from violent disorder or criminal activity.'[27]

Community involvement was vital if this was to be achieved and, in the run-up to the 1988 Carnival, the police had 'wide ranging consultation with all sections of the Notting Hill communities about both the present problem of the Carnival and its future.' Roach described how it was necessary to create 'a popular consensus on which police strategy to reduce crime and conflict was developed.' Pointing out that this approach was consistent with the tradition of policing in Great Britain, he went on to say that any consent 'the community affords to its police under this tradition must always be freely and knowingly given.' It must come, claimed Roach, from the police and the community, working together, to 'establish what goals that community seeks to achieve and what policing measures that community is actively prepared to support in order to attain those agreed goals.'[28]

It was dangerous to 'leave groups of young people aimlessly "milling" around the Carnival area when effectively it was over.'[29] Therefore intense efforts were made to genuinely 'work with community representatives and other opinion makers to establish what the goals of the community' were and how the police could effectively contribute to a successful Carnival.[30]

---

26. The author attended the 1988 Carnival on both days. See Moore, Tony (1988). 'Carnival Saves the Day'. *Police*, Vol. XXI, No. 1, September 1988, pp.36–37.
27. Roach, Lawrence (1992). 'The Notting Hill Carnival: An Exercise in Conflict Prevention'. In *Community Disorders and Policing: Conflict Management in Action* Tony F. Marshall (ed.)). London: Whiting & Birch, p.102.
28. *Ibid*, pp.102/103.
29. *Ibid*, p.106.
30. *Ibid*, p.103.

Various interest groups such as the CAC, the British Association of Sound Systems, the Local Authority and others, came together in a formal multi-agency body known as the Carnival Support Group and they were 'actively encouraged to involve themselves in supporting the management of the Carnival' by providing stewards, adopting a pre-determined route for the floats, controlling street traders and sound systems, and 'organizing a pro-grammed and orderly closure to the event.'[31] Unfortunately, 'some of these organizations did not fulfil their early promise—for instance far fewer stew-ards were forthcoming than had been promised and it fell to the police to make good the shortfall.' But, stressed Roach, 'the importance of the Car-nival Support Group was that the police were seen to be acting to make the Carnival safe and crime-free manifestly with the consent of the majority of Carnival supporters, a perception reinforced as before by steps taken well in advance to inform the public and the media of developments in the Car-nival preparations.'[32]

For the first time, the CAC, and the police signed a Notice of Agree-ment which outlined the routes the bands would take,[33] together with the positioning of stewards and police, and a commitment to prevent unauthor-ised street traders and amplified sound systems. More importantly, it was agreed festivities would end at 8 p.m. each day.[34] But, as was to be expected in an event of this size, particularly after the controversy of 1987, there were problems. Both Kensington and Chelsea, and Westminster Councils again refused to issue licences for street trading. Also, in a controversial proposal, demands were made that the police should refrain from tackling 'muggers', leaving them, initially, to the stewards. However, with less than two weeks to go, none of the 500 stewards promised by the CAC in March had attended training sessions with the Metropolitan Police and the St John Ambulance

---

31. *Ibid*, p.106.
32. *Ibid*, p.106.
33. For the first time, the use of a circular route became compulsory for all masquerade, steel pan bands and mobile sound systems. The judging point was to be located in Westbourne Grove. Official entry and exit points for floats were designated. Mayor of London (2004). *Notting Hill Carnival: A Strategic Review*. London: Greater London Authority, pp.42–43, para. 1.39.
34. *Evening Standard*, 24 August 1988.

Brigade.[35] Eventually, although still claiming that 500 stewards had been recruited, only 150 attended a briefing session three days before the carnival.[36]

The contingency plans to deal with crime were similar to the previous year. However, subtle additions were made. For instance, the 'arrest squads of specially trained officers' worked 'under the direction of a computer-supported Intelligence and Information Cell.' Making arrests, sometimes 'in the most dangerous of circumstances in a confident professional manner' they met with little 'significant opposition' because, Roach suggested, 'they were perceived as acting in the best interests of the Carnival and the wider community.' When five or six groups of youngsters, each about 30-strong, were seen in the northern part of the carnival area at around 5 p.m. on the Sunday, the police immediately deployed a large number of officers to that area; senior officers spoke to the gangs and they dispersed.[37]

As a result of these initiatives, 'more arrests were affected in 1988 than ever before, while the organization of the Carnival, as negotiated between police and the Carnival organizers with the help of the Carnival Support Group, resulted in a reduction in the number of offences reported over the Carnival period to 193 compared with the 1,161 the year before.' Finally, there were comparatively few injuries to the public or police officers.[38] Although there was no disorder to speak of, the occasion did test the contingency plans to deal with crime to the limit but they held up. Roach claimed the reason for this was twofold. Firstly, it was well commanded and professionally policed. Secondly, and more importantly, perhaps, 'the police priority of public safety was consistent with the goals of the community itself—a goal that the public not only subscribed to but was prepared to support actively.'[39] Nevertheless, the Commissioner of the Metropolitan Police was quick to point out, it took 'considerable cost and effort' to achieve this success; the financial cost of policing the Carnival, which included the pre-event and post-event duties of the police and its support services, amounted to almost

---

35. *The Guardian*, 9 August 1988; *The Independent*, 17 August 1988.
36. *The Guardian*, 27 August 1988.
37. *The Times*, 29 August 1988; *Daily Telegraph*, 29 August 1988.
38. Roach, Lawrence, *op. cit.* 27, p.106.
39. *Ibid.*

£3.5 million.[40] Still, chairman of the CAC, Alex Pascall, was not satisfied. At the end of the first day, he blamed the reduced attendance on 'over-policing and bad pre-publicity'.[41]

The Coopers and Lybrand Report

Following the 1987 event, accusations of financial mismanagement had begun to undermine the confidence of those who sponsored the Carnival such as the Arts Council, the Commission for Racial Equality, Kensington and Chelsea Council and the London Boroughs Grants Committee. Therefore management consultants, Cooper and Lybrand, were asked by the CAC to carry out an organizational review, funded by the Commission for Racial Equality.[42] Completed in July 1988, the subsequent report made a number of criticisms of existing arrangements and recommendations as to how things might be improved, but it was too late to alter the arrangements for the 1988 Carnival. Explaining how it had started as an unfunded event, totally dependent on voluntary participation, which attracted little outside interest, it had grown to become a high profile event, attracting up to one million people and, as a result, was now the largest street festival in Europe and the largest black organized event in the western hemisphere.[43]

Safety and security had become major concerns and there was dissatisfaction amongst both performers and the local community as to how the event was organized. In addition, there was an increasing demand for performance and financial accountability.[44] In its findings, Coopers and Lybrand stated that all the activities associated with the organization of carnival were done on a 'near voluntary basis by an under-resourced organization' which meant that the carnival 'was not professionally managed.'[45] In terms of structure, it found that although there was a dedicated board, it was not representative of the Carnival or the community, that the executive team was not equipped

40. 'Report of the Commissioner of Police of the Metropolis for the Year 1988'. Cm. 670. London: Her Majesty's Stationery Office, 1989, pp.26/27.
41. *Daily Telegraph*, 29 August 1988.
42. Cohen, *op. cit.* 2, p.65.
43. Coopers and Lybrand. 'Carnival and Arts Committee—Organization Review: Summary of Findings and Recommendations'. Typescript, June 1988, p.2.
44. *Ibid*, p.4.
45. *Ibid*, p.11.

to manage an event of this magnitude and the board and executive team had merged functionally, making performance and financial accountability awkward.[46]

The report made a number of recommendations:

- The CAC should become a registered charity.[47]
- The board should have wider membership and skills, representatives being appointed from Carnival participants, funding agencies, community groups, local interest groups and skilled individuals.[48]
- Control should remain with the local black community who should have a strong representation on the board.[49]
- The Executive Management Team should, as a minimum, consist of a Director, Finance and Administration Manager, Public Relations Manager and Operations Manager. Secretarial, clerical and book-keeping support should be added.[50]
- Sound administrative and financial systems should be put in place.[51]
- Realistic sources of finance should be determined[52] which should include merchandising initiatives to generate interest in and income from Carnival.[53]
- A development strategy should be prepared and ratified.[54]

In March 1989, Claire Holder, a black barrister, was elected to replace Alex Pascall as the head of the CAC; another prominent member of the new committee was Colin Francis, a black civil servant who was director of the Notting Hill Task Force. Cohen described them as 'part of a new breed of second generation West Indians who had adjusted to the institutional

---

46. *Ibid*, p.12.
47. *Ibid*, p.15.
48. *Ibid*.
49. *Ibid*.
50. *Ibid*, pp.15/16.
51. *Ibid*, p.18.
52. *Ibid*.
53. *Ibid*, p.17.
54. *Ibid*, p.18.

structure of the British system and succeeded in making the most of the opportunities provided within it.'[55]

Finding that the Committee was £133,000 in debt and its books were under investigation by the Fraud Squad,[56] Holder persuaded the CAC to go into liquidation at its May meeting and formed a new organization called the Carnival Enterprise Committee (CEC). A meeting at the House of Commons to launch the new committee was disrupted by some who opposed it, particularly a small group from the Mangrove led by Frank Crichlow. Pointing out that 'Carnival belonged to the community,' Crichlow accused Holder of 'selling out to the big business people,' suggesting that 'when entrepreneurs come in, the little man goes out the window.'[57] Shortly afterwards, the rebels, led by Crichlow, held a meeting at the Tabernacle Community Centre in Powis Square, at which members of the new committee were described as 'yuppie capitalists', 'coconuts' and 'black lackeys' amidst claims that the new committee was intent on handing black heritage 'on a plate to the establishment' and was 'part of a conspiracy involving the police, the local council, property developers and the government's Task Force' which ultimately aimed to drive 'the black community away from North Kensington.' The rebels also announced they would hold an alternative Carnival in All Saints Road. Most of the new committee restrained from comment but one member, Francis, who had personal experience of what was going on in All Saints Road through his work on the Task Force, 'poured scorn on "the conspiracy theory"' and described the Mangrove Community Association as 'a group of ageing state-welfare dependent blacks', 'old guard' whose behaviour placed the black community in a ghetto. At the same time, 'he urged the community to escape from the "culture of dependency" and make the most of the opportunities that were open to them within the system.' In the event, other community leaders persuaded 'the rebels' not to hold a rival carnival on the undertaking that the issues would be debated once it was over.[58]

---

55. Cohen, *op. cit.* 2, p.67.
56. Without warning, the police raided the CAC office and the home of the CAC treasurer, Victor Crichlow, in March 1989 and seized all financial records. See Cohen, *op. cit.* 2, p.66. Crichlow was exonerated of all wrongdoing. See *The Caribbean Times*, 12 February 1991.
57. Correspondence from former Deputy Assistant Commissioner Charles Rideout, dated 22 January 2011.
58. Cohen, *op. cit.* 2, p.68.

The 1989 Carnival

As they had done for the previous two years, the police planned their operation meticulously but this time there had been a change of personnel at
senior level. Charles Rideout had replaced Condon as Deputy Assistant
Commissioner and David Cooke had replaced Roach as Commander. At
Notting Hill, Havard had been replaced by Clive Pearman.

The Notice of Agreement, first signed by Pascall and Condon the previous
year, was this time signed by Rideout, on behalf of the police, and Holder,
on behalf of the CEC. The Agreement laid down:

- The processional route for bands.
- The location of each of the 40 sound systems as agreed with the British
  Association of Sound Systems. No sound system was to be allowed on the
  processional route.
- The roads would be closed to all traffic.
- The locations where stalls would be allowed, as agreed with the Royal
  Borough of Kensington and Chelsea and the Borough of Westminster.[59]
- The times of commencement and close-down on each of the two days.
  This year the agreement stipulated that nothing would start before 10
  a.m., that Sound Systems should close down at 7 p.m. and the Carnival
  itself should be finished by 8.30 p.m.[60]

On the Sunday morning Holder joined Rideout, Cooke and the police
sector commanders for an 'operational breakfast'.[61] The Carnival opened on
a subdued note on the Sunday with the attendance slightly down on the previous year. The crowd was particularly thick in All Saints Road, dancing to
the amplified sound systems. Crichlow expressed his unhappiness with the
'large police presence', claiming that 'the whole community' was 'steward-
ing the streets' and, as soon as a problem was seen 'we zoom in.' More than
40 floats of masqueraders and musicians toured the streets and, in addition
to the 40 amplified sound systems, there were three stages, at Powis Square,
Portobello Green and Great Western Road were more than 20 live bands

---

59. Both councils had finally agreed to grant licences for stalls at the Carnival.
60. *Police Review*, 1 September 1989, p.1750.
61. Rideout, *op. cit.* 57.

performed. The police 'declared themselves "very happy" with the "lowest crime figures for a very long time".' Holder, too, expressed her satisfaction with the way things had gone.[62]

Monday was different. The crowds flocked in and, in the afternoon, three incidents occurred which, in the light of events in Trafalgar Square on New Year's Eve 1987 and, in the aftermath of the Hillsborough Disaster only four months previously,[63] gave Commander Cooke some cause for concern. Predictably, perhaps, the Mangrove Steel Band became involved in a dispute with the police in Westbourne Park Road when they refused to keep to the route agreed with the organizers. A short while later, in Great Western Road, in a protest against the handling of the incident with the Mangrove Steel band, two other bands, Ebony and Eclipse, moved side-by-side along the street. In both cases, this resulted in a build-up of people causing severe congestion which would not have occurred had the bands complied with the original arrangements agreed between the organizers and the police. Finally, by late afternoon, Westbourne Park Underground Station, which, fortunately is at ground level and not underground, was unable to cope with the large numbers of people flocking to and departing from the Carnival. There was severe crushing inside the station on one of the platforms and on the stairs leading down to that platform. London Transport Police officers on duty at the station requested the assistance of the Metropolitan Police and a number of children were lifted bodily to safety through broken windows.[64]

In addition to the safety issues, steaming returned. The police had devised a plan to deal with these gangs based on the wedge which had been used in the mid-1970s and-late-1970s to divide up tightly-knit disorderly crowds. It involved, in this case, deploying arrest squads consisting of 15 officers in a wedge formation into the crowd with the intention of arresting at least one individual in a group of steamers. This was relatively successful.[65]

Most of the amplified sound systems closed down as agreed at around 7 p.m. and many people started to make their way home through the maze of

---

62. *Police Review*, 1 September 1989, p.1750.
63. Ninety-six people had been crushed to death.
64. Much of the information relating to the disorder during the evening of 28 August was obtained in a subsequent meeting with Commander Cooke on 10 May 1990.
65. Rideout, *op. cit.* 57.

streets that make up this part of London. Others, however, moved towards All Saints Road to join the already large crowd. When the trouble came, it was predictable, both in time and place.[66] Shortly before 7.45 p.m., a group of about 20 black youths, deprived of music on the streets, tried to gatecrash a private 'blues' party at 19 Lancaster Road, which had been ongoing for most of the weekend. A struggle developed between those wanting to gatecrash the party and others who were equally determined to keep them out. As police moved in to restore order they were pelted with bottles and bricks. One person was arrested before the senior officer present, Chief Superintendent Pearman, 'ordered a tactical withdrawal as community leaders tried to calm the mob outside the house.' However, as the arrested youth was being taken away, Police Constable McMorran was stabbed by another youth. Fortunately, his body armour deflected the knife away from the vulnerable part of his body but the knife entered his thigh.[67] In an attempt to defuse the situation, Chief Superintendent Pearman sought out Crichlow and other self-styled community leaders but they merely demanded that the police withdraw from the area altogether, something the police neither would nor could be reasonably expected to do, given the situation that then existed.

Thirty minutes later police officers at the junction of All Saints Road and Westbourne Park Road came under attack. A request was made for shield serials to be deployed to clear the area but this was initially refused by Commander Cooke, hoping to contain any disorder within the sector in which it had originated. However, it became clear that around 200 predominantly black youths were out to cause trouble. Staying together as a group, they would run to one junction make a quick missile attack on police and then run to another junction. As a result there were successively four areas of disorder at the junctions leading into All Saints Road. Some shield serials were deployed under Chief Superintendent Crawford who requested Cooke to implement a complete close-down of the Carnival area. Aware of the criticism likely to be directed at the police, Cooke refused. As far as he was concerned the disorder was still relatively contained and he ordered a return to normal policing as soon as possible.[68]

---

66. It started on Sector 3 quite close to All Saints Road.
67. *Daily Express*, 30 August 1989.
68. Interview with former Commander David Cooke, *op. cit.* 64.

However, at around 8.15 p.m., the police came under attack from missile throwing youths at two other locations; firstly in Westbourne Park Road at the junction with Ledbury Road and then in Great Western Road at the junction with Elkestone Road. This raised the number of seats of disorder to six, but, more significantly, three different sectors were now affected. At the same time, youths began climbing to the roof of a block of flats, Clydesdale House, which was located opposite the southern end of All Saints Road, and bombarding the police officers below with missiles. By now officers had been injured and Commander Cooke received a joint request from Chief Superintendents Crawford and Pearman to have the Carnival area cleared. This he reluctantly agreed to do after a brief discussion with Deputy Assistant Commissioner Rideout, and he ordered out all officers held on reserve, including the remaining shield serials. The sector commanders each introduced a number of pre-arranged one-way filter cordons to ensure everyone was moved away from the Carnival area in the agreed directions. Sector commanders north of the Westway channelled the crowd in a north-westerly direction whilst sector commanders south of the Westway directed people in a south-easterly direct towards Notting Hill Gate and onwards. Meanwhile, other serials were deployed to take the ground behind the shield serials as they moved forward, to prevent crime and arrest anyone committing offences.[69]

But, whilst the crowds were channelled away in the desired directions and the central sector on which the disorder had originated was completely cleared shortly after 9 p.m., the plan did not work quite as well as was hoped, simply because a number of bands and masqueraders were still on the processional route and were caught up in the crowds as they were pushed away from the carnival area. At about 9.30 p.m., the police came under missile attack at both ends of Elkestone Road, in Ladbroke Grove and in Great Western Road but it did not last for long. Further disorder occurred in Queensway at about 11 p.m. but by 11.30 p.m. all shield serials had returned to their vehicles and were available for mobile patrol.[70]

Although on the surface, the events at the end of the 1989 carnival were similar to those in 1987 there was one fundamental difference. The police operation to clear the Carnival area in 1989 was mounted in the interests of

69. *Ibid.*
70. *Ibid.*

public safety whereas in 1987 it had been mounted in response to an unacceptable level of crime as gangs of steamers forced their way through the crowds, and, in many cases, used extreme violence to rob people.

Once again the newspapers on the days following the Carnival were full of sensational headlines:

> Notting Hill Carnival ends in violence (*The Times*, 29 August)
>
> Police battle with gangs at carnival (*Daily Telegraph*, 29 August 1989)
>
> Riots wreck the Carnival (*Daily Mail*, 29 August 1989)
>
> 210 Carnival Rioters Held (*Evening Standard*, 29 August 1989)
>
> Carnival marred as riot police clash with youths (*The Guardian*, 29 August 1989)
>
> Police blamed for fanning violence (*The Guardian*, 30 August)
>
> Carnival organizer critical of police riot charge tactics (*The Independent*, 30 August 1989)
>
> Party scuffle sparked off carnival violence (*The Times*, 30 August 1989)
>
> Carnival riot police charged 'at random' (*The Independent*, 1 September 1989)

Despite the violence, for a second successive year crime figures were down, with only 132 being reported, compared with 193 in 1988 and 1,161 in 1987. The number of people arrested was 310 but most of these were in relation to the disorder that broke out on the Monday evening. Thirty-two officers were injured, amongst them Chief Inspector Ray Williams, who was hit on the back of the head by two bottles as he attempted to steer a children's Carnival float to safety.[71] A subsequent article in the *British Medical Journal* accused the tabloid press of grossly inflating the injury figures 'in a sensational manner' leading people to believe that, because of the disorder on the last evening, attending the Carnival in future years 'could pose a risk of serious personal injury'. In fact, the St John Ambulance Brigade treated 269 people over the two days of which only 24, ten fewer than in 1988, were referred to hospital. Virtually all the newspapers reported the injury to Chief Inspector

---

71. *Police Review*, 1 September 1989, p.1750.

Williams as being serious when in fact he received 'a small scalp laceration that did not require suturing.'[72]

Once again, the complaints about the police were predictable; so, too, was the police response. Claire Holder, Head of the CEC, criticised the way people were herded out of the area.[73] Frank Crichlow claimed police numbers were provocative.[74] Joel O'Loughlin, a worker at the Mangrove Community Association, blamed 'police harassment of black youths in the All Saints Road for the trouble.[75] Labour member of Kensington and Chelsea Council, Ben Bousquet, accused the police of going 'wild' and over-reacting, claiming that 'they charged through the area and scared a lot of people who were just trying to make their way home.'[76]

Chris Boothman, chairman of the Society of Black Lawyers 'accused the police of failing to distinguish between troublemakers and the public' and of using what he called 'early resolution' indiscriminately. He said:

'When there is trouble at a football match early resolution does not mean stopping the match. It means isolating the troublemakers and removing them. No one can complain about the police coming down hard on those involved in criminal acts. The complaint is that I saw many innocent people being swept up in their path. If you have a large crowd, you know almost inevitably there will be troublemakers. The Metropolitan Police should be able to isolate them from ordinary people. What became apparent from the manner and timing of the operation was that the police were using the trouble to shut down the carnival at a particular time. The police have got to change their attitude. They have seriously to consider the means they can adopt to ease tension. If you have a major event you can't suddenly say "stop". There has to be an escape valve, a winding down of the carnival.'[77]

---

72. Cugnoni, H, Challoner, T and Touquet, R (1989). 'Medicine and the Media: Notting Hill Carnival 1989 — the Facts from the Accident and Emergency Departments, St Charles and St Mary's Hospitals'. *British Medical Journal*, Vol. 299, 11 November 1989, p.1229; see also Dalton A M, Sharma, A and Touquet, R 'Notting Hill Carnival 1988'. Arch Emerg Med 1989, 6, pp.146–148.
73. *The Guardian*, 30 August 1989; *The Times*, 30 August 1989.
74. *The Times*, 29 August 1989.
75. *The Times*, 30 August 1989.
76. *Daily Telegraph*, 30 August 1989.
77. *The Independent*, 1 September 1989.

There were also allegations from African-Caribbean sources that the disturbances in All Saints Road at the conclusion of Carnival 'were due to Mr Pearman's obsession with destroying the community by any means possible' and the suggestion that his 'continually fermenting interest' in this particular road 'had almost become a crusade.[78] Later the same month, at a meeting of the Kensington and Chelsea Borough Council, Labour members alleged that 'the police had made "Gestapo-like" raids on blacks homes and that the Carnival had been broken up "South African-style",' and called for a public inquiry into policing at Notting Hill. This was rejected as the Tory-controlled council voted along party lines.[79]

In response, Deputy Assistant Commissioner Rideout denied an excessive police presence, claiming that 'the action of these people marred what we thought was one of the most successful days yet.'[80] A police spokesman pointed out that right at the outset, the police did withdraw for nearly 20 minutes in the hope that local community leaders could bring the situation under control. They failed to do so and police cordons were bombarded with missiles.[81] Police action was supported by Barry Irving, director of an independent research body, the Police Foundation, who claimed that they had little option once disorder broke out, particular in the aftermath of Hillsborough where, arguably, people died because of ineffectual decision-making by senior police officers.[82]

Subsequently, an organization calling itself the Association for a People's Carnival (APC), who apparently adopted its constitution on 5 December 1989, issued a report, entitled 'Police Carnival 1989', which was a catalogue of complaints about police action and behaviour. In summary this included:

- Initially refusing some bands entry into the Carnival area when they first arrived;

78. *Caribbean Times*, Friday 15 to Thursday 21 September 1989. Further mention of this is made in *Chapter 17*.
79. *The Guardian*, 22 September 1989.
80. *Evening Standard*, 29 August 1989.
81. *Daily Telegraph*, 30 August 1989.
82. *The Independent*, 30 August 1989.

- The formation of barriers across the Carnival route which either impeded the progress of bands, or split them in two, or prevented spectators from following the bands to dance to the music provided;
- The giving of conflicting instructions to bands by police officers on the street;
- Accusations that because of the number of streets that had been blocked off by the police, crowd congestion was caused unnecessarily;
- Accusations that the police deliberately tried to 'engineer' a scuffle with black youth by trying to close down the Carnival early;
- At the end of the Carnival, bands were prevented by police from returning to where their clothes and belongings had been left or where they were to pick up their transport;
- Police officers on the street were generally intimidating and aggressive, and there was inconsistency in who was arrested and who was not.[83]

Whilst the report was highly critical of the police, its main purpose was to discredit the newly formed CEC and set itself up as a rival organization. Indeed, the report makes mention of the formation of yet another committee, this time by a number of the bands, the Notting Hill International Carnival Committee (NHICC).[84] But the *Caribbean Times* warned that, despite the criticisms it, too, made of the police, the foremost lesson that the black community must learn is that there is no room for disunity and petty squabbles.'[85] In the event, neither the APC nor the NHICC had any impact on future carnivals.

The 1990 Carnival

The 1990 Carnival was uneventful insofar as the police were concerned. In response to complaints about the noise made by helicopters monitoring it, the police used an airship for the first time to get an aerial view of the Carnival. The police continued with the policy of 'keeping the number of officers actually available on the streets to a minimum, while maintaining

---

83. Association for People's Carnival, The. 'Police Carnival 1989'. Typescript. Appendix 7. (Copy in the author's possession), pp.1–7.
84. *Ibid*, Appendix.
85. *Caribbean Times*, 1–7 September 1989.

a strong reserve to deal with any contingency.' The Home Secretary, David Waddington paid a two-hour visit on the Sunday. Although it was estimated that nearly a million people attended the two-day event, crimes were again down—only 84 were reported—but there were 151 arrests, mainly for drug offences. In a statement made after the carnival, Deputy Assistant Commissioner Rideout pointed out that the police's approach had been to concentrate on the safety of the public and police officers but, at the same time the aim was, 'keeping crime to a minimum and reducing inconvenience for residents.'[86]

---

86. *The Job*, 31 August 1990.

CHAPTER 17

A CHANGE OF DIRECTION

Introduction

Superintendent Clive Pearman had been posted to Notting Hill as Rod Havard's deputy in March 1987 and was the Silver Commander during the raids on the dealers' homes during Operation Trident in the July. When Havard left at the end of 1987, Pearman was promoted to take command of the Division. During a subsequent press interview he claimed that, despite the success of Operation Trident, 'morale was on the floor.'[1] Later, in another interview shortly after he left Notting Hill two years later to take up a position at New Scotland Yard, he suggested that, when he took over as Divisional Commander, he 'inherited problems caused by poor leadership and management at very senior level in the division and beyond.' He went on to describe All Saints Road as,

> 'a cancer. If there was an unwritten policy about how to police the area it was one of appeasement, also tinged with idealism that if you treat people nicely, eventually they will be nice back to you. The officers on the streets knew this was a cop-out, betraying the community they were there to protect.'[2]

Because 'operational officers were not getting the support they needed,' this 'inevitably lowered morale' and 'encouraged people to 'interpret the rules and regulations differently.'[3]

---

1.   Graef, Roger. 'Saints and Sinners'. *Evening Standard Magazine*, August 1990, p.27.
2.   Waterhouse, Rosie. 'Inquiry into police assaults suppressed'. In *The Independent on Sunday*, 24 June 1990.
3.   *Ibid.*

Crichlow Arrested Again

According to one report, Pearman believed the Mangrove was the planning headquarters for all that happened in and around All Saints Road[4] and, because he saw this as primarily being concerned with criminality, he saw little value in encouraging a multi-agency approach. Roger Graef suggested that 'the tension between blacks and the police [became] personalised between Crichlow and Pearman and Pearman decided to revoke the Mangrove leader's special status and crush the club.'[5]

In trying to resolve the problems that he believed he had inherited, Pearman 'provided very forceful leadership' and drafted in 'new recruits fresh from training schools.'[6] It was important to him that he had the support of the constables and sergeants who regularly patrolled the streets and showed that 'he cared about them.' He regularly walked round the police station, finding out what was going on and generally listened to their views.[7] However, some evidence was forthcoming which indicated that he did not always make the best use of his senior management team insofar as delegating responsibility was concerned. Instead, he preferred to be 'in the driving seat'[8] and 'leading from the front'.[9] He addressed 'the drugs problem with a series of high profile operations in All Saints Road to cut off the supply,'[10] instigating two raids on the Mangrove in the first five months of 1988. The first occurred at the beginning of February, under the code name Operation Vulture, when 18 people were arrested in a late-night raid on the premises. Four were charged with dealing in drugs and nine with possession; the remaining five were released without being charged. More significantly, perhaps, a large number of weapons, including pickaxe handles, knives and a swordstick,

---

4. Interview with former Chief Superintendent Rod Havard on 1 February 2011.
5. Graef, Roger, *op. cit.* 1, p.27.
6. Waterhouse, Rosie, *op. cit.* 2. In correspondence to the author, dated 10 September 2011, Alan Shave, who served under Pearman as a chief inspector, wrote that 'Pearman was very bright and a clear leader of men. Leading the charge from the front.'
7. In correspondence from Alan Shave to the author, dated 10 September 2011.
8. In correspondence from Tim Hollis to the author, dated 10 September 2011. Tim Hollis served as a chief inspector at Notting Hill before eventually becoming Chief Constable of Lincolnshire and Deputy President of the Association of Chief Police Officers.
9. Shave, *op. cit.* 7.
10. Waterhouse, *op. cit.* 2.

were seized.[11] The second, in mid-May, under the code name Operation Falcon, was carried out by an elite squad, known as PT18 which had been set up to carry out difficult raids. A 48-strong team dressed all in black, it had, amongst other things, the capability to make a rapid entry. In a subsequent interview, Pearman claimed that Crichlow had never been 'lifted' before; on this occasion he was among the 21 people arrested and was subsequently charged with possessing heroin and cannabis with intent to supply and allowing the premises to be used for supplying drugs.[12] The others faced charges ranging from the possession of cocaine and cannabis to criminal damage.[13]

Crichlow claimed he had been 'framed by Notting Hill police officers in a conspiracy to destroy his community association'; he was eventually acquitted by a jury at Knightsbridge Crown Court after a five-week trial in 1989 during which 66 police officers gave evidence. Defending Crichlow, Michael Mansfield QC, referred to the arrangement already commented on by the stipendiary magistrate at Wells Street Magistrates' Court,[14] as 'an extraordinary gentleman's agreement' under which Crichlow or an assistant accompanied anyone arrested locally on drugs charges' to Notting Hill Police Station. However, Mansfield pointed out that all this had changed when Pearman took command of the Division.[15]

Pearman was 'unrepentant' about the operation, suggesting that Crichlow knew about 'all the crime going on in his neighbourhood' and 'he could have stopped it if he wanted to.' He decided 'it was time to do something about it,' so, as he subsequently commented 'we went in and arrested him.' By doing so, Pearman claimed that the officers on the street were no longer confused about what was expected of them.[16] Commenting on Crichlow's acquittal, Pearman apparently observed that, 'because the jury didn't find

---

11. *Kensington News and Post*, 11 February 1988.
12. *Daily Mail*, 21 May 1988, *The Mail on Sunday*, 22 May 1988, *The Observer*, 22 May 1988, *Caribbean Times*, 27 May 1988, *Daily Telegraph*, 28 May 1988.
13. *Kensington News and Post*, 26 May 1988.
14. See *Chapter 15*.
15. *The Independent*, 7 June 1990. See also Batha, Emma. 'Saints and Sinners'. In *Time Out* magazine, 21–28 August 1991, p.11.
16. Graef, Roger, *op. cit.* 1, p.27.

the case proven beyond reasonable doubt' did not 'mean that they believed the allegations against the police.'[17]

Pearman's comment that Crichlow had never been 'lifted' was inaccurate. As has already been described, Crichlow had faced major trials in 1972 and 1977. He was acquitted on both occasions. In addition, he faced a number of trials for less serious offences, in some of which he was convicted. In his autobiography, Michael Mansfield accused the police of 'hostile policing and harassment' and of mounting 'heavy-handed and repeated police raids' on the Mangrove. The first trial, suggested Mansfield, had 'highlighted the oppressive treatment and policing of black people in Britain'. In the third trial, Mansfield claimed that Crichlow was 'falsely accused of dealing in heroin.'[18]

Throughout most, if not all of his time at the Mangrove, Crichlow was able to turn to solicitor Gareth Peirce,[19] whom Mansfield described as 'unique [with] a deep sense of injustice.' More importantly, perhaps, in terms of representing Crichlow, her preparation in defending anyone when she believed an injustice had occurred, was 'immaculate and immense [with] each brief or set of instructions' reading 'like a book'. She entered each case, suggested Mansfield 'with a quiet and deliberate persistence [that was] unnerving'. Thus 'every dimension of a case [was] explored' and she was 'capable of unravelling the most complex situations.'[20] There is no doubt that a number of divisional commanders at Notting Hill, and, indeed, police officers elsewhere, under-estimated Gareth Peirce over the years.

Whether or not the raid in 1988 was justified, in police eyes 'the general perception amongst the local black community' was that Crichlow had been 'fitted up' and this naturally widened the 'rift' between them and the police.[21] For the police, Pearman's raid on the Mangrove and subsequent prosecution of Frank Crichlow had all the hallmarks of failure that had been seen in 1977. It was as if the police had learnt nothing and, once again, the prosecution case was sloppy to say the least. A police inspector admitted in court that he

---

17. Waterhouse, Rosie, *op. cit.* 2.

18. Mansfield, Michael (2009). *Memoirs of a Radical Lawyer*. London: Bloomsbury, pp.275/276.

19. The author first met Gareth Peirce when he was a chief inspector at Caledonian Road Police Station in the early 1970s.

20. Mansfield, *op. cit.* 18, pp.39–40.

21. In correspondence from former Deputy Assistant Commissioner Charles Rideout, to the author, dated 22 January 2011.

failed to complete some required details relating to the search warrant;[22] the packets of drugs allegedly thrown onto the floor by a number of the arrested people were never fingerprinted; and, in addition, Crichlow's clothes were not tested for drugs and neither was his home searched.[23] The result was that it brought yet more criticism on the police at Notting Hill. Although there may have been a brief feeling of euphoria at the station immediately following Crichlow's arrest, there would have ultimately been a feeling of dejection and resentment following his acquittal. Further dejection would have been apparent in October 1992 when Crichlow accepted a £50,000 settlement at the High Court from the Commissioner of the Metropolitan Police for false imprisonment, battery and malicious prosecution.[24] Rather than reduce his status within the black community, the circumstances surrounding his prosecution, eventual acquittal and the award of damages increased it.

'Blinkered Police Officers'

Pearman put Inspector Caroline Nicholl in charge of the All Saints Road unit in 1988. Described as 'a forceful woman with clear ideas',[25] she conceded that 'the behaviour of constables left a lot to be desired,' adding that a

> 'lack of leadership meant the PCs were on their own, so of course they may have done things which they shouldn't have. They were making things up as they went along according to their own ideas of what needed to be done.'[26]

Claiming it was an uphill task to start with, she set about changing their attitudes to All Saints Road by trying 'to give them a sense of purpose other than just nicking blacks for small amounts of cannabis.' She suggested the officers were 'blinkered' in believing 'everyone' in the area was 'black and hostile' so she made them call at houses within the immediate vicinity and speak to the occupiers. The result was that 'they learnt that most of the residents were white' and 'virtually all of them, black and white, supported'

---

22. *The Guardian*, 11 May 1989.
23. *The Independent*, 17 June 1989. The Metropolitan Police also paid his legal costs. *Police Review*, 16 October 1992, p.1917.
24. *Kensington News*, 14 October 1992.
25. Graef, Roger, *op. cit.* 1, p.27.
26. *Ibid.*

the police. As a result, she claimed, even the cynical police officers began to take a different view![27]

Controversy

At the end of January 1989, Pearman caused controversy by withdrawing police participation in the All Saints Road Community Association, claiming that it no longer represented the views of residents. This decision was criticised by Labour Councillor, Ben Bousquet, who pointed out that 'it was the only forum where the black community were able to put forward their points of view.' At the same time he suggested that the withdrawal was a 'well-orchestrated attack on the black community'. Pearman countered this by pointing out that there was a police consultative committee covering the whole area of Notting Hill that met on a regular basis.[28]

Two months later, Pearman was involved in more controversy when a proposal for an ex-prisoners' hostel in All Saints Road was submitted to Kensington and Chelsea Council. On hearing about the application, Pearman wrote to six prominent people in Notting Hill—leader of the Council, Nicholas Freeman, Colin Francis, the North Kensington Task Force Leader, John Sienkiewicz from the Inner Cities Unit at the Department of the Environment, Dave Moran of the Portobello Trust, and Geoffrey Murray and Steve Howlett, directors of the Kensington Housing Trust and Notting Hill Housing Trust respectively.[29] His letter expressed his opposition to the application and, at the same time, suggested that community groups which were critical of authority should not receive financial support:

> 'I am concerned that organizations which create divisiveness in the community are not encouraged by receiving public funding. Highly emotive and politically extremist organizations would never be integrated within the community .... and on the basis of long and bitter experience, should be isolated from public funding.'[30]

---

27. *Ibid.*
28. *Kensington News*, 2 February 1989.
29. *Caribbean Times*, 17 February 1989.
30. *Police Review*, 10 March 1989.

Pearman further 'questioned the morality of accommodating former prisoners' in an area 'whose symbolism is still one of lawlessness, crime and public disorder.' Pearman then invited the six people to meet with him to discuss 'corporate strategy' surrounding the issues raised in the letter. Declining the invitation, Freeman wrote:

> 'You may think it would be wise for you to decline to become involved in such questions. The function of the police is to prevent crime and to preserve the Queen's peace. I am not convinced that a meeting between us and the people to whom you copied your letter would serve any useful purpose.'[31]

The leader of the Labour opposition suggested Pearman's letter was 'extremely offensive' because 'many of the organizations' he was criticising 'were ethnic minority-based'. Paul Boateng, by now the Member of Parliament for Brent, described the letter as 'subversive and sinister'; local councillor, Ben Bousquet suggested Pearman was being 'divisive' and had gone 'way above his remit', whilst Lee Jasper from the National Black Caucus accused him of having 'a political analysis' and being involved in 'a corporate conspiracy to deny black groups and businesses the opportunity to develop in the way they saw fit.'[32] Pearman responded to the criticism by suggesting that the police needed to let people know what their concerns were and what 'the consequences [were] of giving public money [to a] particular group or section of the community'.[33]

The furore within some sections of the local community was such that the Notting Hill Social Council, which represented 20 local voluntary groups, wrote to the Metropolitan Police Commissioner, Sir Peter Imbert, calling for Pearman's resignation.[34] Pearman subsequently defended his actions at a meeting of the Police Consultative Committee, claiming they were based purely on a desire to ensure that the improvement brought about as a result of police action in All Saints Road was maintained. Whilst he received support from some members, the chairman, Christopher Carstairs, felt bound

---

31. *Ibid.*
32. *Caribbean Times*, 17 February 1989.
33. *Police Review*, 10 March 1989.
34. *Kensington News*, 30 March 1989.

to comment that, 'by singling out certain North Kensington groups for criticism', he had 'breached his proper role as a police officer.'[35] Interestingly, three years earlier, Benyon had warned that police officers 'seemed to be increasingly prepared to take part in political debate' which might undermine 'the previous impression of impartiality.'[36] But, in becoming part of a multi-agency approach, as both Pearman's predecessor had and his successor did, the police, of necessity, entered the political arena. Arguably, given what had already occurred during his time as Divisional Commander, Pearman's error in involving the police in this particular issue was that this was seen as yet another example of his hard-line 'law and order' approach to criminality in All Saints Road.

The War on Drugs Continues

By the beginning of 1989 there were signs that some drug-dealers were vacating All Saints Road but plying their trade elsewhere in Notting Hill. Pearman kept up the pressure, organizing a raid, under the codename Operation Harrier, on a house in Kensal Road in which ten people—some of whom were believed to be Yardies—were arrested.[37] Following their arrest, having been given bail, a number fled to Jamaica before they could be brought to trial. However, one female member of the group, found in possession of cocaine, was, later in the year, sentenced to four years' imprisonment at the Old Bailey.[38]

In May, Pearman announced the next phase of his strategy in the clampdown on drugs, at the same time claiming the 'war against drugs was well on the way to being won'. There had, he said, been a dramatic decline in the amount of cannabis, cocaine and heroin on the streets since Operation Trident and he now invited breweries to take action against those pubs which harboured drug pushers.[39] However, less than a month later, he warned that the cocaine-based drug, known as crack, could be available in Notting Hill in the near future. Pointing out that it was 'highly addictive' affecting 'peoples'

---

35. *Kensington News*, 27 April 1989.
36. Benyon, John (1986). 'A Tale of Failure: Race and Policing'. Policy Papers in Ethnic Relations No. 3. Warwick: Centre for Research in Ethnic Relations, University of Warwick, p.63.
37. *Kensington News*, 2 February 1989.
38. *Kensington News*, 14 December 1989.
39. *Kensington News*, 25 May 1990.

mental faculties' to a greater extent than any other hard drug, he promised he would drive out anyone who dealt in crack.[40]

Meanwhile, three operations were mounted during the remainder of 1989. Firstly, in May, four dealers were arrested under Operation Plate.[41] Secondly, in July, two premises in Lancaster Road, which is just off All Saints Road, were raided under Operation Buccaneer Two by officers from Notting Hill, under the command of Superintendent Ian Hutcheson, supported by Six Area Territorial Support Group. A mob of about 100 youths threw stones at police vehicles as 17 people were arrested suspected of being in possession of drugs and public order offences. As was quite common, the action resulted in 'allegations of police brutality' from sections of the community but Superintendent Hutcheson claimed that the police 'were responding to the concerns of the Notting Hill community' and it was yet another example of a 'continuing determination to rid the area of dealers.'[42]

Finally, in December, Pearman mounted his last operation on All Saints Road. Following the pattern that had grown up since 1982, the police, using a covert observation post, merely collated information for the first week under Operation Mint. Three weeks followed in which information was passed to waiting officers on the periphery of the area about people who had purchased drugs. As a result, 62 people were arrested of whom 18 were found to be in possession of crack. It was suggested by one academic that, by arresting those who had bought drugs the police were involved in a form of demand reduction because, it was claimed, once news got back to their acquaintances, they would be put off coming to the area to buy drugs.[43] This was certainly not the case at Notting Hill, neither on this nor on any previous occasion; indeed, some would say the opposite was the case. The more it appeared in the news, the greater its reputation as a source of illegal drugs, added to which the penalties for the mere possession of drugs were generally so derisory that few, if any, people were put off. At the end of the four weeks, 16 dealers had been identified and a considerable amount of evidence had

---

40. *Kensington News*, 15 June 1989.
41. *Kensington News*, 14 May 1990.
42. *Daily Telegraph*, 26 July 1989; Today, 26 July 1989.
43. Dorn, Nicholas; Karim Murji and Nigel South (1992). *Traffickers: Drug Markets and Law Enforcement*. London: Routledge, p.110.

been accumulated. Dawn raids on eleven West London addresses by more than 100 police officers, led to the arrest of nine dealers; another five were arrested subsequently. Officers were accompanied on the raids by members of the Kensington and Chelsea Police Consultative Committee and the Borough Crime Prevention Panel.[44]

Some details of what was involved in the operation were subsequently revealed. It relied 'heavily on the detailed observation logs' in which the surveillance officers recorded the clothes worn by the dealers, in addition to what actually took place. Subsequently, when the police raided the dealers' houses, any clothes that the dealers had been seen wearing during the period of the observation were photographed. In common with many operations of this nature, the officers could not subsequently provide the courts with photographic evidence of deals taking place because this would have revealed the location of the covert observation post.[45] A judgement three years previously by the Court of Appeal had upheld 'the long established rule that police or other investigating officers should not be required to disclose the sources of their information in order to protect the identity of a persons who had allowed their premises to be used for surveillance, and the location of the premises from which the surveillance had been kept.'[46]

Black Leaders Should Accept More Responsibility

Just prior to the 1989 Carnival, an article by Ferdinand Dennis, the 1988 winner of the Martin Luther King Memorial Prize, highlighted some of the problems faced within the African-Caribbean community in England and, in doing so, supported views already expressed by Newman back in 1973 and others afterwards. Pointing out that the 'Caribbean family was in crisis' at the end of this 'controversial riot-torn decade', he described how, in England, 'a third of all Caribbean families' had 'only one parent' and a 'disproportionate number of black children' were 'in local authority care.' He went on to claim that 'when the family crumbles, wider troubles follow' and, in particular he cited 'the hold that hard drugs like cocaine and heroin' had 'on many black communities.' Supporting what senior police officers

44. *Kensington News*, 14 December 1989.
45. Dorn, *op. cit.* 43 pp.109–110.
46. *Regina v. Rankine, Times Law Report*, 4 March 1986.

had been saying for years, Dennis claimed that 'black community leaders' remained 'silent on this issue'; instead 'drugs raids' were seen 'as an occasion to condemn the police for harassment' and the fault lay with an 'uncaring and hostile' white society.' But, says Dennis, 'the Caribbean community' had 'reached a point where it' needed 'to be more self-critical' and 'the next decade' of 'black leaders should demand that their community takes greater responsibility for its own development.'[47]

A New Divisional Commander

Chief Superintendent Pearman was replaced by Chief Superintendent Denis O'Connor in February 1990. Described as 'energetic' and 'shrewd',[48] O'Connor's approach was less confrontational than Pearman's had been. He was not only concerned, as previous divisional commanders had been, with the ready availability of illegal drugs on the streets and in some premises, but also with the number of civil actions being brought against officers from Notting Hill, as described towards the end of *Chapter 16*. But he was also aware of the need to gain the support of 'critical local partners'.[49] He, therefore, decided on a broad two-fold strategy. Firstly, he would engage 'without prejudice' with the Mangrove, with the various community groups on the estates surrounding All Saints Road, and with the Kensington and Chelsea Council. Secondly, and equally importantly, he had to win over the sergeants and constables who, he claimed, could broadly be divided into three when he arrived.

Firstly, there were those who were 'quite hard-nosed about everything that had happened'; then there were those who were intimidated by the threat of complaint and going to court and the hostile reaction they got from some individuals, particularly in All Saints Road; and lastly, there were those who were newly arrived and quite bewildered by it all! Therefore, he set out to convince officers that a more 'calculated approach was needed, in which intelligence about who was doing what and to who and with what drugs', was the way forward towards understanding local drug networks. He told them that the problems on the street and in some premises would only be

---

47. Ferdinand, Dennis. 'The black family in crisis'. *Evening Standard*, 23 August 1989, p.7.
48. Hollis, *op. cit.* 8.
49. *Ibid.*

dealt with successfully by careful planning, and senior management would be involved throughout. In so doing, he wanted to ensure that there was sufficient evidence to convict those who were arrested and taken before the courts.[50]

In May 1990, in an internal memorandum to police and customs, the Home Office drugs inspectorate announced, amongst other things, that Notting Hill had become 'a confirmed centre of crack dealing', reporting that there had been 'forty-three crack seizures' in the first two months of that year, 'compared with 138 in the whole of 1989 and 27 in 1988.'[51] As part of O'Connor's strategy to involve other agencies, in July 1990, the Kensington and Chelsea Council set up a Substance Abuse Action Group. With a budget of £5,000 per year, the group was made up of health, education and police experts. Strongly supporting the multi-agency approach, O'Connor pointed out that, up until then, the police had effectively been dealing with the drug problem on their own. But, he claimed the police could 'only ever have a small impact on drug-taking' if they tackled it on their own because, whilst they could 'do something about supply' they had virtually no effect 'on demand.' Therefore the way forward, he claimed, was in the 'education, counselling and care' of the youngsters who dabbled in drugs.[52]

The main thrust of police action under this scheme was to reduce the availability of drugs whilst the other agencies, such as health and education, acted within their own areas of expertise. Not surprisingly, perhaps, a spokesperson from the Mangrove, Jebb Johnson, was critical of the whole idea, claiming that he was 'not sure that the police' were 'the best people to run this sort of thing'. Instead, he commented: 'If the police and the borough have the money to worry about substance abuse then why don't they give some of it to the voluntary groups in the area who put forward plans for drug rehabilitation centres?'[53] However, by the end of October, Johnson, felt bound to comment positively on the relationship between the police and the black community, suggesting it had improved considerably under Chief

---

50. From correspondence received from former Chief Superintendent Denis O'Connor, dated 6 April 2011.
51. *The Guardian*, 3 May 1990.
52. *Kensington News*, 19 July 1990.
53. *Ibid.*

Superintendent O'Connor. Whereas previously, the police had been 'arrogant' and seen All Saints Road as 'a battle ground', there was now an 'increase in consultative policing.' But he warned the mood was still 'far from utopic.'[54]

Beginning of the End for the Mangrove

A significant event was played out during the first months of 1991. In late-January, officers from the Kensington and Chelsea Council boarded up the windows and installed shatter-proof doors to the premises of the Mangrove Community Association at 10–12 All Saints Road, because, it claimed, the council was owed £71,643 in mortgage arrears. As was to be expected, there was a furore from the black community. Jebb Johnson suggested it was a 'conspiracy between the police, the council and other business interests' because 'they wanted to get rid of us.' Pointing out that it had never been 'discussed at any council committees', local councillor, Ben Bousquet called it 'a deliberate and premeditated attempt ... to silence the Mangrove once and for all.' A number of local organizations such as the Notting Hill Housing Trust and the Council of Churches for Britain and Ireland joined with the Mangrove Community Association in an effort to keep it open[55] but it was finally closed when the Kensington and Chelsea Council evicted the owners for defaulting on its mortgage repayments. The building was put up for auction and bought by two young businessmen, Peter Cross and Simon Rose, who turned it into a restaurant, the Portobello Dining Rooms. Frank Crichlow claimed that some council members were racist and suggested that they did not 'want Carnival' or 'the Mangrove' or 'black people.'[56] As a result, the Mangrove Community Association was left with the very much smaller premises at No.3 All Saints Road.[57]

The Battle Against Drugs Continues

June 1990 saw the culmination of a three-year undercover operation by Customs officers, stretching from North Africa to Notting Hill and codenamed Operation Beagle, when five men, including East End gangster, Robert Tibbs,

---

54. *Kensington News*, 1 November 1990.
55. *The Guardian*, 25 January 1991; *Kensington News*, 31 January; 21 February; 28 February 1991.
56. Batha, Emma, *op. cit.* 15, p.10.
57. *Ibid*, p.11.

and Francis Morland from Westbourne Grove in Notting Hill, were jailed for a total of 46 years at Guildford Crown Court, after being caught trying to smuggle one and half tons of cannabis, valued at around £3.5 million, into Britain via the west coast of Scotland.[58]

But real progress came in the first half of 1991. In April and May, in a succession of trials at Knightsbridge Crown Court, the 14 dealers arrested during Operation Mint were convicted and given terms of imprisonment with the longest sentence, six years, going to George Roberts of Bonchurch Road.[59] The attitude of the courts towards street drug-dealers was, at last, hardening and the majority of those arrested were being remanded in custody to await trial. According to one officer who was at Notting Hill at the time, the removal of these dealers from the streets led to a marked decrease in the level of drug activity in All Saints Road for up to six months.

It was claimed that 'this form of preventative custody' was 'worthy of note' because the prosecution merely had 'to convince a court that remand while waiting trial [was] justified in the light of the available evidence.'[60] O'Connor kept the pressure on. In June, there was another surveillance operation, under the codename, Daffodil, this time lasting six weeks culminating in local officers, together with members of the Territorial Support Unit and officers from the Drug Squad at New Scotland Yard, raiding six addresses. Six people were arrested and faced a total of 44 charges relating to drugs, including cocaine, crack, heroine and cannabis. O'Connor took the opportunity to remind the public that, since November 1989, 24 of the 27 dealers that had been arrested were convicted. However, although there had been 'a noticeable increase of crack on the streets' in the previous 12 months, there was 'good reason to be optimistic' because the police had developed their techniques to deal with it and were having far greater success.' He continued, 'the level of activity on the streets is minimal compared to what it used to be but sadly people have begun to switch to more profitable drugs like crack.'[61]

Chief Superintendent O'Connor also instituted some changes in the policing of All Saints Road. He retained the 24-hour watch on the road but used

58. *Kensington News*, 27 June 1991.
59. *Kensington News*, 14 May 1990.
60. Dorn, *op. cit.* 43, p.110.
61. *Kensington News*, 4 July 1991.

more plainclothes officers thus keeping it discrete. In an interview just before the 1991 Carnival, he described how the police had 'learnt' to undertake 'a lot of surveillance work before acting rather than trying to do it on a one-off basis,'[62] and pointed out that three operations in 1990, Mint, Plate and Coope, had resulted in the arrest of 29 people for dealing in drugs of which 25 were convicted.[63] Continuing Pearman's initiative, invited representatives of the Kensington and Chelsea Council and other important community groups accompanied the police on these raids, acting as 'observers' to see how and where the drugs were discovered. This helped to repair the reputation of the police in the eyes of some of these groups, particularly when convictions followed. More importantly, the increased success of these raids and subsequent convictions, meant that the key leaders of officers operating on the streets, the sergeants and inspectors, became convinced this was the way forward.[64]

But, there were still confrontations. In early-August, two police officers attempting to arrest two people in Powis Square, suspected of having cannabis in their possession, were confronted by a crowd that emerged from a pre-Carnival meeting being held in the Tabernacle Community Centre and released the prisoners. The police officers called for assistance and several police vehicles, including the units on stand-by for the whole of the Metropolitan Police area in Central London, together with police dogs, converged on the area. The duty officer, Inspector Melanie Bailey, arrived to take charge and a stand-off developed with officers, some of whom were wearing protective clothing and carrying shields at one end of the street and a large crowd at the other end. The late senior duty officer, Chief Inspector Alan Shave, arrived and instructed the police officers to withdraw to side streets out of sight of the crowd. He then walked into the crowd at the other end of the street, found some people with authority and persuaded them, in the interests of Carnival, which was only three weeks away, to return to the Tabernacle and carry on with the meeting.[65] The next day, allegations that the police

---

62. Batha, *op. cit.* 15, p.11.
63. *Ibid.*
64. O'Connor, *op. cit.* 50.
65. In correspondence from Alan Shave to the author, dated 5 October 2011. See also *Caribbean Times*, 13 August 1991.

had set dogs onto people within the crowd and that people had been indiscriminately arrested were denied; rather, as Chief Inspector Shave pointed out, the police had, in fact, shown 'a tremendous amount of restraint.'[66]

Strategy for Dealing with Illegal Drugs

Shortly after leaving Notting Hill, O'Connor addressed the Association of Chief Police Officers' National Drug Conference, and suggested there were 'three strategy tests' when constructing local responses to deal with illegal drugs. Firstly, it was necessary to invest in any police operation that was concerned with supply reduction to ensure that it was conducted according to best practice and was properly controlled. This meant it had to be properly researched, planned, staffed and controlled from the very start of the operation right up to the point when it went to the Crown Prosecution Service.[67] Secondly, a multi-agency approach was both desirable and necessary, and O'Connor pointed out that 'the District Drugs Advisory Committee structure, as part of the Government strategy' at that time, provided 'a vehicle locally to co-ordinate and direct work at the relevant health, education, social services and police' levels. However, in the case of Kensington and Chelsea such a Committee did not exist and a number of reservations emerged when attempts were made to set one up:

- In order 'to retain street credibility' some agencies felt that they should 'remain at a 'cordial distance' from police.'
- Because most agencies appeared to have a 'reactive nature', there was little room 'for developing a pro-active approach.'
- Often, there was 'an absence of a shared understanding or agenda for action between the various agencies.'

However, three elements helped to overcome these reservations and get things moving in Notting Hill. Firstly, the police made huge efforts to build personal relationships with key personnel in other agencies. Secondly, the

---

66. Correspondence from Alan Shave, *op. cit.* 65. See also Batha, Emma, *op. cit.* 15, p.11.

67. O'Connor, Chief Superintendent Denis. 'Notting Hill—Developing a Local Strategy'. A Presentation given to the Association of Chief Police Officers Eleventh National Drug Conference in 1992, p.34. Copy in the author's possession.

Kensington and Chelsea Council were already considering setting up a Crack Committee and were persuaded to widen this to a Substance Abuse Action Group, as already described. But, according to O'Connor, the third element was 'the most significant factor in moving forward'. This was 'the clear acceptance by police' that 'enforcement' was not the only solution; the multi-agency approach also needed to address 'harm reduction' and 'demand reduction'.[68]

O'Connor stressed the importance of 'setting realistic goals' and, whilst it might have been possible, in theory, to conceive of elimination and reduction, some agencies in Notting Hill felt that 'anything other than containment' was 'totally unrealistic.' However, all the agencies did sign up 'to a common strategy' that identified 'a whole series of actions starting with schools and working right the way through to assisting those who [had] become embroiled in the process.' As a result 'a multi-agency drugs "Helpline"' was set up, the purpose of which was 'to provide easy access' for those who dabbled in drugs, their parents, neighbours, friends who lived on estates, 'the whole objective being to make it easy for people to opt out or to get help.'[69] The third strategy test and perhaps the most crucial involved the police having access 'to an enormous amount of information in the fight against drugs misuse.' Locally, control could be exercised over the way that information was released so that particular locations were 'not easily labelled as problematic' when raids were carried out or arrests were made.[70]

Conclusions

According to local officers, Operation Mint was the point when the police at Notting Hill began to turn things around insofar as drugs were concerned and the point at which All Saints Road 'became less of a symbolic location'.[71] This may be true but it was another few years before the police could claim to have been totally successful.

Although it was announced by the police that they still considered All Saints Road to be the 'Front Line', the convictions of 18 drug-dealers, arrested

---

68. *Ibid*, p.35.
69. *Ibid*, pp.35–36.
70. *Ibid*, p.36.
71. Dorn, *op. cit.* 43, p.108.

in operations carried out in 1989 and 1990, at Knightsbridge Crown Court in the first half of 1991, would it was hoped lead to a 'quieter period through the summer.'[72] However, the eviction of the Mangrove Community Association from its traditional premises and the failure to find any alternative premises of an equivalent size, led some black community leaders to warn that 'a rising sense of hopelessness in the area' could 'boil over into rioting.' In the event, Chief Superintendent O'Connor claimed that the area was quieter than at any time since he had come to the area over a year ago.[73]

The multi-agency approach was beginning to have an effect. Despite the fact that it was still the most heavily policed street in Europe, Emma Batha described how, in All Saints Road and the surrounding area, 'the crumbling Victorian buildings' had been 'renovated and taken over by chi-chi restaurants and designer workshops.' Suggesting that it was 'a prime example of social engineering,' she claimed, to the casual observer, the changes were impressive. Indeed, in the preceding few years, the Government, the Royal Borough of Kensington and Chelsea and the local task force spent thousands of pounds on cosmetic improvements. Coupled with this, arrests by the police for drug offences had been significantly reduced.[74]

On taking up command of Notting Hill Division, Denis O'Connor had stressed the importance of reducing the availability of illegal drugs. In summing up what he had achieved he said 'this was easier said than done.' There had been considerable success in taking drugs off the street in All Saints Road and reducing the availability of drugs from certain premises but, initially, the availability had merely relocated to betting offices and other premises and there had been a resort to 'using kids on bicycles to courier the drugs.'[75]

72. *Kensington News*, 14 March 1991.
73. *Kensington News*, 11 April 1991.
74. Batha, Emma, *op. cit.* 15, p.10.
75. O'Connor, *op. cit.* 50.

CHAPTER 18

FROM TURBULENCE TO GENTRIFICATION

Changes at the Top

During the last seven years of this turbulent period, from September 1991 to 1998, Notting Hill Division was commanded, firstly by David Gilbertson, until September 1994, and then by Graham Sharp. Gilbertson, who had recently completed the Senior Command Course at the Police Staff College, replaced Denis O'Connor as the Divisional Commander. Prior to his appointment, he spent six months in the USA with the New York Police, getting an insight into the effects drug abuse, particularly crack, had on the community. Sharp arrived in 1993, initially as Gilbertson's deputy but when the latter left in 1994, he was promoted and took command. He already had experience of Notting Hill, having been there as an inspector from 1981 to 1985 during some of the most turbulent times.

Gilbertson's first impression was that Notting Hill was, to some extent, 'living on its reputation.'[1] But others continued to describe All Saints Road in 'iconic' terms and suggested that the All Saints Road (ASR) Squad 'was considered to be at the 'cutting edge' of policing on the Division.'[2] A huge amount of gentrification had taken place with a number of well-known people and various celebrities moving into the area; but there were still areas north of the Westway that were disadvantaged and in need of investment. Like his predecessors, Gilbertson found the vast majority of officers at Notting Hill were 'good coppers', serving the public in a way to which all police forces aspire. However, there was a small minority who displayed racist tendencies and who had a disproportionate influence on many of the

---

1. In correspondence with former Chief Superintendent David Gilbertson, dated 1 March 2011. He retired from the Metropolitan Police in the rank of deputy assistant commissioner.

2. In correspondence with Colin Searle, who served at Notting Hill as a constable from 1992 to 1995, dated 2 August 2011. Colin Searle held the rank of superintendent in the Dorset Police at the time of the correspondence.

young officers, particularly those who were in their probationary period.[3] But another senior officer, who served at Notting Hill at this time, offered a note of caution, suggesting that, although there may well have been officers with racist tendencies, a number of 'unfounded complaints were made against good officers.' He described how they 'were goaded and provoked by some of the black prisoners ' but, generally, the officers 'were acutely aware of the need for restraint because of complaints, the media siding with the black community, and the general reputation of the Hill.'[4]

Getting to Grips with Allegations of Assault

About four months after he arrived, Gilbertson's concern with those who showed racist tendencies came to a head when a number of complaints were made in rapid succession against Notting Hill officers alleging that prisoners, mainly black, had been assaulted in police vans conveying them to the police station. Gilbertson issued an instruction to all inspectors and sergeants that such allegations would be investigated by a CID officer, no matter what time of the day or night it occurred, the police van was to be treated as a crime scene and examined by a scenes of crime officer, and the uniforms of the officers concerned were to be seized and sent for forensic examination. Gilbertson also said that he was to be informed immediately any such allegation was made. This was not a popular move with some officers, and he received a few 'dead' calls at home in the early hours of the morning for the first couple of weeks, but it worked. There were no more allegations of assault by prisoners. The attitudes of some officers changed too; where they did not, Gilbertson progressively ensured that they were transferred or, if they applied to transfer to other departments, he did everything to ensure that they were successful.[5]

City Challenge

In 1991, Michael Heseltine, then the Secretary of State for the Environment, set up a scheme, City Challenge, which provided funds to regenerate urban

---

3. Gilbertson, *op. cit.* 1.
4. In correspondence with former Chief Inspector Alan Shave, dated 5 October 2011. Alan Shave retired from the Metropolitan Police in the rank of Commander.
5. Gilbertson, *op. cit.* 1.

areas by encouraging partnerships between private enterprise and the public sector, and enabled community safety groups to be set up to develop crime prevention initiatives. Gilbertson was part of the bid team put together by the Kensington and Chelsea Council to lobby for some of the money available and it was eventually awarded £37.5 million.[6] The plan was for the money to be spent over the following five years and two projects had a direct bearing on policing in Notting Hill.

The community safety group came up with a plan to create two safe thoroughfares in Notting Hill, one, Ladbroke Grove, going from north to south and a second, which was undetermined, going from east to west. Increased street lighting and constant police patrols were proposed to enable pedestrians to walk safely through the division without fear of being accosted to buy drugs or robbed. Initially this received considerable support until the police suggested making everywhere in Notting Hill safe. The debate that followed created a healthy discussion between all the parties, some of whom had 'very fixed views'. With some gentle nudging from the police, the one initiative that did eventually make a huge difference, was the introduction of fixed closed circuit television (CCTV) cameras in various areas where crime was prevalent and where people resided. CCTV was becoming increasingly popular at the time but, in the main it was confined to communal areas, such as shopping centres and car parks, and having cameras on posts outside people's houses was a step into the unknown. Following a survey of Notting Hill residents, which found that most gave the idea their full support, it was finally announced, in May 1996, that 16 hi-tech cameras would be installed in an area which included Acklam Road, Basing Street, Lancaster Road (at its junction with All Saints Road), Portobello Road and Tavistock Road by March 1997, to assist the police in cracking down on muggings, robberies and thefts in the area. The police were delighted because it enabled them to have court clarity video of crimes taking place—particularly drug-dealing—without the necessity of mounting covert operations.[7]

The CCTV programme, was funded over a two-year period with £250,000 from City Challenge and £35,000 from Kensington and Chelsea Council. The cameras themselves were operated by the council from a dedicated

---

6. Gilbertson, *op. cit.* 1.

7. *Kensington News*, 23 May 1996; Sharp, *op. cit.* 17.

location, which was opened by Nick Ross from the BBC's 'Crimewatch' programme, but the pictures were also displayed in the control rooms at both Notting Hill and Kensington Police Stations, where the police controllers could, if necessary, over-ride the operation of the cameras from the council's dedicated location. Both the chief superintendent at Kensington, Peter Rice, and Graham Sharp had clauses inserted into the conditions of use to the effect that the cameras must never be directed into peoples' houses and that footage must never be shown on television or used for any kind of public entertainment.[8]

Needless to say, the CCTV programme had its detractors. Golborne ward councillor, Pat Mason, was not convinced of its long-term value. He felt that, whilst it would 'reduce crime and have a dramatic effect in its first year ', it was 'not the solution to the crime problem' in Notting Hill. Suggesting that criminals would find a way round the cameras, he claimed that only 'jobs, better benefits, training and something to do' would do that.[9] But Sharp took the view that the installation of the CCTV cameras, which were also used to monitor events at the Notting Hill Carnival, was a major step forward in moving Notting Hill towards complete gentrification.[10]

Later that summer, a more controversial security system was installed around the Swinbrook Estate to prevent 'dealers and criminals' from 'using the estate as a 'drug traffic highway'. Funded by £80,000 from City Challenge and £50,000 from Kensington and Chelsea Council, the Tenants Management Organization (TMO) of the estate arranged for installation of an iron-barred fence and security gates around the estate. Some residents were bitterly critical of the arrangements, suggesting that it had turned the estate into a virtual fortress, but a representative of the TMO claimed that when all the 490 residents on the estate had the opportunity to examine and comment on the plans, only five turned up![11]

Announcing in October 1997 that there had been 359 burglaries in Kellfield and Avondale wards of Notting Hill in a year, a considerable increase in the previous 12 months, Notting Hill police offered free security, including

---

8. In correspondence with former Chief Superintendent Graham Sharp, dated 18 January 2011.
9. Kensington News, 23 May 1996.
10. Sharp, *op. cit.* 8.
11. *Kensington News*, 5 September 1996.

locks, bolts and, in some cases, new doors to hundreds of residents. The scheme, known as Safe Homes, was funded by another project, Safe Cities, with contributions from the Metropolitan Police, the Royal Borough's environmental health department, the housing association and the TMO.[12]

Sector Policing

Sector policing was introduced in 1993. It was similar to the Neighbourhood Policing scheme that had been tried at Notting Hill in the 1980s and failed. But, whereas the initial scheme had been experimental, Sector policing was now being introduced force-wide. It effectively disbanded the relief system that had been in operation for many years and Notting Hill Division was divided into three sectors. Each sector was under the control of an inspector, who had 24-hour responsibility. Policing each sector were six teams of officers led by a sergeant. Instead of there being an equal number of officers on duty for much of the 24 hours as there was under the old relief system, sector policing ensured that the most officers were on the streets when demand for police services was at its highest.[13]

To many, All Saints Road was still a place from which illegal drugs could be readily obtained,[14] but Gilbertson felt that committing an entire team of 15 to 20 officers — the ASR Squad — solely to the small area surrounding this one road was a waste of resources at a time when manpower in the Metropolitan Police was being cut-back.[15] However, the Deputy Assistant Commissioner and senior management team at Area Headquarters took 'an inordinate amount of interest' in All Saints Road, largely, it was suggested, because the then Commissioner, Paul Condon, had been responsible for the area from 1986 to 1988, and Gilbertson was unable to persuade them to allow him to change the system by which this small area was policed. So he waited until the introduction of sector policing and then, without notifying Area Headquarters, disbanded the ASR Squad and incorporated it into

---

12. *Kensington News*, 2 October 1997. The Safer Cities Programme (SCP) was designed to address various crimes, such as domestic and commercial burglary, domestic violence and the like. It was part of a larger initiative, Action for Cities.
13. Metropolitan Police (undated). 'Sector Policing: Why Did We Need to Change our Style? An explanatory leaflet.
14. Shave, *op. cit.* 4.
15. *Ibid.*

the Northern Sector, giving the inspector in charge, Ian Dyson, 'absolute discretion to police All Saints Road in any way he thought appropriate.' The only condition Gilbertson imposed on him 'was that he had to be personally visible at all times to the main "players".'[16]

It was about this time that Sharp arrived as Gilbertson's deputy. He immediately saw that doing away with the relief 'family' system, which had been extremely popular with police officers, had caused a dip in morale, as it did at many police stations throughout London.[17] The uniformed constable was the most important 'cog' in the police wheel and Sharp believed that all other departments, squads and central services should work towards supporting the officer on the street. Recognising that they had 'top/down' support, the inspectors, sergeants and constables were encouraged to tackle the problems on their respective sectors, writing their own action plans, bidding for divisional, area and force services to assist them, and being provided with the finances to achieve them. Finally, they were given credit for end results. As a result, morale was restored and arguably improved.[18]

Street Robberies Reach 'Epidemic' Proportions

Periodically, street robberies continued to be a problem during the early-1990s. Indeed, Gilbertson took over at a time when attacks on people were on the increase to the extent that it was claimed that they had reached 'epidemic proportions' in an area which included Westbourne Park Road, St Lukes Road, Powis Terrace and Powis Square. Throughout December, therefore, 17 officers under Detective Sergeant Brian Henderson, set up a number of covert observation points in areas where this type of crime was prevalent, targeting individuals, mainly those between 14 and 25 years. The offenders' method was simple. They merely walked along the street, snatching handbags, picking pockets, taking money at knifepoint or slashing open bags before running away with the contents. In cases where the crime was not seen from an observation point, within minutes a response car would pick up the victim and details of the suspect, including his description and what he was wearing, were circulated. Meanwhile a crime analyst at the

---

16. Gilbertson, *op. cit.* 1.
17. Sharp, *op. cit.* 8.
18. *Ibid.*

police station tried to connect various crimes with a suspect, particularly if his clothes had unusual features. In December 1991 alone, the police made 27 arrests.[19]

A similar problem arose 18 eighteen months later when another crime wave, again involving young criminals, occurred during which a range of offences, from stealing from motor vehicles to violent muggings and burglary took place. This outbreak highlighted a weakness in dealing with young criminals that had existed for years. For a number of years, the case of any juvenile arrested for crime was merely referred to the juvenile bureau. But, as soon as they were released the youngsters committed further crimes. Pointing out that one youngster had come into contact with police at Notting Hill, 45 times, Chief Inspector Barry Clark explained that they were not able to deal effectively with persistent juvenile offenders and suggested that they should have 'the power to charge them and bring them before the courts the next day'.[20] Senior officers at area level and at New Scotland Yard were lobbied for a change in force policy in relation to persistent juvenile offenders, but none was forthcoming.[21]

In October 1995, a London-wide initiative by the Metropolitan Police, codenamed Eagle Eye, aimed at combatting street robberies, had some dramatic results in Notting Hill. In less than three months, 66 people were arrested of which 38 were prosecuted. Chief Inspector Anthony Wills suggested that the success of the operation was 'not only as a result of extra police on the streets' but was also due to diligent work by both investigators and interviewers, who made substantial contributions by obtaining 'good descriptions of the suspects—including their clothing,' from the victims, as a result of which they were, more often than not, identified, traced and arrested.[22]

Guns on the Streets

Dominated by the 23 storey Grenfell Towers, the Lancaster West Estate was built in the early 1970s. Like many such estates in Britain at around that time, it suffered from a number of problems, 'many of them drug related'.

---

19. *Kensington News*, 16 January 1992.
20. *Kensington News*, 15 July 1993.
21. Gilbertson, *op. cit.* 1.
22. *Kensington News*, 5 October 1995.

In February 1993, two officers patrolling the estate, in a police van, were shot at twice as they emerged from the underground car park beneath Grenfell Towers. Fortunately, both bullets ricocheted off the roof of the van just above the driver. A third bullet smashed the side window of a police patrol car that responded to a call for assistance from the occupants of the van. When interviewed by the press, Gilbertson pointed out that it was 'an extremely serious incident' in which officers' lives were at risk.[23]

In an effort to reassure the residents, Gilbertson's response was to flood the estate, including the walkways, staircases and other public places, with pairs of uniformed officers. However, it had the reverse effect because, about a week later, he was approached by the tenants committee and asked to withdraw the patrols because the presence of so many officers made the residents 'feel uncomfortable.'[24] Later that month, in an unrelated operation, police swooped on a Notting Hill flat, where seven handguns and ammunition were found in a holdall under a bed.[25] By April, a total of 16 illegally-held weapons had been seized by police in a relatively short time, which, suggested to Gilbertson a 'growth in the number of guns circulating in the criminal underworld.'

In a major inquiry launched after the incident on the Lancaster West Estate, four men were arrested and, amongst the weapons seized, were a pump action shotgun, a harpoon gun, knuckle-duster and baseball bats. However, the gun used to fire at the police officers was not amongst them.[26] Firearms continued to be a problem throughout the remainder of the year to the extent that, in November, the police issued a statement suggesting that weapons had overtaken fast cars and Rottweiler dogs as the latest status symbol.[27]

Crack on the Rise

In April 1992, despite some local opposition, the Mangrove set up its own independent advice line in an attempt to rid Notting Hill of drugs.[28] Three

---

23. *Kensington News*, 10 February 1993.
24. Gilbertson, *op. cit.* 1.
25. *Kensington News*, 24 February 1992.
26. *Kensington News*, 14 April 1993.
27. *Kensington News*, 11 November 1993.
28. *Kensington News*, 22 April 1992.

years later, in May 1995, building on the drugs line concept, a drop-in centre for drug addicts, funded by the Westminster Drugs Project, was opened by the Mangrove at its premises at No.3 All Saints Road. Pointing out that 'the crack problem had escalated in West London, particularly around Ladbroke Grove' over the previous few years, the Mangrove's Housing, Welfare and Drugs Adviser, Annette Larande, suggested that opening such a place in the heart of the black community' meant that 'addicts, who might not feel comfortable going anywhere else' could come to the Mangrove and, hopefully, 'make the vital first steps towards recovery.'[29] There is no evidence that this was the case.

Meanwhile, drug-dealing continued in All Saints Road, but, by this time, it had become a little more 'sophisticated' although it was still sometimes carried out on the street. The dealers themselves carried no drugs. Someone wishing to purchase drugs would approach and pay the dealer who would then point out a girl to the client. These girls were the couriers and despite the health risks would often store the drugs, in separate deals, in their vaginas until needed, with possibly one deal in their mouths. Once approached by the client, the girl took him or her into a nearby doorway or even into an adjacent street where often they would end up kissing and it was at this moment the drugs were passed over from mouth-to-mouth.[30] At the end of a two-month surveillance operation, under the codename Operation Hosea, culminating in April 1992, five dealers were arrested and charged with various drug offences, including supply.[31] Almost a year later, at Knightsbridge Crown Court, three of the dealers were each jailed for four years; one was jailed for two years and recommended for deportation and a fifth was jailed for 18 months.[32] Gilbertson claimed that 50 rocks of crack had been seized from buyers during the operation and suggested that, 'despite the high profile policing in All Saints Road,' the presence of crack cocaine 'had got worse.'[33]

The availability of crack was to continue to present the police with problems in a number of inner city areas, including Notting Hill, over the next

---

29. *Kensington News*, 18 May 1995.
30. Gilbertson, *op. cit.* 1.
31. *Kensington News*, 22 April 1992.
32. *Kensington News*, 3 March 1993.
33. *Kensington News*, 22 April 1992.

decade. The increased involvement of Jamaican Yardies in the drug trade was highlighted at the 1994 National Drug Conference when Detective Sergeant Brennan, from the South East Regional Crime Squad, told the audience that they were 'mainly responsible for the huge increase in the supply and circulation of crack cocaine from which a dealer could make up to £20,000 a week.' Brennan pointed out that it was common knowledge that using 'armed intimidation and violence to terrorise people, particularly in law-abiding black communities', these Jamaican crime gangs controlled 'certain areas' but suggested it would be reckless to name them in the open forum of the conference. Announcing that Yardies were responsible for 'crack seizures by the police going 'through the roof' he pointed out that the 'increase in violent crime involving firearms in Britain' was largely attributable to them. Brennan went on:

> 'Their motivation was greed and status … but it was important to understand there was no hierarchical structure to the group such as you would see in the Mafia. Jamaican crime groups "lived for today" and wealth in the form of cars and expensive jewellery could be lost very quickly.'[34]

The growing violence amongst drug-dealers, particularly those dealing in crack cocaine, had been emphasised in Notting Hill in July 1993, when Peter Turner, an illegal immigrant from Jamaica had eight bullets pumped into him while he stood on the corner of All Saints Road and Westbourne Park Road. The assailant was another black man, Delroy Johnson. Turner and Johnson were both Jamaican Yardies. Johnson, known as 'Notches' because of the number of people he had killed in his home country, had been sent from Kingston, Jamaica, to kill Turner because the latter was 'skimming' too much profit from the deals he was involved in. Johnson was jailed for nine years at the Old Bailey the following April, by which time Turner, who made a complete recovery from the attack, was dead, murdered in an unconnected drugs shooting in New York.[35]

The year following Brennan's presentation to the National Drugs Conference, between 21 June and 10 July 1995, two London men carried out a

---

34. *Police Review*, 17 June 1994, p.12.
35. *Kensington News*, 5 May 1994; Gilbertson, op. cit. 1.

series of gun attacks in Birmingham, Peckham, Stoke Newington and Notting Hill. The incident in Notting Hill occurred on 8 July when the two men pulled up in a car and, using a 9mm pistol, shot 17-year-old Adrian Francis who was standing outside a betting shop in All Saints Road; as a result Francis suffered a severe spinal injury and was confined to a wheelchair. The drug-related incident led Labour councillor and All Saints Road resident, Pat Mason, to write to the Notting Hill police, requesting that the patrols withdrawn by Gilbertson three years earlier be restored, claiming that All Saints Road was 'knee-deep in prostitutes, drug addicts and dealers', and suggesting that something needed to be done before there was 'permanent gang warfare.'[36] Whilst this was an exaggeration, later the same month, in the early hours of 14 July, two police officers were attacked by a mob of about 30 youths carrying bottles and knives as they tackled a fight in All Saints Road. One officer was knocked to the ground but his colleague was able to radio for assistance and, within minutes, about 30 police officers arrived. The crowd immediately scattered.[37]

On taking over as Divisional Commander, Sharp claimed that, although there was still a problem with All Saints Road, it was a lot quieter than it had been during his earlier time on the division between 1981 and 1985. But, it was still 'necessary to be sensible' when taking action. It was, he claimed, 'perfectly possible to walk up and down' the road but it could still 'blow up without warning.' Also, residents continued to express their concern about the lack of police action.[38] Operations continued, and, as a result, four men were arrested in a crack house after a three-week, undercover operation, codenamed Operation Falcon. All were charged with possessing drugs with intent to supply. A number of others had been arrested during the operation prior to the raid on the crack house. However, two of the dealers fled the country following the raid. Four months later, one man was jailed for five years and another for four years, for dealing crack.[39]

Two people were murdered in 1996. The first was Clifford Angol, who was sitting in a BMW, owned by one of London's most notorious gangsters, Mark

<hr>

36. *Kensington News*, 13 July 1995; *The Job*, 15 September 1995, p.1.
37. *Kensington News*, 20 July 1995.
38. Sharp, *op. cit.* 8.
39. *Kensington News*, 17 November 1994.

Lambie,[40] outside the Warwick Castle public house in Portobello Road when a yellow car pulled up beside him and the driver pumped six bullets into him, in what was believed to have been a gangland 'tit-for-tat' revenge killing.[41]

The second was Russell Christie, brother of one of Britain's most famous sprinters, Linford Christie, who was fatally stabbed in Portobello Road near its junction with Lancaster Road. The local newspaper described it as 'an area renown for drug dealing,'[42] and a national newspaper, as an area controlled by black Yardie gangs who fought for control of the lucrative market in crack cocaine.[43] It later transpired that he had been stabbed by Simon Williams, after Christie had stolen £20 worth of crack cocaine from him, which the former had bought earlier 'at a drug den in Notting Hill.' Williams subsequently pleaded guilty to manslaughter and was sentenced by the court to four years' imprisonment after the court heard that Christie had a history of violence.[44]

The Community Take Action

In September 1995, residents and businesses, with police support led by the Sector Inspector, Stan Davies, formed the All Saints Road and Community Association. Explaining why this action was taken, Notting Hill Housing Trust area director, Ros Spencer, said:

> 'There was shouting, screaming and fighting at all times of the night and residents were frightened. They would hear someone being beaten up but were distressed because it was unsafe to go out and help. The place was being ruled by crack and we didn't feel like we could even walk down the street.'[45]

Members of the association began gathering information on the dealers, which was then passed to the police. At the same time, the police increased

---

40. As a juvenile, Mark Lambie was one of the six people prosecuted for the murder of PC Keith Blakelock at the Broadwater Farm riot in 1985.
41. McLagan, Graeme (2009). *Guns and Gangs: The Inside Story of the War on Our Streets*. London: Allison & Busby, p.94.
42. *Kensington News*, 26 December 1996.
43. *The Mail on Sunday*, 22 December 1996.
44. *Mirror*, 16 December 1997.
45. *Kensington News*, 2 October 1997.

their patrols in the area and, between June and December 1996, made around 300 arrests, mainly for drug-related offences. This included a 30 per cent increase on the number of dealers arrested during the preceding six months, a 43 per cent increase in the number of people arrested for possessing drugs and a 32 per cent decrease in the number of reported burglaries. Also, the Kensington and Chelsea Council used the civil law to close down a 'notorious crack-house', when on 11 November 1996, at the Central London county court, evictions orders were granted against two addicts who lived there.[46]

Members of the Community Association had read an article where the residents of a community living in a red light district had banded together and stood in the street, as a group, stopping prostitutes plying their trade and frightening-off prospective clients. Ros Spencer decided this was what was needed to finally drive prostitutes and drug-dealers out of All Saints Road and other similar areas. Concerned about accusations that this might be seen as a vigilante movement, Sharp was, at first, unsure of the wisdom of such a move but he nevertheless sent Sergeant Maurice Kiddle to interview the community that had apparently successfully mounted this operation, and some of the prostitutes who had suffered as a result. Kiddle reported favourably and Sharp decided to risk it. After having been carefully briefed as to what they could and could not do, members of the community safety group took to the streets. Their action, basically, was to stand as a group near people they knew to be dealers or prostitutes, or outside a house which was being used as a drug den. Somewhat to Sharp's surprise, it worked. All Saints Road was eventually clean and one year later, the Community Association held a street party to celebrate their success.[47]

Carnival

With two exceptions, Carnival throughout the 1990s went reasonably well, from the point of view of both the police and organizers. The downward trend in crime generally continued so that, by 1993, despite reported increases in attendance, only 85 crimes were reported; this compared with 99 the previous year. The police claimed they were pleased with the way things had

46. *Kensington News*, 27 February 1997.
47. Sharp, *op. cit.* 8.

gone particularly at the 1993 Carnival; it had been peaceful and they were now more concerned with public safety.[48]

However, the apparent success of this Carnival was disputed by two consultants who were on duty in the casualty unit at St Mary's Hospital at Paddington over the weekend. They revealed that 115 people had attended the unit from the Carnival of whom 88 per cent had been brought in by ambulance. Some were children, others had suffered panic attacks in the large crowds and around 12 were so drunk they were unconscious. In 39 per cent of the cases, the injuries had been sustained as a result of assaults. Twenty-six patients required stitches, 20 of them because they had been attacked with glass or knives. The average number of stitches for these patients was 15 and three-quarters of the lacerations were facial.

Three of the victims suffered life-threatening haemorrhaging, the assaults having transacted arteries in the head or neck, and three major facial lacerations required more than 30 stitches each. In addition, six of those assaulted had broken noses. Many of those who had been injured described the attacks on them as being completely unprovoked.

Sixteen people were admitted to the hospital as in-patients. These included a person with a fractured skull, another with a broken thigh bone, and four with stab wounds. One was to the neck causing shock; another was to the chest; the third had sustained severed tendons to several fingers of one hand and in the fourth case a stab wound had penetrated the knee joint. [49] Pointing out that the carnival had resulted in a 35 per cent increase to their normal workload over the August bank holiday weekend and some of those who were treated would have permanent injuries, including disfiguring scars, Jane Fothergill and Robin Touquet suggested, in a letter to *The Independent* newspaper, that 'any other social event attended by similar numbers of people and resulting in 115 casualties' would not be 'described as peaceful,' and claimed the 'level of violence' was 'unacceptable.'[50]

In 1995, the Carnival was again attended by more than a million people. More than 6,000 police officers and 150 stewards ensured that it was relatively trouble-free. However, things turned nasty yet again early on the

---

48. *Evening Standard*, 7 September 1993.
49. Quoted in the *Evening Standard*, 7 September 1993.
50. *Ibid.*

Monday evening when a gang of youths, carrying knives and handguns, shot a 20-year-old man in the arm and stabbed his 25-year-old friend in the stomach. Both men were taken to hospital along with five police officers who suffered cuts and bruises. Later, there was a second shooting, this time in the Malvern public house in Bevington Road. In total more than 620 people were treated, mainly for minor injuries, but 71 were taken to St Mary's Hospital. Ninety-six people are arrested for a variety of offences, including robbery, the possession of drugs and offensive weapons and drunkenness. This was one fewer than the previous year. Pointing out that 'the vast majority of people enjoyed a spectacular Carnival,' Commander Tony Rowe claimed that 'a small number of incidents marred what was otherwise a successful event[51] and, in a letter to the Metropolitan Police's own newspaper, Sharp claimed that he had received a number of favourable letters about the policing of the event.[52]

However, not for the first time, there was disagreement between senior and junior officers as to what success was. In the same edition, Sergeant Andrew Mellows, from Barkingside Police Station, took issue with the comments attributed to Commander Rowe. Pointing out that there had been 13 reported stabbings and two shootings, Sergeant Mellows suggested that whilst it was 'not politically correct to knock' the Carnival, he could not 'think of any other situation where such figures would be treated in such a blasé manner.' He continued:

> 'The time has come to take a firm grip of the situation. We must employ many more officers on duty at the Carnival, especially on the Monday. We will then be able to put our hand on our heart and say honestly that we have enough police on duty to deal with or prevent a major incident, such as crowd crushing, and also deal with violent criminals who seek refuge in the dense crowds, knowing full well that they vastly outnumber the few officers who may chance their luck by entering the crowd to make an arrest.'

---

51. *Kensington News*, 31 August 1995; *The Job*, 15 September 1995, p.1.
52. *The Job*, 29 September 1995, p.12.

Pointing out that the police had 'been relatively lucky so far' he called for the police to wear body armour the following year, otherwise 'the list of stabbings and shootings may include police officers.'[53]

Once again more than one million people thronged the streets of Notting Hill for the 1996 Carnival. Crime again fell as did the number of arrests, down from 96 to 80. Nevertheless, nine people were stabbed, fortunately none fatally. This was four less than the previous year. The most serious occurred on the Monday afternoon, when a 17-year-old youth was found in St Luke's Road. There were also a number of other knife attacks on people between 18 and 30-years-of-age.[54] Safety issues again raised their head. In some areas the crowd was so dense that people were in danger of being crushed.[55] A total of 763 members of the public and five police officers were treated, mainly for minor injuries, but 66 were taken to hospital.[56] Following these crushing incidents, the question of safety was again raised with some community leaders prior to the 1997 Carnival[57] but, in the event both this one and the one that followed in 1998 passed off without serious incident.

Conclusions

Writing towards the end of the 20th century, Mike and Charlie Phillips suggested Notting Hill had 'changed further and faster than almost anywhere else' you could name in London:

> 'The impetus for that change came from the Caribbean immigrants in the sixties and by the richest of ironies, the same changes made it impossible for them to hold on to the ground which they had gained at such cost. On the other hand, change is fundamental to the nature of city life. People ebb and flow like the tides, buildings decay, are rebuilt and renovated, turned to other uses. The big wheel turns.'[58]

---

53. *Ibid.*
54. *Kensington News*, 29 August 1996.
55. *Kensington News*, 22 May 1997.
56. *Kensington News*, 29 August 1996.
57. *Kensington News*, 22 May 1997.
58. Phillips, Charlie and Mike (1991). *Notting Hill in the Sixties*. London: Lawrence & Wishart, p.108.

The combined efforts of the Notting Hill Task Force, City Challenge, various agencies and community groups, together with those of the Notting Hill police finally drove the drug-dealers and prostitutes from All Saints Road. The street lost its status as a Front Line amongst the black community and it was no longer regarded as a Symbolic Location by the police. Matt Nicholls, who arrived as a newly promoted sergeant in November 1997 and stayed until September 1999, described Notting Hill as a fairly typical division with some development taking place around All Saints Road and Golborne Road and, in general, as a place that 'was becoming very trendy.' Whilst he was there, the girl-group named All Saints, after the infamous All Saints Road, had their first song in the charts and the film, 'Notting Hill', starring Hugh Grant and Julia Roberts, was filmed on location.[59] Jim Busby, who arrived at Notting Hill as a superintendent in 1998 agreed that the area had lost its iconic status and described the previous management teams as leaving an excellent legacy in terms of morale and professionalism.[60]

Tim Hollis, was quick to suggest that it was all too easy to make Notting Hill the story of All Saints Road and vice versa, because the whole division was 'a diverse and interesting place to work.' Nevertheless, as he also pointed out, what happened on Notting Hill Division absorbed a good deal of time and energy for the Deputy Assistant Commissioner and his team at Area Headquarters.'[61] And that was primarily because of what occurred in and around All Saints Road and the publicity that accompanied it.

Graham Sharp took a similar view, suggesting that there was a tendency to believe that All Saints Road was 'full of violence and law breaking' but, such an impression did 'a great disservice to the officers policing brilliantly on a daily basis.' Nevertheless, he became convinced during his six years at Notting Hill in the 1990s that 'in order to achieve anything long term and worthwhile there needed to be three Ps in policing—partnership, partnership,

---

59. In correspondence from Matt Nicholls, who served as a sergeant at Notting Hill from 1997 to 1999, dated 8 March 2011. Matt Nicholls was a superintendent in the Hertfordshire Police at the time of the correspondence.
60. In correspondence with former Superintendent Jim Busby, dated 28 March 2011. Jim Busby was the acting chief superintendent at Notting Hill for a few months in 1998.
61. In correspondence with former Chief Inspector Tim Hollis, dated 9 September 2011. Tim Hollis was the Chief Constable of Humberside at the time of the correspondence.

partnership.'[62] Of course, attempts had been made to involve other agencies since 1983 when the Web of Affiliation was first identified. But, to start with, the path was slow and difficult. Some agencies did not wish to be seen to be getting too close to the police. But the two initiatives funded by central government, the Notting Hill Task Force and City Challenge changed that. By the mid-1980s, the Royal Borough of Kensington and Chelsea, too, had taken some positive steps towards multi-agency initiatives. Without such initiatives and the involvement of other agencies, Sharp suggested the police would 'still be pushing the snowball uphill.'[63]

---

62. Sharp, *op. cit.* 8.
63. *Ibid.*

EPILOGUE

A Racist Police Force

A significant event in 1999 was the public inquiry conducted by Sir William McPherson into the Metropolitan Police Service's handling of the investigation into the murder of Stephen Lawrence in 1993. A number of instances of police incompetence were identified in the report but the most crucial finding, insofar as the way Notting Hill was policed during this turbulent period, was his suggestion that the police service was institutionally racist. He went on to define what he meant by this. It was

> 'the collective failure of an organization to provide an appropriate and professional service to people because of their colour, culture or ethnic origin. It can be seen or detected in processes, attitudes and behaviour which amount to discrimination through unwitting prejudice, ignorance, thoughtlessness and racist stereotyping which disadvantages minority ethnic people.'[1]

This definition of institutional racism could explain much of what went on during those 50 turbulent years.[2] Perhaps the only thing that can be said in defence of the police, however, is that if the definition is accepted, then it applied to virtually every organization that had some influence over the lives of the ethnic minorities from 1958 onwards, and even before. Nevertheless, this does not absolve those black leaders who, for years, failed to actively oppose, or even speak out against, the criminal element amongst them.

Carnival

The Carnival continues. For just two days in each year over the August Bank Holiday, Notting Hill resembles its historic past. Despite a number of innovations, including the introduction of pre-Carnival intelligence teams in an

---

1. McPherson, Sir W (1999). 'The Stephen Lawrence Inquiry'. London: Her Majesty's Stationery Office, para. 6.34.
2. See Rowe, Michael (2004). *Policing, Race and Racism*. Cullompton: Willan, for an analysis of police attitudes towards race since McPherson's report.

attempt to pre-empt those likely to cause trouble from attending,[3] the use of screening wands at certain entry points[4] and of automatic number plate recognition around the Carnival area,[5] at least three people have been murdered; others have been shot or stabbed, well over 200 people have been robbed and many others have had property stolen from them.

Two of the murders occurred in 2000,[6] the other in 2004. In 2000, junior officers were 'angry' at being told to keep a low profile. The *Independent on Sunday* accused the Metropolitan Police of 'undue leniency prompted by political correctness.'[7] Interviewed by the BBC, an anonymous officer claimed they were 'discouraged' from getting involved with crimes which 'were not necessarily violent.' He also claimed that the police were not in a position to control the crowds, particularly in the latter part of Bank Holiday Monday, describing how 'a false impression' was given 'to members of the public' that it was 'safe to come to carnival and have a good time' but that certainly was 'not the case.'[8] Such allegations were rejected by a Metropolitan Police representative who was quick to point out that there had been an 84 per cent rise in the number of arrests over the previous year. But Assistant Commissioner Ian Johnson, who had overall responsibility for the policing of the Carnival, did say the it was, unfortunately, 'a good operating environment for criminals.' Not for the first time, the Metropolitan Police claimed that the Carnival had become too big for the streets of Notting Hill and should be held over a much wider area.[9]

Partly as a consequence, Mayor Ken Livingstone set up the Notting Hill Carnival Review Group under the Chairmanship of Lee Jasper, former development officer of the Mangrove Trust, who had become the Mayor's Director for Policing and Equalities. As a result, changes were made to the

---

3. See Clark, James, and Jonathon Carr-Brown (2000). 'Walking a Thin Blue Line' in *The Sunday Times*, 3 September; *The Independent*, 2 September 2000; *The Times*, 1 September 2004; *Daily Mail*, 26 August 2008.
4. Metropolitan Police Bulletin 0000000581 dated 12 December 2006.
5. BBC News, 30 August 2011. See www.bbc.co.uk/news/uk-england-london-14706924. Accessed 16 October 2012.
6. Judd, Terri, and Ian Burrell (2000). 'How two young men, and the spirit of the Carnival, died on the streets of Notting Hill'. *The Independent*, 2 September, p.3.
7. *Independent on Sunday*, 3 September 2000.
8. Clarke and Carr-Brown, *op. cit.* 3.
9. *Sunday Telegraph*, 3 September 2000.

route and the judging point[10] and a new Operational Planning and Safety Group (OPSG) was set up.[11] However, it seemed to have little overall effect.

The murder in 2004 was particularly vicious. The man was killed when at least six members of 'the notorious "Mus Luv Crew" gang pulled out guns, a minimum of which three were fired.' The incident marred what was described as a relatively peaceful carnival at which, in addition to the murder, only two people were stabbed. Six members of the Mus Luv Crew were subsequently each sentenced to life imprisonment.[12]

In 2008, the Carnival was largely trouble-free until the Monday evening when youths fought running battles with riot police for two hours in scenes reminiscent of the disorder that had marred the 1987 and 1989 carnivals.[13]

Periodically since its inception, the smooth running of the carnival has been disrupted by upheavals in the management arrangements. The first decade of the 21st century was no exception. In 2002, after having successfully led the management team since 1989, Claire Holder was suddenly ousted by the Trustees, amidst accusations of nepotism, 'fraudulent practices' and incompetence but, following a protracted legal battle, she was awarded 'a five-figure sum' by the High Court in 2005, when it was found there was no substance in the allegations.[14] But the ousting of Holder meant that, in February 2003, a new body, the London Notting Hill Carnival Limited was set up under the chairmanship of Professor Chris Mullard.

In October 2011, the Carnival faced another crisis after the co-directors for the event, Chris Boothman and Clive Barclay resigned, blaming 'a lack of funding and disagreements over policing levels.' However, in June 2012, a

---

10. Mayor of London (2004). *Notting Hill Carnival: A Strategic Review*. London: Greater London Authority, pp.43–46, para. 1.42.

11. *Ibid*, p.45, para. 1.46. Members of the OPSG who were also members of the CSLG were the Royal Borough of Kensington and Chelsea; City of Westminster; Metropolitan Police Service; British Transport Police; Transport for London; London Underground Ltd; London Buses Ltd; St John Ambulance; London Ambulance Service; London Fire Emergency and Planning Authority; Notting Hill Carnival Trust/London Notting Hill Carnival Ltd. The Greater London Authority became a member of the Safety Group (and its successor, the OPSG) as a consequence of the Mayor of London's Review.

12. Metropolitan Police Bulletin 0000000581 dated 12 December 2006. http://cms.met.police.uk/met/layout/set/print/content/view/full/6098. Accessed 23 January 2011.

13. *Daily Mail*, 26 August 2008; BBC News, 26 August 2008. http://news.bbc.co.uk/2/hi/uk_news/england/london/7580562.stm. Accessed 16 October 2012.

14. *The Guardian*, 10 April 2004.

new organization, the London Notting Hill Carnival Enterprises Trust was set up under the chairmanship of Vincent John consisting of five directors 'each representing a different strand of Carnival.'[15]

Crack Again

Despite the efforts by police to curb such places, including on one occasion, officers abseiling down a tower block in North Kensington in February 2001, the area continued to be plagued by crack houses. The drug dens would be set up by dealers who targeted vulnerable people, such as the mentally-ill or disabled, frequently living in council property. Kensington and Chelsea Council therefore set up a multi-agency working group, which included representatives from the police and major landlords, which developed a Rapid Reaction Protocol to tackle crack houses. The overall aim was 'to ensure a quick response' as soon as a crack house had been identified, to prevent those already closed down from re-establishing themselves and 'to protect the most vulnerable communities and residents from drug-related crime.' Under the protocol, 'a co-ordinated multi-agency response' was triggered 'within seven working days of a crack house being identified' with the intention that, by taking legal action, it would be closed within 42 days of it being known to exist.[16]

An example of just how corrosive these crack houses were became public in May 2003 when five people, who ran a multi-million pound drugs-empire across London, including 12 crack houses in Notting Hill, finally met their match. Georgette Williams, Joanna Dowling and Theresa Chase, together with two men, were banned by a court from entering the area of North Kensington between Holland Park in the south and Harrow Road in the north, for life under Section 222 of the Local Government Act 1972. The police had records of Williams, dubbed the 'Queen of Crack' and who had convictions for supplying crack cocaine, possessing weapons and violence, being involved in drug-related activities between May 1999 and October 2002

---

15. *The Voice*. http://www.voice-on-line.co.uk/print/1872 and http://www.voice-online.co.uk/print/9573. Both accessed 16 October 2012.
16. Royal Borough of Kensington and Chelsea, The (2004). 'The top of the agenda: cracking down on antisocial behaviour'. Newsletter 03/May – http://www.rkbc.gov.uk/rbkcdirect/rdbe-haviour/asbo404.asp. Accessed 17 October 2012.

on 333 occasions. On 101 occasions she had been seen to visit drug dens in Notting Hill. Dowling had three separate convictions concerning Class A drugs and was seen to visit the Notting Hill dens on 15 occasions. The third woman was Theresa Chase, a mother of five children, all of whom were in care. She had more than 150 convictions, mainly for soliciting but also for the possession of heroin. Concealing between £700 and £1000 worth of crack internally, the women transported it from where it was manufactured to the dens.[17] The two men, Brian Ellis and Frankie Charles, were used as security guards to protect the premises from other drug-dealers. Ellis had nine firearms and shotgun offences against him and had been convicted of assaulting police officers on five occasions; Charles had been sentenced to four years imprisonment in 1998 on five counts of supplying crack cocaine. Police recorded 340 visitors to one crack den, a one-bedroom maisonette, over a 24-hour period. It was estimated that their activities were bringing them in £6,800 per day or £2.5 million a year.[18]

Any person that breached a banning order under Section 222 of 1972 Act is in contempt of court. Police seeing such a breach could report it to the council who could then start proceedings against the person who was liable to a term of imprisonment of up to three years. In 2004, the Council did take four people who were in breach of such an order back to court and each was sentenced to six months' imprisonment. Claiming that it was a 'trailblazing approach', the council said it highlighted 'imaginative policies and partnerships between key agencies', and had paved the 'way for communities across Britain to fight back against the crack dealers'.[19]

The August Riots

Notting Hill did not escape the riots which swept across London following the shooting of Mark Duggan in Tottenham on 4 August 2011. Three gangs, from Queens Park, Lisson Green and Ladbroke Grove, normally

---

17. The police were unable to conduct intimate searches without the consent of the person to be searched.
18. *Evening Standard*, 6 May 2003 — http:www.standard.co.uk/news/londons-crack-queens-7224259.html. Accessed 16 October 2012.
19. Royal Borough of Kensington and Chelsea, *op. cit.* 16. It should be noted that, since then, the Anti-Social Behaviour Act 2003, the Police and Justice Act 2005 and the Criminal Justice and Immigration Act 2008 have all come into force.

rivals, combined forces and the 70-strong group met in the Brunel Estate in Westbourne Park, before setting out 'on a trail of destruction.' The group first stole cash and left one member of staff with a broken arm at the Gala Casino in Queensway; next they went to the Supersave Grocery Store in Westbourne Park Road, where they seriously assaulted the owner, and stole bottles of tequila. Some of the group then moved south into Kensington and Chelsea where they robbed a taxi-driver and two passengers, attacked a police car and tried to set a double-decker bus on fire, before heading back to Notting Hill, where they looted some shops in Portobello Road, before entering the Michelin-starred restaurant in Ledbury Road where they terrorised and robbed both customers and staff. In August 2012, 16 of those involved, all of whom were, with one exception, aged between 16 and 25, were sentenced to terms of imprisonment from 16 months to nine years. The one exception, a 15-year-old Asylum seeker from Sudan was sentenced to three years in detention.[20]

Drawing the Story to an End

On the 50th anniversary of the murder of Kelso Cochrane in 2009, a memorial service took place at his graveside in Kensal Green, followed by a procession along Ladbroke Grove and the unveiling of a plaque close to the place where he was murdered in Southam Street.[21] An even more sombre event occurred when, on the 50th anniversary of Oswald Mosley's attempt to become the elected Member of Parliament for North Kensington in 1959, his grandson, Alex, died of a drugs overdose in a house in St Luke's Mews, off All Saints Road.[22] Another high-profile person to succumb to drugs, again in St Luke's Mews, was the former wife of Bob Geldorf, Paula Yates, who died in September 2000, although, on this occasion, the coroner found that it was not suicide but rather the 'foolish and incautious' taking of heroin.[23]

---

20. *The Guardian*, 8 August 2012; also *Kensington and Chelsea Chronicle*—http://kensington. londoninformer.co.uk/2012/08/notting-hill-rioters—-the.ful.html. Accessed 16 October 2012.
21. Antigua and Barbuda High Commission (2009). Official newsletter—Issue 133—May.
22. *Daily Mail*, 6 May 2009. See www.dailymail.co.uk/news/article-1177954 accessed 12 December 2012.
23. BBC News, 8 December 2000—http://news.bbc.co.uk2/hi/uk-news/1013404.stm. Accessed 16 October 2012.

In the 15 or so years since Notting Hill was 'gentrified' some of the principle characters in this story have passed away. Ben Bousquet, eventually retired to South Africa with his English-born wife, Mary, where he died in June 2006.[24] Gladstone 'Sledge' Robinson died of smoke inhalation at the age of 77 in December 2008 after his basement flat caught fire.[25] Frank Crichlow[26] and the second of the three hustlers, Johnnie Edgecomb,[27] both died in September 2010. A blue plaque, dedicated to Crichlow, describing him as a human rights campaigner, community organizer and restauranteur, now adorns the wall of the old Mangrove Restaurant.[28] Similar plaques were unveiled at the junction of Tavistock Square and Portobello Road dedicated to the memories of the principal founders of the Carnival, Claudia Jones, who died in 1964, and Rhaune Laslett-O'Brien, who died in 2002,[29] whilst two more were unveiled in Carnival Square dedicated to two people who had a major influence on the development of carnival, Russell Henderson and Leslie Palmer.[30]

Life in Notting Hill goes on. Already those 50 turbulent years are slipping further into history. But it is a very different life to that which the first post-war immigrants from the Caribbean saw when they arrived. And, it is unlikely that the officers who policed the area during much of this period would recognise it as the same place if they were to visit today.

---

24. Amongst other places an obituary appeared in *The Guardian* on 26 June 2006. See http://www.guardian.co.uk/news/2006/jun/26/guardianobituaries.politics/print. Accessed 1 June 2011.

25. London Obituaries: Gladstone Robinson — http://www.fulhamchroncile.co.uk/2008/12/24/london-obituaries-gladstone-robinson. Accessed 11 October 2012.

26. An obituary to Frank Critchlow appeared in *The Independent* on 23 September 2010.

27. *Daily Telegraph*, 4 October 2010; *New York Times*, 10 October 2010 on page A30 of the New York edition.

28. London Remembers. http://www.londonremembers.com/memorials/frank-critchlow. Accessed 27 October 2012.

29. http://www.bbc.co.uk/news/uk-england-London-14682187. Accessed 12 December 2012. Rhaune Leslett's plaque carries her married name which she took after her association with the Carnival had ceased.

30. Davies, Lizzie (2012). 'Notting Hill carnivalgoers hope to put on London's summer-long party'. *The Observer*, 26 August 2012.

INDEX

G

H

M

N

S

Y

Police Leadership in the 21st Century: Philosophy, Doctrine and Developments
Edited by Robert Adlam and Peter Villiers
With a Foreword by John Grieve QPM

Contains the 'Golden Rules' of Police Leadership. In Police Leadership in the Twenty-first Century the editors bring together a collection of authoritative and innovative contributions to show that: Leadership is less of a mystery than is often supposed; Much mainstream leadership theory can be adapted to police leadership; The qualities required can be developed by education and training; There are certain 'Golden Rules' for police leaders.

'Addresses the practical challenge of leadership at all levels ... an understanding of the underpinning principles and conflicting values of policing is vital for organizational survival': *John Grieve QPM (from the Foreword)*

Paperback | ISBN 978-1872870-24-3 | 2003 | 246 pages

Principled Policing: Protecting the Public With Integrity
by John Alderson

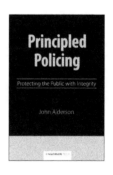

John Alderson demonstrates how it is all too easy for everyday police officers to fall into behaviour which becomes difficult to comprehend-as a result of police practices, working cultures and a lack of values for decision-making. Through his description of what he calls 'high police' and by way of worldwide examples he calls for decency, fairness and morality to act as touchstones for police officers everywhere. Principled Policing - which is dedicated to 'the innocent victims of the world's unprincipled policing' is now in wide use on courses for police training.

Paperback | ISBN 978-1-872870-71-7 | 1998 | 185 pages

Lightning Source UK Ltd.
Milton Keynes UK
UKHW020139101122
411923UK00007B/475

9 781904 380610